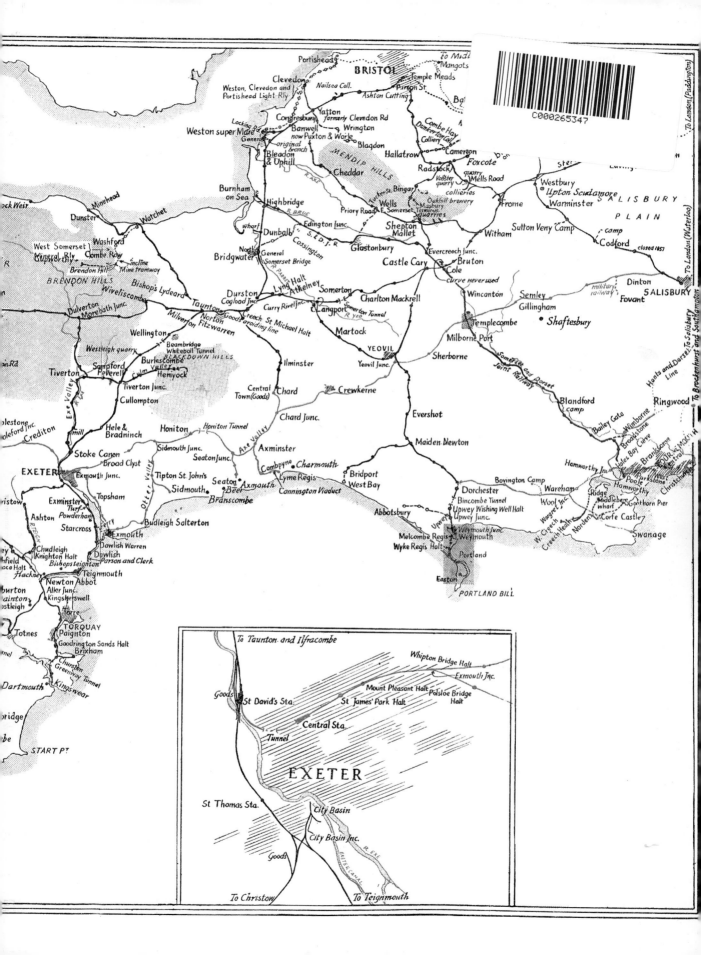

SOUTHERN RAILWAY

HANDBOOK

1923-47

SOUTHERN RAILWAY

HANDBOOK

THE SOUTHERN RAILWAY 1923-47

DAVID WRAGG

First published in 2003 by Sutton Publishing, Thrupp, Stroud, Gloucestershire
This edition re-issued in April 2011 by Haynes Publishing

David Wragg hereby asserts the moral right to be identified as the author of this work.

A catalogue record for this book is available from the British Library

ISBN 978 0 85733 011 6

Endpaper, front: The Southern's lines in the south-west were inherited from the London & South-Western Railway, which was locked in competition with the Great Western for traffic between London and Exeter, Plymouth and Weymouth. The lengthy and meandering Southern line to North Cornwall has become known as 'the withered arm' in railway circles.

Endpaper, back: The Southern inherited lines in the south and south-east of England from its three main ancestor companies, the London & South-Western , London Brighton & South Coast and the South-East & Chatham, but on the Isle of Wight no less than three companies operated, as well as a stretch of track between Ryde Pier Head and St Johns owned jointly by the LSWR and LBSCR.

Title page photograph: Ventnor, the 'English Madeira', was at one end of the route of 'The Tourist', the cross-Isle of Wight express, and also of the 'Invalids' Express', although the latter was an unofficial title. This view is from the turntable end. When in use, the island platform was reached by a moveable gangway from platform 1. *(HRMS AES801)*

A continental express is headed by 4–6–0 'Lord Nelson' class *Sir Walter Raleigh* through Knockholt in 1929. *(HRMS AAG311)*

Published by Haynes Publishing,
Sparkford, Yeovil, Somerset BA22 7JJ, UK
Tel: 01963 442030 Fax: 01963 440001
Int.tel: +44 1963 442030 Int.fax: +44 1963 440001
E-mail: sales@haynes.co.uk
Website: www.haynes.co.uk

Haynes North America Inc.,
861 Lawrence Drive, Newbury Park, California 91320, USA

Designed and typeset by Dominic Stickland

Printed in the USA by Odcombe Press LP,
1299 Bridgestone Parkway, La Vergne, TN 37086

Contents

Bulleids' wartime utility 'Q1' class were far from being the most attractive of locomotives but still had many features that clearly associated them with his more famous express engines. This is No. 33039 after nationalisation, but still proclaiming Southern ownership, at Wandsworth Road. *(HRMS AER206)*

Below: Despite the growing threat of nationalisation, the Southern continued to look ahead as the war ended. It was clear that not every line could justify electrification, so diesel traction was considered, including this 1600 hp diesel mechanical locomotive, whose lower axle loadings could have made it ideal for the many secondary routes. The lack of a cab at both ends seems strange, especially in the light of the Southern's work on electric locomotives and the 'Leader' class steam locomotive. *(NRM Brighton Collection B246)*

Acknowledgements

In writing any book such as this, an author is always indebted to those who help with such important matters as, for example, the quest for photographs. In this case I am especially grateful to the late Mr A.E.W. 'Bert' Colbourn of the Historical Model Railway Society for the use of their considerable archive of material on the Southern Railway, its predecessors and heirs. Thanks are also due to the staff of the National Railway Museum, especially Mrs Lynne Thurston, Reading Room Supervisor, and her colleague Martin Bashforth, and to Kevin Robertson for his photograph of the 'Leader' class prototype.

Times are given throughout as am and pm as the 24-hour clock was not in use on public transport during the period covered by this book, and also to make references to the timetable extracts easier. In the photograph captions HMRS refers to the Historical Model Railway Society, and NRM to the National Railway Museum.

David Wragg
Edinburgh

Southern pride! The docks at Southampton, and local bus companies as well, in the 1947 timetable. Had the Southern not been nationalised, airlines would have appeared before long. (*Southern Railway*)

Introduction

Railways in the South

Most people who have any affection for a particular railway do so for reasons that go beyond the simple achievements of the line in question. My first remembered contact with trains was standing on the platform at Winchester as first one and then another express thundered through towards London, and even at that tender age I noticed that while the two Bulleid steam engines seemed almost identical, one looked smaller than the other. No doubt I had seen a 'Merchant Navy' class hauling an express from Bournemouth, while either a 'Battle of Britain' or a 'West Country' pulled a boat train from Southampton Docks. I went to a boarding school on a Southern ferry and then down the old main line of the Isle of Wight Railway, and started work as a weekly commuter on the Portsmouth Direct, before commuting regularly from Haslemere and then from Woking.

In my day, much of the Southern's rolling stock was still around, but seeming increasingly neglected and eventually dated. British Railways invested heavily in lines to the north and Scotland, first of all modernising with diesel electrics, and then repeating the process with electric trains, first on the lines to the north-west and on the West Coast route, while travellers in the south made do with increasingly unreliable pre-war rolling stock. This was the penalty for the Southern having got it right first time round, while British Railways, flush with money from the taxpayer, needed two bites at the cherry! It is always easier to spend someone else's money, and the other great attribute of the Southern Railway, lest we forget, was that under the shrewd general managership of Sir Herbert Walker, it attempted to make every penny count.

To those with only a fleeting knowledge of the south of England, it is overcrowded commuter territory, dominated by London, the 'Great Wen' as it has been called. In effect, it is an extended suburb. Then there are those who see it as 'holiday' country, with a chain of seaside resorts running from north Kent and down through Sussex, Hampshire and Dorset to Devon. Others see it as a part of the country to pass through on their way to France. The consensus is that the south has been spared the heavy industrial development that has marred so much of the rest of the country. To some extent, that much is true.

Looking at the south like this is about as misleading as describing, say, Northumberland as a county dominated by slag heaps and shipyards, and ignoring the attractive countryside, small towns and villages, such as Alnwick, Hexham and Warkworth, and the coastal scenery.

It is true that the south has been spared the worst excesses of the industrial revolution, with the possible exception of parts of north Kent; equally true that it is resort country. The London commuter area has also grown. First with the advent of the railway, which must have contributed so much to London's urban sprawl by enabling people to move out of the overcrowded centre of early Victorian times to what were, at first, small towns and villages. Then a second deepening of the commuter belt came with the electric train, spurred on as property prices closer to the centre became too expensive for those working there. It also

'Change at Brading for the Bembridge branch' may have seemed a good idea in the days of horse-drawn road traffic, and when the train ferry operated from Langstone to Bembridge, but increasingly it was vulnerable to competition from the motor bus on the more direct route from Ryde to Bembridge. Despite this, is took nationalisation to close the line. On one occasion, the porter was approached by a well-dressed stranger. 'I can't bother with you now, can't you see I have two trains to deal with?' said the harassed porter. 'I can quite understand your predicament,' replied the stranger. 'I am the stationmaster at Waterloo!' *(Kershaw Collection, HRMS ACM414)*

became apparent to those of us who commuted over longer distances that it took no longer to commute from Guildford than from Teddington, and that it was more comfortable. But, during the early 1970s at least, more people commuted into Guildford than out of it.

The south is also home to the Royal Navy and the British Army, and during the period covered in this book, the former had bases at Chatham, Portsmouth, Portland and Plymouth, with a considerable overspill from Portsmouth into neighbouring Gosport, and naval aviation was at one time at Ford and Lee-on-Solent, and still clings on at Yeovilton. Apart from the Channel ports, the south also included the large docks at Southampton, which again during the period covered started its steady rise to becoming Britain's largest deep-sea passenger port, displacing Liverpool and London. Aldershot was, and remains, a garrison town, proclaiming itself to be the 'Home of the British Army', while the area around Andover and Salisbury is also heavily influenced by the army.

Industry in the south has tended towards the more modern industries, such as commercial vehicle manufacturing at Guildford. The aircraft industry scattered itself across

Opposite: The railways had to fight Admiralty objections to get to the waterfront at Portsmouth, but the Royal Navy quickly found the railways useful. This is the Admiralty Pier at Portsmouth leading into the dockyard from Portsmouth Harbour. Another connection with the Southern into the Royal Dockyard ran from the High Level station in the city centre. *(HRMS ABW107)*

the south from Yeovil to Weybridge and beyond to the Medway, until Hitler's bombers forced Shorts to relocate. Agriculture has also been very important, with fishing less so, and even then it has tended to be offshore rather than deep-sea.

This is the story of the smallest of the 'Big Four' railway companies formed out of the groupings in 1922 of more than a hundred smaller companies. It is also the story of a railway in transition, and indeed there are some contradictions arising from this.

It is the story of a railway that more than almost any other started to instil a uniformity to its trains, earning the contempt of many traditional railwaymen by producing even express trains that seemed 'more like trams', as its electric multiple units whirled and cranked busily and frequently into its termini, and then rolled out again on their return journey having spent all too short a time at the platform. The sense of occasion associated with the arrival or departure of a great train seemed to get lost. On the other hand, this was the railway company that sought to introduce a great number of titled trains, bringing high standards of comfort and service on its main routes; a company almost wedded, it would seem, to the Pullman service, which was always just a little more than simply having a meal served at one's seat. The magnificent Bulleid locomotives provided high standards of comfort for the enginemen and, while short on range, reflected the need for powerful steam traction even over short and medium distances.

At a time when airports are seen as great traffic generators for the railway, the Southern was miles and years ahead, with the first airport station at Shoreham and plans for a station for the new airport at Gatwick. The LNER, by contrast, closed its station at Turnhouse, the site of the airport for Edinburgh, during the late 1930s. The Southern even operated a special train for the famous Imperial Airways Empire Air Service. Through trains to Europe have been a reality for some years now, following the opening of the Channel Tunnel, but the Southern managed a genuine through train as early as 1936, eliminating the need to change from train to ship and back again, for a small number of passengers. For others, the boat trains were accelerated and new ships introduced.

The Southern Railway also made great strides in developing the port of Southampton, and became involved in some of the first domestic air services, as well as taking a stake in Imperial Airways. It had its own narrow-gauge railway, as did the Great Western, but uniquely among the main-line companies it also had its own tube, the Waterloo and City, known familiarly as 'The Drain'.

Chapter One

The Ancestors

The Railways Act 1921 enforced the grouping of more than a hundred railway companies into four big concerns and saw the Southern Railway take over the operations and assets of three substantial companies and many smaller ones. Of the three largest, the London & South Western Railway had main lines from Waterloo to Exeter, Southampton, Bournemouth and Weymouth, and Portsmouth, and a London suburban network that stretched to Reading and Horsham, and many points in between. Then there was the London, Brighton & South Coast Railway, which was based on the main line from Victoria and London Bridge to Brighton, but whose tentacles spread as far as Portsmouth in the west, with an offshoot of a couple of miles on the Isle of Wight operated jointly with the LSWR, and Hastings in the east. It had a suburban network that covered much of south London, greatly helped by the curious inability of the London underground system to penetrate this area deeply, other than by an extension of the Northern Line to Morden. The LBSCR had been one of a trio of railways, the others being the Midland and the Great Western, which had what would today be described as an 'up-market' image. The third major concern was the South Eastern & Chatham, in effect the marriage of two impoverished railways, the London, Chatham & Dover and the South Eastern Railway, that had tried to destroy each other through their networks of competing lines and copied

The Southern inherited a wide variety of coaching stock from its predecessors. Here is the unusual ex-SECR S4147. *(HRMS AEN235)*

initiatives, operating from some of the smaller but well-placed London termini, including Charing Cross, Cannon Street, Holborn Viaduct and Blackfriars. The SECR extended as far west as Hastings, down a line that had been so jerry-built that during the 1850s Mountfield Tunnel, near Battle, had to be relined. This necessitated the use of special narrow-bodied rolling stock, since a rebuild would have been out of the question, and allowed the LBSCR a significant share of the traffic travelling to Hastings on the less direct route via Lewes. Despite serving the Channel ports closest to France, the SECR failed to make the most of this, for not only had cross-Channel traffic still to develop as fully as it is today, but there was serious competition from the LBSCR at Newhaven and the LSWR at Southampton.

The Southern also inherited many smaller companies, of which the most impoverished must have been the Freshwater, Yarmouth & Newport, with just three steam engines, one of which was rented. It was the smallest of the three railway companies on the Isle of Wight. The Southern directors must have envied their opposite numbers at the Great Western, able to bolt other companies such as the Taff Vale on to just one substantial trunk railway. Even the London Midland Scottish and the London & North Eastern could build on their pre-grouping structures that had been so essential to making the West Coast and East Coast Anglo-Scottish services work, despite the number of companies involved, and face the demands of the occasional outbreak of real competition on these two routes, as well as from the longer Midland route from St Pancras.

An idea of the task that awaited the new board of management can be gathered from the following list of the minor, or subsidiary, companies absorbed into the Southern:

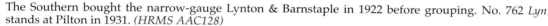

The Southern bought the narrow-gauge Lynton & Barnstaple in 1922 before grouping. No. 762 *Lyn* stands at Pilton in 1931. *(HRMS AAC128)*

Bridgwater Railway Company
Brighton & Dyke Railway Company
Freshwater, Yarmouth & Newport (Isle of Wight) Railway Company
Hayling Railway Company
Isle of Wight Central Railway Company
Isle of Wight Railway Company
Lee-on-Solent Railway Company
London & Greenwich Railway Company
Mid Kent Railway Company
North Cornwall Railway Company
Plymouth & Dartmoor Railway Company
Plymouth, Devonport & South Western Junction Railway Company
Sidmouth Railway Company
Victoria Station & Pimlico Railway Company

In fact, the Plymouth, Devonport & South Western Junction Railway Company had already been acquired by the LSWR, which had used its line to reach Plymouth once it opened in 1890, freeing the LSWR from having to use the South Devon route of its rival for London to Plymouth traffic, the Great Western.

London, Brighton & South Coast Railway

Railways had come to the south of England early. The Surrey Iron Railway had been authorised by Parliament in 1801 as the world's first public railway, running from the banks of the River Thames at Wandsworth to Croydon, some 8¼ miles, and following the course of the River Wandle. The track consisted of cast-iron plates of L-section fixed to stone blocks, with a gauge of 4 ft 2 in. Traction was provided by horses, which because of the lack of any substantial gradient could move five or six wagons, each weighing 3½ tons fully loaded, at around 2½ mph. The line was supported by the many mills and factories spread along its route, showing that some at least of London's urban sprawl pre-dated the arrival of the railways. The promoters of the line were keen to see it extended to Portsmouth, but only succeeded in extending the tracks as far as the quarry at Merstham, a further 8½ miles. Part of its route was later to be used by the London, Brighton & South Coast Railway.

The LBSC, or the 'Brighton' as it was commonly known, first appeared in 1846 on the amalgamation of the London & Croydon and London & Brighton Railways, and already had a network that included Brighton, from which a line had opened to Shoreham in 1840, while the main line to London Bridge was opened throughout the following year. Having its main line to London, the company set about making the most of the 'South Coast' in its title, reaching Chichester to the west and St Leonards to the east in 1846, and then continuing to Portsmouth in 1847. Newhaven was also reached in 1847, with Horsham in 1848 and Eastbourne in 1849. A second terminus in London was achieved in 1860 with the opening of Victoria, so that the railway was reasonably well placed to serve the West End and the City, although it was not actually within either.

The company was not above making the most of circumstances to expand its business. It was no coincidence that when the Crystal Palace was demolished after the Great Exhibition of 1851 it was moved from Hyde Park to Penge Park, sold by its owner, an LBSCR director, to a company associated with the LBSC, which opened a new branch ready for the official re-opening of the re-erected building by Queen Victoria in 1854. That this was an astute move can be judged by the fact that in a single day in 1859 112,000 passengers visited the palace.

A problem arose when the Brighton & Continental Steam Packet Company was found to be a wholly owned subsidiary of the LBSCR and had to be liquidated, as railways were

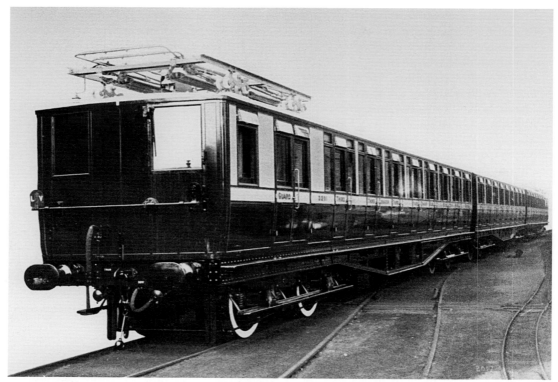

The new railway had different braking systems to rationalise, and different ideas on electrification. The LBSCR favoured overhead electrification, or 'elevated electric' as it was known, and the SECR would also have used an overhead system had grouping not gone ahead, but it would have been different from that of the 'Brighton' line. This is a three-car suburban electric multiple unit, with the driving brake third closest to the camera. *(HRMS ABV125)*

barred at the time from running shipping companies. Despite this setback, railway companies were later allowed to operate shipping services and, as with all of the major companies in the south, shipping soon became very important for the LBSCR, which introduced its first shipping services from Newhaven to Dieppe in 1867 in partnership with the Ouest Railway of France, and also operated shipping out of Littlehampton from 1867 until 1882. Nevertheless, all was not well, and by 1867 the line was in danger of bankruptcy, partly through having paid over-generous dividends of 6 per cent (at a time when the standard rate of interest was around 2½ per cent). More prudent policies over the next seven years led to far healthier finances, so that during the final quarter of the nineteenth century dividends of 5 per cent or even higher could be afforded.

The Brighton line was not always the fastest in the country, but still produced an acceptable performance, with through non-stop journey times of 90 minutes in 1844, reducing to 75 minutes in 1865 and 60 minutes by 1898 making twentieth-century timings look fairly lame and unexciting by comparison. This of course marked one big difference between steam trains and the first generation of electric trains, with the former performing at speeds that electric trains found hard to match on longer distances, while the electric trains came into their own on services with many stops because of their far superior acceleration.

To maintain high end-to-end speeds while not neglecting the needs of intermediate stations, the LBSCR introduced the first slip carriages in the British Isles, serving Haywards Heath from 1858. Pullman cars were introduced in 1875, and electric lighting was

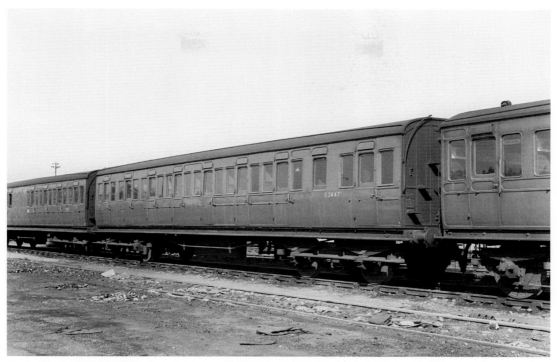

Probably one set of slam-door non-corridor compartment stock seemed much the same as any other to the casual observer, which may explain why ex-LBSCR S2447 was still in service in 1958. *(HRMS AEN228)*

introduced from 1881, while the 'Brighton' also rated highly for braking and signalling practice. Yet, in common with the Great Western, the 'Brighton' was also criticised during the late nineteenth century for its poor provision for third-class passengers.

The LBSCR enjoyed a monopoly on its main lines, although there had been competition with the LSWR for Portsmouth traffic prior to the opening of the Portsmouth 'Direct' in 1859, which settled the matter in the latter's favour once and for all. It cooperated with the LSWR at Portsmouth and at Ryde, where the two companies were responsible for the line from the pierhead through to St Johns and jointly owned the Portsmouth–Ryde ferry service. It also sought a similar relationship with the South Eastern Railway at Redhill and London Bridge, but found working relations difficult, and eventually resolved this at Redhill through the construction of an avoiding (or bypass) line for fast traffic, the 'Quarry' line, in 1900. This would have been needed sooner or later anyway to avoid the flat junction at Redhill with its branches off to Guildford and Tonbridge.

The LBSCR built a substantial suburban network dominating the suburbs between Dulwich and Purley. Yet this extensive network was vulnerable to competition from the new electric tramways, which often provided a more direct route for travellers, and had the advantage of passing closer to the doorstep and to the destination. This was the spur for early electrification. There was also the threat of a new London & Brighton Electric Railway shortly after the turn of the new century. The LBSCR struck back, quadrupling its main line as far as Balcombe Tunnel and obtaining parliamentary powers for electrification in 1903. The first electric services were introduced on the London Bridge to Victoria South London Line in 1909 using a 6,700 volts AC overhead system, and after this proved successful the lines to Crystal Palace and Selhurst were electrified in 1912. Including joint lines, in 1922 the LBSCR had a total mileage of 457 miles.

Typical of early third-rail electric stock was two-car electric multiple unit 4559, seen here at Durnsford Road in 1957, shortly before withdrawal. *(HRMS ACD210)*

London & South Western Railway

The largest of the constituent companies that formed the Southern Railway, the LSWR had its origins in the London & Southampton Railway, which received parliamentary approval in 1834 and was opened from Nine Elms to Southampton in 1840, by which time the name had been changed to the London & South Western Railway. The new railway set about a vigorous programme of expansion, doubtless anxious to get as far west as possible before any rival appeared. It reached Dorchester in 1847, Portsmouth from Eastleigh in 1848, the same year as it also reached Salisbury, and then secured its position as one of the two main routes to the West Country when it reached Exeter in 1860. The LSWR had already acquired the Bodmin & Wadebridge Railway in 1847, giving a clear indication of its ambitions, but did not reach Plymouth until 1876 and Padstow, the end of the line, until 1899. The London terminus was moved from Nine Elms to Waterloo in 1848, recognising that the former was too remote. In the light of the town's subsequent growth, it seems strange that the original line westward from Southampton to Poole and Dorchester avoided Bournemouth, and it was not until 1888 that the town was served by a direct route.

The variety of services operated by the LSWR was greater than that of the other ancestor companies of the Southern. Like the others, it had its London suburban network, in this case covering the western end of Surrey, part of Middlesex and much of Berkshire, and had a longer distance main-line network extending from Portsmouth to Exeter, but it also had the sprawling network to the west of Exeter which ensured that it was the main railway to serve North Devon and part of North Cornwall. Essentially, after Woking the Southern split into three main lines: the Portsmouth Direct which branched off at Woking; the Exeter line that branched off at Basingstoke; and the original Southampton line that eventually went all the way to Weymouth. An important secondary main line served Aldershot and Farnham, and provided an alternative route to Winchester, while the network of lines serving the Thames Valley centred around the core Waterloo to Reading line.

Military and naval traffic was important from the start, with the LSWR area including Portsmouth, Portland and Aldershot, and also running through Salisbury Plain. The importance of this first became apparent during the Boer War, when all the traffic for South Africa was shipped through Southampton, where the docks had been acquired in 1892, and again during the First World War, although in this conflict the railways were effectively taken over by the government. In peacetime it meant that on the Portsmouth line, for example, heavy weekend and holiday traffic was balanced by a reverse flow of servicemen travelling home on leave or for the weekend, and in later years this was to become one of the most profitable routes in the south. In fact, in retrospect it seems strange that the LSWR never seemed to accord the Portsmouth line the heavy service that it seemed to deserve, nor spent more providing easier gradients, which left the line difficult to work with steam traction and prone to earth slips.

The LSWR had competed with the LBSCR for the important London–Portsmouth traffic, with the line through Eastleigh challenging that through Arundel, but the extension of the line from Guildford to create the Portsmouth Direct placed Portsmouth firmly in LSWR territory. However, the LSWR was only just in time as the South Eastern had planned a branch to Portsmouth off the line from Redhill to Guildford – the embankment can still be seen just south of the junction for Shalford, but it never carried track. There was also competition with the Great Western, for although the LSWR route to Plymouth was circuitous, as far as Exeter the route was the most direct. The LSWR route to Reading was never as fast as that of the GWR from Paddington, although it could be a better bet for those with the City as their ultimate destination. Windsor was another destination served by both companies.

The suburban network was completed in 1885 with what has become known as the 'New Guildford Line', running through Cobham.

One of the greatest achievements of the LSWR, and one for which many passengers have had cause to be grateful over the years, was the construction of flying and burrowing junctions, with a total of seven on the 42 miles west of Raynes Park, although the last of these, Worting Junction, was a Southern achievement. The major omission from this programme, and one that would have saved many conflicting train movements, was the flat junction at Woking, almost certainly due to space constraints as the town quickly coalesced around the station, and this has always been the Achilles heel of the South Western main line, with as many as six trains an hour coming off the Portsmouth Direct in addition to those starting from Guildford.

At one time it was the practice for transatlantic liners to put passengers and mail ashore at Plymouth, saving a day in the journey to London, and the LSWR was spurred on by this to provide fast boat trains to Waterloo. Timings were eased considerably after one of these trains derailed at Salisbury in 1906 in the LSWR's worst accident, killing twenty-four of the forty-three passengers on the train.

Shipping services were an important feature of the LSWR's expansion, and here too at first it competed with the GWR, the LSWR's Channel Island services from Southampton competing with the GWR services from Weymouth, although the LSWR line to the town was the more direct. Eventually, the two companies operated a combined service to the Channel Islands. Southampton was also the base for a network of ferry services to Le Havre and St Malo, while a Lymington to Yarmouth, Isle of Wight, ferry service was also established. At first, because legislation barred the railway companies from operating shipping services directly, services were developed at arm's length through shareholdings in shipping companies, in this case the South Western Steam Navigation Company, formed

The old LSWR electrics. This is the view from the driving cab of an electric multiple unit at Queen's Road in 1923. Another electric train is just passing and can be seen on the left. (HRMS AAZ204)

in 1842, but before the end of the decade railways were allowed to operate shipping services provided that they specified the route, and by 1863 complete freedom was granted.

The LSWR was a profitable railway, paying a dividend of 5½ per cent or more from 1871 onwards. Surprisingly, while mainly a passenger railway, freight, docks and shipping business provided almost 40 per cent of turnover by 1908. Innovations included the first track circuits, installed between Woking and Basingstoke between 1902 and 1907. While not a fast railway overall, the LSWR did have some fine locomotives from 1878 onwards, with a growing degree of standardisation under a succession of chief mechanical engineers, including Adams, Drummond and Urie. Nevertheless, it was not until Herbert Walker was poached in 1912 from the London & North Western to become the LSWR's last general manager that suburban electrification started. This included the rebuilding of Waterloo, until that time a collection of four stations built at different times to cope piecemeal with expansion, and its subsequent distinction of becoming the first major railway terminus in the world built for an electric railway. In 1922 the LSWR completed a new marshalling yard at Feltham, with electrically controlled points and hump shunting.

The LSWR operated a number of joint lines, but the most important of these was the Somerset & Dorset Line, which the company acquired in partnership with the Midland Railway in 1875, much to the anger of the GWR which had its eyes on this important cross-country route that linked the South Coast with the West Country and provided a good through route to the Midlands and north-west. In 1907 it also acquired the Waterloo & City Railway, completed in 1898, helping to ease the isolation of Waterloo by giving a through non-stop direct link with the City of London, taking passengers to just outside the Bank of England. Waterloo's position was also helped by the completion of the Bakerloo and Hampstead (now the Northern Line) tubes in 1906 and 1926 respectively. One final acquisition before grouping was the Lynton & Barnstaple Railway, a 2 ft narrow-gauge line providing an important link across a sparsely populated part of north Devon, but which, ironically, was to be one of the few closures during the Southern's reign.

In 1922 the LSWR operated 862 miles, and was involved in joint ventures that covered a further 157 miles.

South Eastern & Chatham Railways Managing Committee

The ruinous competition between the London, Chatham & Dover Railway and the South Eastern Railway was brought to an end on 1 January 1899 by the creation of the South Eastern & Chatham Railways Managing Committee.

The South Eastern Railway came into existence as the result of legislation passed in 1836 to build a line from London to Folkestone and Dover, but the London & Brighton Act, 1837, required both the SER and the LBSCR to enter London on the same route from Redhill, forcing the SER to abandon plans for a route via Oxted. The result was that the SER reached the capital by paying tolls to the London & Croydon and Greenwich railways. The initial route from Redhill was to Tonbridge, reached in 1842, Ashford and Folkestone, reached in 1843, with the line extending along the coast to Dover the following year, and Tunbridge Wells served from 1845, the same year that the SER started cross-Channel operations through a wholly owned subsidiary using small paddle steamers that took 2½ hours. For the most part, the SER concentrated its efforts south of the Weald, prompting the creation of the London, Chatham & Dover Railway by the disappointed people of north Kent. Even so, the SER reached Ramsgate and Margate in 1846, Deal in 1847, Gravesend in 1849, Hastings in 1851 and Maidstone via Strood in 1856, as well as extending west to Reading via Redhill and Guildford in 1858, an incredibly indirect route through a sparsely populated area that contributed to the SER's financial weakness. One of the best-positioned London termini was opened at Charing Cross in 1864, the only terminus actually in the West End, followed by Cannon Street, ideal for the City, in 1866, but it was not until 1868 that a direct route to Tonbridge was opened, bypassing Redhill and cutting 13 miles off the London to Folkestone and Dover route.

A vision for the future of the SER came with the appointment of Sir Edward Watkin as chairman in 1866; he remained until 1894. Watkin wanted a route from Manchester to Paris using three railways including the SER, and a Channel Tunnel. Stirling's appointment as chief mechanical engineer (CME) in 1878 marked the start of a series of locomotives with much-improved performance. However, passenger rolling stock continued to be poor for the most part, though the situation was helped by the introduction of 'American' cars for the Hastings service, and by similar British-built carriages for the Folkestone route in 1897.

The SER's concentration on the Weald route and its failure to extend the North Kent Line beyond the Medway left the field open for a rival, with the creation of the East Kent Railway in 1853, mainly supported by business interests in Faversham. The line opened

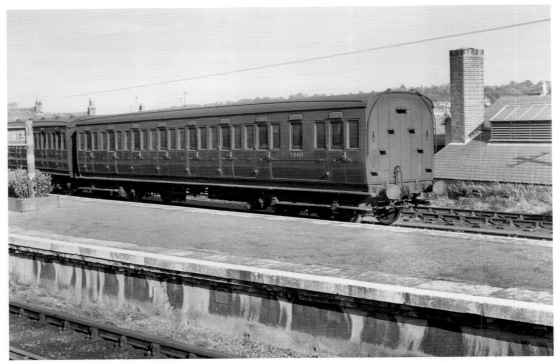

S2438, ex-SECR rolling stock still in service at Cowes in 1964. *(HRMS ACM803)*

between Strood and Faversham in 1858, and was extended not at first in the direction of London but instead to Canterbury and Dover, which the EKR reached in 1862 and introduced its own continental sailings with a service to Calais. The EKR's expansion had been noted with concern by the SER, and the intensive competition that ensued enabled the contractors to persuade the directors to extend the line towards London, changing the EKR's name to the London, Chatham and Dover Railway in 1859. The extension reached Bromley in 1860, Victoria in 1862 and Farringdon in 1866. This rapid expansion and the reliance on contractors who had been the driving force in the development of the LCDR, placed the company under great financial strain, especially after a bank failure in 1866, which forced the company into a bankruptcy that lasted until 1871. After James Staats Forbes became chairman in 1874, the competition with the SER became bitter, and extended to opening new lines to capture a share of the other company's traffic, often regardless of the likely financial benefits.

A working union between the two companies was proposed as early as 1890, by which time the LCDR's financial position was, if anything, stronger than that of the SER. This became clear later as the SER objected to the LCDR demanding 37 per cent of the overall receipts in 1890, but had to accept the LCDR having 41 per cent in 1899. In 1898, before the combining of the two companies, the LCDR had receipts of £142 per mile per week, against £87 on the SER. On the other hand, the SER had far better rolling stock, especially locomotives. Had the SER taken a more comprehensive approach to the provision of railway services throughout Kent, the outcome could have been different, and it could even have enjoyed a monopoly within its area.

To prepare for the union, a Joint Committee was set up in August 1898 under the chairmanship of Cosmo Bonsor. While the plan was that from 1 January 1899 the two companies would operate as one, there seems to have been little stomach for strong measures. Obsolescent LCDR carriages and locomotives were scrapped, but considerable savings could have been made by eliminating competing routes, especially those to Margate and Ramsgate. Many lines had been built too quickly and too cheaply, and suffered from narrow tunnels and bridges with weight restrictions. One positive step was the linking of the two main lines by constructing four long spurs where they crossed at Bickley. Meanwhile, the new CME, Wainwright, produced a series of 4–4–0 locomotives and new carriages, with Pullmans introduced in 1910. In 1919 Dover Marine station opened, easing the transfer from train to ship, but before this, while still unfinished, the station handled hospital trains bringing home First World War wounded and departing for destinations throughout England.

While the improvements enhanced the quality of the continental trains, suburban operations continued to be dismal, and plans for electrification were not implemented until after the grouping.

Isle of Wight

It would be wrong to omit the railways of the Isle of Wight from any consideration of the Southern Railway's predecessors. While these were small companies, they were fiercely independent, with three operating 56 miles of railway on an island with a population of around 85,000 and an area of just 127 square miles. The ambitions of the LSWR and LBSCR had not ignored the island, with the line from Ryde Pier Head to St John's owned jointly by the two companies, even though neither ran any trains on the island.

Of the three island companies, the only one with a reasonable level of traffic and capable of producing adequate returns was the Isle of Wight Railway, whose main line from Ryde to Ventnor opened as far as Shanklin in 1864, and then reached Ventnor through a tunnel cut under St Boniface Down in 1866, a distance of 12½ miles including the section along the pier at Ryde, essential so that ferries from Portsmouth could come alongside at all states of the tide. The IWR also operated the 2¾ mile branch from Brading to Bembridge Harbour,

Mainstay of the Isle of Wight lines under Southern ownership was the 'O2' class. Here is No. 22 *Brading* heading a train to Ventnor on Ryde Pier. The pier tramway tracks can be seen in the foreground. *(HRMS AEP312)*

opened in 1882 by the Brading Harbour Company, which was initially operated in conjunction with a wagon ferry from Langston on Hayling Island provided by the LBSCR, but abandoned in 1888. In 1898, the IWR took over the branch.

The Isle of Wight Central Railway had opened as the Cowes & Newport Railway in 1862, and this remained an isolated operation until the opening of the Ryde & Newport Railway in 1875. The two companies did not amalgamate until 1887 to create the IWCR, which also took over the struggling Isle of Wight (Newport Junction) Railway which operated from Newport to Sandown, where it shared the station with the IWR. When a branch was built from Merstone, on the Newport–Sandown line, to Ventnor West between 1897 and 1900, that also became part of the IWCR. Traffic even on the line from Ryde to Newport and Cowes was never substantial, although there was some freight at Medina Wharf between Newport and Cowes. Altogether, it is not surprising that no dividend was paid until 1913.

Between them, the IWCR and the IWR did at least link major centres of population on the Isle of Wight, but the third company, the Freshwater, Yarmouth & Newport, used a 12 mile route to reach places no bigger than a village. The ferry from Yarmouth to Lymington was the least well placed of the three main ferry routes for traffic from London and the main South Coast cities. Opened during 1888–9, the Freshwater, Yarmouth & Newport Railway was worked by the IWCR until 1913, when it decided to work on its own, purchasing and hiring three tank engines. To be fair, there were schemes to provide a tunnel to link the line to the LSWR just north of Lymington, but these never came to fruition. Even if they had, there would have been a major bottleneck at Newport, where trains to west Wight had to reverse out of the station before making their way through remotely populated countryside. Space at Newport, the island's principal town, would also have been a problem.

Chapter Two

The London Termini

None of the Big Four had as many termini in London as the Southern, with the huge terminus at Waterloo and one almost as big at Victoria, where the LBSCR and LCDR had adjoining, but separate, stations, joined later by a narrow opening. There were smaller but important termini at London Bridge, Charing Cross, Cannon Street, Blackfriars and Holborn Viaduct, and until 1929 there was also the small and cramped terminus at Ludgate Hill, through which trains could also reach Farringdon. By contrast, the much larger Great Western had just one terminus at Paddington, while the LNER had three, at Liverpool Street, Kings Cross and Marylebone. The LMS came nearest, with four, at Euston, St Pancras, Broad Street and Fenchurch Street. A purist might argue that the Southern had an eighth terminus, at Bank for the Waterloo and City tubes! Others maintain that Blackfriars, Holborn Viaduct and Ludgate Hill were really a 'three-in-one' terminus, and certainly they were built and operated by the same company, the LCDR.

The small size of many of the Southern termini was in part a reflection of the poverty of the companies serving Kent, but also because a compromise had to be made. No railway station of any company was as well placed as Charing Cross, but this was already a tightly congested site. There was much more room at Waterloo, but this was hardly the most convenient location – only Paddington was more remote from the ultimate City or West End destinations of most travellers. In some ways the size of the stations serving the City was a relief, since they were never fully utilised seven days a week. In fact, once Saturday morning working ended in the City, they were really only used five days a week, and even then only at peak periods, making them busy for ten or perhaps fifteen hours a week. Even if it had been possible to locate a station as large as Waterloo in the heart of the Square Mile, it could have proved to be a costly white elephant.

The image of the Victorian railway companies is that they were essentially freebooting and highly competitive. This is only part of the picture, as not only did companies collaborate when it was in their interests to do so, but Parliament also had to approve the authorising legislation needed for new railway works. As early as the 1840s there was a Royal Commission on Metropolitan Termini to try to ensure some semblance of order as the railway companies raced towards the capital, and eventually, in 1855, the House of Commons created a Select Committee on Metropolitan Communications. Among the many ambitious schemes that were rejected was one by Joseph Paxton, architect of the Crystal Palace, for a covered shopping arcade running from Regent Street to the City, with an overhead railway running its entire length!

In this review of the Southern's London termini, Ludgate Hill is omitted as much of its history is tied up with that of Holborn Viaduct and in particular Blackfriars, the jerry-built station that only came into being as an overflow for Ludgate Hill.

Blackfriars

From its opening in 1886 until 1937, the station now known as Blackfriars was known as St Paul's. The current name was adopted in 1937 to allow London Transport to rename the Central Line station until then known as 'Post Office' as St Paul's.

The construction of Blackfriars, or St Paul's, was brought about by the success of the London, Chatham & Dover's extension towards London. The LCDR had been allowed to extend to London by its Metropolitan Extension Act of 1860, which gave it powers to reach Victoria and, more ambitious still, to a junction with the Metropolitan Railway at Farringdon Street, offering considerable long-term potential that was not to be realised for many years. In fact, there was an earlier station named Blackfriars, opened on 1 June 1864 on the south bank of the Thames at the junction of what is today Southwark Street and the approach to Blackfriars Bridge. It served as a terminus for a little over six months until the railway bridge over the Thames was completed, allowing trains to stop at a temporary station at Little Earl Street on the north bank from 21 December 1864. It was not until 1 June 1865 that Ludgate Hill was opened, it too becoming a terminus until the Metropolitan Extension was completed to Farringdon Street on 1 January 1866. The LCDR had persuaded both the Great Northern Railway and LSWR to subscribe more than £300,000 each towards the cost of the extension with the promise of through running powers, which they soon exercised, along with the Midland Railway, which started running trains through to Victoria in 1875. The LCDR itself sent trains from Herne Hill through to Kings Cross and then as far as Barnet.

The new station at Ludgate Hill and the extension through the City was a considerable success, although it was not used by anything so ambitious as the Brighton–Rugby services of recent years. Unfortunately, a shortage of space meant that Ludgate Hill offered just two island platforms, which soon proved insufficient for the traffic on offer, and, as expansion was out of the question given the high cost of property and the LCDR's over-stretched finances, an additional station was built on a spur off the Metropolitan Extension. It was this that was named St Paul's when it opened on 10 May 1886, despite the fact that the name Blackfriars was already in use as the name of the adjacent District and Circle Line station.

Before the opening of St Paul's, the LCDR lines south of the Thames had been widened and a second bridge built across the Thames alongside the original bridge and to the east of it, carrying seven tracks. The new terminus was a necessity forced on the railway and was built as cheaply as possible without any great architectural pretensions, even having a wooden booking office. The cramped surroundings, and the presence of the District Railway immediately under the station, meant that there was no forecourt and no cab access to the tar-coated wooden platforms, which were reached by a dark and drab staircase. Only two of the platforms were given numbers, simply 1 and 2 between the eastern siding and the up and down loops. Despite this, in incised letters on the stones surrounding the doors, the names were given of fifty-four destinations that could be reached from the station, including St Petersburg and Vienna, with nothing to suggest that the intrepid traveller could expect to make several changes along the way! Rather more practical was the inclusion in this list of Westgate-on-Sea and Crystal Palace. Two through lines were routed through the station, with another three terminating tracks. The roof was kept as short as possible and constructed of iron and glass, although canopies were provided above the outer ends of the platforms.

Trains running to Holborn Viaduct generally stopped at Blackfriars, while it also took the City portions of trains from the new Gravesend branch, opened on the same day as the new terminus, which were later joined by those from the Greenwich Park branch, opened in October 1888. The new station was the only one operated by the LCDR with direct access to the underground network. Ludgate Hill continued to prove inadequate for the traffic on offer and became the butt of much press criticism as it was the most convenient station for Fleet Street, then the home of almost all the national newspapers and the London offices of many provincial dailies. Holborn Viaduct was generally regarded as useless, being inconveniently sited. Despite these criticisms, it was not until well after the formation of the South Eastern & Chatham that any attempt was made to remedy the situation, with a minor reconstruction of Ludgate Hill between 1907 and 1912.

The First World War saw a dramatic reduction in services, reflecting both the need to save resources and also to allow for the large number of military specials. These reductions hit Ludgate Hill, jammed between Blackfriars and Holborn Viaduct, especially hard, and the station was open only during rush hours from 1919. Electrification failed to save the station, with closure on 2 March 1929. Part of the problem was that the station was in too tight a spot for expansion, and its platform was too short for an eight-car electric train by some 80 ft – roughly a carriage length and a third.

The Southern Railway introduced electric suburban trains to both Holborn Viaduct and St Paul's on 12 July 1925, initially from the latter station to Crystal Palace (High Level) and Shortlands via the Catford loop, while a service from Holborn Viaduct to Shortlands and Orpington via Herne Hill also called at St Paul's. The running roads at St Paul's were re-arranged so that trains on the local lines to Holborn Viaduct could operate in parallel with the main-line trains terminating at St Paul's. There were also some modifications to the platforms, including extending all of them to take eight-car trains, and at the river end these now provided some fine views of the Thames downstream. St Paul's, later Blackfriars, saw a steady extension of its electric services until the outbreak of the Second World War, culminating in the extension to Gillingham and Maidstone on 2 July 1939.

The services using Blackfriars were reduced as a wartime emergency measure from 16 October 1939, including the complete withdrawal of rush-hour services to Dartford via Lewisham. The First World War had spared the City termini from the worst of German bombing, with only the Great Eastern's Liverpool Street being hit, but the Second World War saw considerable damage inflicted, especially at the height of the 1940/41 blitz. The worst night of the blitz was that of 16/17 April 1941, when a bomb wrecked the old Blackfriars signal cabin on the south side of the river. Immediately, flagmen were put into position to signal trains through the section and work the points, but worse was to come when either a large bomb or landmine destroyed the bridge over Southwark Street and seven flagmen seeking refuge in a shelter were caught by the blast, with three being killed outright, another three dying in hospital from severe burns, and just one surviving to make a slow recovery. With military help, a temporary bridge with two running roads was ready in fifteen days, but a permanent replacement was not in place until 9 October 1942. The terminal roads at Blackfriars were locked out of use until the end of the war, while temporary signalling arrangements were provided.

It was not until 12 August 1946 that a full restoration of services could be made at Blackfriars, with wartime cuts in services reversed, a new signal cabin opened and the terminal roads re-opened. The station's platforms were numbered 1 to 5 from east to west at the same time.

Cannon Street

Cannon Street was opened in 1866 as the City terminus for the South Eastern Railway, which had previously decanted its passengers at London Bridge, on the wrong side of the Thames. Earlier plans had been to provide two other stations on the extension line running to Charing Cross, but when the LCDR was authorised to provide an extension to Ludgate Hill, the SER realised that it also needed a terminus on the north bank of the Thames. It was even felt that there could be local traffic between Cannon Street and Charing Cross from those anxious to avoid the heavy congestion on the streets of London; these were the days before the construction of the Circle and District lines and the prediction was to prove correct before these underground lines were built.

The extension to Cannon Street was authorised by an Act of 1861, with a bridge across the Thames and a triangular junction on viaducts with the line between London Bridge and Charing Cross. At first, and for many years, all trains running to and from Charing Cross called at Cannon Street. The triangular junction led on to an engine shed and turntable, so cramped that locomotives had to run over the turntable to enter or leave the shed, and coaling stages.

There were five tracks – four running roads and an engine road – on the bridge, which had pedestrian walkways on either side, with that on the east reserved for railway personnel, and that on the west available to the public on payment of a ½d toll. The station itself abutted immediately on to the bridge, with nine roads. It was a handsome building offering stunning views over the Thames, with a hotel fronting the street. The roof was a single span of 190 ft more than 100 ft above the rails and glazed over two-thirds of its surface, surmounted by a 22 ft-wide lantern running almost the whole 680 ft length. There were seven platform faces, varying in length between 480 and 721 ft, with the two longest faces incorporating a cab roadway. Another set of platform faces was separated by three tracks to include a spare for rolling stock. The two longest platforms extended beyond the roof and on to the bridge.

The hotel, the City Terminus, was operated by an independent company and opened in May 1867, but was later acquired by the SER, and later renamed the Cannon Street Hotel. It was, for reasons that remain obscure and can be nothing more than a coincidence, the venue for the creation of the Communist Party of Great Britain in July 1920. Falling business led to its closure in 1931, and while the public rooms were retained for meetings and functions, the remainder was converted to offices and let as Southern House.

When first opened on 1 September 1866, Cannon Street fulfilled its promise of being served by all trains proceeding to and from Charing Cross, including boat trains, and with these and a shuttle service between the two stations, there was a five-minute-frequency service between the West End and the City, taking seven minutes, and costing 6d first class, 4d second class and 2d third class, compared with 3d for the horse bus. The local traffic was considerable, with 3.5 million of the 8 million passengers using Cannon Street in 1867 travelling solely between the City and the West End. This all came to an end with the opening of the District Railway between Westminster and Blackfriars in May 1870, and which reached Mansion House in July 1871, while the completion of the Circle Line on 6 October 1884 saw a station opened under the forecourt of Cannon Street.

One kind of specialised traffic had already disappeared before this. The seven-minute run had proved a great draw to certain ladies who found that it combined with the comfort of a first-class compartment to provide the ideal environment for the entertainment of their clients. Once a stop was introduced at Waterloo from 1 January 1869, the number of drawn blinds on trains running into and out of Charing Cross dropped dramatically!

Cannon Street was the exclusive preserve of the SER, except from late 1867 until the end of July 1868, when the LBSCR operated two up morning and two down evening trains to and from Brighton.

Growing traffic, with a train being handled every minute at peak periods, meant that the approach bridge had to be widened to ten tracks, including a siding on each side. This was completed on 13 February 1892. Inside the station, the cab road was shortened to provide another platform, while three platforms were extended further on to the first pier of the bridge. On the south bank, the locomotive facilities were extended.

The First World War saw the continental boat trains removed to Victoria, an arrangement that continued until the late 1930s, while severe reductions in services to save fuel also saw the practice of running Charing Cross trains into and out of the station finally come to an end on 31 December 1916. This must have been a welcome cut in journey times for passengers travelling to and from the West End terminus, and certainly could not have continued during the postwar years as traffic levels continued to rise. The next year saw the station closed on Sundays, and after 1 May 1918 it also closed on Saturdays after 3 pm, and between 11 am and 4 pm on weekdays. While these changes reflected the nature of the passenger traffic at Cannon Street, they also enabled the station to be used as a crew interchange point for the goods trains operating between the Midlands and north of England and the Channel ports via Farringdon and Ludgate Hill, and provided a marked improvement in productivity on these services.

Plans to electrify the suburban services were overtaken by the grouping, even though the SECR had first obtained powers for this as early as 1903.

Post-grouping, the Southern Railway remodelled the track, with electrification ending the need for light engine movements and the old layout designed to facilitate the operation of trains to and from Charing Cross being redundant. An extension of the system of non-conflicting parallel movements pioneered by the SECR in 1922 also increased the number of trains that could be handled at peak periods. The changes required Cannon Street to be closed from 3 pm on Saturday 5 until 4 am on Monday 28 June 1926. The bay platform was abolished and the eight remaining platforms rearranged, providing lengths of between 567 and 752 ft, with numbers 1 to 5 electrified. Under the new timetable introduced with electrification on 19 July 1926, there were eight electric trains an hour off-peak and seventeen during the peak, with a total of just thirty-six steam trains daily, mainly for Chatham and stations beyond. Two further platforms were fitted with third rail in July 1939, when the services to Gillingham and Maidstone were electrified. The station reopened on Sundays in summer 1930, and a few trains returned between Charing Cross and Cannon Street in 1933, some of which continued until 1956. Continental boat trains returned during summer 1936, to relieve pressure on Victoria, and this continued up to the outbreak of the Second World War.

Once again, wartime saw restrictions on the station's operating hours, closing between 10 am and 4 pm and after 7.30 pm daily, and from 3 pm on Saturday until Monday morning with effect from 16 October 1939. Even rush-hour services were severely curtailed in wartime, so that by 1944 there were just twenty-four peak hour departures, only one of which was for the Kent coast. Before this, on the night of 10/11 May 1941, the station was bombed and caught fire, with railwaymen braving molten glass dripping from the roof to rescue locomotives and carriages, but one of the former, *St Lawrence*, was caught by a bomb on the bridge.

Postwar, Southern House was patched up, but the station had to operate as a shell of its former self, as it was judged too badly damaged to carry the weight of the single-span roof. Weekend services resumed after nationalisation, but after a period of ten years were dropped again.

Charing Cross

No London railway station is as well situated for the traveller as Charing Cross, at the end of The Strand and with Trafalgar Square just around the corner. It is the only railway station actually in the West End, since Victoria and Marylebone are located on the fringes. The substantial forecourt and the impressive façade of the Charing Cross Hotel all serve to disguise the fact that this is not at all a big station, and indeed is smaller than many termini to be found in even medium-sized provincial cities. Its small size means that any delay or disruption in the evening peak immediately sees a massive crowd overflowing from the cramped main concourse and through the booking hall into the forecourt. At such a time it no longer shares with Marylebone the distinction of being one of the capital's nicest stations.

Plans for a railway terminus in this part of London were mooted as long ago as 1846, when the South Eastern Railway promoted an ultimately unsuccessful bill for an extension from Bricklayers' Arms to Hungerford Bridge. While the SER continued to promise a West End terminus and made unsuccessful attempts to enter Victoria, the company finally managed to obtain the approval of the LBSCR for a line from London Bridge in the direction of the West End, and in 1857 the SER decided that the site of the Hungerford Market was the preferred option, especially since the route also held the prospect of a link with the LSWR at Waterloo. The SER's determination was fuelled by some early market research, which showed that around 60 per cent of the passengers alighting at London Bridge were heading for the distant West End. At first the SER also planned to incorporate two other intermediate stations, other than Waterloo, in the extension to serve passengers heading for the City, and these would have been just west of London Bridge and at the southern end of Blackfriars Bridge, but the first was discarded in favour of the far more attractive option of the station at Cannon Street, and the second opened with Charing Cross, but closed after a very short life on 31 December 1868.

As with Cannon Street, the thinking was that the two stations would pair well with a lucrative traffic between the City and the West End, and this was indeed the case until the District and then the Circle lines came into existence.

The Charing Cross Railway Company Act 1859 authorised the construction of a line 1 mile and 68 chains in length, mainly on viaduct except for Hungerford Bridge which took it across the Thames and into the terminus. The new company was separate from the SER in theory, but obviously linked to it, with the SER providing £300,000 of the initial £800,000 capital, and later raising this investment to £650,000 as land purchase costs over and above those of construction proved to be far heavier than originally anticipated. The land purchase costs were not simply those of the then already fashionable West End, since much of the money was spent south of the river. The governors of St Thomas Hospital exacted the heavy price of £296,000 and despite the poverty of the area at the time the many slum landlords followed this example. Yet not all of the increases were down to the cost of property, as the Charing Cross Railway Company wisely decided to build three running tracks instead of two on the viaduct, and to build Hungerford Bridge with four tracks instead of two. Urban railway construction was not for the faint-hearted, and this was an extreme case, for despite running on viaduct to both minimise disturbance to existing property and ensure level running, the SER had to pay for the reconstruction of Borough Market as well as a 404 ft iron viaduct over it, and oversee the removal and reinterment at Brookwood of more than 7,000 corpses from the College Burial Ground of St Mary, Lambeth – which must have been a welcome additional business for the LSWR. All in all, the viaduct had 190 brick arches, including fourteen crossing streets, seventeen iron bridges and two iron viaducts, including that at Borough Market. Later, in June 1878, a new junction was opened to provide a link, Metropolitan Junction, with the LCDR line to Blackfriars and beyond.

The line also resulted in the removal and scrapping of Brunel's original Hungerford Bridge, intended to encourage those on the south bank of the Thames to patronise Hungerford Market. Nothing was wasted, however, as the bridge and ironwork was used for the construction of Clifton Suspension Bridge across the Avon Gorge at Bristol. As at Cannon Street, the bridge included a pedestrian walkway, in this case on the eastern side, for which a toll of ½d was charged until 1878, when the Metropolitan Board of Works paid the SER £98,000 for pedestrians to enjoy free access in perpetuity.

On 11 January 1864 Charing Cross opened, initially with just a limited service of trains to Greenwich and Mid-Kent, but on 1 April trains from the north of the county started to use the new station, and on 1 May main-line services followed. The train shed had a single arch, a pattern repeated at Cannon Street, with a span of 164 ft and a length of 510 ft, and was 98 ft above the track. The station was not immediately popular. For every one of those who appreciated the location overlooking the Thames, there was another who found Charing Cross and Cannon Street monstrous. There was an additional edge to the opposition to Charing Cross, as there were those, including some town planners, who favoured closing the station so that a new road bridge could be built over the Thames to take traffic directly into Trafalgar Square. How times change!

As at Cannon Street, there were tracks against both walls, but Charing Cross was smaller, with just six platforms, all built in wood and ranging in length up to 690 ft and extending on to the bridge. Platforms 1 and 2, the most westerly and reserved for main-line departures, incorporated a cab road with an exit through the front of the station under the hotel, and a ramp to bring cabs up from Villiers Street. Accommodation was provided in the station building for Customs officers, in anticipation of continental traffic from Dover and Folkestone. At first there were no engine sidings, but two were eventually provided, known as 'gussets', at the end of platforms 1 and 6.

The Charing Cross Hotel was designed by the architect E.M. Barry. With 250 bedrooms, it almost wrapped itself around the station by extending down Villiers Street, and later had an annexe across the street reached by a covered footbridge.

As always with the SER and LCDR, whatever one company did, the other had to rival it, no matter how worthwhile or practicable. In this case, the SER was jealous of its rival's links to the north, between Holborn Viaduct and Farringdon Street, and so powers were obtained in 1864 in The North Western & Charing Cross Railway Act to provide an underground line running just below the surface for goods and passenger trains from Charing Cross to Euston. The LNWR and SER both gave guarantees to raise 5 per cent of the capital, but this was not enough to encourage investors and the scheme was abandoned in the financial crisis of 1866 that pushed the LCDR into chancery. Even after recovery in 1871, a similar scheme to link with the Midland at St Pancras was so hedged around by Parliament with clauses to build new streets and minimise vibration that investors were not attracted and it was abandoned in 1874. The Euston link resurfaced in 1885, with the two railway companies by this time prepared to provide a third of the capital each, but floundered again as the outside parties providing the remaining third expected to have preference over the railway companies should the company fail. Had either line been built, they could have undermined financial backing for the Hampstead tube, but on the other hand could also have provided the basis for a modern-day regional express across the centre of London, and no doubt at far lower cost than the Cross Rail proposals. At the same time, weaknesses in the scheme would have included the congested approaches to Charing Cross and the only slightly less difficult approach to Euston.

While any expansion at Charing Cross was likely to be difficult, Hungerford Bridge was widened in 1887 on the western or upstream side to provide another three tracks, and later, in 1901, a fourth track was laid between Waterloo and Metropolitan Junction, with scissors crossings east of Waterloo Junction. Meanwhile, the SER started to busy itself buying the freehold of property on either side of the station in readiness for much-needed expansion. In 1900 powers were obtained to widen Hungerford Bridge on the east side and also to enlarge the terminus. Having got this far, the SER was discouraged from any further move by the plans to replace the station and bridge with a road bridge. But then a further and unexpected problem intervened.

During the afternoon of 5 December 1905, workmen were busy on a programme of roof maintenance work that had started in June. At 3.45 pm there was a sudden noise; passengers and railwaymen looking up saw the workmen rushing to safety, and naturally enough followed their example. Shortly afterwards, at 3.57, there was a deafening roar as 70 ft of the roof at the outer end of the station collapsed into the station, while pushing outwards the western wall on to the Avenue Theatre in Craven Street. Inside the station, three men were killed as rubble, ironwork and glass crashed on to the 3.50 express to Hastings, while at the Avenue Theatre, three men out of a hundred who, by unhappy coincidence, were also working on renovations to that building, were crushed under the rubble. The SECR closed Charing Cross at once, traffic on Hungerford Bridge was stopped, and then the trains sent back, one at a time, to Waterloo Junction.

Investigation soon showed that a weakness in a wrought-iron tie rod next to the windscreen at the southern end of the roof was the main cause. The weakness was due to a fault that doubtless had occurred at the time of manufacture, and had grown worse over the years as it expanded and contracted with changing weather conditions. Despite claims by some engineers that the remaining roof would be safe for another forty years, the SECR decided to take no chances, rebuilding the roof and walls at a reduced height and dispensing with the single span. Meanwhile, trains were diverted to Cannon Street and Charing Cross could not reopen to traffic until 19 March 1906, when a partial service was restored. However, the closure did have one beneficiary, as it enabled the Charing Cross, Euston & Hampstead Railway, precursor of today's Northern Line, to dig down through the forecourt, something which the SECR had prohibited for fear of causing difficulty and inconvenience to their passengers, and press ahead with building what became known as the Strand underground station. When opened on 22 June 1907, the dream of a direct railway link between Charing Cross and Euston was realised, but, of course, this was far from being a through route between the SECR and the LNWR.

Once the new roof was up, the opportunity was also taken to enhance many of the facilities at Charing Cross, with new booking offices and waiting rooms, including the then customary ladies' waiting room. These works were not completed until 1913. By this time the suburban services were beginning to feel the competition from the trams, while the underground network had already long removed the once heavy volume of traffic between Charing Cross and Cannon Street.

The First World War saw the SECR become Britain's frontline railway, with the heaviest responsibility for the movement of men and materials to the coast. Charing Cross also had the role of being Westminster's local station, and a special train, code-named Imperial A, was held ready at all times for VIP journeys, being used for 283 journeys during the war years. The train was a short-formed but luxurious operation, usually consisting of just a Pullman car and a brake composite. In addition, there was a military staff officers' train that operated daily from Charing Cross to Folkestone, leaving at 12.20 pm. Less happily, but an incredible achievement nevertheless, after the start of the Battle of Messines at dawn on 7 June 1917, the first wounded arrived at Charing Cross at 2.15 pm on the same day.

The SECR displayed some considerable foresight during the war years. As early as late October 1914, a lookout was posted on Hungerford Bridge watching for Zeppelin raids, and if an air raid seemed possible, no trains were to be allowed on to the bridge. As it was, all continental boat trains were diverted to Victoria for the duration of the war, but there were many fewer of these as Dover was closed to civilian traffic on the outbreak of war, and the boat trains disappeared the following year when closure was extended to include Folkestone. It was not until some time after the Armistice that continental civilian traffic was allowed once again, starting on 18 January 1919 with Dover–Ostend, then Dover–Boulogne the following month, and Dover–Calais on 8 January 1920. Folkestone reopened to civilian traffic on 1 March 1919.

When the Southern inherited Charing Cross, it also took on the old controversy over the question of a road or rail crossing of the Thames. In May 1925 the SR and the London County Council met to consider what could be done, but without any agreement. Meanwhile, a Royal Commission on Cross River Traffic in London had been established by Parliament, and in 1926 this reported, proposing that Charing Cross station be relocated slightly to the east, while Hungerford Bridge would be replaced by a new bridge with an upper deck carrying a 60 ft wide road, above a six-track railway line. This appealed to the Southern, appreciating that it would mean a new terminus purpose-designed to meet the changing needs of railway operation and the growth in traffic since the original station had opened. There would also be compensation for any disruption incurred during the work. Attitudes changed when the engineering report was published in 1928, moving beyond its terms of reference to find that while the proposed double-deck bridge was feasible, a road bridge with a new railway terminus at Waterloo would be much cheaper, at about three-quarters of the cost. The Southern objected strongly, but after the LCC offered a riverfront site at the southern end of Waterloo Bridge, plus substantial compensation of £325,000, on 30 July 1929 the Southern's directors recommended the plan to the shareholders as the best that could be achieved. It was all for nothing, as the bill authorising the works and the compensation was thrown out by the House of Commons on 6 May 1930. The scheme had depended on a 75 per cent government contribution, and when the financial crisis of the early 1930s began to bite, this was withdrawn. The scheme resurfaced once or twice before the war in one form or another, but by this time the benefits of railway electrification had swung the balance of opinion back in favour of the railway, and then the Second World War intervened and nothing more was heard of the idea.

One reason for the Southern's consideration of the various plans for the Hungerford Bridge and Charing Cross was that the bridge itself was beginning to show signs of weakness, and restrictions had to be imposed on the weight of trains and locomotives using it. Electrification proved the saviour of the bridge, as the lighter weight of electric multiple units and the more even spread of weight throughout the train gradually made the restrictions superfluous. All that was necessary was to swap around the main-line and suburban services, with the former using the newer and stronger 1887 bridge, while the latter took over the original bridge. The changeover was made during the weekend of 22–24 August 1925, ready for the start of electric services to Addiscombe, Beckenham Junction, Bromley North, Hayes and Orpington on 28 February 1926, with services to Dartford following on 6 June. The success of the scheme can be judged by the fact that daily traffic increased from 48,800 in 1925 to 71,200 in 1930. For electrification, the platform numbers were reversed with the lines into platforms 1 to 3 electrified, number 1 now being at the eastern or Villiers Street side of the station. A carriage road between the lines serving platforms 4 and 5 was removed and this enabled platform 4 to be widened, while all of the platforms were lengthened, so that lengths varied between 610 and 750 ft. The station enjoyed some further modest improvements during the 1930s under Southern management, including setting back the buffers of platforms 2 and 3 to bring them into line with the exit to Villiers Street and providing a much-needed increase in circulating area. Ticket barriers were improved with metal barriers replacing wooden gates. No less important, growing traffic resulted in additional trains during peak hours in 1932.

The Second World War found Charing Cross left on the sidelines, as with the evacuation of the BEF from Dunkirk there was no longer any need for senior officers to make hasty trips to France. During 8 October 1940 a daylight raid inflicted serious damage on a train standing in the station, but the worst raid of all was during the night of 16/17 April 1941, with the hotel and station both badly damaged by fire and other fires started on Hungerford Bridge. Three trains in the terminus were set alight along with a fourth on the bridge, while further disruption was caused when a landmine was discovered near the signal cabin with its parachute caught on the bridge girders. The mine was eventually defused and removed, but not before a fire under platform 4 had come within 4 yards of it. Charing Cross was closed throughout 17 April. Another closure followed a further raid on the night of 10/11 May. On 18 June 1944 a flying bomb blew out a span of the original bridge near the south bank, but trains managed to continue using the station by using the newer section of the bridge, although a full service could not be resumed until 4 December.

Holborn Viaduct

By 1870 the congestion at Ludgate Hill was such that it was clear that another station needed to be built, and although the LCDR was still in chancery, the sale of its telegraph system to the Post Office for £100,000 provided the necessary funding, although to avoid possible problems with creditors a front company, the Holborn Viaduct Station Company, was formed to raise the rest of the money. The use of small companies to achieve extensions to the railway network or to cover new projects such as termini or bridges was not in any case uncommon at this time. Holborn Viaduct was reached by a 264 yd spur off the through line and was intended for main-line trains, with just four short platforms, each of 400 ft, serving six roads. The idea was that all trains would be half length, as they would have been split en route into City and West End portions. Sometimes described as a 'mini-terminus', Holborn Viaduct opened on 2 March 1874. It was used by boat trains for Dover and Sheerness, the latter having a service to Flushing, as well as trains to Maidstone and Ashford.

A few local trains used Holborn Viaduct, but most were relegated to a low-level station with two platforms used by trains running through to Farringdon, and known initially when it opened on 1 August 1874 as Snow Hill, but changed to Holborn Viaduct (Low Level) on 1 May 1912.

Despite the cramped accommodation, a hotel was built and leased to the LCDR's caterers, Spiers & Pond, for 6 per cent of its capital cost and 10 per cent of its profits. The hotel was requisitioned by the government during the First World War, afterwards becoming offices, and was never reinstated as a hotel. It was destroyed during the blitz in 1941.

Holborn Viaduct was not a popular station for the City, being criticised by the Corporation as 'the great useless station called Holborn Viaduct' at a time when Ludgate Hill was also suffering criticism as being dangerous for the great number of people using it. It was not until 1907 that reconstruction of Ludgate Hill was started, removing the main-line island platform, whose trains now used Holborn Viaduct, and slewing the tracks to provide a much larger platform for local trains. The staircases were also widened to help passengers clear the platforms more quickly. This took until 1912 to complete, by which time the local traffic had slumped dramatically as passengers switched to electric trams and to the developing network of underground services. Even before work had really started in 1907, the GNR removed its trains, and the Midland followed in 1908. Wartime demands on the only north–south link through the centre of London meant that SECR trains stopped running through to Moorgate and Farringdon in April 1916.

Electrification came to Holborn Viaduct in 1925, with services to Shortlands and Orpington via Herne Hill, but because of the constraints on space, only two platforms, 4 and 5, could be lengthened to take eight-car trains. Further electrification followed, ending with services to Gillingham and Maidstone on 2 July 1939. The old hotel building was hit on 26 October 1940. Services were badly affected following the collapse of the bridge over Southwark Street during the heavy raid on the night of 16/17 April 1941, and while services were reinstated when a temporary bridge was erected, more was to follow. On the night of 10/11 May, the old hotel building was hit again, and completely gutted by fire, with the damage to the station itself so extensive that it could not be used by trains until 1 June, and a temporary booking office had to be provided.

Postwar, the services withdrawn as wartime austerity measures were gradually reinstated, but the station remained a gutted mess for many years after nationalisation. It was not until the late 1950s that rebuilding started, and was completed in 1963.

London Bridge

The oldest of the London termini, London Bridge grew in a haphazard way, a situation not helped by being used by two railway companies with an uneasy relationship since Waterloo also grew piece by piece, but benefited greatly from the massive rebuilding of 1910–20 that created an elegant and functional station.

Railway development in this part of London came as early as 1832 when a 3½ mile railway was planned between Greenwich and Tooley Street, close to London Bridge. In many ways this set the fashion for many of the later railways in the area by being built on a brick viaduct with 878 arches, creating a valuable investment income from the business premises and stables developed within many of the arches, while the remainder enabled the line to travel easily over the roads and lanes in this already built-up area. The first section of the new line was completed on 8 February 1836 between Spa Road, Bermondsey, and Deptford, making the former London's first terminus, although, of course, a purely temporary one. The line was opened to the first London Bridge station on 14 December 1836, with a grand opening attended by the Lord Mayor of London, even though it was outside his jurisdiction, the Common Council and sheriffs and around 2,000 guests. The grandeur of the opening was in stark contrast to the reality of the station, which was basically little more than the end of the viaduct, with low platforms and with the railway offices and booking offices below. The railway service started at noon, but still only ran as far as Deptford, and it was not to reach Greenwich until 1838. Plans for a triumphal arch at the entrance to this crude station were never fulfilled.

A 'J2' locomotive with an ex-SECR birdcage brake waits at London Bridge. *(Kershaw Collection, HRMS ACM500)*

Despite the awfulness of these arrangements, the new railway was not short of ambition, and had bought more land than it needed for the short line to Greenwich, with the London Bridge end of the viaduct able to take eight roads. For the immediate future, the London & Greenwich saw potential in allowing other railway companies to reach London through using its terminus. The first of these was the London & Croydon Railway, authorised in 1835, which joined the Greenwich line at Corbett's Lane, Bermondsey, and then ran to London Bridge, paying the then not inconsiderable sum to the LGR of 3*d* per passenger carried. A similar arrangement was proposed for the SER, authorised by an Act of 1836, which would effectively extend the London & Croydon to Redhill and Dover.

While the LCR had to operate over the LGR's tracks, it had its own three-road platforms immediately to the north of the LGR's terminus at London Bridge when it opened on 5 June 1839. This station obviously had the SER's needs in mind as it was far beyond the needs of the initial service of twelve trains daily. The LCR station was a grander development than that of the LGR, with a train shed 170 ft long and 48 ft wide, but again the booking office was in the street below, with the unusual refinement of separate staircases for first- and second-class passengers. A small goods station was also provided.

The SER was not to be the only user of the LCR facilities, as these were also to be shared with the new LBSC, but before this could happen, Parliament insisted on additional tracks on the Greenwich viaduct, preferring widening of an existing route to a new construction. It also persuaded the LGR and LCR to swap stations so that the LCR, SER and LBSC would not have to cross the LGR's tracks. Bearing in mind the basic nature of the LGR station, the LCR probably welcomed the 1840 permission to build a new station for itself and its two guest companies.

The additional lines into London Bridge were ready on 10 May 1842, although the first sections of the Brighton line had been open since 12 July 1841. On 26 May 1842, SER trains began to operate into the new station from Tonbridge. The new joint station was not ready until February 1844, and was operated by the Brighton, Croydon & Dover Joint Station Committee. Had it not been overtaken by later expansion, it could have been an attractive station, with a two-storey frontage with a booking office and waiting rooms on the ground floor, and the station offices in a separate building. There were three train sheds, one on the site of the old LGR station, with another two, one for arrivals and the other for departures, each with two platforms and three tracks. Access to a four-road carriage shed was by traversers. Platforms varied between 240 ft in the old LGR station now intended for the North Kent Railway, to 338 ft for the main departure platform and 531 ft for the main arrival platform.

The LGR, ever keen to make an extra penny out of its strategic position, now demanded 4½d per passenger, forcing the LCR with its short journeys to refuse to carry third-class passengers between New Cross and London Bridge, while also considering introducing a horse bus service between New Cross station and London Bridge. These measures were hardly conducive to increasing the traffic, and a slightly more practical measure was the construction of a new terminus for the LCR and SER at Bricklayers' Arms, near the junction of the Old Kent Road and what is now Tower Bridge Road, which opened on 1 May 1844. The new station had one big advantage in that there was enough room to expand the goods facilities and also introduce those for sheep and cattle. Using a new 1¾ mile branch from the Croydon's line, the new station also meant that the LGR lost its toll revenue, while the LCR at last felt free to introduce an hourly service, and was able to charge less than it had for trains to London Bridge. This at last had the desired results, forcing the LGR to charge more reasonable tolls and at different levels to reflect the fare paid, while the LCR responded by standardising fares and frequencies to both termini until it realised that London Bridge was the more attractive destination for its customers and pulled passenger traffic out of Bricklayers' Arms, which became a goods-only station.

Named after a nearby coaching inn, doubtless made redundant by the arrival of the railways, Bricklayers' Arms was neat and compact rather than grand, and many saw that it had greater potential as a goods terminus than as a passenger one, being even further from the West End and City than London Bridge. It started life as a true joint venture between the LCR, which contributed a third of the cost, and the SER, but the latter had powers in its Act to purchase the LCR share and did so in 1849, thereafter charging the smaller company a toll of 1¼d per passenger.

Bricklayers' Arms was far too remote to be acceptable as a London terminus, even though for a while it served as a station for royal trains, but even royalty soon began to appreciate the convenience of Victoria and Charing Cross when these opened. An attempt to use it as the terminus for a frequent service on the SER's north Kent lines between 1849 and 1852 failed to stimulate sufficient business among the travelling public, and so once again the focus of attention for all of the companies involved became London Bridge.

The LGR had started life with great promise, and considerable ambition, although the latter was based not on expanding its own network but in providing a way into London for other companies, and its greed in handling this potentially lucrative traffic was its downfall. The Bricklayers' Arms affair, literally as well as metaphorically a diversion, showed its weakness. The SER agreed to take over the running of the LGR on lease from 1 January 1845, and this arrangement continued so that the LGR was one of the companies acquired by the Southern in 1923.

Effectively under new management if not new ownership, London Bridge now became the focus of one of the many inter-company squabbles that so marred the early development of the railways. It was true that the still-new joint station was far too small for the SER and LBSC, and demolition was probably inevitable, but no attempt was made to create an enlarged joint station, something that might have worked as a cohesive whole. The SER built a boundary wall and established a new terminus on the north side of the site; a three-storey building at the street end with a canopy supported by iron pillars to provide shelter for travellers boarding or alighting from cabs. The main building was joined by another also of three storeys stretching down the approach road and dividing it from Tooley Street, with shops on Tooley Street and further shops and refreshment rooms on the approach side.

Inside the main building were separate booking offices for the Greenwich, north Kent and Dover lines, with the Greenwich lines using the narrow shed built for the LCR as their station. Immediately adjoining these to the south was the station for the north Kent lines, with two platforms providing an arrival and departure road which were separated by a road used as a siding for rolling stock. To the south of this was the 'Dover Station' of similar layout, with its own single-span roof and sitting on the site of the original 1836 station. Frequencies were not great at first, with the early years seeing just thirty departures daily to Greenwich and another fifty for the rest of the SER network.

The SER and LBSC had come to a truce, allowing each company toll-free running rights over key sections of the other's territory, with occasional exceptions. The SER's willingness to accommodate the LBSC could not disguise the fact that the available facilities were inadequate, so the Brighton company built its own new station to the south of the boundary wall, and by 1854 a three-storey building with an Italianate frontage was completed. It had a number of features in common with the SER building, including a flat roof and a canopy, although the latter was replaced in the mid-1880s by a glass shed extending over part of the station yard. The platforms were covered by a train shed with a single span about 100 ft wide and 700 ft long, covered by glass. This station was still only half complete when the Great Exhibition of 1851 produced a tremendous upsurge in traffic. The original Greenwich viaduct was widened with a third pair of lines in 1850, and an additional track built to the junction at which the north Kent line diverged.

In 1860 the LBSC had established a second London terminus at Victoria, and on 13 August 1866 the south London line was opened via Denmark Hill to connect the two termini and also to serve the densely populated area between them. This required three more approach roads into London Bridge, one for Victoria trains and two for inbound traffic. Three additional platforms were also added at this time, giving the LBSC station a total of nine. Meanwhile, in 1861 a hotel had been built close to the station but independently of the railway companies. Known as the Terminus Hotel, it never justified itself commercially, doubtless because of the remoteness of the station from the business of the City and the attractions of the West End, and in 1893 it was purchased by the LBSC and converted into offices. It had to be demolished in 1941 as a result of heavy damage suffered during the blitz.

Despite its location, London Bridge was a success commercially, with the Commons Select Committee on Metropolitan Communications reporting in 1855 that the number of passengers using the two stations had risen from 5.5 million in 1850 to 10 million in 1854. Nevertheless, all was not well, and certainly not good enough, for Sir Joseph Paxton told the committee that it took longer to travel from London Bridge to the GWR terminus at Paddington than to travel from London Bridge to Brighton. The Commons had already extracted a promise from the SER that it would build a West End terminus, and this was the basis for the extension to Charing Cross and, later, Cannon Street.

The two extensions required substantial changes to London Bridge, requiring it to become a through station despite the fact that it was now on a very cramped site. A route for the through roads was found on the north side of the SER station, but the shopping arcade on the approach road had to be demolished and replaced by a railway viaduct which led on to a girder bridge carrying the line over the station approach. The line then had almost immediately to swing south-west to avoid Southwark Cathedral, taking it into the grounds of St Thomas Hospital. The amount of land required from the hospital was exceedingly small, a sixth of an acre, for which the Charing Cross Railway Company offered the generous sum of £20,000, but the enabling Act had granted to the hospital the power to insist that the railway acquire the entire site, and the governors used this, demanding £750,000, and only reduced this to £296,000 after arbitration. The money was used towards the cost of the new Albert Embankment Hospital, completed in 1871.

In constructing the extension, the original Greenwich station disappeared, and the lines leading to it were raised on a viaduct to provide a high-level station with five platforms, two for Down traffic and three for Up traffic. The high-level station started to handle Greenwich and Mid-Kent trains from 11 January 1864, and was opened for all lines on 1 May. The surviving parts of the old SER station became a new Continental Goods depot with eight tracks under one roof.

The two new termini satisfied the SER's traffic demands for the time being although, as mentioned in the piece on Charing Cross, expansion was soon to come to the fore. The LBSC meanwhile saw its traffic continue to increase and put pressure on its station, but expansion in the 1870s was rejected because of the cost. Instead, tracks were rearranged and signalling improved to get the maximum capacity out of the limited space, and by rearranging the approaches to the platforms, many of which were extended, so that these could be used both for arrivals and departures. In some cases platforms could be used by two trains at the same time, as at Victoria. The cab road was shortened to allow the construction of two more short platforms. To increase capacity at London Bridge for passengers, the Continental Goods depot was moved in 1899 to Ewer Street, Southwark, on the Charing Cross extension line, and four low-level terminal platforms were constructed between the LBSCR station and the high-level viaduct, with canopies replacing the old depot's wooden roof. These platforms were ready for use from 2 June 1902, initially numbered separately as 1 to 4. A further benefit for passengers came with the City & South London tube on 25 February 1900, although it was not until 2 December 1901 that lifts were available, making London Bridge just a little less remote. There were further changes at the turn of the century following the joint working of the SER and LCDR, with the new SECR providing two more tracks on the north side of the approach viaduct.

The tracks on the approaches became, north to south:

SECR No. 1 Down
SECR No. 2 Down
SECR No. 3 Down
SECR No. 2 Up
SECR No. 1 Up
SECR Down main (also used by LBSCR)
SECR Up main (also used by LBSCR)
SECR Up local (also used by LBSCR)
LBSCR South London Down
LBSCR South London Up main
LBSCR South London Up local

Even these arrangements were far from permanent, with the LBSCR Up main being resignalled for reversible working on 19 October 1909, ready for the electrification of the south London line. This also relieved the congestion on the SECR Down main, which in 1912 was carrying fourteen LBSCR and five SECR trains between 5 and 6 pm. Meanwhile, electrification started on 1 December 1909, with the south London line using the 6,600 V AC system with overhead wires, described somewhat confusingly by today's standards as the 'elevated electric'. With the six most southerly platforms in the LBSC station electrified, this was a clear indication of the company's intention to proceed with electrification on a grand scale. The next phases of electrification were completed during 1912, with services to Crystal Palace Low Level via Tulse Hill on 1 March, and to Streatham and Victoria via Tulse Hill on 1 June. What today would be described as the 'sparks effect' resulted in a tremendous increase in activity, with pre-electrification services into the LBSCR station running at 663 trains a day, but rising to 901 in 1912.

London Bridge was spared any damage from air raids during the First World War, and no significant development occurred in the years before the SECR and LBSC passed to the Southern Railway. The bringing together of the companies operating trains across the whole length of southern England, if one accepts that the south coast of Cornwall is in the west, was publicly demonstrated by the knocking-through of an opening in the wall between the former LBSCR and SECR stations. However, this had to wait until 1928, as did a second footbridge over the low level to expedite movement across the station, as now, more than ever, it was realised that many arriving off the Brighton trains needed to continue their journey to Cannon Street, Charing Cross or Waterloo. The platforms were renumbered in a single consecutive sequence 1 to 22 from north to south, with the omission of any platform 5, although there was a fifth road for light-engine movements between the tracks served by platforms 4 and 6. Platforms 1 and 2 are believed to have been the first in London to have had the benefit of a loudspeaker system when this was installed as an experiment in 1927.

The new owners of the complete system were heavily influenced by the LSWR, but did at least go through the motions of assessing rival forms of electrification before deciding on the third rail DC system favoured by the LSWR. The initial electrification of what was now the Eastern Section of the Southern Railway saw third-rail electrification of services running through London Bridge to Addiscombe, Beckenham Junction, Bromley North, Hayes and Orpington from 28 February 1926, with services to Dartford via Blackheath, Bexleyheath and Sidcup all electrified on 6 June, although full services were not operated until 19 July. Services to Caterham and Tattenham Corner on the Central Section were electrified from 25 March 1928, with a full service from 17 June. This was accompanied by conversion of the Brighton overhead to third rail, with the services to Crystal Palace (Low Level) switching on 25 March 1928, and those to Victoria via the south London line, Crystal Palace via Tulse Hill, Coulsdon North, Epsom Downs via West Croydon, Streatham Hill, Selhurst and Sydenham changing to the DC system from 17 June. From 3 March 1929 third rail also covered services to Dorking North and Effingham Junction via Mitcham. At any time in railway history, such activity would have been impressive, but this was not the best of times.

The changes also necessitated modifications to the working of the approach tracks, and in 1936 the locomotive turntable opposite the ends of what were by now platforms 15 and 16 was removed, leaving the few remaining steam locomotives working the Kent coast and Hastings via Tonbridge trains to turn at New Cross Gate shed. It would be reasonable to think that the space so freed up would have been used for a beneficial operational purpose, but instead a large 'London Bridge' nameboard was erected and illuminated at night – and this at a station whose travellers were almost all daily commuters!

Given financial incentives by the government which abolished taxation on railway travel on condition that the money was spent on modernisation, the Southern next turned its attention to the south Coast, where many of its longer-distance trains operated at peak period frequencies that rivalled some suburban lines. Platforms 14 and 15 were lengthened to 800 ft. As an interim measure, electric trains started to operate to Reigate and Three Bridges from 17 July 1932, but from 1 January 1933 main-line electric trains operated from London Bridge to Brighton and West Worthing. Seaford and Hastings via Eastbourne services followed on 7 July 1935, and from 3 July 1938 those to Littlehampton and Bognor, the latter reached by the Portsmouth No. 2 Electrification Scheme.

As the Second World War approached, London Bridge handled 250,000 passengers daily, although of these 80,000 were on the trains continuing through to the City and West End. It seems surprising that there were not more of them, since although London Bridge was by this time served by the Bank branch of the Northern Line, access from the surface to the tube platforms was by lift and not one of the quickest or pleasantest places to make this transfer. Another way of looking at these figures was that the station handled 2,407 railway movements daily, and in the morning peak hour received 94 trains, of which 46 terminated while 29 continued to Cannon Street and another 19 to Charing Cross. One seasonal movement was that of Londoners to work in the Kent hopfields each summer, often taking their household effects with them as they camped out on what was a working holiday at a time when paid holidays were very limited. This was a useful off-peak business with an annual average of 33,000 passengers during the 1930s, but it was business that was treated to the oldest available rolling stock with goods vans for the household effects. One gets the impression that the Southern was ashamed of the clientele, and wished to shield the City workers alighting from Pullman cars and first-class carriages from this sight of the working man.

The Second World War brought air raids on a scale that could not have been imagined in the earlier conflict, and the railways were a prime target because of their strategic importance. On 9 December 1940 the signal-box had a parachute mine settle against its wall with its parachute caught on a signal. Displaying great heroism, the three signalmen continued working while a naval officer and a rating defused the mine. Worse was to follow, as on the night of 29/30 December 1940 the station, while not in the City, was caught in the massive raid using incendiary bombs. At just after midnight the former hotel and the upper floors of the station buildings were gutted by fire, which also destroyed many station offices. In an attempt to get the station working again, the ticket office became the parcels office and a temporary wooden ticket office was sited on the main concourse.

Post-nationalisation, London Bridge was badly neglected by British Railways for several decades, even leaving the wooden ticket office functioning. The only substantial changes for some thirty years were those associated with the spread of electrification to the Kent coast. It took London Transport until 1967 to replace the lifts for the underground station with escalators.

Victoria

Although not quite in the West End, Victoria was closer to it than any other station for the southern companies until the opening of Charing Cross. It also had the advantage of good surface transport links with the substantial bus station outside and, in later years, Victoria coach station nearby and the Greenline terminus on Eccleston Bridge, although both of these may be seen as competitors, the former for the longer-distance traffic and the latter for suburban custom. On the other hand, Victoria was dependent on the slow and indirect services of the District and Circle lines for many years until the opening of the Victoria Line.

The LBSCR was unhappy with its shared terminus with the SER at London Bridge, as much because of the friction between the two companies that broke out from time to time as for the remoteness of the location. So desperate was the situation that the Brighton company had even made overtures to the LSWR about using Waterloo or pursuing a new terminus. As happened so often in the early days of the railways, progress came from the initiative of a newcomer, and when the LSWR refused to support the planned West End of London & Crystal Palace Railway proposed in 1853, the LBSCR saw its chance. The WELCPR was a scheme to link the LBSCR's new Crystal Palace branch to a junction with the LSWR at Wandsworth, with a further branch, running for a short distance over LSWR metals, to a riverside terminus on the south bank of the Thames opposite Pimlico. The new railway opened its first stage on 1 December 1856, running from Crystal Palace to a temporary terminus at the northern end of Wandsworth Common, and was worked by the LBSCR, which introduced a new service between London Bridge and Wandsworth. The WELCPR had ambitions to extend to Farnborough in Kent and take a share of the Kent coast business, using powers obtained in 1854, while the company obtained its second connection with the LBSCR at Norwood Junction on 1 October 1857. The through line to the riverside terminus at Battersea opened for traffic on 29 March 1858, and rejected by the LSWR, simply touched that system at what is now Clapham Junction, running parallel to it without any running connection, before passing under the LSWR towards the river. It was perhaps not quite the 'con' that it seemed, since passengers could reach the north bank of the Thames by using the new Chelsea Suspension Bridge.

Although the riverside terminus was meant to be permanent and the site amounted to 22 acres, the station buildings were constructed of timber. It was later to become a goods depot. The temporary buildings indicated the sudden lack of confidence on the part of the WELCPR, because the railways were now being offered a number of schemes to take them closer to the West End. These included a Westminster Terminus Railway, which aimed to reach Horseferry Road, authorised in 1854, and in 1857 the Victoria Station and Pimlico Railway was actively promoted, with the necessary legislation passed the following year. This new arrival immediately made much of the WELCPR plans redundant, and was immediately embraced by the LBSCR. The new plan was for a junction with the WELCPR at Stewarts Lane, just before it ceased running alongside the LSWR, with the line climbing to cross over the main line to Waterloo and then continuing on a bridge over the Thames to the western end of Victoria Street, using the disused basin of the Grosvenor Canal. Construction started in 1859 and the LBSCR obligingly acquired the WELCPR line to Battersea on 1 July. The other line, the extension to Farnborough, was acquired by the East Kent Railway.

Partly to show its independence, and partly to help raise capital from investors, the Victoria Station and Pimlico Railway claimed that it would be building a terminus not only for the LBSCR, but also for the SER, the East Kent Railway (the predecessor of the LCDR) and the LSWR. The WELCPR also had another branch from Norwood to Bromley, now Shortlands, opened on 3 May 1858, with an adjoining section built by another railway. This was worked initially by the SER, but later the lease was transferred to the LCDR, and enabled the company to operate from Canterbury to Victoria. Despite its poverty, the LCDR realised that the new arrangement still left it at the mercy of other companies, and in 1860 obtained the necessary powers to build its own new routes to both the West End and the City of London, with the former being achieved through a new line to the WELCPR from Beckenham to Battersea.

Such were the changing fortunes and ambitions of the railway companies, that the Victoria Station and Pimlico Railway found itself building a major terminus for the LBSCR and the LCDR plus the Great Western, which meant that the line from Longhedge Junction, Battersea, where the GWR would approach over the West London Extension Railway, had to be of mixed gauge to accommodate the broad-gauge GWR trains. The LBSCR provided two-thirds of the Victoria line's capital and secured its own terminus and access lines, taking 8½ acres of the 14 acre site, so that eventually, despite the magnificent façade of the Grosvenor Hotel, Victoria was really to be two stations in one! The LBSCR was also to encourage other railways to use its portion of Victoria, which must have necessitated some interesting detours around London.

The approach to Victoria from Clapham Junction required both a tight curve and a steep climb, with the bridge over the river built high enough to allow passage of the largest ships likely to use the Thames. Indeed, the bridge was unrealistically high. This was the LBSCR approach, but it also had to be shared with the GWR despite that company's connection with the LCDR. On crossing the bridge, the line then had a steep descent to the station, as it had been decided that an approach on a viaduct to an elevated station would have been unacceptable to the wealthy landowners in the area. Other concessions to this element included extending the train shed beyond the platforms, and mounting the early sleepers, of longitudinal design, on rubber to minimise vibration.

The new station opened for LBSCR trains on 1 October 1860, the WELCPR having closed its riverside terminus on 30 September. The station was built from the outset on a generous scale, being 800 ft long and 230 ft wide, with a ridge-and-furrow roof having 50 ft spans covering ten tracks and six platform faces. There was a cab road from Eccleston Bridge, with an exit into Terminus Place. Facilities were provided for horses and carriages to be unloaded from trains. A turntable was provided by Eccleston Bridge. The main-line trains

The first electrification was the south London line linking Victoria and London Bridge, but this is the service at Wandsworth after conversion to third rail. *(HRMS AER210)*

used the eastern side of the station. The Grosvenor Hotel was constructed independently, despite its obvious attachment to the terminus. The presence of several railway companies had convinced its promoters of success, and it was completed in 1861. The original hotel was built along the west side of the station but could not conceal the distinctly unattractive, even primitive, entrance with offices in a series of wooden huts, for while the LCDR was indeed poverty-stricken, even the more affluent LBSCR had found the cost of the move into the centre of London expensive. Matters were not improved when in February 1884 the Fenian Brotherhood deposited a bomb in a bag in the left-luggage office, which also wrecked the LBSCR's cloakroom and ticket office. Fortunately the police were able to prevent similar outrages at Charing Cross and Paddington.

Last of all came the LCDR and GWR station, completed on 25 August 1862, although the LCDR had made use of a temporary station since December 1860. The LCDR had a modest side entrance into the station, which had nine tracks on its smaller acreage, of which four were mixed gauge. The GWR started services to and from Victoria on 1 April 1863, with what was essentially a suburban service from Southall, where connections could be made with its main-line services. Trains running through to Reading, Slough, Uxbridge and Windsor were also provided at times over the years that followed, while there were experiments with slip coaches off trains from further afield, such as Bristol and Birmingham, special trains to Henley and to the Wycombe line, and finally, between 1910 and 1912, a daily train in each direction between Birmingham and Wolverhampton and Victoria. Wartime restrictions saw the end of the Southall service in 1915, and in any case such a service was superfluous with the opening of what is now known as the Circle Line between Victoria and Paddington in 1868.

Other railway companies operating into Victoria included the Great Northern Railway, operating from Barnet via Ludgate Hill from 1 March 1868, and the Midland Railway from

South Tottenham and Hendon via Ludgate Hill from 1 July 1875, both of which used the LCDR station. London & North Western trains operated into the LBSC station from Broad Street via Willesden Junction and the West London Railway from 1 January 1869, and survived as an occasional service between Willesden Junction and Victoria until 1917.

Meanwhile, much had been happening with the arrangements for handling the traffic for the fast-growing station. The LBSCR opened a cut-off between Balham and East Croydon, one effect of which was that the distance between that station and the two London termini became more or less the same. The LCDR also bypassed the WELCPR route by building its own lines, opened in two sections, between Stewarts Lane and Herne Hill on 25 August 1862, and Herne Hill and Penge Junction at Beckenham on 1 July 1863, leaving the original WELCPR approach as a purely local line. Despite these changes, or even perhaps because of them, Victoria's traffic continued to grow apace, and the approaches became a serious bottleneck, so that a leading consulting engineer, Sir Charles Fox, was asked to prepare proposals, eventually recommending new lines, including extra tracks over the Thames, and junctions. The companies accepted Fox's proposals and Parliamentary approval was obtained.

The new layout entailed removing the broad-gauge tracks from two of the approach lines, providing an additional line for the LBSC, while providing three new mixed-gauge lines and a standard-gauge line for the GWR and LCDR. A new bridge was constructed alongside the existing Grosvenor Bridge on the downstream side. Everything was completed for normal services on 20 December 1865. The new layout meant that stations could be built at each end of the bridge, with the northern station known as Grosvenor Road and opened on 1 November 1867 for the LCDR, while the southern station was called Battersea Park and Steamboat Pier for the LBSCR, and was in effect a rebuild of a station opened in 1860 as a substitute for the old WELCPR terminus. Battersea Park only survived until 1 November 1870, when the LBSCR opened its own platforms at Grosvenor Road. The new station at Grosvenor Road was really too close to Victoria to be of much commercial value, with the LBSCR using it by stopping Up trains for ticket inspection, and only a few local trains called in both directions. The LBSCR stopped using it on 1 April 1907 and was followed by the LCDR on 1 October 1911.

Further additional approach lines came when the LCDR opened a new high-level line with three tracks built on a mile-long viaduct running from Wandsworth Road to Battersea Pier Junction, at the southern end of Grosvenor Bridge, on 1 January 1867. This line also had a connection to the LBSCR's new south London line.

It was soon time to consider tidying up and expanding the station itself, especially as by 1890, with all of its lines completed, the LBSCR was producing a steady return on its capital, with the annual dividend running at 6 or 7 per cent. Starting in 1892, the LBSCR acquired the houses on the west side of the station, and also bought the freehold of the Grosvenor Hotel when the owners refused to sell houses owned by them. The LBSCR let the hotel to a new operator and built an impressive 150-room wing across the front of the station. The initial development of the station during the 1890s produced another 90 ft in width, but only at the southern end of the station between Eccleston Bridge and the hotel. Even this was judged, rightly, to be insufficient. Unable to expand further west because of Buckingham Palace Road, or east because of the LCDR station, the only solution was to extend the station towards the river, and for this the powers were obtained in 1899, so that the station could increase from ten roads and eight platform faces to thirteen roads with nine faces, several of which could be used by two trains at once. Work started in 1901. The old roof was removed and five new ridged roofs were erected to cover the north station with a similar arrangement for what was to become the south station between Eccleston Bridge and Elizabeth Bridge. The vast project was completed in instalments, starting on 10 June 1906 and followed by the five western platforms and a new cab road on 10 February 1907. Before the end of the year the new wing for the Grosvenor Hotel was completed across the front of the station. By 1 July 1908 the four eastern platforms were ready and the new station enjoyed a formal opening. The LBSCR station was now worthy of the Brighton line, with its luxurious trains and well-heeled clientele.

Innovations included a large departure board which showed the departure times, platforms and stops for up to eighteen trains at a time, behind which was an underground 'gentlemen's court', which was actually a public lavatory with a hairdressing saloon. The small telegraph office became the first post office on a London station on 2 October 1911. The station was screened off from Buckingham Palace Road south of the hotel by a wall of Portland Stone and red brick with niches for busts of the great, although these were never filled. All in all, the new station was 320 ft wide and 1,500 ft long and occupied 16 acres, almost double the area of the original. It had coaling stages at the ends of four of its platforms. It was lit by gas, and remained so until 1927, even though by then many of the trains were electric.

Of even greater value than all of the changes to the station, long overdue though many of them were, was the introduction of the first electric service on 1 December 1909, over the south London line via Denmark Hill to London Bridge. This was an immediate success, with its 6,600 V AC overhead system, and countered the growing competition from the electric tramways. Electrification was clearly the way ahead for the suburban services, with Victoria–Streatham Hill–Crystal Palace Low Level electrified from 12 May 1911 and, on 1 June 1912, Victoria–Norwood and Victoria–Streatham Hill–London Bridge.

Meanwhile, the Chatham station, now operated by the SECR, also underwent rebuilding, although its four storeys were dwarfed by the adjoining new wing of the Grosvenor Hotel. This work was completed in 1907, but most of the rest of the interior remained unchanged, the one area of big improvements being that for international passengers.

That the station was in mixed ownership was made clear by the signs greeting intending passengers. The Chatham boasted 'The Shortest and Quickest Route to Paris & the Continent Sea Passage One Hour', while the Brighton proclaimed 'To Paris and the Continent via Newhaven and Dieppe Shortest and Cheapest Route', all of which indicated that these were the days before advertising and trading standards since the latter route meant a sea journey of almost four hours!

The First World War saw Victoria become the main station for troop movements between London and France, with special trains for leave traffic to and from Folkestone starting in November 1914 and eventually increasing to twelve daily, with another two for Dover. A free buffet provided by voluntary workers served refreshments for up to 4,000 men every day. The SECR station also handled mail for the Western Front, which meant a train with some thirty vans remaining in the station each day from 11 am to 11 pm while letters and parcels were loaded. Inward mail was divided between Victoria, Cannon Street and Charing Cross. The station escaped serious damage during the air raids, although on one occasion an anti-aircraft shell case crashed through part of the roof, and on 1 October 1917 around 100 ft of the northern end of Grosvenor Bridge was set alight when an anti-aircraft shell pierced the gas main under the disused platform.

Wartime meant disruption to traffic, with Dover being taken over by the army and all the remaining boat trains redirected to Victoria. The Folkestone to Boulogne boat train ceased on 29 November 1915, although the Dieppe service diverted to Folkestone away from Newhaven until withdrawal on 13 April 1916. This left Southampton–Le Havre as the only route handling civilian traffic.

The SECR concentrated its cross-Channel boat trains on Victoria from 8 January 1920, as there had been a gradual reinstatement of cross-Channel services throughout 1919 and 1920, helped by the completion of the new Dover Marine station in January 1919.

The SECR main arrival platforms, then designated 1 and 2, were lengthened in 1921 to 764 ft and 735 ft, and the following year platforms 3 and 4, now too narrow and too short, were replaced by a new platform designated 3 and 4, which at 550 ft long and 37 ft wide was more than a third longer and three times the width.

The Southern Railway designated the two stations as Victoria (Eastern Section) and Victoria (Central Section), but it was not until 1924 that the first passageway was opened between the two parts of the station, with a second later in the year, and a single stationmaster appointed. The platforms were renumbered, reversing the order used by the SECR so that platform 1 was no longer against the dividing wall, but instead its number was taken by the most easterly platform to allow numbers to run across the station. For many years the SECR platforms had been numbered 1 to 9, with no platform 7, but now they were 1 to 8. The Central Section platforms were 9 to 17. The main arrival platform for continental trains became platform 8, and in 1930 this was roofed over and the Customs examination area heated for the first time.

There was an element of tokenism about many of these changes, as separate booking offices remained and there was no operational connection between the two sections until a new line and points were installed in 1938. Some further overhead electrification continued, using equipment ordered before the grouping, with electric services introduced to Coulsdon North and to Sutton on 1 April 1925.

In 1926 the Southern announced that it had decided to standardise on the third rail 600 V DC system, and started wholesale electrification of the lines out of Victoria so that only services to Hastings via Tonbridge and the Kent coast, including the boat trains and the 'Night Ferry', were still steam-hauled by the outbreak of the Second World War. Before the announcement, a third-rail service had been launched to Herne Hill and Orpington on 12 July 1925, while the south London line became third rail on 17 June 1928 and the Crystal Palace Low Level service followed on 3 March 1929, working beyond to West Croydon and Beckenham Junction, as well as a new service to Epsom via Mitcham Junction. In its haste to ensure a single standard system, the Southern completed the transfer to third rail on 22 September 1929, when the last overhead train left for Coulsdon North thirty minutes after midnight.

Now electrification was spreading out of the suburbs, although a cynic might remark that that description suited the Sussex coast! After running services to Reigate and Three Bridges from 17 July 1932, electrification through to Brighton and West Worthing began on 1 January 1933. There was also a tremendous increase in frequencies, with four trains an hour along the main line from Victoria, including an hourly non-stop. Electric services to Hastings via Eastbourne and to Seaford started on 7 July 1935, and to Littlehampton on 3 July 1938, as well as to Bognor and Portsmouth via Arundel on the Portsmouth No. 2 Electrification Scheme on 3 July 1938, just in time for the start of the summer peak. Almost a year later, on 2 July 1939, Gillingham and Maidstone East services became electric, the last scheme to be completed before the outbreak of war.

As mentioned elsewhere, the 'sparks effect' produced a dramatic increase in traffic, with the numbers arriving at Victoria in the height of the peak rising from 10,200 in an hour in 1927 to 17,200 in 1937. There would also have been a significant saving in costs, with fewer operational personnel and the end of shunting mileage as locomotives moved to turntables.

Growing competition from air transport led to a number of developments intended to improve the quality of the continental services, with an all-Pullman train introduced to Dover in 1924. In 1929 the famous 'Golden Arrow' was introduced, followed on 14 October 1936 by the 'Night Ferry' through sleeping-car service with specially built Wagons Lits rolling stock.

Imperial Airways opened a London terminal in Buckingham Palace Road in 1939, and the so-called Flying-Boat Train from Waterloo was augmented by a service from Victoria during that summer. This was replaced during wartime by Air Specials from Victoria to Poole to connect with flights by the newly formed British Overseas Airways Corporation, BOAC, to Baltimore, on which accommodation was usually reserved for VIPs.

The Second World War brought about major restrictions, with train services cut back. Not only did the continental traffic end on the outbreak of war, but trains carrying service personnel to Europe also disappeared with the fall of France. The heavy air raids during the Blitz of 1940 and 1941 saw Victoria shut down at times as bombs and parachute mines closed the approaches. However, the station itself was spared serious damage, despite a crashing Dornier Do17 hitting the Eastern Section on 15 September 1940. A flying bomb hit the Eastern Section on 27 June 1944, destroying offices and also damaging the booking office.

The invasion of France soon brought back the daily leave trains, and a limited service for civilian traffic to Europe started after the German surrender, but a more complete service did not follow until 15 April 1946, including the reinstatement of the 'Golden Arrow'. The 'Night Ferry' was reinstated only a little more than a fortnight before nationalisation.

Waterloo

In some ways the history of Waterloo is similar to that of London Bridge, with the station being fairly remote from the destinations of most of the travellers arriving off its trains, but having replaced an earlier and even less satisfactory terminus, in this case at Nine Elms. The station also grew piecemeal, with four separate stages of construction. It was also extended to provide through running, and with the creation of a station just outside at Waterloo Junction on the line from London Bridge to Charing Cross, it was also used by two railway companies. Here, however, the histories of the two stations differ considerably. The through connection for trains to run beyond Waterloo was relatively short-lived. More importantly, Waterloo was taken in hand and the LSWR terminus completely rebuilt by a vigorous and determined new general manager, Sir Herbert Walker. For more than eighty years it has represented a dignified and cohesive whole, with a gentle sweep to the broad concourse so that the entire station can be seen at a glance from the office windows, and clearly shows that it was the first terminus designed for electric trains. It is an indictment of the other grouping companies and of British Railways that for almost fifty years this was the most modern of London's termini.

The predecessor of Waterloo, Nine Elms, was chosen as the terminus for the new London & Southampton Railway, first mooted in 1831, largely because it meant that costly disturbance to business and residential property would be minimal. Its position, close to the southern end of Vauxhall Bridge, meant that passengers could make their way to the West End, while boat services were envisaged for those travelling to the City. The new terminus was opened on 21 May 1838, by which time the railway was open as far as Woking. The following year the London & Southampton unveiled its ambitions with a new name, the London & South Western Railway, although it did not reach its original objective until 11 May 1840. The first train, carrying guests, took three hours for the journey of just under 80 miles between Nine Elms and Southampton.

Nine Elms was a simple station occupying 4 acres and fronted by a neoclassical building just two storeys high, but there seems to be little evidence that it was conceived as a temporary structure. There were separate platforms for arrivals and departures, which was a fairly common practice at the time. Departure of the five daily trains operated from the opening of the station was signalled by the ringing of a bell mounted on the station roof five minutes before the due time. Nevertheless, anxious to stimulate excursion traffic, the then L&SR decided to operate eight trains in connection with Derby Day at Epsom racecourse on 30 May 1838, even though its nearest station was 6 miles from the course. For a guinea, passengers could have a return journey by train and coach, but for those paying the ordinary fare there would be a long walk. Failing to appreciate the distance between the railway and the racecourse, the small station was besieged by a crowd of thousands, far more than could be carried. As many as possible were put on the train, and the doors of the terminus shut, at which point the crowd rioted, broke down the doors and besieged the train. The police were called for and managed to calm the situation, but all trains were cancelled for the day.

The new railway soon found that its heaviest traffic was short-distance between what would now be the outer suburbs and London. Many of the station names of the early LSWR differ from those of today, with the original Kingston now being Surbiton. The first branch line was opened on 27 July 1846 from Clapham Junction to Richmond, and soon provided a

Unrebuilt 'Merchant Navy' class but renumbered 35017, *Belgian Marine*, arrives at Waterloo with the Up 'Bournemouth Belle'; in the background a 4 COR heads a Portsmouth fast. (HRMS AAZ424)

quarter of the company's traffic. The lack of appeal of the railway for much of the other traffic was largely due to the remote location of Nine Elms, and the LSWR admitted to the Metropolitan Termini Commission in 1846 that road coaches had survived between Chertsey and the City because of this. The original promoters of the branch to Richmond had also proposed a line from Nine Elms to a supposed 'West End' terminus near Hungerford Bridge. Having taken over the Richmond branch before its completion, the LSWR obtained powers in 1845 for a new terminus in York Road, close to the southern end of Waterloo Bridge, and a further act in 1847 increased the number of lines to the new terminus to four and also the size of the site. The reasons for the LSWR choosing Nine Elms in the first place can be the more readily understood when it is realised that the extension to Waterloo, then requiring far fewer tracks than exist today, required the demolition of 700 houses and the crossing of 21 roads, despite the 1¾ mile railway using viaduct with more than 200 arches for most of its length. Obstacles that affected the alignment included Lambeth Palace, Vauxhall Gardens and a gas works. One intermediate station was built at Vauxhall, while a bridge over Westminster Road was on the skew with the then unprecedented span of 90 ft. The size of the undertaking was partly because the LSWR was encouraged by earlier negotiations with the LBSCR that would have seen the latter share the new terminus, but despite legislation being passed, the concept was dropped, largely because of objections from the London & Croydon Railway before that company was absorbed by the LBSCR. A few years later another scheme surfaced that would have seen the LBSCR use Waterloo, but this was also dropped and eventually Victoria became the objective of the Brighton company's ambitions. The SER also considered an extension to Waterloo from Bricklayers' Arms, but Parliament rejected the proposal. The interest in using Waterloo can be understood, with Robert Stephenson telling a Royal Commission in 1846 that there was 'no point on the South side of the Thames so good for a large railway station, as the south end of Waterloo Bridge.'

The first Waterloo station opened on 11 July 1848, with Nine Elms having closed the previous day, although still being available for VIP use and visiting royalty. Initially, Waterloo was designed not as a terminus but as a through station. Under a two-span 280 ft iron and glass roof were six tracks and six 300 ft platform faces, although the length of these was soon doubled, while a spur towards the river suggested that the LSWR was attempting to keep every option open. The catchment area for the new terminus was soon growing again, with an extension of the Richmond branch to Windsor on 1 December 1849, by which time an additional Up line had been installed.

The LSWR itself, notwithstanding the opinion of Stephenson and the interest displayed by other companies, was not content with Waterloo, and instead wanted to get closer to the

City. Even at this early stage, the LSWR claimed that there was no room for goods traffic at Waterloo, especially since access to the river was blocked by the Lion Brewery. Acts of 1846 and 1848 provided for an extension to a site just west of London Bridge and property acquisition started, but a financial crisis in 1848–9 undermined these plans. The plans for an extension and the financial crisis doubtless also delayed the construction of permanent buildings on the site.

By this time the rapid expansion of London and the tremendous growth in population combined to put extreme pressure on cemetery space. This was solved in 1854 when the London Necropolis & National Mausoleum Company opened a private cemetery at Brookwood, conveniently on the LSWR main line west of Woking, and a private station was built at Waterloo for the special trains with their hearse carriages.

Expansion continued at Waterloo as the LSWR network grew. Four additional platform faces were built in 1860, in what was to become known as the Windsor station, and separated from the original station, now known as the 'Main station', by their own cab road. The opening of the Charing Cross extension in 1864 was accompanied by a short spur into Waterloo. This could have enabled passenger trains to work through to London Bridge and, later, to Cannon Street, thus providing the long sought-after City extension of the LSWR. However, it was rarely used by passenger trains, although it was the route taken by Queen Victoria when travelling from Windsor to the Channel ports. In 1868 a service from Kensington to Cannon Street was introduced over the connection, but this was cut back to Waterloo in February 1869, no doubt influenced by the opening of an SER station, known as Waterloo Junction for many years, on the Charing Cross extension, although at first passengers changing between the two companies were forced to rebook, and only later were through fares offered for those attempting to reach the City. For the most part, the connection was used for the occasional goods working.

Yet another Waterloo station was added in 1878, opening on 16 December, but on this occasion new offices were opened and a refreshment room, with a cab yard under a new 300 ft frontage on Waterloo Road. In November 1885 a further final extension was added, with the North station built as an extension of the Windsor station with six new platform faces. By now Waterloo had a total of eighteen platforms, and unusually for the day, all of them were suitable for arrivals and departures. However, they were still served by just four approach tracks, which were the cause of much delay as by this time Waterloo was handling 700 trains daily. As was the custom at the time, and as we have seen at Victoria, Waterloo was an open station, with tickets being checked at Vauxhall, and this no doubt added to the delays. The station itself was a mess, not least because of an eccentric platform numbering system that meant that many platforms used the same number for two faces, and this, with a paucity of departure information, meant that even if the intending passenger found the right platform, there was a 50 per cent risk of boarding the wrong train. Between 1886 and 1892 a further two approach tracks were added for trains off the South Western main line and a third for trains on the Windsor line, necessitating the rebuilding of Vauxhall station. Once again, there was massive destruction of housing, so that the LSWR had to provide new property in 1890 for more than a thousand people. In 1900 the number of approach lines was increased to eight for part of the approach, reducing to seven as far as Queen's Road. Progress was uneven, and it was not possible to ease the lot of all passengers at once. Passengers for the City were growing in numbers, and were also people of considerable influence. The need to rebook at the South Eastern station was a nuisance, and although through season tickets did become available later, the service from Charing Cross to Cannon Street was unreliable, especially in thick fog since the railways of the day depended entirely on enginemen being able to see signals, and Cannon Street was not by any means a convenient terminus for all City workers. An idea of the character of the typical LSWR City-bound passenger can be gained from one event in 1880, when a group of them formed the Metropolitan Express Omnibus Company to operate horse buses between Waterloo and the City. Even though this company was taken over within a year by the Railways & Metropolitan Omnibus Company, within five years it was operating eighteen 26-seat buses and carrying 2.5 million passengers annually. The LSWR itself calculated that of the 50,000 daily arrivals at Waterloo, a quarter of them were heading for the City, divided equally between the buses and the SER. As early as 1882, plans were considered for an overhead railway, but rejected as too costly, and no doubt hazardous given the technology of the day. The plans were revived in 1891, but were still considered too costly. Relief was soon found in plans for a Waterloo and City tube line, authorised in 1893. The new company was clearly attractive to the LSWR, which provided much of the capital and five of the eight directors, and agreed to operate the line for 55 per cent of the gross receipts after payment of a 3 per cent dividend. The line opened in 1898, providing a direct non-stop link between a station not strictly deep underground but in Waterloo's basement and a point just across the road from the Bank of England, appropriately enough known as Bank. Open-air carriage sidings were constructed at the Waterloo end, and rolling stock could be moved using a hoist. This was also the LSWR's first experience with electric train operation. In 1907 the company took over the line completely.

Even earlier plans had attempted to introduce a tube line between Waterloo and the West End. A pneumatic tube was begun, but this, the Waterloo and Whitehall, was abandoned in 1868. At this stage the LSWR was probably being cautious in the middle of a depression in railway financing, but there seems little explanation for its neglect of the Baker Street & Waterloo Railway, which opened on 10 March 1906 between Lambeth North and Baker Street, with a station deep below Waterloo which was reached at first by means of lifts.

Waterloo was to experience the demands of wartime traffic before any other London terminus, simply because all of the troops sent to the Boer War between 1899 and 1902 passed through Southampton, and the majority of them also went through Waterloo, while the cavalry boarded with their horses at Nine Elms.

The LSWR was not blind to the shortcomings of its only London terminus, and as the 1890s drew to a close and the railway enjoyed considerable prosperity, powers were sought from Parliament to extend the station by purchasing an additional 6½ acres to the south of the terminus, including six streets and parts of two others, a church and church schools. In return the LSWR would erect six blocks of flats to accommodate 1,750 people, allegedly more than the number displaced by the expansion. From contemporary accounts, little of worth was lost in the exercise since the area around Waterloo was as much a mess as the stations themselves, with such an unsavoury reputation that it was sometimes known as 'whoreterloo'.

Site clearing had already begun in 1901 when the new chief engineer, J.W. Jacomb-Hood was sent to the USA to study American termini. He returned to design a magnificent twenty-three platform station with a single roof, a wide passenger concourse running uninterrupted across the platform ends, and opposite them a substantial office block that also accommodated the station facilities. This was thinking on a grand scale that had no precedent in the design of the London termini at the time, or, some might suggest, since! It required massive strengthening of the foundations, with additional foundations being dug 30 ft deep to get below the marshy ground, while the bridge over Westminster Bridge Road was widened to take eleven approach roads. The Necropolis station was demolished, with a new structure built on the south side of Westminster Bridge Road, and opened on 16 February 1902, and powers were obtained to buy more land to the north of the terminus and to abandon the through line to the SER. When Herbert Walker joined the LSWR in 1912, the plans were scaled back, but only slightly, since Walker, who was a man who knew how to get the best value out of any investment, decided that the 1885 North station, still relatively new, should be untouched and retain its own roof, although the concourse would still continue unbroken across the station, and this reduced the number of platforms to twenty-one.

Much of the new roof had already been completed by the end of 1907, followed by a new cab road that ran from Westminster Bridge Road along the side of the new terminus and then turned left to run in front of what were to be the new offices. The first four platform faces were ready in stages during 1909, with another early in 1910, all with conventional numbering of each face. Parts of the new frontage block were also ready in 1909, although the new booking hall was not ready until 11 June 1911, with doors both to the cab road and to the main concourse. The LSWR obviously had other priorities, as a 'gentlemen's court' was opened under the new building and reached by a stone staircase from the main concourse: described by *Railway Magazine* as 'perhaps the finest in England', it also included a hairdressing saloon, shoe cleaning room and bathrooms, while the air could be changed by electric fans.

A far-sighted feature of the first fifteen of the new platforms was steps running down to a subway that ran under them and provided access to the tube stations, speeding up the progress of those wanting to travel on the underground and also easing pressure on the platform barriers. Less far-sighted were the platform lengths, and given the amount of work undertaken both within the new terminus and on the approach roads, this oversight is all the more difficult to understand. Already, main-line trains often consisted of twelve corridor carriages and a locomotive at each end, with that at the buffers having brought the train into the station. Trains could easily be 750 ft in length, but the platforms were as short as 635 ft, with those for the West Country and Portsmouth at 728 ft and 735 ft. Just one, reserved for boat trains to Southampton, was 860 ft, and later extended to 946 ft, and another platform across the central cab road from this was 843 ft. The end of the cab road also had two short loading docks. The legacy of the Southern and its predecessors on nationalisation would have been almost perfect but for this, especially in recent years as pressure on existing train lengths has led to calls for longer trains. Additional office accommodation was provided in a two-storey block completed in 1920 between platforms 15 and 16, marking the boundary between the all-new platforms and the Windsor station, which also had a further loading dock on its north side, beyond which the carriage and engine sidings, hoist to the Waterloo & City and locomotive turntable were little affected by the changes. Changes to the approaches allowed greater flexibility in operations and allowed parallel working at some of the platforms.

Once completed and opened on 21 March 1922 by Queen Mary, Waterloo stood comparison with the best anywhere, and there could be no doubt that this was a single large terminus, since the concourse, 120 ft deep, ran for 770 ft across the platform heads with a single long block of offices and amenities behind it, including the first London terminus branch of a bank when the National Provincial (now RBS NatWest) opened in 1923. The economy made by Walker on the Windsor platforms was not apparent to the casual observer, and represented good housekeeping with so much else to spend money on, modernising and standardising the now grouped railway. In addition to access from the cab road, there was the Victory Arch, the war memorial to the LSWR dead in the First World War, and staircases opposite platforms 8 and 12 leading down to Waterloo Road. Given the SER's penchant for building riverside termini in prominent positions, it seems a shame that the view of Waterloo, set back somewhat from the banks of the river, was marred by the viaduct carrying the former SER lines from Waterloo to the Hungerford Bridge.

During the First World War Southampton had handled the embarkation of the British Expeditionary Force in 1914, followed by many of the reserves in 1915, and was the main port for those going to other theatres of war, especially in the Middle East. The presence of the Royal Navy at Portsmouth, as well as the flood of men going for training on Salisbury Plain or into the many garrisons in the south, meant that there was considerable strain on the entire system. As at Victoria, there was a free buffet for troops at Waterloo staffed by volunteers which opened in 1915 and didn't close until 1920, some 8 million meals later. The numbers returning from leave were such that on Sunday nights as many as thirty extra trains had to be organised.

Despite its importance, Waterloo suffered bomb damage just once, when on the night of 29/30 September 1917 a number of bombs dropped on the sidings to the north of the station – the damage was repaired within a day.

The LSWR was an energetic proponent of the electric railway, and Walker's eye for value meant that this system of transportation was introduced on the 600 V DC system using a third rail. This was certainly economical and straightforward. Wimbledon via East Putney was electrified on 25 October 1915, and on 30 January of the following year it was joined by the Kingston Roundabout and its Shepperton branch. On 12 March 1916 the Hounslow Loop was electrified, followed by the Hampton Court branch on 18 June. The so-called 'new' Guildford line, running via Cobham, was electrified as far as Claygate on 20 November 1916, and initially there was a steam push-pull service beyond for stations to Guildford. However, the line had to revert to steam working in July 1919, as demand on the other routes meant that the rolling stock could be used more effectively elsewhere. After grouping, the line through to Guildford via Cobham was completed, as was the line from Raynes Park to Dorking North, and electric services started on these routes on 12 July 1925. After some delay while competing methods of electrification were evaluated, services to Windsor were electrified on 6 July 1930.

In 1924 improvements were made to the Waterloo booking hall, with the original woodblock floor replaced by coloured glass tiles and plaster columns replaced by marble capped with bronze, while the doors to the cab road were replaced by windows. Of possibly greater importance, on 13 September 1926 the Hampstead Tube, now the Northern Line, opened an extension from Charing Cross to Kennington, with a station beneath Waterloo, providing a direct service from Waterloo to Euston, but it was not until the following year that the escalators were ready with a new booking hall beneath the Windsor platforms.

Possibly bearing in mind that many longer-distance passengers would have to wait for a train, and of course catering for those waiting to greet arriving passengers, a newsreel and cartoon cinema was built at the end of the concourse next to platform 1 and opened on 27 August 1934. Announcements of arriving trains would be flashed up at the side of the screen if requested from the cashier.

In 1935, twelve years after the grouping, the name Waterloo Junction was dropped for the old SER station, which had lost its line into the terminus in 1911, and platforms were designated A to D to avoid confusion with those of the terminus. As at Victoria, the process of integration seems to have been piecemeal and patchy.

New signalling and layouts were brought into use on 17 May 1936 as steady growth in traffic, boosted by electrification, required changes to be made to the approaches to the station. Given the congested nature of the surrounding area, this required a flyover at Wimbledon, the nearest point at which the work could be carried out, to carry the Up main local over the Up main line. This meant that the arrangement north of Wimbledon became:

Down main local
Up main local
Down main through
Up main through

joined at Clapham Junction by:

Down Windsor local
Down Windsor through
Up Windsor local
Down Windsor through

These lines were joined at Vauxhall by a relief line between the Up main through and the Down Windsor through, while at Waterloo electrification was extended to platforms 7, 8 and 9. Colour light signalling was introduced between Hampton Court Junction and Waterloo, although those at the terminus were delayed until 18 October 1936.

Electrification had continued to spread, so that from 3 January 1937 Windsor electrics divided at Staines, with the rear portion serving Chertsey and Weybridge. Next came Waterloo's first main-line electrification, and the longest on the Southern, with the introduction of the third rail for the Portsmouth Direct, the line running through Woking and Guildford to Portsmouth Harbour, and becoming operational on 4 July 1937. This was done in conjunction with electrification to Aldershot and Alton, with the stopping trains dividing at Woking into Portsmouth and Alton portions. Once again there was a massive increase in frequencies, with summer Saturdays seeing four fast trains an hour on the Portsmouth line, which had seen just four fast trains a day under steam traction. As war approached, further electrification followed, with services to Reading from 1 January 1939. These trains divided at Ascot, with a portion continuing to Guildford by the roundabout route of Camberley and Aldershot. As the suburbs grew, a new line was needed branching off the Dorking North line to Tolworth, reached on 29 May 1938, and Chessington South, reached on 28 May 1939, and of course electrified throughout.

Loudspeakers had been introduced and used from 9 March 1932, which was probably an ideal day since the Oxford and Cambridge boat race coincided with a rugby international at Twickenham. Waterloo's business could be sporty as well as commuting, for there were also occasions when trains were needed for races at Ascot and Epsom. In 1937 the Southern experimented with playing music over the loudspeaker system, often using light opera, the idea being to have marches to encourage arriving passengers to leave the station briskly in the morning and something soothing to calm them and entertain them as they waited for their evening train home. The announcer was also responsible for the musical programme – although recordings were never announced – and at first was based in a booth over the newsstand opposite platforms 8 and 9. This was later moved to a position above the station offices between platforms 15 and 16.

As war approached, the Southern started to take precautions, with air raid shelters for around 6,500 people constructed in the arches underneath the station, doubtless with the idea that there could be trainloads of passengers to protect at busy periods. In fact, many of the users were to be local people, and those bombed out of their homes sometimes took up permanent residence.

The Second World War was one in which few places escaped the bombs, and Waterloo was a primary target. On 7 September 1940 a bomb fell just outside the station and seriously damaged the viaduct over John Street. Railwaymen and the Royal Engineers worked to restore services, but the station was closed until 19 September and services could not be fully restored until 1 October. The disruption affected more than just passengers, and at one stage there were 5,000 bags of unsorted mail. The overnight newspaper trains switched to Clapham Yard, and after further enemy action moved to Wimbledon, and then to Surbiton after bombing destroyed the roads around Wimbledon station. Waterloo was one of the worst affected of the Southern termini in London, as it was out of action because of incendiary bombs from the night of 29/30 December 1940 until 5 January 1941, which itself was not a quiet night as the old LSWR offices in York Road were destroyed and the underground lifts and booking hall badly damaged. A further closure came after the raid on the night of 10/11 May 1941, when around fifty high-explosive and incendiary bombs and parachute mines set fires blazing and destroyed the Necropolis station, and penetrated to the basement arches, setting alight large quantities of spirits stored there: the station could not function until a partial reopening on 15 May. The disruption to services was severe, with many passengers delayed by several hours as the crowds overwhelmed the replacement bus service from Clapham Junction, with a queue of more than a mile at one point and the road towards Waterloo difficult to drive over as it was cluttered with many fire hoses. One unexploded bomb was to remain undetected until work started on an office building in York Road in 1959: at 2,000 lb, had it exploded during the intervening years the destruction and loss of life at the height of the rush hour would have been terrible. The original LSWR terminus at Nine Elms also lost its roof on 10/11 May.

There were few changes at Waterloo after the war, and only the most essential tidying up between the end of the war and nationalisation. For many years, Waterloo was largely neglected by the new British Railways, and it took almost twenty years before any further electrification, with the line through to Bournemouth finally being electrified in 1967.

Chapter Three

Southern Destinations

The Southern served a wide variety of destinations, most of which had one thing in common – the sea – but they could also be grouped into certain categories. There were the naval bases at Chatham, Portsmouth, Portland and Plymouth; the Channel ports at Dover, Folkestone, Newhaven and Southampton, with the latter also serving the Channel Islands and under Southern ownership developing a strong ocean liner business; and, finally, the resorts, such as Brighton and Bournemouth, as well as many of the towns on the Isle of Wight and in north Kent. Of course, some of these destinations could lay claim to belong to more than one category, with Portsmouth having its own resort at Southsea. Even when grouped together, one could argue that Brighton, so much in commuterland, differed from Bournemouth, not least because the Sussex resort was a great favourite with day trippers and Bournemouth, then in Hampshire, a little too far away for most of them. The north Devon and north Cornwall resorts were certainly different from either Bournemouth or Brighton, and from the Isle of Wight resorts as well, not least in the frequency of train services. Exeter was an exception, for despite having its own docks and those at Exmouth, it was notable as a junction and one of the places where the Southern met the Great Western. Weymouth, both a resort and a ferry port for the Channel Islands, was a Great Western, rather than Southern, port, although the latter had the more direct service to London.

Obviously, space considerations mean that it is not possible to provide a potted history of the railway in every town and village served by the Southern, but an outline of the railway in the major centres is necessary to understand much of the history of the railway, and of the relationships with other railways and other modes of transport.

Bournemouth

Effectively a backwater until the arrival of the railway, Bournemouth was bypassed by the main coaching routes and by the first railway in the surrounding area from Ringwood to Poole, which opened in 1847. Local opposition meant that the Ringwood, Christchurch & Bournemouth Railway did not reach Bournemouth until 1870, and was leased to the LSWR from the outset. Five years later, the Somerset & Dorset Railway reached the town and the following year was leased and worked jointly by the Midland Railway and the LSWR, much to the dismay of the GWR, although this used the 'West' station while the LSWR had the 'East'. In 1888 the LSWR opened a shorter route from Brockenhurst to Christchurch and Bournemouth, reducing the distance from London to 108 miles, and finally linked its line to Bournemouth West as well as building the new Central station on a branch off the main line.

Prior to grouping, Bournemouth was just 2 hours from London and also had four trains a day from the Midlands. Post-grouping, the Southern improved services by accelerating trains and introducing the all-Pullman 'Bournemouth Belle' and, had it not been for nationalisation, would have expected to electrify the line during the mid-1950s.

Brighton

Brighton was a fashionable seaside resort well before the arrival of the railway, owing to the popularity of sea bathing and the patronage of the Prince Regent. By the time the first

The Southern and the LBSCR before it even arranged steam-hauled rolling stock in sets to ensure standardised formations and to facilitate rapid composition of trains. This is unit 861 at Bournemouth West, consisting of the main-line version of Bulleid's 'wide-bodied' rolling stock. *(HRMS ACD903)*

railways were proposed for the town, with six rival schemes mooted between 1834 and 1835, there were no fewer than sixteen coach services a day between London and Brighton, with the 50 mile journey taking 5½ hours.

In 1836 Parliament approved the LBSCR scheme, which was the most direct but also the costliest, and the railway opened in 1841. The resort was by this time no longer fashionable, but the railway created the day-tripper market and the commuter market. The LBSCR made Brighton its railway town by moving its rolling stock and carriage works there in 1852, bringing to the resort its sole industrial activity. Both the SER and LCDR proposed routes to Brighton, but failed. Having reached Brighton, the LBSCR spread itself east and west along the coast, but also ensured that these towns received direct trains from London.

The LBSCR had what would be regarded today as an up-market image, although sometimes this seems to have been at the price of neglecting its third-class passengers. Pullman trains were operated and even on ordinary expresses a Pullman car could often be found. This was not so extravagant as it might seem, since the short distances of even its trunk services were such that a conventional dining car would have been able to take just one sitting.

After the grouping the Brighton line became Britain's first main-line electrification, and in true LBSCR tradition, many of the comforts of the 'Brighton Belle' all-Pullman train were to be found on other services as Pullman cars were inserted into standard electric multiple units.

Dover

At first, the influence of the railways on sea traffic was not always fully appreciated, and a factor in this was the unsuitability of many of the older facilities for railway use, with

The 'Brighton Belle', usually comprising two 5 BEL Pullman electric multiple units, arrives at Brighton in 1933, with a 4 LAV in the background. *(HRMS AAF125)*

narrow quays and piers rather than the long quaysides, as in the Western Docks at Southampton, that allowed the railways easy access. The construction of warehouses close to the dock sides and the congested residential areas close to the older port areas also contributed to the problems.

It soon became apparent that the railways could combine with shipping to produce new and more direct routes, saving time and often bypassing significant areas of danger. A good example of this was the way in which travel to the continent through Dover or Folkestone avoided the hazards of the North Foreland, and also enabled the traveller to take the shortest route between England and France.

The SER invested heavily in Dover, where the older part of the harbour was owned by the Admiralty, especially after railways were allowed to operate their own shipping. The transfer of passengers, their luggage and mail between train and ship was eased considerably by the new Dover Marine station. This was sufficiently developed to be usable by the military during the First World War, and was completed for civilian traffic after the war, shortly before grouping. Dover and Folkestone were completely taken over by the military during the First World War. During the Second World War they played an important role in the evacuation from Dunkirk, but were then used only by the Royal Navy until after the Normandy Landings.

Under Southern ownership, Dover became the main port for the short cross-Channel services, including such up-market operations as the famous 'Golden Arrow' Pullman express, which in more prosperous times had the luxury of its own ship, and the now virtually forgotten 'Night Ferry' through sleeper service between London and Paris. Southern backwardness in developing drive-on car ferries, for which the train ferry configuration pointed the way forward, allowed a certain Captain Townsend to develop competition.

An unidentified 'U1' locomotive waiting to leave Dover Marine after the end of the Second World War with a train for Edinburgh. *(HRMS AAL809)*

Exeter

While Exeter was not a terminus station, it could fairly be described as the gateway to the south-west of England, for here the Southern and GWR met and the former crossed over the other's territory, switching from the south coast to the north coast of Devon and part of Cornwall. Of the two railway stations in the city, the GWR's St David's was on the natural route through the area, and while the Southern's Queen Street, renamed Central in 1933, was the better placed for the city, it could only be reached in the Up direction by a steep climb out of St David's and through a tunnel. The GWR insisted that all LSWR and, later, SR trains heading further west, and especially those going to Plymouth, stopped at St David's, a delaying tactic, but one that must have benefited at least some passengers needing to change trains. The LSWR arrived in the city during the early 1860s from Salisbury and reached Plymouth in 1876. Between 1862 and 1864 Exeter was one of the trans-shipment points between the broad and standard gauge.

While in theory in competition for the London custom, 170 miles away, in many respects the railways served different markets. The LSWR routes were most useful for the villages that acted as dormitories for the city, including Exmouth and Budleigh Salterton, while the GWR provided fast direct routes to the other two major cities of the west, Plymouth and Bristol, as well as the prospect of travel beyond to the Midlands.

An LSWR plan to bypass St David's was blocked by the GWR in 1905, but the Southern managed to gain Parliamentary approval in 1935, and preliminary work was in hand when the Second World War and then nationalisation put an end to the scheme. The new route can be regarded as a missed opportunity, missed most of all by those travellers whose journeys between Plymouth and Exeter have been disrupted in bad weather by the failings of the notorious Dawlish sea wall.

A very mixed rake of boat train rolling stock in 1957, with even such a premium service comprising ex-SR and BR Mk I carriages. *(HRMS ADS118)*

Folkestone

Like Dover, Folkestone was developed by the SER, which purchased the port in 1844 and established a route to Boulogne. As at Dover, the port prospered with many of the ferry services operated in conjunction with French, and later Belgian, railways. Both ports were heavily used by the military during the First World War, with a steady shutdown of services to civilian passengers, and in the Second World War played an important part in the evacuation from Dunkirk. After that, they virtually ceased to function as ports apart from naval use, and even that was limited by the proximity of both to Luftwaffe bases in France. They returned to service after the Normandy landings.

Plymouth

Plymouth was first served by the broad-gauge lines of the GWR and its associates, such as the South Devon Railway, which reached the town from Exeter in 1849. The LSWR reached Plymouth in 1876, running over mixed-gauge track on the Launceston branch of the North Cornwall Railway. The LSWR built its own terminus at Friary, but was allowed to use the SDR through station at North Road from 1877. A better route came with the opening of the standard-gauge Plymouth, Devonport & South Western Junction Railway in 1890, but when the GWR converted to standard gauge in 1892, and then shortened the route from London to 225 miles in 1906, that became the better and faster service. This didn't prevent the LSWR operating fast special boat trains for the mails put ashore by transatlantic liners, with the mail trains also being used by those passengers wanting to save a day or so on the journey to London, but a serious derailment at Salisbury in 1906 put an end to the LSWR's only real attempt at running fast trains.

Plymouth was the farthest extent of the Southern's main-line system, with its north Devon and north Cornwall system operated primarily as a series of branches.

Civic dignitaries eagerly await the arrival of the inaugural train of the 'Portsmouth No. 1 Electrification', which is clearly terminating at Portsmouth & Southsea low level station, although the 4 COR/4 RES units usually operated through the high level station to Portsmouth Harbour and carried an '8' headcode. Postwar, the headcodes were change to 7X and 8X, so a fast became an 81. *(NRM 5/95)*

Portsmouth

Portsmouth was already a substantial town and Britain's major naval base before the railways arrived. Despite this, in 1842 the first railway in the area ran from Eastleigh on the Southampton main line via Fareham to Gosport, a short ferry trip across the harbour. The first line into Portsmouth did not arrive until 1847, with the LBSCR extending its line from Brighton, and the following year the LSWR line arrived via Fareham. Both routes were about 95 miles from London, and the two companies operated a pooling agreement from 1848, the LSWR using its rival's station in the town. The opening of the Portsmouth Direct line in 1859 cut the distance from London to 74 miles by extending the LSWR branch from Guildford and Godalming, while in 1867 the LBSCR provided an 87 mile route via Arundel.

While the services to the city were now much faster, passengers for the Isle of Wight still had to be conveyed by road between the train and the ferry, as the Admiralty refused to allow the companies to extend their line to the harbour, even though it had its own internal railway system. This eventually changed in 1876, when a high-level station with an island platform was built alongside the town station, later known as Portsmouth & Southsea, to carry the line to Portsmouth Harbour station, which was built on a pier with direct access to the Isle of Wight ferries across the concourse. The ferries themselves had been operated independently, but passed into railway control to be operated by the LBSCR and LSWR in 1880.

The resort of Southsea was reached by an independently promoted branch line from Fratton from 1885 and operated by the two main-line railways. It was never a success, being worked by railcars in competition with a comprehensive tramway system, and the Southern was allowed to close it in 1923 after it had been out of use for most of the First World War.

Portsmouth itself was the target for two pre-Second World War electrification schemes, when the 'Direct' route was electrified in 1937 and the Arundel line, along with that from Brighton, the following year. The main service to Waterloo, which had enjoyed just four fast trains a day before electrification, enjoyed as many in an hour on a summer Saturday afterwards.

Reading

The LSWR reached Reading in 1856, running over SER metals from Wokingham, although it was to be another two years before the SER line from Farnborough was connected through Guildford to the rest of the company's network at Redhill. Reading was already an important calling point and junction on the GWR by this time. The LSWR line to Waterloo has never rivalled that of the GWR to Paddington in terms of speed, and the opening of the

Ex-LSWR 0–4–2 'A12' class locomotive No. 638 at Southampton West, now simply Southampton, in 1929. *(HRMS AAG309)*

Metropolitan Railway also placed the latter in a better position for those travelling onwards to the City of London. However, the towns along the LSWR line soon became some of the smarter London dormitories. In addition to being slightly longer, the LSWR line also suffered from severe bottlenecks, especially at Richmond. While the SER line must have counted as one of the most pointless in the country, and a millstone around the neck of the company and its successors, it took the emergence of London Gatwick as an important international airport for the line to show serious potential, and that was long after the demise of the Southern.

Southampton

Linking Southampton to London was the reason why the LSWR came into existence. Although the town had a history as a commercial port, by the early nineteenth century this business had declined and the town was a quiet resort. The introduction of steamship services to the Channel Islands and France during the 1820s was the start of the restoration of the town's maritime trade, while new piers and docks were opened during the 1830s. The London & Southampton Railway was authorised in 1834, with Manchester businessmen taking up 40 per cent of its shares, opened as the London & South Western in 1840 and extended to Dorchester via Poole in 1847.

As at Bournemouth, under the LSWR and then the Southern Railway, there were two main stations: the original Southampton terminus just outside the docks and, with the Poole extension, Southampton West, later renamed Central. The former station has long been closed. The railway lines were also taken into the docks, but suffered from weight restrictions, so that when the 'Merchant Navy' class was introduced, these powerful Pacific locomotives could not be used on boat trains!

The railway contributed as significantly to Southampton's prosperity as the town contributed to that of the railway, with shipping services diverting to the port, cutting the long and often dangerous passage around the North Foreland to London with a railway journey of 3 hours. Initially much criticised for poor service and for its wider ambitions, the LSWR service improved once trains operated through the town to Bournemouth.

The LSWR bought the docks, with their own railway system, in 1892. The port was the first, probably anywhere, to experience wartime traffic pressures, as it handled troops bound for the Boer War between 1899 and 1902, and then was a major port in both World Wars, being heavily blitzed during the Second World War.

Under the Southern, the new West Docks were built and the port much improved, while the railway service benefited from new rolling stock and more powerful locomotives. The port also became the departure point for the Imperial Airways services to the Empire from 1937 onwards, with special Pullman carriages attached to a Bournemouth express and detached at Southampton (see the Flying-Boat Train).

Post-nationalisation, the Southern's new Ocean Terminal was completed, bringing fresh business to the old docks, but plans for electrification were long delayed, not being implemented until 1967.

Chapter Four

A New Railway for a New Era

The challenge facing the directors of all of the 'Big Four' companies was considerable, for they had to cope with a wide variety of equipment, with not just locomotives and rolling stock differing between the constituent companies, but also such matters as braking systems and signalling. Working practices varied, and so new rule books were important. There were differences in the inherited cultures and long-established rivalries and jealousies. In many towns station names had to be changed, and each new company's house magazine published an extensive list of these. In the Southern's case, and no doubt it was not unique in this, geography also played a part, so that there were two towns called Ashford in its area, and two towns called Gillingham. As mentioned in the chapter on the termini, the Southern approach to rationalisation and standardisation tended to be intermittent and somewhat patchy. The problem was that this required a lot of senior management time, and there was so much else to consider. Some have suggested that the post-grouping restructuring into sections, Eastern, Central, Western and London, with only the last mentioned being 'new', while the others were very much 'old' railway, was to blame for the poor progress in rationalisation, and that in effect three, or possibly even four, railways were operated. But given the size of the operation and the differing characteristics, it is hard to see what other form of organisation could have been contemplated.

The rush to modernise included the installation of mechanised coal hoists, but the tight confines of the shed at Guildford meant that such a structure was out of the question. In any case, electrification had already reached Guildford via Cobham when this photograph was taken in 1925. *(HRMS AAF204)*

To ease the transition and in recognition of the vast amount of work to be done, the general managers of the LSWR, LBSCR and SECR all remained in post throughout 1923, but with effect from 1 January 1924 Sir Herbert Walker became the sole general manager of the new company. Sir William Forbes of the LBSCR and Sir Percy Tempest of the SECR both retired. This was not a complete takeover by the LSWR, even though it had been the largest of the old companies, since the SECR's chief mechanical engineer, R.E.L. Maunsell, became the first to hold that post for the Southern Railway.

The True Picture

The Southern Railway published its own magazine, called simply *The Southern Railway Magazine*, but from start to finish the masthead always mentioned that it incorporated the *South Western Railway Gazette*, first published in 1881. Those who believe that there are no such things as true mergers, merely disguised takeovers, will feel vindicated by this example. The LSWR dominance of the SR showed itself in other ways, no less obvious. The third-rail system of electrification was chosen, officially after taking independent advice, but it was also the LSWR system. The LSWR had owned a cement works, so it is not surprising that the SR quickly settled on concrete structures as it undertook station rebuilding and modernisation. None of this should have been surprising, since Walker was of course the last general manager of the LSWR as well as the first for the SR.

The first issue of *The Southern Railway Magazine* in 1923 showed a steam locomotive hauling an express from a station and proclaimed '"Right away" for 1923 and a prosperous future for the Southern Railway'.

In fact, the start seemed nothing like prosperous. In 1922, the last year before the grouping and the first outside Government control, prices were reduced from 100 per cent above the First World War levels to 75 per cent above, with the 'pre-Southern' companies affected by £3 million.

The Southern Railway Magazine started by giving its readers a true picture of the new railway. Among the news about personalities, gardening clubs and amateur dramatics, there was always business news and at first it also included articles on the predecessors of the SR, so that the employee working in Portsmouth knew about the Brighton line and vice versa. It was unusual for a house publication in that at first advertisements were carried, but for the most part these were not advertisements aimed at staff or their families, but really those by the suppliers of equipment who obviously felt that the directors' favour would be gained. The practice was discontinued after a year or so.

The magazine set the scene early on with a feature on 'Our Railway'. The readers were told that the SR had:

7,490 passenger carriages, of which 467 were electric.
3,071 non-passenger vehicles, as well as
36,749 goods wagons
1,948 service vehicles

It also put this into perspective by showing how the SR compared with other railway companies.

	Passenger Journeys	% of Total	Freight Tons	% of Total
SR	17.27m	70.81	6.11m	29.19
GWR	13.73m	43.05	18.11m	56.96
LMS	32.63m	41.07	46.25m	58.63
LNER	21.98m	37.80	36.14m	62.20

Ex-LSWR 'T9', No. 312 heads a Bognor train during the early 1930s, with a Pullman car sixth in the rake. *(HRMS AAA634)*

It was clear that this was the smallest of the Big Four companies, and the most dependent upon passenger traffic. Not only that, the average journey would have been shorter than those on the long-distance railways such as the LMS and LNER, with their Anglo-Scottish traffic. The LMS was claimed to be the largest private enterprise in the British Empire during its existence.

In addition to the passenger carriages and goods wagons, the new company inherited 2,281 steam locomotives from its predecessors. Appendix III shows the classes present in January 1923. Steady rationalisation was achieved by a combination of rebuilding and retiring those that might be described as oddities, notably the Drummond 4–2–2–0 divided-drive four-cylinder 'T7' and 'E10'-class locomotives. There were in any case only a handful of these, and although dating from 1897 and 1901 they were hardly old. On the other hand, the faithful little Adams 02 0–4–4Ts of 1889 continued working on the Isle of Wight, where they did everything, until the end of steam in December 1966, a working life of seventy-seven years!

During the first five months of 1924, the SR claimed to have lost £382,000 in revenue owing to road competition. The following year, using *The Southern Railway Magazine* to communicate with his employees, Walker, by this time the sole general manager, noted that the combined profits for the railway companies in 1913 had totalled £45m, but that by 1920 these had dropped to less than £7m, owing to improved rates of pay during the First World War, when the railways were under direct government control for the first time. During 1921, immediately prior to government control ceasing, the railways were running at a loss overall. Railway wages in 1913 had totalled £47m, but by 1920 had risen to £160m. For the southern railway companies, the operating ratio of costs to revenue was 64 per cent in 1913, but this had risen to 82 per cent after the First World War.

At first some modest improvement in revenue took place. Between 1924 and 1925 passenger revenue increased by £40,000 to £17,396,000, while that for goods traffic rose by £33,000 to £6,069,000.

The new railway had a great deal of work to do, standardising locomotives, rolling stock and working practices. A new rule book was issued and *The Southern Railway Magazine*

'L1' No. 1787 heads a Hastings train through an electrified section in 1935. *(HRMS AAA709)*

explained many of the changes. Just how urgent standardisation was can be judged by the fact that the constituent companies had two incompatible braking systems, with the LSWR and SECR companies using vacuum brakes, while the LBSC used the Westinghouse brake, which used compressed air. There were no fewer than 135 different classes of steam locomotive in service. Not only was the LSWR system of third-rail electrification incompatible with the overhead or 'elevated' system used by the LBSCR, but the latter's overhead system was incompatible with that proposed for the SECR.

The new railway inherited works at Ashford, Brighton, Lancing and Eastleigh. The Brighton works was reduced to running repairs only in 1928, with its locomotive-building work transferred to Ashford and Eastleigh, leaving half of the works unused.

A consistent identity for the new railway was much-needed, and the Southern chose green for its locomotives and rolling stock, showing that here at least the old LSWR was not to have complete sway. The choice was a bold move, replacing the colour schemes of each of the major pre-grouping companies, so that no one could be shown to have scored points over their former rivals. Nevertheless, at first the green was fairly dull and consistency in application was lacking. It was not until 1936 that a more consistent approach was applied. According to Charles Klapper in Sir Herbert Walker's *Southern Railway*, on a visit to the Isle of Wight with some of his officers in 1936, Walker listened to a debate between them over the Southern livery. Of his three companions, one, Edwin Cox, wanted a bright green with gold lining, another, Frank Bushrod, wanted plain green all over, while the third, Richard Maunsell, soon to retire as CME, almost unbelievably wanted dark grey without any relief, a scheme originally introduced in 1917 under wartime austerity conditions. Today, a team of corporate image consultants would be hired at heavy expense and given a year or two to produce a solution. Walker's answer was as always highly cost-effective. On passing an optician's premises, he suddenly dived inside and emerged a couple of minutes later with a reel of green spectacle cord, cutting a length for each officer, and saying: 'Now argument will cease; that will be the colour Southern engines and coaches shall be painted in future. This reel shall remain in my office safe as the standard to which reference shall be made.' Walker would be as appalled at the cost of modern corporate identity projects as he no doubt would have been puzzled by references to Pantone shades!

Productivity

Productivity left a lot to be desired at first, and *The Southern Railway Magazine* told the story. In 1925 the number of shunting miles per 100 train miles was between 7.73 miles and 8.31 miles for passenger trains, but for goods trains the figure varied between 99.13 miles and 103.77 miles, so that unproductive and non-revenue-earning shunting miles exceeded train miles. This can only be explained in any satisfactory way if non-revenue-earning movements – 'bringing back the empties' as it were – were to be included in the figure for shunting miles. The backlog of maintenance during the war years was still being felt by 1925, as was the fact that the system was already very crowded. The Southern also inherited many problems originating in the fact that the two south eastern companies, the London & South Eastern and the London, Chatham & Dover, had been poverty-stricken, and that this had been alleviated, not completely cured, by their collaboration as the SECR. In 1925 just 36 per cent of passenger trains arrived on time, while the same percentage arrived between 1 and 5 minutes late. Another 14 per cent were between 6 and 10 minutes late, 9 per cent between 11 and 20 minutes late, and 5 per cent were more than 20 minutes late. On a weekday, steam trains were an average of 2.55 minutes late, compared to an average of 1.69 minutes for electric trains.

In January 1923 Philip Gibb of the Pennsylvania Railroad had been asked for advice on the best means of electrification, and in 1926 he recommended third rail, largely because of its advantages on a suburban system. It was cheaper to install, since tunnels and other structures over the line did not need to be rebuilt to provide clearance for overhead equipment. While overhead systems could be AC or DC, the former required transformers which took up a great deal of space on trains, while the latter suffered from the third rail's drawback of needing many more trackside substations. There was another advantage for the third rail while steam operations continued – it was free from the corrosive effect that the frequent passage of steam trains caused to the overhead wires.

There was a paradox in that it was the Southern more than any other railway that was in its short life to standardise train formations and timetables, reintroducing the concept of an even-interval service that had somehow been lost over the years, and which had first appeared on the London & Blackwall Railway as early as 1840 with an even 15-minute headway. Many traditional railwaymen were contemptuous of the Southern electric multiple units, seeing them simply as glorified trams. Yet it was also the Southern that put so much effort into luxury trains with character and prestige, such as the 'Golden Arrow' and the 'Night Ferry'.

Railway in Transition

The Southern marked the transition not between the early railway and the modern railway, because the railways had become very sophisticated even by the start of the twentieth century, but between the Edwardian railway and the modern railway. The idea of longer-distance trains running backwards and forwards all day rather than making a single journey or, at most, a return journey, showed the pattern of train services for the future, so that today longer-distance trains often work more than a thousand miles a day. This was the real start of the electric railway, less romantic and less glamorous than the age of steam, but more efficient and much cleaner. Even steam operations were marked by modernisation, with the Bulleid Pacifics incorporating many advanced features and being among the best in terms of crew comfort, although the 'Leader' class that was to follow was very deficient in this respect, at least from the fireman's point of view. The 'Leader' class was an attempt to see if the same flexibility offered by electric trains could be found in a steam locomotive design, capable of being driven at speed in either direction and

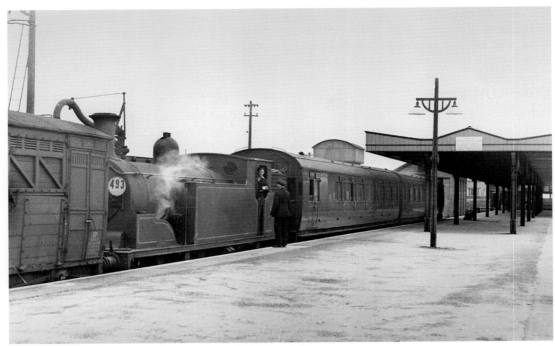

One of the Southern's many branch lines was that to Seaton in south Devon, here seen catering for passengers and for horses. *(HRMS AES523)*

eliminating the need for turntables, which in many cases, including Waterloo, often involved running light some distance over the congested approaches.

None of the tremendous modernisation of the Southern Railway was without cost, and inevitably the impact of modernisation was uneven. The most potent example has to be the delay in producing powerful steam locomotives, something for which Maunsell frequently pressed, but was denied, partly because of objections from the civil engineers who were all too well aware of the deficiencies of the track in many places, as we will see later in the case of the accident at Sevenoaks, and partly because of the high priority accorded electrification, which both cut costs and produced dramatic improvements in passenger receipts. It was left to Maunsell's successor, Oliver Bulleid, to introduce the high-powered Pacific locomotives, managing to achieve this despite strict wartime restrictions on what could be built.

In many cases, services off the main routes were improved by what today would be described as 'cascading', most significantly on the Isle of Wight, where the Southern improved services by boosting frequencies and sending over carriages and locomotives from the mainland that were already elderly. No doubt the Southern got away with this because, for many years, local and suburban services were operated using slam door non-corridor stock, and to the layman the carriages of the 1890s looked little different from those of the 1930s. As it was, the Isle of Wight had little running on the rails that belonged to the twentieth century, even when steam was withdrawn at the end of 1966.

It also has to be remembered that the Southern was not simply a railway, and had to allocate funds for the modernisation of its shipping services and ports, where the new West Docks and the Ocean Terminal at Southampton were both the result of heavy investment and long-term planning.

The Southern also saw the future for shunting as being diesel, not steam, and delay in this respect was no doubt due to the difficult economic conditions of the inter-war years

An ex-LSWR 4–4–0 'T9', on a Waterloo–Portsmouth royal duty near Haslemere between the wars. (HRMS AAC306)

and the desire to press ahead with electrification that had proven revenue-earning and business growth benefits. There was also the point that many small tank engines could be 'cascaded' at zero capital cost on to shunting duties. Where the Southern did improve its goods operations was in building new marshalling yards with a 'hump' that allowed goods wagons to use gravity, the genuine fuel-free and economic form of energy, for at least part of the time.

The Southern was flexible over the future, and while pursuing one means of retaining steam traction with the 'Leader' class, also collaborated with the LMS in the design of a diesel locomotive for main-line work. It was made clear that this was the most likely way ahead for the train services west of Basingstoke. Even if electrification could, in Southern days, be justified as far as Exeter, that was the extreme limit as the lightly used and infrequent operations on the lines in Devon and Cornwall precluded it.

Modernisation

Modernisation of a kind less obvious to the passenger was also taking place. From the beginning railway carriages were washed by hand, a labour-intensive and costly business. By 1933 the first carriage-washing machine was operational in a shed at Brighton. This move also reflected the fact that electric trains could be driven through a wash, in a way that steam locomotives with their open cabs could not.

There was expansion in the electric railway, and both road and air transport, but contraction elsewhere. In 1930 the Southern withdrew services from Lee-on-Solent and closed the historic Canterbury and Whitstable line, the oldest in the south of England. In 1931 it closed the line between Hythe and Sandgate in Kent. One wonders just how much these moves were the result of having a virtual monopoly in local public transport in these areas following the move into road transport. On the other hand, the company could be judged as

Ex-Kent & East Sussex 0–8–0T No. 849 *Hecate* at Nine Elms. The relatively short distances operated by many of the companies that were grouped into the Southern meant that tank engines accounted for a high proportion of locomotives at the grouping. *(HRMS ACM321)*

being flexible and changing with the times. Many railway lines had been built in the day of the horse-drawn wagon but were in fact for journeys better suited to buses than to trains.

By 1933 timekeeping still varied. Trains on time in the busy London South-West area were the worst, at 67.07 per cent, whereas despite much single-line working, 82.59 per cent of trains on the Isle of Wight arrived on time. To be fair, these were true 'on time' figures, not 'within five minutes', as today.

In looking at productivity, direct costs were an important factor, but so too were those over which the company had little control, such as local authority rates. To show how important this was, in 1935 the directors were able to report that a rating appeal had caused the Net Value Rating Authority to reduce the value of the company from £2,180,000 to £1,077,131, saving the Southern £300,000 per annum. As was later demonstrated, savings such as this could contribute a considerable amount towards modernisation.

This was the first railway company to foresee air travel becoming increasingly important in the future, and this was reflected in plans for airport stations at Gatwick and Shoreham. Before the Second World War, Bungalow Town Halt had been closed, only to reopen as Shoreham Airport Halt, although it was closed soon after the war started. No one can really blame the company for failing to foresee that the latter airport was likely to have a short life. It is simply strange that the potential for Eastleigh wasn't also foreseen, especially for Channel Islands traffic, while at the time, Hilsea, just outside Portsmouth, would also have appeared to show potential. Perhaps, once Heathrow was chosen as the site for London's primary postwar airport, it would have been advantageous to incorporate an airport spur off the Hounslow Loop, or possibly from Feltham, but by this time the railways were nationalised, as were the airports and the main scheduled airlines, with the private sector limited to charter operations or scheduled services as 'associates' of the state-owned BOAC and BEA.

Chapter Five

The Managers

The new railway company had all three general managers inherited from the constituent pre-grouping companies working together during the first year of the grouping. This made sense as the consolidation of three major companies and the absorption of several smaller ones was a major undertaking. Nevertheless, it was soon clear that there could only be one general manager and one chief mechanical engineer, respectively Herbert Walker from the London & South Western Railway and Richard Maunsell from the South Eastern & Chatham Railway. The Southern Railway was to be shaped by these two men, and although Maunsell's locomotive and electric multiple unit designs have been eclipsed by those of his successor Oliver Bulleid, it was Maunsell who was in charge during the formative years. Walker's successor was constrained by the demanding conditions of wartime operation and by nationalisation.

The first general manager was Sir Herbert Ashcombe Walker, the last general manager of the LSWR, who was followed by Gilbert Szlumper and then by Sir Eustace Missenden. After the latter was seconded to become chairman of the Railway Executive in the run-up to nationalisation, Sir John Elliot took over. Szlumper's father is also mentioned here since he was directly responsible for the reconstruction of Waterloo station, which, with the exception of the addition of the Eurostar terminal, is still in its essentials much as he left it.

The other figure who helped to shape any railway was the chief mechanical engineer. Throughout its existence, the Southern Railway had just two, starting with Richard Maunsell who had held the same post with the SECR, and who was succeeded on retirement by Oliver Bulleid.

These personalities are taken here in alphabetical order.

Oliver Bulleid

Oliver Vaughan Snell Bulleid (1882–1970) was, like his predecessor Maunsell, a man of considerable experience at home and abroad. He started his career as an apprentice under Henry Ivatt on the Great Northern Railway, but in 1908 moved to become the assistant manager of the Westinghouse works in Paris, before returning to the UK in 1911 to become personal assistant to Nigel Gresley, again on the GNR, for which company he was assistant carriage and wagon engineer in the three years before the grouping. Bulleid continued as assistant to Gresley in 1923 when Gresley became the chief mechanical engineer of the new LNER.

Bulleid took over as chief mechanical engineer at the Southern Railway in 1937, and inherited a railway in which development of larger and more powerful locomotives of the kind favoured by the LNER had been neglected, partly owing to the demands of electrification, but also because of weight restrictions on many lines. He pressed successfully for the introduction of powerful 4–6–2 locomotives, and despite severe wartime restrictions on the type and size of locomotives that could be built, by claiming that his new designs were for general-purpose duties, he succeeded in building no fewer than 140 Pacific locomotives of the 'Merchant Navy', 'West Country' and 'Battle of Britain' classes, introducing many new features such as completely enclosed chain-driven valve gear and welded fireboxes, and an improved working environment for the enginemen. At

Oliver Bulleid is the Chief Mechanical Engineer most usually associated with the Southern Railway, largely because of the impact of his 'Merchant Navy', 'West Country' and 'Battle of Britain' classes of air-smoothed Pacific locomotives, and for his 'wide-bodied' passenger rolling stock. *(NRM 119/97)*

the other end of the scale, he produced an austerity 0–6–0 freight locomotive, the 'Q1' class, of outstanding ugliness. The Bulleid Pacifics incorporated many features that were to be introduced into post-nationalisation designs, and were also more economical in their use of coal than the 'Britannia' class which in rebuilt form they closely resembled. However, they also had their weaknesses, including poor forward visibility and being prone to often catastrophic mechanical failures. Bulleid's attempt at producing a steam locomotive capable of working at express speeds in either direction and based on current thinking on electric and diesel designs resulted in the 'Leader' class of C-C or 0–6–6–0 layout, which failed to pass the prototype stage, not least because of the great discomfort suffered by the fireman.

Far more successful and enduring was Bulleid's work on new passenger rolling stock, using a design with widened bodies to provide greater comfort on main-line stock, and additional seating on suburban stock in the 4 SUB classes, with these features being carried over post-nationalisation to the early 2 and 4 EPB and 2 HAP classes.

Postwar, Bulleid worked on a successful design for a prototype 1Co-1Co diesel-electric locomotive, the precursor of 350 locomotives for British Railways, but his anger at the rebuilding of his own Pacific classes, despite some of their features being incorporated in the new British Railways standard classes, led him to resign in 1949 and join CIE, the Irish transport undertaking, as CME for the railways. He introduced diesel locomotives to Ireland and worked on new carriages and railcars as well as goods vehicles using welded production, and, as a final gesture to the steam locomotive, built yet another C-C design, but on this occasion designed to run on peat. He retired in 1958 to live in Malta.

Sir John Elliot

Sir John Elliot (1898–1988) started life as a journalist, becoming assistant editor of the London *Evening Standard* after the First World War. Elliot was wooed away from journalism in 1925 to join the Southern Railway as public relations assistant to Sir Herbert Walker. In complete contrast to the career paths of modern PR people, he became assistant traffic manager in 1930 and in 1938 assistant general manager to Gilbert Szlumper. Postwar, he became acting general manager when Sir Eustace Missenden was appointed to the Railway Executive, and after nationalisation he became chief regional officer of the new British Railways Southern Region. He took over from Missenden in 1951 as chairman of the Railway Executive and, when that body was abolished, filled a number of other roles in the nationalised transport industries.

Richard Maunsell

Richard Edward Lloyd Maunsell (1868–1944) was the Southern Railway's chief mechanical engineer, and a contemporary of Walker. Like Walker, Maunsell was an import, having started his career at the Inchicore Works of the Great Southern & Western Railway of Ireland. He moved in 1891 to the Lancashire & Yorkshire Railway, where his experience was broadened, and three years later he became assistant locomotive superintendent of the East Indian Railway, although not for long as he returned to Inchicore as works manager in 1896.

Maunsell joined the SECR as its chief mechanical engineer in 1913, inheriting a mixture of locomotives of differing quality from its two cash-starved constituent companies. He immediately created a new engineering team, bringing Clayton from Derby and both Pearson and Holcroft from the GWR works at Swindon. This team set about improving the existing 4–4–0 locomotives as well as introducing modern 2–6–0 and 2–6–4 tank engines ideally suited for the shorter-distance expresses and commuter trains of the south-east. The team was augmented by Lionel Lynes, a carriage specialist, when Maunsell became chief mechanical engineer for the new Southern Railway in 1923.

During his time at the Southern, Maunsell continued the improving work started at the SECR by tackling the ex-LSWR Urie 4–6–0s and in the process introducing a degree of standardisation. He was responsible for the highly successful 'Schools' class, as well as heavy 4–6–0 and 0–6–0 locomotives for goods, but his main work was on electrification and during his tenure the Southern limited funds for steam locomotive development because of the capital demands of electrification. A major disappointment for Maunsell was the rejection by the civil engineer of his plans for a four-cylinder 4–6–2 express locomotive and for three-cylinder 2–6–2 locomotives, with the former having to wait for his successor, Oliver Bulleid. Nevertheless, in addition to building new rolling stock for the main-line electrification programme, it was also possible to update the steam-hauled passenger carriages along similar lines.

Maunsell concentrated locomotive work on Ashford and Eastleigh, introducing modern line-production methods, and effectively sidelined the old LBSCR works at Brighton and Lancing, although these were run down rather than closed.

He retired in 1937 and died in 1944.

Sir Eustace Missenden was the last Southern Railway General Manager, and continued the tradition set by Walker and Szlumper by taking on important national responsibilities as the first chairman of the new Railways Executive. *(NRM BTC-collection 835/68)*

Sir Eustace Missenden

Sir Eustace J. Missenden (1886–1973) came from a railway family. His father was a stationmaster in Kent. He joined the South Eastern & Chatham Railway in 1899 as a junior clerk, but made rapid progress to district traffic superintendent and became a divisional operating superintendent for the Southern in 1923. In the years before the Second World War Missenden was assistant superintendent of operations in 1930, docks and marine manager at Southampton in 1933, and traffic manager in 1936. He became acting general manager in 1939 when Gilbert Szlumper was seconded to the War Office, and became general manager in 1942 with Szlumper's transfer to the Ministry of Supply.

In the preparations for nationalisation, Missenden became chairman of the Railway Executive, as second choice to Sir James Milne of the GWR who had rejected the post. Missenden was a Southern man through and through, and, not surprisingly, he found the Railway Executive uncongenial. In addition, he found the relationship with the British Transport Commission, the 'catch-all' body for all the nationalised transport industries, difficult, and retired in 1951.

Missenden's life centred around the railway. A shy man with few outside interests, he was a competent and conscientious railwayman, a sound if not always inspiring leader, and an opponent of nationalisation, with a healthy disregard for politicians and civil servants.

Albert Szlumper

Albert W. Szlumper (1858–1934) joined the civil engineering department of the LSWR and in later years did much of the preparatory work for the reconstruction of Waterloo, including both the terminus itself and the widening of the congested approaches. He became chief engineer in 1914 following the death of his predecessor in a riding accident, and became chief engineer of the Southern Railway in 1923. He was responsible for the remodelling of Cannon Street and for the reconstruction of the lines in the Ramsgate and Margate areas.

Father of Gilbert Szlumper, Albert Szlumper was described in one account as 'bluff, chunky and capable'; he retired in 1927 to become a consulting engineer.

Gilbert Szlumper

Gilbert Savill Szlumper (1884–1969) was that rare breed at the LSWR, someone who reached senior level having started inside the company. Furthermore, he was the son of Albert Szlumper, the LSWR's chief engineer and the brains behind the reconstruction work at Waterloo.

Gilbert Szlumper's early career was in engineering, working in his father's department from the time he joined the LSWR in 1902, but in 1913 he became assistant to the new general manager, Herbert Walker, and during the First World War he followed Walker on to the Railway Executive Committee as its secretary. Returning to the LSWR after the war, he became its docks and marine manager and started the planning for the massive extension of Southampton Docks. He rejoined Walker as assistant general manager of the Southern Railway in 1925, and eventually replaced Walker when he retired in 1937.

As general manager, Szlumper completed most of the Southern's electrification programme with the exception of the direct line to Hastings, for which work was prevented by the outbreak of the Second World War. Once again, Szlumper was required for the wartime railways, being loaned by the Southern to become Director-General of Transportation at the War Office shortly after war broke out, and he was retired officially from the Southern in 1942 to become Director-General at the Ministry of Supply until the war ended.

Szlumper is remembered as being quietly efficient, tireless and a clear thinker. He was very much in the mould of his predecessor and no doubt had war not intervened would have considerably extended the Southern electrification, possibly following Hastings with the lines throughout Kent, starting with the Thanet coast, and then probably taking on Southampton and Bournemouth.

Sir Herbert Walker

Sir Herbert Ashcombe Walker (1868–1949) was the last general manager of the LSWR, and followed in that company's tradition of recruiting its general managers from outside, in his case from the London & North Western Railway which he had joined at the age of seventeen. He joined the LSWR in 1912 when he was forty-three years old, at a time when it had already started on third-rail electrification and on the massive and desperately needed reconstruction of Waterloo. Despite being one of the youngest general managers, during the First World War he became acting chairman of the Railway Executive Committee, the body that ran the railways on behalf of the government, and his valuable work was recognised by a knighthood in 1917.

Walker has become famous for his extensive system of third-rail electrification, completing that of the suburban network and extending it to the coast so that by 1939 the third rail covered the Sussex coastline as far east as Hastings, extended into Hampshire as far as Portsmouth, and well inland to Aldershot and Alton. He also took the credit for the extension of the docks at Southampton that enabled it to become Britain's premier

The architect of main-line electrification, Sir Herbert Walker, who oversaw the rebuilding of Waterloo station, making it the world's first terminus designed for electric trains, and the building of the West Docks at Southampton. *(NRM BTC-collection 3592/64)*

passenger port at a time when overseas travel meant travel by sea. Others credit him with even-interval or 'clockface' scheduling, on which he insisted, but many of the early railways had operated on such a basis, especially on suburban services where high frequency lent itself to even-interval operations.

It is true that Walker deserves acknowledgement for all of these, and indeed for the strong leadership that he provided throughout his time at the Southern Railway. Yet, to confine any appraisal of him to these matters alone is to overlook his other qualities. He had a strong grasp of financial matters coupled with what can only be described as common sense. Typical of him was the decision not to rebuild the whole of Waterloo because the 'Windsor' station was at the time a new structure and could be incorporated into the design for the reconstruction without damaging the completeness of the new terminus. Equally, one suspects that his enthusiasm for third-rail electrification was based on the economy of a system that did not require the wholesale reconstruction of tunnels and overbridges, the cost of which could well have changed the economics of the programme completely. In many cases, carriages originally built for steam haulage were rebuilt as suburban electric multiple units, again a worthwhile economy, especially as the newer rolling stock was selected that otherwise could have been wasted by premature retirement. Walker also had an eye for publicity and recruited the young journalist John Elliot to handle the Southern's publicity. The LSWR had no great history of named trains, but the Southern Railway soon established a range of named expresses, showing that Walker did not adhere blindly to every LSWR tradition.

That Walker also took the long view and was aware of developments in transport generally can be gathered from the Southern's keen interest in acquiring bus companies, and where the entire company could not be purchased, taking a substantial shareholding. The Southern also took an interest in air transport and airports. The enthusiasm for main-line electrification has led many to believe that Walker's ultimate ambition was that of complete electrification of the Southern, but this seems unlikely given the sparse service and poor business prospects of many of the lines in Devon and Cornwall.

As a man, Walker has been described as quiet but authoritative, a consummate professional with a strong grasp of all aspects of railway operation, and a leader who always got the best from his management team. He had a strong sense of duty towards his shareholders and the travelling public. A weakness was the failure not to look for greater integration of the old companies, that could have rendered economies in management. Integration was carried through efficiently in such places as the Isle of Wight, where the three companies rapidly became one, but this did not involve upsetting traditionalist elements in the three constituent companies, possibly because, once the SECR had been created and the feuding between the two South Eastern companies ended, what resulted were three geographically distinct railway companies. It also has to be accepted that communications and automation were less sophisticated than today, so that keeping distinct divisions would have been seen as a practical approach rather than allowing over-centralisation. Undoubtedly, the network could have taken more line closures than was in fact the case, with branches such as those to Bembridge and Ventnor West proving a drain on the finances of the Southern Railway at a time when market conditions were far from buoyant, while those closures that did take place could have been accelerated. There was a curious contradiction in that the man who managed a railway and shipping concerns, and several ports of which the most significant by far was Southampton, believed that airports should be provided by the state, rather like roads.

Walker retired in 1937 and became a non-executive director of the Southern until nationalisation. He died in 1949.

Chapter Six

The 'Sparks Effect' – Electrification

The electrification work of the Southern Railway's predecessors has already been described. Further suburban electrification was to be a high priority for the new company, not just because of the competition from the electric trams and, now, the increasingly reliable motor bus, but because between 1913 and 1923 the number of passengers carried by the Southern and its predecessors had grown by 26 per cent. In addition, after the war, working hours were shortened, so that the morning and evening peaks became more concentrated than had been the case pre-war or during the war years. This made steam working extremely difficult over the congested approaches to the London termini, and left electrification of suburban services as the only viable solution since widening the lines would have been hopelessly uneconomic given the dense residential and commercial development that had taken place alongside the tracks.

A 3 SUB leads an Up train at Wimbledon in 1926. The rest of the train consists of a two-car trailer unit and another 3 SUB. Even as early as this all four roads were electrified, some time before main-line electrification was considered. *(HRMS AAQ624)*

One problem with the LSWR system of direct current, DC, electrification was that it required a substantial number of substations, and at first these had to be manned, the cost of which was a marked disadvantage. However, railway grouping more or less coincided with the advent of the automatic substation, remotely controlled and requiring no manning. Electric trains needed a crew of two, a motorman and a guard, compared with the two enginemen and guard of a steam train, required less maintenance and dispensed with stops for coaling and taking on water, and on stop-start suburban working were considerably faster than steam trains, all of which meant a considerable improvement in productivity. In addition, there was the inestimable benefit of dispensing with the shunting run to and from the sidings and turntables, with the almost constant demand for paths for light engines over already congested tracks.

The Southern must have been sorely tempted to press ahead with the LSWR system of third-rail electrification, not least because the LBSC overhead system differed from that planned by the SECR which had been delayed by the war. Nevertheless, in 1923 a consultant engineer was asked to consider all three systems and report on the best one. Meanwhile, work went ahead so that even after grouping a new overhead, or in LBSC terms 'elevated', electric scheme was introduced.

Cost and value for money were certainly always to the fore on the Southern Railway during Walker's term of office. Naturally, bids for the company's business were always keenly examined as simple good business practice, but when Raworth, the engineer in charge of electrification, reported that manufacturers were dictating just which company would make what, Walker smelt a rat and hence many contracts were noted in the board minutes as being left in the 'hands of Chairman and General Manager'. These were tangible signs of the Southern's dissatisfaction with the eventual award of contracts to English Electric for traction equipment, and to ASEA in Sweden for substation equipment in 1935. This was at a time when British business was more nationalistic than is the case today, and when Britain still believed that it could make anything and everything.

Electrifying the Suburbs

The occasion for announcing the Southern Railway's plans for electrification was at the first annual general meeting, held in March 1924. Sir Hugh Drummond, the chairman, confirmed that the SECR programme of electrification was approved and supported by the new board. In addition, the Western Section electrification would be extended from Surbiton to Effingham Junction and Guildford, Raynes Park to Leatherhead, and from Effingham Junction and Leatherhead to Dorking North. This theme was taken up again at the following AGM in February 1925 by the new chairman, Brigadier-General Baring, who explained that the electrification scheme was the largest ever on a suburban system. Plans to open the 'elevated' extension to Coulsdon North and Sutton on 1 March 1925 had been delayed by a month because of electricity supply problems. Nevertheless, the other extensions to Guildford and Dorking North were expected to follow in July, while the Eastern Section was being electrified within a 15 mile radius of London.

Accompanying electrification, a number of suburban stations were rearranged or had their platforms extended. New stations were built at Motspur Park and Carshalton Beeches, while those at Wimbledon and Sutton were rebuilt.

This was one vital aspect of the Southern Railway's approach to electrification. It never confined itself to simply installing third rail, but instead whenever possible considered changes to track and station layouts, and to signalling, while also rationalising and removing redundant facilities, especially those of the steam age such as turntables, coaling stages and watering facilities. This has since become known as 'whole route modernisation', and its absence in many Treasury-dominated postwar modernisation schemes has often meant that the full economic potential of, for example, investment in new trains could not be realised, either because of poor passenger appeal in old and badly

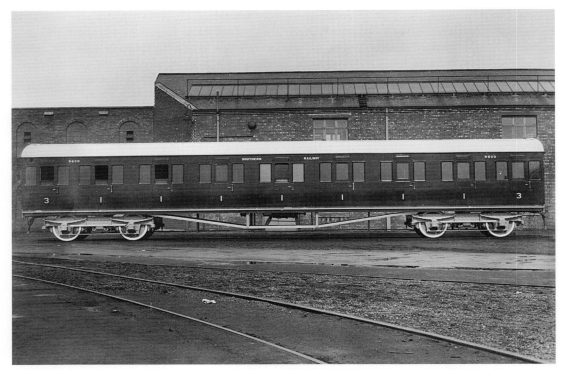

SR9600, a composite trailer for Eastern Section suburban electrification, clearly showing the way in which the company signed its rolling stock, although as a wartime economy the third-class marking was later dropped. *(HRMS AEP702)*

maintained stations, or because the new trains could not be used at their most productive due to speed limits and signals that were either out of date or suffered from poor spacing for higher-speed operation.

The Southern's programme of rolling electrification also meant that the teams engaged in this work were continuously employed, led by the Southern's two electrical engineers, Alfred Raworth and Herbert Jones, ensuring that not only did they acquire considerable expertise, but also that the company received good value for its money that could not have been obtained with any 'stop-start' system. The one failing was that at the time it was felt that the gaps in the conductor rails would preclude working by electric locomotives, so while passenger services were electrified, goods continued to be worked by steam trains. It would not be until the Second World War that the potential of electric locomotives would be realised, and this meant that the potential for economy and efficiency of a complete changeover was completely wasted for a period of between sixteen and twenty-two years.

The official start of the Coulsdon North and Sutton extensions of the 'elevated' electric on 1 April 1925 was marred by a broken conductor wire at Battersea Park, which severely disrupted the morning peak service. No doubt many frustrated and delayed commuters must have felt that the April Fool had been played on them!

New rolling stock had been supplied for these extensions by the Metropolitan Carriage Wagon & Finance Company at Birmingham. This included 21 motor vans, in reality electric locomotives, 60 driving trailers, and a further 20 trailer carriages. The configuration of these trains is given in Appendix IV. Trains operated at 20-minute intervals except between 11 am and 1 pm and after 9 pm Monday to Friday, when the service was half hourly, but on Saturdays there was a 20-minute interval service until 6 pm, after which trains were half-hourly until Monday morning.

The Southern introduced destination boards on the front of the leading carriage on each suburban electric train other than those on the south London line, and in addition new headcodes were devised for all suburban electric services. These were:

SL South London line (Victoria to London Bridge)
7 Victoria–Selhurst
8 Victoria–West Croydon via Crystal Palace
9 Victoria–Sutton via Selhurst
10 Victoria–East Croydon via Crystal Palace
11 Victoria–Coulsdon North via Selhurst
12 Victoria–Coulsdon North via Crystal Palace

The LSWR system of headcodes was continued on services out of Waterloo. These were:

V Waterloo–Malden–Kingston–Richmond–Waterloo (the 'Kingston Circular')
S Waterloo–Malden–Kingston–Shepperton
H Waterloo–Malden–Hampton Court
P̱ Waterloo–East Putney–Wimbledon
V̱ Waterloo–Richmond–Kingston–Malden–Waterloo
Ō Waterloo–Richmond–Hounslow–Brentford–Waterloo
O Waterloo–Brentford–Hounslow–Richmond–Waterloo

The compartments carried advertisements and this encouraged one famous baker to create an advertisement reading HōVIS, and underneath listing the headcodes used!

It was not until August 1926 that the decision to standardise on the third-rail DC system was announced, although in the meantime further work had been carried out on an additional AC scheme linking Victoria and Streatham Hill, which opened on 17 June 1928, the same day that the south London line, and the original Victoria to Streatham Hill and Crystal Palace services, were converted to third rail. The second Victoria and Streatham Hill service and the Crystal Palace services were converted on 3 March 1929, and their stock used to augment the Coulsdon North and Sutton sets until these too switched on 22 September 1929. Some of the wires remained in place for some time afterwards so that sets could be moved to the works for conversion to direct current, but the motor vans lay idle for four years at Streatham Hill sidings before being converted to bogie goods brakes, weighing 27 tons, at Eastleigh.

The cost of conversion was put officially at £1,456,328 in 1932, and gradually written off over the next ten years, with the write-off of the final remaining £205,473 in 1942. Meanwhile, progress had continued in extending the third rail. The extensions to Guildford and Dorking North, involving 67 track miles, were formally opened on 9 July 1925, with a special train conveying the directors and senior management as well as local civic dignitaries from Waterloo to Dorking North, before returning to Leatherhead and continuing to Guildford for a civic luncheon attended by the Minister of Transport. The new services started on 12 July. One feature of these extensions was that many of the new power substations were unattended.

The new trains shortened the journey times, with Waterloo to Guildford taking 52 minutes, compared with 73–79 minutes by steam train. Today it takes 59 minutes, with the off-peak frequency dropping from every 20 minutes to half-hourly. So much for progress, although part of the problem lies in the longer station dwell times required for sliding door stock, compared to the rapid boarding and alighting possible with slam doors to every set of seats.

The first electric services on the Eastern Section also started on 12 July 1925. Little incidental works had been required for the extensions to Guildford and Dorking, but the same could not be said for the initial Eastern Section electrification, where the poor state of

Mls	Down.	mrn	mrn	mrn	mrn	mrn	mrn	mrn	mrn	mrn	mrn	mrn	mrn	mrn	mrn	mrn	aft	aft	aft	aft	aft	aft	aft
	Waterloo dep.	6 7	...	6 10	6 45	7 7	7 45	7 55	8 7	8 45	9 7	9 45	10 7	1045	11 7	1145	12 7	1245	1 7	1 14	1 38	1 45	2 7
1¼	Vauxhall	...	...	6 13	...	...	...	7 58	...	...	...	...	...	...	...	...	...	...	...	...	Saturdays only.	...	...
4	**Clapham** Junction **	...	...	6 18	...	...	...	8 3	...	...	...	...	...	...	...	...	...	...	...	...		...	...
5½	Earlsfield, for Summers-	...	...	6 22	...	...	...	8 7	...	...	...	...	...	...	...	...	...	...	...	1 25		...	...
7¼	**Wimbledon** [town	...	...	6 26	7 1	...	8 1	8 11	...	9 1	...	10 1	...	11 1	...	12 1	...	1 1	...	1 30		2 1	...
8¾	**Raynes Park**	...	...	6 32	7 5	...	8 5	8 16	...	9 5	...	10 5	...	11 5	...	12 5	...	1 5	...	1 34		2 5	...
10¾	Worcester Park	...	...	6 38	7 10	...	8 10	8 21	...	9 10	...	1010	...	1110	...	1210	...	1 10	...	1 39		2 10	...
13	Ewell *	...	...	6 42	7 15	...	8 16	8 27	...	9 15	...	1015	...	1116	...	1216	...	1 16	...	1 45		2 16	...
14½	Epsom	...	...	6 49	7 22	...	8 21	8 32	...	9 20	...	1023	...	1122	...	1221	...	1 21	...	1 50		2 21	...
16½	Ashtead	...	...	7 0	7 28	...	8 27	...	...	9 28	...	1029	...	1128	...	1227	...	1 27	...	1 56		2 27	...
18¼	Leatherhead	...	7 0	7 7	7 34	...	8 33	8 45	...	9 35	...	1036	...	1134	...	1233	...	1 33	...	2 1		2 33	...
20¾	Bookham	...	...	7 12	7 40	...	8 39	8 50	...	9 41	...	1042	...	1140	...	1239	...	1 39	...	2 6		2 39	...
9¾	Malden, for Coombe	...	...	Change at Raynes Park.	...	...	...	Change at Raynes Park.	...	...	...	...	...	...	...	...	...	...	...	Saturdays only.	...	...	...
12	**Surbiton**	6 28	...		...	7 28	...		8 28	...	9 28	...	1028	...	1128	...	1228	...	1 28		1 58	...	2 28
15¼	Claygate, for Claremont	6 36	...		...	7 36	...		8 36	...	9 36	...	1036	...	1136	...	1236	...	1 36		2 6	...	2 36
17	Oxshott, for Fairmile	6 42	...		...	7 42	...		8 42	...	9 44	...	1042	...	1142	...	1242	...	1 42		2 12	...	2 42
18¾	**Cobham** †	6 47	...		...	7 47	...		8 47	...	9 48	...	1048	...	1147	...	1247	...	1 47		2 17	...	2 47
21¼	Effingham Junction	6 54	...		7 45	7 54	8 44		8 54	9 46	9 55	1047	1055	1145	1154	1244	1254	1 44	1 54		2 24	2 44	2 54
22¼	**Horsley** ‡	6 59	7 12		7 49	7 59	8 48		8 59	9 50	10 0	1051	11 0	1149	1159	1248	1259	1 48	1 59		2 29	2 48	2 59
25¼	**Clandon** ‖	7 6	...		...	8 6	...		9 6	...	10 7	...	11 7	...	12 6	...	1 6	...	2 6		2 36	...	3 6
28½	London Road [197	7 13	...		...	8 13	...		9 13	...	1014	...	1114	...	1213	...	1 13	...	2 13		2 43	...	3 13
30	**Guildford 150, 158** arr.	7 17	...		...	8 17	...		9 17	...	1018	...	1118	...	1217	...	1 17	...	2 17		2 47	...	3 17

Down. **Week Days**—*Continued.*

Down.	aft	aft	aft	aft	aft	aft	aft	aft	aft	aft	aft	aft	aft	aft	aft	aft	aft	aft	aft	aft	aft	aft	aft
Waterloo dep.	2 14	2 45	3 7	3 45	4c7	4 45	5 4	5 14	5 34	5 45	6 4	...	6 14	6 38	6 45	7 8	7 15	7 45	8 10	8 45	9 7	9 45	10 7
Vauxhall	...	...	...	...	...	...	...	...	Except Saturdays	...	Except Saturdays.	Saturdays only.	...	Except Saturdays	...	...	...	...	...	...	...	9 50	...
Clapham Junction **	...	...	...	...	...	...	...	...		...			...		...	...	...	...	...	...	...	...	...
Earlsfield, for Summers-	2 25	...	...	...	...	...	...	5 25		...			6 25		...	...	7 26	...	...	...	...	...	...
Wimbledon [town	2 30	3 1	...	4 1	...	5 0	...	5 30		6 1			6 30		7 0	...	7 31	8 1	...	9 1	...	10 2	...
Raynes Park	2 34	3 5	...	4 5	...	5 4	...	5 34		6 5			6 34		7 4	...	7 35	8 6	...	9 5	...	10 6	...
Worcester Park	2 39	3 10	...	4 10	...	5 10	...	5 39		6 10			6 39		7 9	...	7 40	8 13	...	9 10	...	1011	...
Ewell *	2 44	3 16	...	4 16	...	5 14	...	5 45		6 15			6 44		7 14	...	7 46	8 18	...	9 16	...	1017	...
Epsom	2 51	3 21	...	4 21	...	5 20	...	5 50		6 23			6 53		7 19	...	7 51	8 24	...	9 21	...	1022	...
Ashtead	2 59	3 27	...	4 27	...	5 27	...	5 56		6 30			7 2		7 26	...	7 57	8 32	...	9 27	...	1028	...
Leatherhead	3 5	3 33	...	4 33	...	5 35	...	6 1		6 36			7 8		7 33	...	8 1	8 39	...	9 33	...	1034	...
Bookham	3 10	3 39	...	4 39	...	5 41	...	6 6		6 42			7 13		7 39	...	...	8 45	...	9 39	...	1040	...
Malden, for Coombe	Saturdays only.	...	...	...	...	...	...	Except Saturdays.	...	...	...	...	Except Saturdays.	...	...	...	Except Saturdays.	...	...	...	...	...	...
Surbiton		...	3 28	...	4 28	...	5 26		5 56	...	6 26	6 28		6 58	...	7 28		...	8 32	...	9 28	...	1028
Claygate, for Claremont		...	3 36	...	4 36	...	5 34		6 4	...	6 34	6 36		7 6	...	7 36		...	8 40	...	9 36	...	1036
Oxshott, for Fairmile		...	3 42	...	4 42	...	5 40		6 10	...	6 40	6 42		7 12	...	7 42		...	8 46	...	9 42	...	1042
Cobham †		...	3 47	...	4 47	...	5 47		6 15	...	6 48	6 48		7 17	...	7 47		...	8 51	...	9 47	...	1047
Effingham Junction		3 44	3 54	4 44	4 54	5 46	5 54		6 22	6 47	6 55	6 55		7 24	7 44	7 54		8 50	8 58	9 44	9 54	1045	1054
Horsley ‡		3 48	3 59	4 48	4 59	5 50	5 59		6 27	6 51	7 0	7 0		7 29	7 48	7 59		8 54	9 3	9 48	9 59	1049	1059
Clandon ‖		...	4 6	...	5 6	...	6 6		6 34	...	7 7	7 7		7 36	...	8 6		...	9 10	...	10 6	...	11 6
London Road [197		...	4 13	...	5 13	...	6 13		6 41	...	7 14	7 14		7 43	...	8 13		...	9 17	...	1013	...	1113
Guildford 150, 158 arr.		...	4 17	...	5 17	...	6 17		6 45	...	7 18	7 18		7 47	...	8 17		...	9 21	...	1017	...	1117

Miles	**Down** **HOUR**	mrn 6	6	6	6	A 7	7	7 32 mrn to 6 32 aft HOURLY from	**And at**	B 7	7	8	8 12 mrn to 11 12 aft HOURLY from	8	8 52 mrn to 6 52 aft HOURLY from	**And at**	aft 7	8	9	10	11	11	12	ngt. 12	29th July and 5th Aug.
--	Waterloo dep.	.	12	.	52	7	32			747	52	12		52			42	42	42	42	0	42	0	20	
4	Clapham Junction **A**	.	.	.	.	.				.	.	.		.			.	.	.	.	8	49	7	30	
7¾	Wimbledon	.	.	.	.	20	Z			758	.	X		Y			52	52	52	52	15	55	13	40	
12	Surbiton	.	28	.	**8**	28	49			.	**8**	28		**8**			**1**	**1**	**1**	**0**	25	**2**	20	53	
14	Hinchley Wood	.	31	.	11	31	52			.	11	31		11			4	4	4	4	29th July only.	5	24	.	
15¼	Claygate, for Claremont	.	34	.	14	34	55			.	14	34		14			7	7	7	7		8	27	.	
17	Oxshott, for Fairmile	.	38	.	18	38	59			.	18	38		18			11	11	11	9		12	30	.	
18¾	Cobham **B**	.	41	.	21	41	**2**			.	21	41		21			14	14	14	14		15	34	.	
21	Effingham Junction 197	25	46	58	26	46	7			831	26	46		26			20	20	19	18		21	39	.	
22	Horsley **C** [Corner **D**	27	48	**4**	28	48	9			833	.	48		28			22	22	21	21		23	42	.	
25¼	Clandon, for Newlands	32	53	9	33	53	14			838	.	53		33			27	27	26	26		28	47	.	
28½	London Road **F**	38	59	14	39	59	20			844	.	59		39			33	33	32	31		34	52	.	
30	Guildford 180, 192 arr.	42	**3**	18	43	**3**	25			848	.	**4**		43			37	37	36	35	.	38	56	.	

Suburban services were the first to benefit from electrification, spurred by competition from electric tramways, but Guildford was first to benefit when the Southern broke out of the inner suburban area in 1925, even before it had officially decided on the third rail. The compact 1938 timetable (bottom) cannot disguise the fact that trains were more frequent and ran for almost an extra 2 hours in the evening. *(Bradshaw)*

the SECR and its constituent companies had meant that there were disused stations to be removed and platform lengthening sometimes involved extra work on bridges as well as the approaches at St Paul's (now Blackfriars) and Holborn Viaduct. The lines covered by the initial scheme included Victoria–Orpington via Herne Hill and Shortlands, as well as Holborn Viaduct to Herne Hill, the Catford Loop between Loughborough Junction and Shortlands, and Nunhead to Crystal Palace High Level. The shortage of running roads also

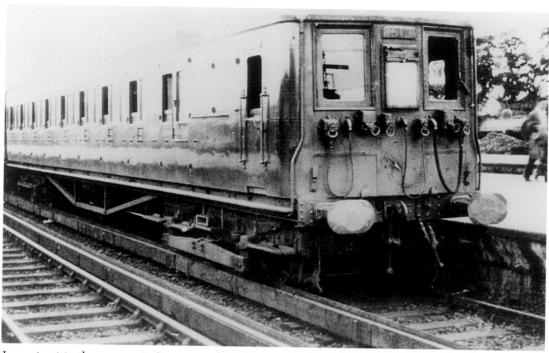

In contrast to the new main-line units, the designations of suburban units often covered a variety of styles, including 3 SUB No. 1513 converted from ex-LBSCR steam-hauled stock. *(HRMS AAC133)*

dictated some less than satisfactory timings, with the section of double track between Herne Hill and Shortlands dictating that services from Victoria and Holborn Viaduct ran just 5 minutes apart, leaving a gap of 15 minutes to accommodate the many steam trains, including continental boat trains, using the same route. The new services started on a Sunday and worked well on the first day, but a number of breakdowns on the second day, some of which may well have been due to staff inexperience, led to serious disruption and it was to be well into the first week before everything was working smoothly. Problems with major timetable changes were to occur time and time again with electrification, largely because operating staff had to constantly refer to new timetables rather than simply working by experience and memory.

On 21 March 1926 the Southern introduced the world's first four-aspect colour-light signalling on the stretch of track between Holborn Viaduct and Elephant & Castle. This was an important advance, but the requirement for four-aspect rather than three was dictated by a combination of intensive traffic and the mix of steam and electric traction. Seven manual signal-boxes were replaced by two larger installations, one of which used the existing building at Holborn Viaduct, but a new cabin had to be built at Blackfriars Junction.

The initial electrification was followed by a much-needed rearrangement and simplification during the second half of 1925 of the approaches to Cannon Street which had been originally designed to allow all trains to and from Charing Cross to work in and out of the station. There was also extensive work at Charing Cross, where the platform numbering sequence was reversed.

Plans to introduce a second group of electric services on the Eastern Section from 1 December 1925 had to be postponed until 28 February 1926, again because of power supply problems. These were the services from Cannon Street and Charing Cross to Bromley North, Orpington, Beckenham Junction, Hayes and Addiscombe, although trains on the Hayes to Elmers End branch switched to electric operation on 21 September 1925 to

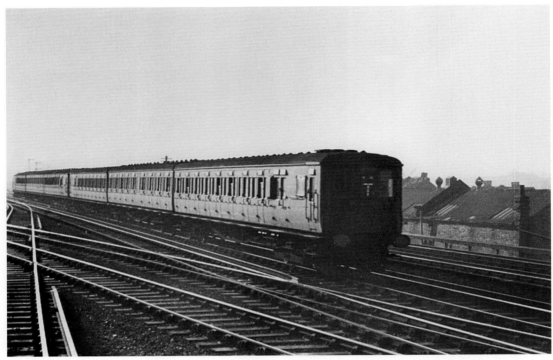

This is a 1939 six-car suburban train comprising two 3 SUB electric multiple units. *(HRMS AAN512)*

allow for staff training. Sufficient electric rolling stock and track mileage was available during the General Strike of 1926 for a service of electric trains to operate between Charing Cross and Dartford from 10 May until 16 May, but steam returned to the route afterwards. Electric trains returned to this route, but again on a temporary basis, from 6 June during the closure of Cannon Street for reconstruction to cope with traffic diverted to London Bridge and Charing Cross. The work at the two old SER termini also saw further colour light signalling installed.

The General Strike and the much longer miners' strike associated with it resulted in the temporary closure of the south London line between 18 May and 20 September 1926. Closure, plus the extension of the City and South London tube line, meant that traffic on the route was found to have fallen away considerably when the line reopened. A major reorganisation of services associated with further electrification that came into effect in 1928 saw the south London line service cut back, probably the only time in the history of Southern electrification that this action was found necessary. This instance of defeat simply reflected the fact that the line really was the wrong type of route to be operated by a main-line railway, and could only have prospered in the longer term as a link in an urban railway, an above-ground section of an underground line, as otherwise it was extremely vulnerable to competition from the modern tramway. The route also ran through a less prosperous neighbourhood, where the impact of recession was probably more heavily felt. Once again a major launch of electric services had to be postponed, but only from 11 July to 18 July 1926, when electric services were introduced from Charing Cross and Cannon Street to Plumstead, and Dartford, permanently at last, via Blackheath and Woolwich, Bexleyheath and Sidcup.

In addition to the conversion of the overhead electrics to third rail, the needs of the Central Section were not being ignored. The announcement of the conversion in August 1926, following the recommendation that third rail was the best and most economical way forward, also mentioned that third-rail electrification would cover the sections between London Bridge and Norwood Junction, Crystal Palace Low Level to both Beckenham Junction and Sydenham, from Purley to Caterham and Tattenham Corner, from Streatham North Junction to Sutton and Epsom, and from Sutton to Epsom Downs, as well as Wimbledon to Herne Hill, Tulse Hill and Haydons Road. A little more than a year later, further colour light signalling was announced, with another nine manual boxes replaced by power-worked cabins at Borough Market Junction and London Bridge. The speed at which these improvements were implemented was astonishing enough, although it no doubt also vindicated the decision to stick with third rail, but what was even more impressive was that a number of services were ready to be operated by electric trains using the steam train timings by 25 March 1928, when the services between Cannon Street, Charing Cross and London Bridge to Caterham and Tadworth changed, as did London Bridge to Crystal Palace Low Level through Sydenham. The new services, with accelerated timings and improved frequencies, were introduced on Sunday 17 June 1928. Once again, the initial service went smoothly, but on Tuesday 19 June a points failure disrupted services during the evening peak, and while delays were not too long, mainly less than 15 minutes, it took until 4 July for a full train service to be reinstated.

The next stage in the Central Section electrification followed on 3 March 1929, with Dorking North and Effingham Junction having electric trains to London Bridge as well as to Waterloo, with the former operating via Tulse Hill and Mitcham Junction. On the same day, electric services were introduced from Victoria to Epsom via Mitcham Junction and from Holborn Viaduct to Wimbledon via Tulse Hill and Haydons Road, while the Victoria to Crystal Palace Low Level service was converted from AC to DC operation and extended to West Croydon and Beckenham Junction, with the latter requiring considerable work as the line between Bromley Junction and Beckenham Junction had not been used by passenger

After conversion from 3 SUB to 4 SUB by the simple expedient of inserting a second trailer, this is No. 4327. *(HRMS AEN114)*

Miles	Down.	mrn	mrn	mrn	mrn	mrn	mrn	mrn	mrn	mrn	mrn	mrn	mrn	mrn	mrn	mrn	mrn
—	Charing Cross .....dep.	3 cl.		5 18		5 57	6 15		6 40		7 2						
¾	Waterloo Junction			5 20		5 59	6 17		6 42		7 4						
—	Cannon Street		4 43		5 53			6 32		6 50		712		7 32	7 40	7 44	7 48
1¾	London Bridge	3 22	4 46	5 25	5 56	6 4	6 22	6 35	6 47	6 53	7 9	715		7 35	7 43	7 47	7 51
5¼	Greenwich .....(wich)	Leaves Holborn Viaduct 3 15 mrn.	4 56		6 7		6 30		6 55		7 20			7 43			
6¼	Maze Hill (E. Green-		4 59		6 10		6 33		6 58		7 23			7 46			
7	Westcombe Park		5 3		6 14	h	6 36		7 1		7 26		3 cl.	7 49			
5	New Cross			5 34		6 11		6 42		7 0			7 27		7 50		7 59
5½	St. John's			5 37		6 14		6 45		7 3			7 29				8 2
6	Lewisham Junction			5 40		6 17		6 48		7 6		725	7 32		7 54		8 5
7	Blackheath			5 44		6 21		6 52		7 10			7 36		7 58		8 9
7¾	Charlton Junction		5 7	5 50	6 17	6 27	6 39	6 58	7 4	7 16	7 29			7 52	8 5		8 15
8¾	Woolwich (Dockyard)		5 12	5 54	6 21	6 31	6 43	7 2	7 8	7 20	7 33		7 44	7 56	8 8		8 18
9½	" (Arsenal)	3 40	5 15	5 57	6 24	6 34	6 46	7 5	7 11	7 23	7 36		7 47	7 59	8 11	8 4	8 21
10	Plumstead		5 20	6 0	6 28	6 37	6 49	7 8	7 15	7 27	7 39		7 50	8 0	8 14		8 24
11½	Abbey Wood		5 26	6 5	6 34	6 43	6 55	7 14	7 21	7 33	7 45		7 56		8 20		8 30
13	Belvedere		5 30	6 9	6 38	6 47	6 59	7 18	7 25	7 37	7 49		8 0		8 24		8 34
14¼	Erith		5 36	6 13	6 42	6 51	7 3	7 22	7 30	7 42	7 53		8 4		8 28	8 14	8 38
15¾	Slades Green		5 42	6 17	6 49	6 55	7 7	7 26		7 46	8 0						
17¼	Dartford 248 .....arr.	4 0	5 48	6 22		7 0	7 12	7 31		7 54						8 21	

Miles	Down.	mrn	mn	mrn	mrn	mrn	3 cl.	mrn	K mrn	mrn	mrn	mrn	mrn	mrn	mrn	mrn	mrn
—	Charing Cross .....dep.		810			8 34	8 38	8 50	Mons., Fris., and Sats.	9 18	9 38		10 2		1010		
¾	Waterloo Junction		812			8 36	8 40	8 52		9 20	9 40		10 4		1012		
—	Cannon Street	8 8		8 24	8 32							9 56		1016		10 50	1058
1¾	London Bridge	8 11	817	8 27	8 35	8 41	8 45	8 57		9 25	9 45	9 59	10 9	1019	1017	10 53	11 1
5¼	Greenwich .....(wich)			8 35			8 56					1010		1028			
6¼	Maze Hill (E. Green-			8 38			8 59					1013		1031			
7	Westcombe Park			8 41			9 2					1016		1034			
5	New Cross	8 18			8 42					9 33			1017		1025	11 1	
5½	St. John's	8 21			8 45										1028	11 4	
6	Lewisham Junction	8 25			8 48					9 38			1021		1031	11 7	
7	Blackheath	8 30			8 52				9 20	9 42			1025		1035	11 11	
7¾	Charlton Junction	8 38		8 44	8 58		9 5	9 11		9 48		1019	1031	1037	1042	11 19	
8¾	Woolwich (Dockyard)	8 41			9 1		9 8	9 14		9 51		1022		1040	1046	11 22	
9½	" (Arsenal)	8 44	836	8 50	9 5	8 58	9 11	9 17	9 30	9 54	10 5	1025	1037	1043	1049	11 25	1119
10	Plumstead	8 47		8 54	9 10	9 2	9 15	9 20		9 58		1029	1040	1046	1052	11 28	
11½	Abbey Wood			9 0	9 16			9 27				1035			1058	11 34	
13	Belvedere			9 4	9 20			9 31				1039			11 2	11 38	
14¼	Erith		846	9 8	9 25			9 35	9 40		1015	1043	1050		11 6	11 42	
15¾	Slades Green			9 12	9 32							1047	1059		1110	11e53	
17¼	Dartford 248 .....arr.		853	9 18					9 47		1022	1053			1115		1133

Week Days—*Continued.*

Down.	mrn	mrn	S aft	mrn	mrn	aft	E aft	S aft	S aft	S aft	S aft	E aft	S aft	E aft	S aft	S aft
Charing Cross .....dep.			3 cl.		11 55			1210			1245					
Waterloo Junction					11 57			1212			1247					
Cannon Street	11 6	11 8		1150		12 8	1212		1224	1234		1250	1 2	1 2	1 8	1 12
London Bridge	11 9	11 11		1153	12 2	12 11	1215	1217	1227	1237	1253	1253	1 5	1 5	1 11	1 15
Greenwich .....(wich)	1117		Runs to Gravesend (C.), see page 248.			12 19		1225		1246				1 13		1 23
Maze Hill (E. Green-	1120					12 22		1228		1250				1 16		1 26
Westcombe Park	1123					12 25		1231		1253	1 4		1 16	1 19		1 29
New Cross		11 19		12 3			1222		1235			1 2			1 18	
St. John's		11 22		12 6			1225		1238			1 5			1 21	
Lewisham Junction		11 25		12 9			1228		1241			1 8			1 24	
Blackheath		11 29		1214			1232		1245			1 12			1 29	
Charlton Junction	1126	11 35		1220		12 28	1238	1234	1251	1256		1 18		1 23	1 36	1 32
Woolwich (Dockyard)	1130	11 39		1223		12 32	1242	1238	1254	1 0		1 21		1 27	1 40	
" (Arsenal)	1133	11 42		1226	12 20	12 35	1245	1241	1257	1 4	1 11	1 24	1 23	1 31	1 43	1 37
Plumstead	1137	11 46		1229		12 38	1249	1245	1 1	1 8	1 15	1 27	1 26	1 34	1 46	1 40
Abbey Wood		11 52		1235			1255	1251		1 14		1 33	1 32		1 52	1 46
Belvedere		11 56		1239			1259	1255		1 19		1 37	1 36		1 56	1 50
Erith		12 0	1212	1243	12 36		1 3	1 0		1 23		1 42	1 40		2 0	1 54
Slades Green		12 7	1215	1251			1 7	1 21		1 28		1 51				1 58
Dartford 248 .....arr.		12e13	1220		12 38		1 12			1 33			1 47			2 3

Down.	E aft	S aft	S 3 cl.	E aft	S aft	S aft	E aft	S aft	E aft	S aft	aft	S aft	aft	S aft	E aft	E aft
Charing Cross .....dep.			1 42			1 47				2 20						
Waterloo Junction	a		1 44			1 49				2 22						
Cannon Street	1 23	1 30		1 45	1 50		2 2	2 8	2 16		2 40		2 50	3 0	3 8	3 16
London Bridge	1 26	1 33	1 49	1 48	1 53	1 54	2 5	2 11	2 19	2 27	2 43		2 53	3 3	3 11	3 19
Greenwich .....(wich)		1 41			2 1				2 27	2 35					3 19	
Maze Hill (E. Green-		1 44			2 4				2 30	2 38					3 22	
Westcombe Park		1 47			2 7				2 33	2 41					3 25	
New Cross	1 33			1 55			2 15	2 20					3 0	3 10		3 30
St. John's	1 36			1 58		2 3	2 18	2 23					3 3	3 13		3 33
Lewisham Junction	1 39			2 1		2 6	2 21	2 26					3 6	3 16		3 37
Blackheath	1 43			2 5		2 10	2 25	2 30					3 10	3 20		3 41
Charlton Junction	1 49	1 50		2 11	2 10	2 16	2 31	2 36	2 36	2 44			3 16	3 26	3 28	3 48
Woolwich (Dockyard)	1 53	1 54		2 15	2 13	2 19	2 34	2 39	2 39	2 48			3 19	3 30	3 32	3 52
" (Arsenal)	1 57	1 57	2 5	2 18	2 16	2 22	2 37	2 42	2 42	2 51	2 59		3 22	3 33	3 35	3 55
Plumstead	2 3	2 0		2 21	2 19	2 26	2 40	2 45	2 45	2 54			3 26	3 37	3 39	3 59
Abbey Wood	2 10	Stop		2 27		2 32		2 51	2 51				3 32	3 43		4 5
Belvedere	2 14			2 31		2 36		2 55	2 55				3 36	3 47		4 9
Erith	2 19	2s20	2 14	2 35		2 40		2 59	2 59			3 25	3 40	3e51		4 13
Slades Green	2 24	2s23		2 43		2 44		3 3	3 3			3 28	3s44	4 26		4 17
Dartford 248 .....arr.	2 30		2 22			2 50		3 8	3 8		3 13		3s50			4 23

Mls	HOUR ☞	B 3	4	5	5	5	5	5	5	5	5	5	6	6	6
—	Charing Cross ....dep.						4		18			57			23
¾	Waterloo .... "						6		20			59			26
—	Cannon Street........ "					2				38	52			13	
1¾	London Bridge ...... "	13				6	11		25	42	**0**	**5**		16	29
5	Deptford											11			35
5¼	Greenwich					14			35			13			37
6¼	Maze Hill A					17			39			16			40
7	Westcombe Park					19			42			18			42
5	New Cross						19			48				22	
5¼	St. John's						22							25	
6	Lewisham						24			51				27	
7	Blackheath						27			54				29	
7¾	Charlton					22	32		47	58		21		33	45
8¾	Woolwich Dockyard					24	34			**0**				36	47
9¼	" Arsenal					28	38		53	4	17	25		39	50
10	Plumstead					31	40		57	7		27		41	52
11½	Abbey Wood					35	44	49	**2**	10		30	39	45	55
13	Belvedere					40	47	52	6	13		33	41	48	58
14¼	Erith					41	50	55	10	17		36	44	52	**1**
15¼	Slades Green					48	53	58	13	21		39	48	55	4
17	Dartford 348	42	59	26	43	52	58	**2**	17	23	35	43		**0**	8
19	Stone Crossing Halt			30	47		**3**			30					12
19¾	Greenhithe		**4**	32	49		5			32					14
20¾	Swanscombe Halt			36	52		8			35					18
21¼	Northfleet [369a		9	38	55		11			38	45				20
24	Gravesend Cen. 348. arr.	54	13	43	59		15			42	51				25

HOUR ☞	6	6	D 6	6	6	7	7	7	7	7	7	8	8	8
Charing Cross ....dep.							11		34	38				
Waterloo .... "							13		36	41				
Cannon Street........ "	36		43	55	58	0		27			48		1	5
London Bridge ...... "	39	46	50	58	**1**	8	16	29	39	48	50		3	7
Deptford	45			**4**				36	45					
Greenwich	47			6				38	47					
Maze Hill A	50			8				40	50					
Westcombe Park	52			11				43	52					
New Cross		52			8		23				57			
St. John's		55			10									
Lewisham		57			12		26				**0**			
Blackheath		**1**			15		28				2			
Charlton	55	5		13	20			45	55		6		13	19
Woolwich Dockyard	57			16	22		34	48	57				16	
" Arsenal	**0**	10	**5**	18	25		37	50	**0**	**4**	10		18	23
Plumstead	2	15		21	28		39	52			12		20	25
Abbey Wood	5	19		24	32		42	56			15		24	29
Belvedere	8	22		28	35		45	59			18		27	32
Erith	11	25	15	33	38		48	**2**	7	12	21		30	35
Slades Green	14	30		37	42		51	5	10		25		33	38
Dartford 348	18		26	41		38	55		14	19		28	37	
Stone Crossing Halt	22						**0**					33		
Greenhithe	24						2					36		
Swanscombe Halt	28						5					39		
Northfleet [369a	30						8					43		
Gravesend Cen. 348. arr.	35					51	12			31		48		

HOUR ☞	8	8	8	8	8	L 8	P 8	N 9	8	8	9	9	P 9	9
Charing Cross ....dep.		5		31										
Waterloo .... "		7		33										
Cannon Street........ "	8		23		39				50	55	8	10	16	21
London Bridge ...... "	10	12	25	36	41				52	57	10	12	20	23
Deptford	16				47					**3**				
Greenwich	18				49					5		20		
Maze Hill A	20				51					8		22		
Westcombe Park	23			45	54					10		25		
New Cross		19							59					30
St. John's		21												
Lewisham		23				54	54		**2**					33
Blackheath		26				56	56		5					36
Charlton		30	35		56				9	13		27		40
Woolwich Dockyard			38		59					15		30		42
" Arsenal	28	36	41	50	**1**	**7**	**7**		12	18	23	32	38	45
Plumstead	30	39	43	52	3				14	20	25	34		47
Abbey Wood	33	42		55	7				18		28			50
Belvedere	36	45		58	10				21		31			53
Erith	39	50		**1**	13				24		34	41		56
Slades Green		55		4					27		37	44		**1**
Dartford 348	45	**0**		8	19	24	24	24	30		41	48	53	5
Stone Crossing Halt				12					35		46			
Greenhithe				14					37		48			
Swanscombe Halt				17					41		51			
Northfleet [369a				20					43		54			
Gravesend Cen. 348. arr.				24		35		35	48		58		**5**	

HOUR ☞	9	S 9	9	S 9	9	9	10	10	S 10	E 10	10	H 10	10	10
Charing Cross ....dep.					E46	53					28			53
Waterloo .... "					E48	55					30			57
Cannon Street........ "	25	29	35	40	S49		6	13	17			44	52	
London Bridge ...... "	27	31	38	42	51	59	11	15	19	19	33	46	57	**0**
Deptford	33	38	44	49		**6**				26	40			7
Greenwich	35	40	46	51		8				28	42			9
Maze Hill A	38	42	48	53		10				30	45			11
Westcombe Park	41	45	51	56		13				33	47			14
New Cross					58			21				52		
St. John's					**0**			E						
Lewisham					2			25				55		
Blackheath					5			28				58		
Charlton	44	48	54	58	9	15		32		36	49	**2**		16
Woolwich Dockyard	46	50	56	**1**	12	18		35		38	52			19
" Arsenal	49	53	59	3	14	20		37	32	41	54	6	**13**	21
Plumstead	51	56	**1**	5	17	24		39	34	44	56	8		23
Abbey Wood	55		5	9	21	28		43	37	47	**0**	11		27
Belvedere	58		8	12	24	31		46	40	50	3	14		30
Erith	**2**		11	15	27	34		49	43	54	6	17		33
Slades Green	6		14		30	37		52	46	59	9	20		36
Dartford 348			17	21	S35	E42		55	51		S13	25	27	40
Stone Crossing Halt			S22			E47		**0**			S17			
Greenhithe			S24			E49		2			S19			
Swanscombe Halt			S27			E52		6			S23			
Northfleet [369a			S30			E55		8			S25			
Gravesend Cen. 348. arr.			S3[illegible]			E59	47	13			S30		38	

mrn ☞ aft ☞ **Week Days**—*Continued*

HOUR ☞	R 11	E 11	E 11	S 11	S 12	S 11	E 11	E 11	S 12	S 11	E 11	S 11	E 11	S 12	S 12
Charing Cross .....dep						24	27						57		
Waterloo.......... "						26	29						59		
Cannon Street....... "	0		14	16				42		43	51	49		10	15
London Bridge .... "	4	13	16	18		30	33	47		45	53	51	**2**	12	
Deptford	12	18				36	39					58	8		
Greenwich		20				38	41					**0**	10		
Maze Hill A	17	23				40	43					2	13		
Westcombe Park		25				43	46					5	15		
New Cross			23	24						52	59			18	
St John's			25											21	
Lewisham			28	27						55	**2**			23	
Blackheath			31	30						57	5			25	
Charlton	23	28	35	34		45	48			**1**	9	7	18	29	
Woolwich Dockyard		30		36			51			4	11	10	20	32	
" Arsenal	29	33	39	39		49	53	**3**	2	6	14	12	23	34	
Plumstead	32	36	41	41		51	55			8	16	14	25	36	
Abbey Wood		39	45	44		54	59			12	19	18	28	40	
Belvedere		42	48	47		57	**2**			15	22	21	31	43	
Erith	40	45	51	50		**0**	5		12	18	25	24	34	46	
Slades Green		49	54	54		3	8			21	28	27		49	
Dartford 348	47		58			7	14	17	20	25	32	31	40		
Stone Crossing Halt															
Greenhithe															
Swanscombe Halt															
Northfleet [369a					7										
Gravesend C. 348, arr.	**0**				10			29	31						53

HOUR ☞	E 12	S 12	S 12	E 12	S 12	S 12	E 12	S 12	S 12	E 12	S 1	E 1	S 1	E 1	S 1
Charing Cross .....dep		13	25	28					52	55				19	
Waterloo.......... "		15	27	30					54	57				22	
Cannon Street....... "	14				37	39	44	48			10	14	18		20
London Bridge .... "	16	19	30	33	39	41	46	50	59	**6**	12	16	20	26	24
Deptford		25	37	39				56		7	19				
Greenwich		27	39	41				58		9	21				
Maze Hill A		30	41	44				**0**		11	23				
Westcombe Park		32	44	46				3		14	26				
New Cross	23				46		53					22	27		
St John's					49								30		
Lewisham	26				51		56					25	32		
Blackheath	29				54		58					28	34		
Charlton	33	35	46	49	58	51	**2**	5	**9**	16	28	32	38		
Woolwich Dockyard	35		49	51	**1**	54	5		12	19	31		41		
" Arsenal	38	38	51	54	3	56	7	9	15	21	33	35	43	43	39
Plumstead	40	40	54	56	5	58	9	11	17	23	35	37	45		
Abbey Wood	43	44		59	9	**2**	13	14	20	27		40	49		
Belvedere	46	47		**2**	12	5	16	17	23	30		43	52		
Erith	49	50		5	15	8	19	20	26	33	42	46	55		
Slades Green	52	53		8	18	11	22	24	29	36		49	58		
Dartford 348	56	57		12	21		26		33	40		53	**2**	56	52
Stone Crossing Halt					26				37						
Greenhithe					28				39						
Swanscombe Halt					31				42						
Northfleet [369a					34				45						
Gravesend C. 348, arr.					38				50					**8**	**5**

HOUR ☞	S 1	E 1	S 1	E 1	S 1	S 1	E 1	E 2	E 2	S 2	E 2	S 2	S 2	E 2	S 2
Charing Cross .....dep		27	29				55				30	28			
Waterloo.......... "		29	31				57				32	30			
Cannon Street....... "	30			44	45	55		14	16	15				45	45
London Bridge .... "	32	33	35	46	47	57	**0**	16	18	17	36	34		47	47
Deptford		39	41			**4**	7				42	40			
Greenwich		41	43			6	9				44	42			
Maze Hill A	40	44	46			8	11				46	45			
Westcombe Park	43	46	48			11	14				49	47			
New Cross				53	54			22		24				54	53
St John's								25		26					
Lewisham				56	57			27		28				57	57
Blackheath				58	59			30		31			56	59	**0**
Charlton	45	49	51	**2**	**3**	13	16	34		35	51	50		**3**	4
Woolwich Dockyard	48	51	53	5	6	16	19	36		37	54	52		6	6
" Arsenal	50	54	56	7	8	18	21	39	31	40	56	55	**5**	8	9
Plumstead	52	56	58	9	11	20	23	41		42	58	57		10	11
Abbey Wood	56	59	**1**	13	14	24	27	45		45	**2**	**0**		14	14
Belvedere	59	**2**	4	16	17	27	30	48		48	5	3		17	17
Erith	**2**	5	7	19	20	30	33	51	39	51	8	6	15	20	20
Slades Green	5	9	11	22	23	33	36	54	42	54	11	10		23	23
Dartford 348	10			26	27	37			45	58	14		25	26	29
Stone Crossing Halt					32				50	**2**	19			31	
Greenhithe					34				52	4	21		31	33	
Swanscombe Halt					38				55	8	24			36	
Northfleet [369a					41				58	10	27		37	39	
Gravesend C. 348, arr.					45				**2**	15	31		42	43	

HOUR ☞	2	E 3	H 3	3	S 3	E 3	E 3	S 3	E 4	E 4	S 4	E 4	S 4	E 4
Charing Cross .....dep	55			27			53	54						
Waterloo.......... "	57			29			55	56						
Cannon Street....... "		4	14		44	44			14	11	14	21	30	36
London Bridge .... "	**0**	9	16	32	46	46	59	**0**	16	13	16	23	32	38
Deptford	7			39			**5**	7				29	39	
Greenwich	9			41			7	9				31	41	
Maze Hill A	11			43			10	11				34	43	
Westcombe Park	14			46			12	14				36	46	
New Cross			23		52	52				20	22			
St John's						55								
Lewisham			26		56	57				23	26			
Blackheath			28		58	59				25	28			
Charlton	16		32	48	**2**	**3**	15	16		29	32	39	48	
Woolwich Dockyard	19		35	51		6	17	19			35	41	51	
" Arsenal	21		37	53	6	8	20	21	29	33	37	44	53	52
Plumstead	23		39	56	8	10	22	23		35	39	46	55	
Abbey Wood	27		43	59	11	14	26	27		38	43	49	59	
Belvedere	30		46	**2**	14	17	29	30		41	46	52	**2**	
Erith	33		49	5	17	20	32	33	37	44	49	55	5	**0**
Slades Green	36		52	8		23	35	36		47	52	59	8	3
Dartford 348	S41	35	56	S12	23	27		39	42	51	56		11	6
Stone Crossing Halt								44		55			16	11
Greenhithe								46		57			18	13
Swanscombe Halt								49		**1**			22	16
Northfleet [369a								52		3			24	19
Gravesend C. 348, arr.		48						56	53	8			29	23

trains for fourteen years. Peak period services were also introduced between Streatham Hill and Victoria.

As a general rule, the pattern of services was three trains an hour at peak periods and half-hourly at other times. It was usual for frequencies to be higher than with the previous steam working, but this was most marked on the services from Holborn Viaduct to Wimbledon, which had enjoyed a rush-hour service only previously, with the electric trains attracting a healthy market away from the trams. The improvements were not without some rationalisation of services and stations, with Ludgate Hill and, on the southern loop from Tooting Junction to Wimbledon, the stations at Merton Abbey and Merton Park all closing on 3 March 1929. A new station was built at Epsom, replacing the separate LSWR and LBSCR stations, while goods trains were concentrated on the former LBSCR sidings. Colour light signalling was also extended, with considerable rationalisation of signal-boxes, providing a welcome economy in staffing to offset the heavy capital costs being incurred.

By this time, all that was needed to complete suburban electrification was a degree of tidying up and infilling, and this was achieved on 6 July 1930 when electric services commenced to Windsor, and between Wimbledon and West Croydon, and reached Gravesend Central from Dartford. The Gravesend services were simply an extension of trains that would otherwise have terminated at Dartford. That same day, Cannon Street reopened on Sundays. Earlier, on 4 May, trains from Victoria to Sutton were extended to Epsom Downs. By this time the Southern Railway had almost 800 track miles electrified, which equated to just under 300 route miles.

On 1 July 1933 the London Passenger Transport Board came into existence, acquiring the entire London underground network, including the District Line that used some of the Southern Railway's metals, as well as buses and trams within its designated area. The new London Passenger Transport Area stretched out to the south as far as Woking, Guildford, Dorking, Horsham, Sevenoaks and Gravesend. Within this area, all suburban railway services were to be coordinated by a Standing Joint Committee consisting of four LPTB members and the four main-line railway general managers, and all receipts from the area, less operating costs, were to be apportioned between the LPTB and the railways. The Southern Railway's share of these receipts was fixed at 25½ per cent, a tribute to the traffic growth generated by its investment, but hardly an incentive to further modernisation.

To the Coast

Sometime, probably during the late 1920s and certainly no later than 1930, Sir Herbert Walker opened a meeting with his officers with the simple statement: 'Gentlemen, I have decided to electrify to Brighton.'

Many believe that Walker wanted an all-electric Southern Railway, but, as already mentioned, this seems unlikely given the infrequent nature of many of the services in Devon and Cornwall, and the limited traffic potential of the services in these lightly populated rural areas. The LBSCR had ambitions to operate all of its passenger services, and possibly goods as well, using its 'elevated electrics'.

There was also an incentive for further electrification. In his budget in 1929, the Chancellor of the Exchequer, the then Mr Winston Churchill, announced the abolition of the Railway Passenger Duty that had first been introduced in 1832 and by the late 1920s was levied on all passenger fares above 1d per mile, on condition that the sum was capitalised and used for railway modernisation. This is probably the only clear instance of political interference with the railways being beneficial, though Churchill hadn't the interests of the long-suffering passenger in mind, but instead was concerned to reduce unemployment by

Opposite: The Dartford service was one of the most intensive, running throughout the night, and again the 1938 timetable (two lower timetables) was more intensive than that for 1922. *(Bradshaw)*

The Brighton electrification was introduced in stages, giving passengers at intermediate stations an early taste of what was to come and also helping with crew training – this poster positively shouts the message. *(NRM 1340/86)*

encouraging investment through this form of 'pump-priming'. The exemption for fares of 1*d* per mile and below was to ensure that workmen's trains, or parliamentary trains as they were also often known, were spared the tax to ensure cheap travel. Some idea of the discount afforded the purchasers of workmen's tickets can be gathered from information that in 1947 the return workman's fare on the Waterloo and City Line, available to anyone travelling before 8 am and which could be used on any return train, was just 3*d*, compared to a standard 3½*d* single or 7*d* return. At the time, the Southern had enjoyed some success in stimulating leisure traffic to the main resorts with its special 'summer fares', offering third-class returns of 1*d* per mile. The Southern Railway's share of the capitalised value of the duty was just over £2 million, while the cost of electrifying the main line from Victoria and London Bridge to Brighton and West Worthing was estimated to cost £2.7 million.

The plans were announced publicly at the Southern Railway AGM in 1930, when the shareholders were told that this first main-line electrification scheme would use the same

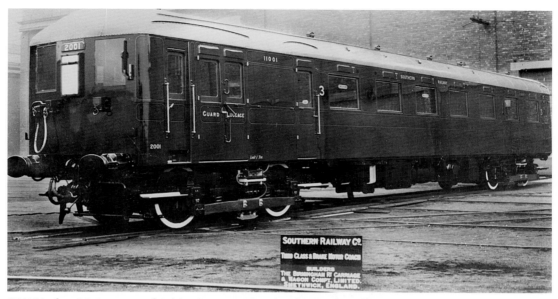

S11001, the driving open third brake prototype for the Brighton line 6 PUL units, in this case unit 2001, had far flatter sides than the versions that followed. It is seen here at the Birmingham Railway & Carriage Works. *(HRMS AEP703)*

660 V DC system already in use, not least because it held the possibility of existing suburban stock being used on weekend excursion trains. Once again, the Southern planned a massive increase in frequency, more than doubling the existing steam-hauled service, and also promised to continue the practice of non-stop expresses between Brighton and London, including the use of Pullman carriages. Not only would electrification take place, but it would be accompanied by a further extension of colour light signalling, although on this route it would be three-aspect, with the colour light signalling for the stretch of track between Coulsdon North and Brighton being the longest in the country. As part of the scheme, at many stations, including Brighton, platforms would be lengthened, while Haywards Heath station would be rebuilt. A former paint shop at Brighton would be converted to a twelve-road carriage cleaning and inspection shed, with a mechanical carriage washer in the sidings, and another carriage shed would be built at West Worthing. To justify the cost of electrification and the enhanced service, a 6 per cent increase in revenue would be required.

Work started in 1931, following on in true Southern fashion from the completion of the suburban network, and 36 out of the 162½ track miles were completed by the end of the year. It was possible to operate an electric train service as far as Three Bridges and on the short piece of electrification between Redhill and Reigate, on the North Downs line to Guildford, on 17 July 1932, and although basically just hourly, this was a great help in training motormen and providing experience for depot staff. Once again, the time taken to complete or commission work seems to have been incredibly short by modern standards. For example, it took just 15 minutes on a weekday morning, 6 October 1932, to commission the colour light signalling from Balcombe Tunnel Junction to Copyhold Junction. At Brighton, it took just 5 hours early on Sunday 16 October to commission a new signal cabin that replaced six manual boxes, and this despite the commissioning taking place during heavy rainfall!

Trial trains were running between London and Brighton from 2 November 1932, and the official inauguration took place on 30 December, when the Lord Mayor and sheriffs of

The 6 PUL electric multiple units continued the Brighton line tradition of inserting a Pullman car in express and fast trains. This was far more suitable than a restaurant car on short services on which more than a single sitting would be impossible and also mean duplicating dining and non-dining seating. This is an Eastbourne to Victoria working with a 6 PUL leading a 6 PAN. *(HRMS AAE521)*

London, the board of the Southern Railway and its senior officers, all travelled to West Worthing on one of the new 6 CITY sets, complete with Pullman car, to meet the Mayor of Worthing, and then back to Brighton to meet that town's mayor, before the entire party moved off to luncheon at the Royal Pavilion.

Provision of rolling stock was very lavish, and all of it was new. The electric multiple units are described in detail in Appendix IV. Basically, they included three 5 BEL Pullman sets, the first electric multiple unit Pullmans in the world, 6 PUL corridor sets with one Pullman car and 6 CITY variants of the 6 PUL with additional first-class accommodation, as well as 4 LAV compartment sets in which one carriage had a side corridor and lavatories. The 4 LAV worked the stopping trains, while the others provided the fast and semi-fast services. Off-peak, six trains an hour were provided, four from Victoria, including one for West Worthing, and two from London Bridge. The non-stop service to Brighton, advertised as 'on the hour, within the hour, every hour', showed little improvement over steam timings, although the working timetable was for 58 minutes to ensure on-time arrival. The other trains, advertised as 'six trains per hour all day – comfort and frequency – you won't need a timetable', were an improvement, with semi-fasts taking 74 minutes to Brighton and even stopping trains just 98 minutes, despite lingering at Redhill to detach a portion for Reigate. Contemporary advertisements show a man waiting for his girlfriend, saying that

Opposite: On the Brighton line, the best timings in 1938 (middle and bottom) were those of the non-stop trains. They were no better than in 1922, although timekeeping would have been more reliable, with the working timetable actually showing 58 minutes for the one hour run. The semi-fast and stopping trains were faster in 1938, thanks to electrification, and there were more than twice as many trains. *(Bradshaw)*

VICTORIA (West End)....dep.
Clapham Junction......"
LONDON BRIDGE (C.)dep.
New Cross......"
Norwood Junction +......"
East Croydon......"
South Croydon......"
Purley 244, 253, 268......"
Red Hill Junction 244......"
Earlswood......"
Horley......"
Three Bridges 188. { arr.
190 { dep.
Balcombe......"
Hayward's Heath 194arr.
Hayward's Heath......dep.
Wivelsfield......"
Burgess Hill......"
Hassocks......"
Preston Park......[188
Brighton (Cen.)184arr.
188Hove......arr.
188Shoreham-by-Sea "
188Worthing......"
188West Worthing "
Hayward's Heath......dep.
Wivelsfield......"
Plumpton......"
Cooksbridge......"
Lewes 194, 196, 197......"
Brighton (Cen.)......dep.
London Road......"
Falmer......"
Lewes 178......arr.
Lewes......dep.
Newhaven Town......"
Harbour......"
Bishopstone......"
Seaford......arr.
Lewes......dep.

VICTORIA......dep.
Clapham Junction......"
LONDON BRIDGE......dep.
New Cross Gate......"
Norwood Junction B......"
East Croydon......dep.
Purley......"
Coulsdon South......"
Merstham......"
Redhill 290......"
Earlswood......"
Salfords......"
Horley......"
Gatwick Airport......"
Three Bridges (below) 261......"
Balcombe......"
Horsted Keynes......dep.
Ardingly......"
Haywards Heath C { arr.
266 { dep.
Wivelsfield (below)......"
Burgess Hill......"
Hassocks D......"
Preston Park......"
Brighton (below)......arr.
Haywards Heath......dep.
Wivelsfield (above)......"
Plumpton......"
Cooksbridge......"
Lewes 266......arr.
Brighton......dep.
London Road (Brighton)......"
Falmer......"
Lewes......arr.
Lewes......dep.
Southease and Rodmell......"
Newhaven Town......[Halt
Harbour......"
Bishopstone Halt......"
Seaford......arr.
Lewes......dep.

VICTORIA......dep.
Clapham Junction......"
LONDON BRIDGE......dep.
New Cross Gate......"
Norwood Junction B......"
East Croydon......dep.
Purley......"
Coulsdon South......"
Merstham......"
Redhill 290......"
Earlswood......"
Salfords......"
Horley......"
Gatwick Airport......"
Three Bridges (below) 261......"
Balcombe......"
Horsted Keynes......dep.
Ardingly......"
Haywards Heath C { arr.
266 { dep.
Wivelsfield (below)......"
Burgess Hill......"
Hassocks D......"
Preston Park......"
Brighton (below)......arr.
Haywards Heath......dep.
Wivelsfield (above)......"
Plumpton......"
Cooksbridge......"
Lewes 266......arr.
Brighton......dep.
London Road (Brighton)......"
Falmer......"
Lewes......arr.
Lewes......dep.
Southease and Rodmell......"
Newhaven Town......[Halt
Harbour......"
Bishopstone Halt......"
Seaford......arr.
Lewes......dep.

he would 'wait for just six more trains'. Brighton was already part of the London commuter belt, so peak services had to be considerably augmented, with five fast trains between 5 and 6.30 pm, four of them running non-stop and one making just three stops. The only stock that was not new was for the Brighton–West Worthing local service, using three-car suburban stock from the Western Section. These ran every 15 minutes, with alternate trains missing the halts. There was one closure, with the halt at Bungalow Town between Brighton and Worthing being closed on the day that electric services started, though it was not to be closed for long as it was also convenient for Shoreham Airport.

A new system of headcodes was introduced for the Brighton electrification, with even numbers used for trains running between Brighton and Victoria, and odd numbers for trains to and from London Bridge. Typical examples were:

4 Victoria–Brighton non-stop via Quarry Line
6 Victoria–Brighton fast via Quarry Line
12 Victoria–Brighton fast via Redhill
14 Victoria–Brighton slow via Redhill

The first month of operations showed an immediate jump in traffic, with revenue up 5 per cent, and at holiday periods traffic grew even more, with 78 per cent more tickets sold over the 1933 Easter holidays, while on Easter Monday passenger numbers rose by 127 per cent, so that on that day between 6 and 10 pm, no fewer than twenty-eight trains left Brighton for London, most of them fast. This was success on a grand scale.

Anxious to make the best use of the investment in the Brighton line, it was decided to extend electrification to Eastbourne and Hastings via the coastal route, rather than taking the direct route to Hastings through Sevenoaks and Tonbridge. This seems strange at first, but it must be remembered that the Southern was pressing ahead with electrification at a time when the British economy was still shaky, and in addition to feeding off the Brighton electrification, the chosen route to Hastings also enabled Lewes, Eastbourne and Bexhill to be served. The direct route to Hastings would have been electrified had the Second World War and nationalisation not intervened, something borne out by both a later announcement on electrification and by the extension of electrification from Orpington to Sevenoaks.

The short section of track between Bickley Junction and St Mary Cray was opened to electric trains on 1 May 1934, while electric services from Sevenoaks via both Swanley Junction and Orpington started on 6 January 1935. Again, the standard 20-minute frequency in peak hours, half-hourly off-peak was adopted, with trains from Charing Cross, Cannon Street and Holborn Viaduct. On eight-coach trains, the three leading carriages only ran beyond Orpington or Swanley Junction. This was an investment in the future, calculating that rapid growth in residential areas would soon fill the then-empty rural spaces beyond Orpington. Once again, the Southern's confidence was to prove to be justified, and the company helped with its advertising campaign with the slogan 'Live in Kent and be Content'.

The Eastbourne and Hastings electrification also included the line from Haywards Heath to Horsted Keynes, and from Lewes to Seaford, and some additional work in the London area, including extra sidings at New Cross Gate. While incidental works were not numerous, a tunnel at the London end of Lewes station had to have one of its curves eased to allow modern rolling stock to use it and an overbridge at the station was rebuilt so that the platforms could be lengthened, while platforms were also lengthened at Eastbourne. There was also some station rebuilding, including elevating the halt at Cooden to station status as Cooden Beach, while ten stations had electric lighting installed for the first time. A new carriage shed with four roads was built at Ore. One unusual aspect of the preliminary work was the replacement with wooden sleepers of track relaid with steel sleepers.

The formal opening took place on 4 July 1935, once again with the Lord Mayor and sheriffs of London accompanied by the usual hosts travelling on a 6 CITY unit to meet the mayors of Eastbourne, Bexhill and Hastings. Services actually started on 7 July. As shown

The 2 NOL electric multiple units were built for local services on the Brighton and Eastbourne electrifications. This is No. 1816. *(HRMS AAE519)*

S11070, one of the first driving open third brakes for the 6 PAN units, intended for the Eastbourne electrification but usually operated on both Brighton and Eastbourne services paired with 6 PUL units. Note the revised windows that almost make this carriage a hybrid between the Brighton and Portsmouth stock. *(HRMS AEP704)*

in Appendix IV, the new electric multiple units for the Eastbourne and Hastings electrification lacked the Pullman car, which was replaced by a first-class coach with a pantry (although the light refreshments were served by Pullman car staff), but these operated with 6 PUL sets as far as Eastbourne, while some of the new sets replaced 6 PUL sets on the Brighton services. The best trains took just 80 minutes to reach Eastbourne.

As with the original Brighton and West Worthing electrification, a much-improved coastal service was introduced, with trains running every half hour from Brighton to Seaford and every half hour to Eastbourne, with both these services serving passengers travelling between Brighton and Lewes. However, all was not well, for despite the frequency of services being more than doubled, passengers east of Eastbourne took exception to trains running into and out of that station instead of dividing at Polegate, as had been the practice during steam working.

Meanwhile, there had been another development on the Brighton line. The opening of what was billed as the 'largest indoor swimming pool in the world' at Brighton on 29 June 1934 was taken as an opportunity to rename the 'Southern Belle' Pullman as the 'Brighton Belle' by the Mayor of Brighton when the train arrived at noon.

The Southern's confidence in electrification was soon justified. At the AGM in February 1936, Mr R. Holland-Martin, the chairman, was able to announce that revenue on the Sevenoaks electrification had risen by 41 per cent, almost 50 per cent more than that estimated to cover the costs of the work, while the Eastbourne and Hastings schemes had seen revenue rise by 16 per cent, more than twelve times the amount needed to cover the costs. It is clear from his statement that in addition to meeting interest on the capital costs, in some cases costs had also risen with electrification because of the enhanced train services provided.

There was yet another incentive for the railways to modernise. The previous November, the government had agreed with the four main-line railway companies to provide funds for major improvement schemes at an interest rate of $2\frac{1}{2}$ per cent, lower than that generally available on the money markets at the time, through a Railway Finance Corporation that would have its initial capital of £30m guaranteed by the Treasury. The Southern, despite its being the smallest of the railway companies, decided to take a loan of £6 million to fund further electrification and improvements at a number of stations, as well as a new line from Motspur Park to Chessington South (see Chapter Eight). The new electrification schemes were to include both routes to Portsmouth, the direct line via Guildford and the old LBSCR line through Horsham and Arundel, as well as the Thames Valley line between Staines and Reading. In Kent there would be additional electrification from Swanley Junction to Gillingham and Gravesend to Maidstone, as well as Sevenoaks to Hastings, but the last-mentioned was delayed by the Second World War and nationalisation, and indeed, only barely managed to electrify a short time before the end of the twentieth century, and even then on a cut-price basis!

The Southern had already started work on the first of the two Portsmouth electrification schemes, the Portsmouth Direct via Guildford, known to the company as the 'Portsmouth No. 1 Electrification Scheme'. The Guildford New Line had already been electrified, but could not be used by the new scheme which had of necessity to use the main line, requiring electrification from a point just south-west of Surbiton to Portsmouth Harbour, the longest main-line electrification scheme at that time, a distance of more than 60 route miles. As with the Brighton and Eastbourne schemes, the Portsmouth No. 1 would include a number of other schemes, including electrification from Woking through Aldershot to Alton, in itself hardly a minor work, and from Weybridge to Staines. All in all, this required a track mileage of 242 miles and was estimated to cost £3m.

The Portsmouth Direct required very extensive incidental works, including rebuilding the station at Woking and extending its four through platforms to 820 ft each, but while the stations at Guildford and Haslemere also received platform lengthening, sadly neither was rebuilt. Havant was also rebuilt, but with the Down platform served by a loop off the running line, and with a bay for the short Hayling Island branch, which was not to be electrified, suggesting that even the optimistic Southern had some doubts over the long-

THE 'SPARKS EFFECT' – ELECTRIFICATION

A Down Waterloo to Portsmouth fast heads towards Woking. The distinguishing feature of the Portsmouth electrification schemes was the introduction of main-line electric multiple units with corridor connections through the driving cabs, so that passengers, guards and ticket inspectors could have access to the whole train. *(HRMS AER320)*

6 PUL 2020 near Polegate, possibly the Hastings section of a train from Victoria via Lewes and Eastbourne. *(HRMS AAN518)*

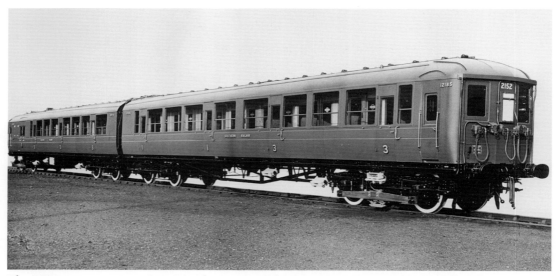

The 2 BIL series was introduced for the Portsmouth stopping trains, but also worked services to Alton and Reading, and postwar often handled rush-hour semi-fast services. *(NRM BTC-collection 115/54)*

term future for this branch with its highly seasonal traffic. There was also platform lengthening at the high-level station at Portsmouth & Southsea, as the town station was now called. Once again, colour light signalling was extended. The goods yard at Portsmouth was moved, providing a relief line between Portsmouth & Southsea and Fratton, while new carriage sheds were built at Wimbledon, Fratton and Farnham, with carriage washers at the first two.

In late 1936 trial trains were operating north of Woking and between Weybridge and Virginia Water, and on 3 January 1937 electric services were introduced between Staines and Weybridge, while electric trains were also operated from Waterloo to Guildford and Farnham but using steam timings, again to help train operating staff. The trial trains were able to operate into Portsmouth Harbour from 11 April, and a limited number of weekend departures were operated by electric trains from 29 May. Finally, the new electric train service from Waterloo to Portsmouth Harbour and Alton was introduced on 4 July 1937, with the first train having the coat of arms of Portsmouth painted on its front corridor connection. This, of course, was the most obvious difference between the new Portsmouth rolling stock and that prepared for the Brighton and Eastbourne lines: the corridor connections through the driving cabs of the 4 COR and 4 RES electric multiple units meant that complete access could be had throughout the train, and this may also have been a factor in using four-car rather than the less flexible six-car multiple units. The citizens of Portsmouth must have been regarded as being less well-heeled than their Sussex counterparts, because a restaurant car was provided in the 4 RES units rather than the Pullmans of the lines to the Sussex Coast towns.

The fast trains on the Portsmouth routes normally ran into the Harbour station, but the inaugural train terminated at Portsmouth & Southsea Low Level for the necessary civic

Opposite: The Portsmouth schedule in 1938 was not nearly as intensive as that for Brighton, but in 1922 (two upper timetables) the entire day saw fewer trains than just the morning and middle of the day in 1938, and the last train in 1938 was later. The lack of quadruple tracks beyond Woking and the importance of Isle of Wight ferry traffic on this route meant that there was some bunching of trains, with fast trains leaving within 5 minutes of one another. *(Bradshaw)*

Miles	Down.	mrn	mrn	mrn a	mrn	mrn Saturdays only.	mrn	mrn	mrn	mrn Saturdays only.	aft d	mrn Except Saturdays.	mrn Saturdays only.	aft Saturdays only.	aft Luncheon Car.	aft	aft	aft	aft Saturdays only.	aft Tea and Light Refreshments served.	aft Sats. only.	aft Except Saturdays.
	WATERLOO ...... dep.	5 50	6 50	7 50	...	8 50	9 50	...	1024	1050	...	1150	1150	...	1250	...	1 50	2 34	2 50	3 50	4 4	4 15
4	Clapham Junction ‖ "	...	...	...	...	...	...	...	...	...	...	...	...	...	...	...	...	...	...	...	...	...
7½	Wimbledon .... "	...	...	...	...	...	...	...	1050	...	...	...	...	...	...	...	...	2 50	...	...	...	...
12	Surbiton .... "	6 11	7 11	8 11	...	...	...	...	11 1	...	...	1212	...	1212	...	...	...	3 1	...	...	...	...
19½	Weybridge § ...... "	...	7 26	...	8 29	...	...	...	1114	...	...	...	...	...	...	...	...	3 14	...	...	...	...
24½	Woking ‡ .... "	6 30	7 38	8 31	8 40	...	...	1026	1132	...	...	1232	...	1232	...	...	...	3 32	...	...	4 45	...
30½	Guildford .... "	6 48	7 56	8 45	8 56	9 36	1035	1045	1149	1155	1240	1250	1235	1250	1 35	1 40	2 35	3 50	3 35	4 35	5 1	4 58
33½	Farncombe	6 56	8 4	...	9 4	...	...	1053	1157	...	...	1258	...	1258	...	1 47	2 43	3 58	...	...	5 9	5 6
34½	Godalming	7 1	8 9	8 56	9 9	...	...	1058	12 2	...	1251	1 3	...	1 3	...	1 51	2 47	4 3	...	...	5 13	5 10
36½	Milford	7 7	8 15	...	9 15	...	...	11 4	12 8	...	...	1 9	...	1 9	...	1 57	2 53	4 9	...	...	5 19	5 16
38½	Witley †	7 14	8 22	...	9 22	...	...	1111	1215	...	1 2	1 16	...	1 16	...	2 3	3 0	4 16	...	...	5 26	5 23
43	Haslemere	7 26	8 34	9 16	9 34	...	...	1124	1228	...	1 15	1 30	...	1 30	...	2 15	3 14	4 29	...	...	5 39	5 36
47	Liphook	7 33	8 41	...	9 41	...	...	1131	1235	...	...	1 37	...	1 37	...	2 21	3 21	4 36	...	...	5 46	5 43
51½	Liss	7 43	8 50	...	9 50	...	...	1140	1244	...	1 29	1 46	...	1 46	...	2 30	3 30	4 45	...	...	5 55	5 52
55	Petersfield (below) arr.	7 49	8 56	9 33	9 56	...	...	1146	1250	...	1 35	1 52	...	1 52	...	2 36	3 36	4 51	...	...	6 1	5 58
	Petersfield dep.	7 54	8 59	9 37	...	...	...	1149	...	...	1 39	1 56	...	1 56	...	...	3 39	4 54	...	...	...	...
63½	Rowland's Castle ...	8 12	9 16	9 54	...	...	...	12 6	...	...	...	2 13	...	2 13	...	...	3 56	5 11	...	...	...	...
66½	Havant **136**, 211 ...	8 21	9 25	10 2	...	...	...	1214	...	...	2 2	2 22	...	2 22	...	...	4 4	5 20	...	...	...	...
73	Fratton 186	8 32	9 36	10 13	...	1050	1142	1225	...	1245	...	2 33	1 43	2 33	2 42	...	4 15	5 31	4 43	5 42	...	...
73¾	Portsmouth **	8 42	9 41	10 18	...	1055	1148	1230	...	1250	...	2 40	1 48	2 40	2 48	...	4 20	5 36	4 48	5 48	...	...
74½	" Harbour 910 arr.	8 47	...	10 24	...	11 1	1154	...	...	1256	...	2 46	1 54	2 46	2 54	...	...	5 42	4 54	5 54	...	...
79	Ryde Pr. *168, 170 "	9 55	1035	12 0	...	1145	1245	1 55	...	1 55	...	...	3 0	...	3 45	...	5 20	6A30	5 40	6 40	...	...

Down. Week Days—*Continued.*

Down.	aft	aft	aft	aft Except Saturdays.	aft Except Saturdays.	aft Dining Car.	aft	aft	aft	aft
WATERLOO .... dep.	4 50	...	5 40	5 50	6 4	6 50	...	...	8 0	9 50
Clapham Junction ‖ ... "	...	...	...	...	...	...	...	...	...	...
Wimbledon .... "	...	...	...	...	...	...	...	...	...	...
Surbiton .... "	...	...	...	...	6 26	...	...	...	8 22	...
Weybridge § ...... "	...	...	...	...	...	...	...	...	...	...
Woking ‡ .... "	...	...	...	6 27	...	...	...	7 35	8 50	1027
Guildford .... "	5 34	5 39	6 25	6 44	7 20	7 35	7 40	7 54	9 7	1043
Farncombe	...	5 46	6&33	6 52	7 27	...	7 48	8 2	9 15	1051
Godalming	5 43	5 50	6 35	6 55	...	...	7 53	8 5	9 20	11 0
Milford	...	5 56	6 41	...	...	...	7 59	...	9 26	11 6
Witley †	...	6 4	6 48	...	...	...	8 6	...	9 33	1114
Haslemere	6 3	6 14	7 0	...	...	8 3	8 18	...	9 44	1126
Liphook	6 10	...	7 7	...	...	...	8 25	...	...	1133
Liss	6 19	...	7 16	...	...	...	8 34	...	...	1142
Petersfield (below) arr.	6 25	...	7 22	...	...	...	8 40	...	...	1148
Petersfield dep.	6 28	...	7 28	...	...	...	8 43	...	...	1152
Rowland's Castle	6 45	...	7 45	...	...	...	9 0	...	...	...
Havant **186**, 211	6 53	...	7 53	...	...	...	9 8	...	...	1213
Fratton 186	7 4	...	8 4	...	...	8 47	9 19	...	...	1221
Portsmouth and Southsea.	7 9	...	8 10	...	...	8 52	9 24	...	...	1226
" Harbour 910 arr.	...	...	8 18	...	...	8 58	...	...	...	...
Ryde Pier *168, 170 "	...	...	9 10	...	...	...	12 0	...	...	...

Miles		mrn (Calls Wimbledon 5 3 and Malden 5 10 mrn)	mrn d	mn d	mrn c	mn c	mrn c	mrn (On 30th July only.)	mrn	mrn c	mrn (Dep Wimbledon 7 26 mrn)	mn	mn	S RC	mrn RC	mn		mrn c	mn	mrn E	S RC	S RC	mrn	mrn c	mrn	mrn S	mn E	mn E	mn	S RC	mrn RC	mrn
	LONDON (Waterloo) .. dep.	4 50	5 27	540	5 57	6 0	6 27	6 50	..	6 57	..	724	727	7 45	7 50	..	..	7 55	8 4	..	8 15	8 20	..	8 25	8 30	8 35	840	842	844	8 45	8 50	..
12	Surbiton	5 18	5 45	6 2	6 15	..	6 45	..	..	7 15	7 33	..	743	..	..	..	..	8 13	..	..	..	..	..	8 43	8U48	8U56	..	858	..	..	..	..
14½	Esher, for Sandown Park ..	5 25	5 49	..	6 19	..	6 49	..	..	7 19	..	..	747	..	..	..	..	8 17	..	..	..	..	..	8 47	..	..	..	9 2	..	..	..	..
16	Hersham	..	5 52	..	6 22	..	6 52	..	..	7 22	7 39	..	750	..	..	..	..	8 20	..	..	..	..	..	8 50	..	..	..	9 5	..	..	..	..
17½	Walton-on-Thames	5 33	5 55	..	6 25	..	6 55	..	..	7 25	..	..	753	..	..	..	..	8 23	..	..	..	..	..	8 53	..	..	..	9 8	..	..	..	..
19½	Weybridge **A**	5 39	5 59	..	6 29	..	6 59	..	..	7 29	7 44	..	757	..	..	..	..	8 27	..	..	..	..	..	8 57	..	..	..	912	..	..	..	..
20½	West Weybridge	..	6 2	..	6 32	..	7 2	..	..	7 32	7 47	..	8 0	..	..	..	..	8 30	..	..	..	..	..	9 0	..	..	..	915	..	..	..	..
21½	Byfleet **B**	..	6 5	..	6 35	..	7 5	..	..	7 35	..	..	8 3	..	..	..	..	8 33	..	..	..	..	..	9 3	..	..	..	918	..	..	..	..
24½	Woking **C**	5 52	6 12	619	6 42	636	7 12	..	..	7 42	7 54	755	8 8	..	..	..	..	8 38	832	8 44	..	..	..	9 8	9 5	9 13	910	922	915	..	..	..
26¾	Worplesdon	..	6 17	..	6 47	..	7 17	..	..	7 47	..	..	813	..	..	..	..	8 43	..	..	..	..	..	9 13	..	..	..	..	..	..	..	..
30½	Guildford 192, 271, 290, 292 arr.	..	6 23	..	6 53	..	7 23	..	..	7 53	8 8	..	820	..	8 25	..	..	8 50	..	8 57	..	8 55	..	9 20	..	..	..	..	..	..	9 25	..
	Guildford dep.	..	6 31	..	7 1	..	..	..	7 31	8 1	..	..	..	..	8 26	831	..	..	..	..	..	8 56	9 1	..	..	..	..	..	..	..	9 26	9 31
33½	Farncombe	..	6 36	..	7 6	..	..	..	7 36	8 6	..	..	..	..	..	836	..	..	..	..	..	..	9 6	..	..	..	..	..	..	..	..	9 36
34½	Godalming	..	6 39	..	7 9	..	..	..	7 39	8 9	..	..	..	..	..	839	..	..	..	..	..	..	9 9	..	..	..	..	..	..	..	..	9 39
36½	Milford	..	6 44	..	7 14	..	..	..	7 44	8 14	..	..	..	..	..	844	..	..	..	..	..	..	9 14	..	..	..	..	..	..	..	..	9 44
38½	Witley, for Chiddingfold ..	..	6 48	..	7 18	..	..	..	7 48	8 18	..	..	..	..	..	848	..	..	..	..	..	..	9 18	..	..	..	..	..	..	..	..	9 48
43	Haslemere **D**	..	6 56	..	7 26	..	..	..	7 56	8 26	..	..	..	..	8 45	856	..	..	..	..	..	..	9 26	..	..	..	..	..	..	..	9 45	9 56
47	Liphook	..	7 2	..	7 32	..	..	..	8 2	8 32	..	..	..	..	..	9 2	..	..	..	..	..	..	9 32	..	..	..	..	..	..	..	..	10 2
51½	Liss	..	7 9	..	7 39	..	..	..	8 9	8 39	..	..	..	..	..	9 9	..	..	..	..	..	..	9 39	..	..	..	..	..	..	..	..	10 9
55	Petersfield 180d	..	7 14	..	7 44	..	..	..	8 14	8 44	..	..	..	..	..	914	..	..	..	..	..	..	9 44	..	..	..	..	..	..	..	..	1014
63½	Rowlands Castle	..	7 26	..	7 56	..	..	..	8 26	8 56	..	..	..	..	..	926	..	..	..	..	..	..	9 56	..	..	..	..	..	..	..	..	1026
66½	Havant **239**, 272	..	7 31	..	8 1	..	..	..	8 31	9 1	..	..	..	9 5	..	931	..	..	..	..	..	..	10 1	..	..	..	..	..	..	10 5	..	1031
67½	Bedhampton Halt	..	7 33	..	8 3	..	..	..	8 33	9 3	..	..	..	..	..	933	..	..	..	..	..	..	10 3	..	..	..	..	..	..	..	..	1033
73	Fratton 239	..	7 41	..	8 11	..	..	..	8 41	9 11	..	..	..	..	..	941	..	..	..	..	..	..	1011	..	..	..	..	..	..	..	..	1041
73¾	Portsmouth & Southsea ..	..	7 43	..	8 14	..	..	8 20	8 44	9 14	..	..	..	..	9 20	944	..	..	..	..	9 45	9 52	1014	..	..	..	..	..	..	..	1020	1044
74½	" Harbour arr.	..	7 50	..	..	..	..	8 25	..	..	..	..	..	9 20	9 25	..	..	..	..	..	9 50	9 57	..	..	..	..	..	..	..	1020	1025	..
79	Ryde Pier 1129 (By Boat) "	..	9A5	..	..	..	..	9 20	..	..	..	..	..	10 5	10 5	..	..	..	..	..	1045	1045	..	..	..	..	..	..	..	1115	1110	..

Down — Week Days—*Continued*

Waterloo,	mrn S	mrn	mrn	S RC	mrn E	S RC	mrn	mrn	mrn	mrn S (Not after 10th September.)	S RC	mrn RC		mrn	mrn	mrn	mrn E	S RC	S RC	mrn	mrn		S RC	mrn RC	mrn	mrn E	mrn	S RC	S RC	aft	mrn
LONDON .... dep	8 54	8 57	9 0	9 15	9 17	9 20	..	9 27	9 30	9 40	9 45	9 50	..	9 54	..	9 57	10 5	1015	1020	..	1027	..	1045	1050	..	1054	1057	1115	1120	..	1127
Surbiton	..	9 13	9U17	..	9 33	..	..	9 43	9U48	..	..	..	..	..	..	1013	1021	..	..	..	1043	..	..	..	..	..	1113	..	..	..	1143
Esher, for Sandown Park	..	9 17	..	..	9 37	..	..	9 47	..	..	..	..	..	..	..	1017	..	..	..	..	1047	..	..	..	..	..	1117	..	..	..	1147
Hersham	..	9 20	..	..	9 40	..	..	9 50	..	..	..	..	..	..	..	1020	..	..	..	..	1050	..	..	..	..	..	1120	..	..	..	1150
Walton-on-Thames	..	9 23	..	..	9 43	..	..	9 53	..	..	..	..	..	..	..	1023	..	..	..	..	1053	..	..	..	..	..	1123	..	..	..	1153
Weybridge **A**	..	9 27	..	..	9 47	..	..	9 57	..	..	..	..	..	..	..	1027	1032	..	..	..	1057	..	..	..	..	..	1127	..	..	..	1157
West Weybridge	..	9 30	..	..	9 50	..	..	10 0	..	..	..	..	..	..	..	1030	..	..	..	..	11 0	..	..	..	..	..	1130	..	..	..	12 0
Byfleet **B**	..	9 33	..	..	9 53	..	..	10 3	..	..	..	..	..	..	..	1033	..	..	..	..	11 3	..	..	..	..	..	1133	..	..	..	12 3
Woking **C**	9 25	9 38	9 34	..	9 58	..	..	10 8	10 5	1012	..	..	..	1025	..	1038	1043	..	..	..	11 8	..	..	..	..	1125	1138	..	..	..	12 8
Worplesdon	..	9 43	..	..	..	..	..	1013	..	..	..	..	..	..	..	1043	..	..	..	..	1113	..	..	..	..	..	1143	..	..	..	1213
Guildford 192, 271, 290, 292 arr.	..	9 50	..	..	..	9 55	..	1020	..	..	..	1025	..	..	..	1050	..	..	1055	..	1120	..	..	1125	..	..	1150	..	1155	..	1220
Guildford dep.	..	..	..	..	..	9 56	10 1	..	..	..	..	1026	..	..	1031	..	..	..	1056	11 1	..	..	..	1126	1131	..	..	..	1156	12 1	..
Farncombe	..	..	..	..	..	..	10 6	..	..	..	..	..	..	..	1036	..	..	..	..	11 6	..	..	..	..	1136	..	..	..	..	12 6	..
Godalming	..	..	..	..	..	..	10 9	..	..	..	..	..	..	..	1039	..	..	..	..	11 9	..	..	..	..	1139	..	..	..	..	12 9	..
Milford	..	..	..	..	..	..	1014	..	..	..	..	..	..	..	1044	..	..	..	..	1114	..	..	..	..	1144	..	..	..	..	1214	..
Witley for Chiddingfold	..	..	..	..	..	..	1018	..	..	..	..	..	..	..	1048	..	..	..	..	1118	..	..	..	..	1148	..	..	..	..	1218	..
Haslemere **D**	..	..	..	..	..	..	1026	..	..	..	..	1045	..	..	1056	..	..	..	..	1126	..	..	..	1145	1156	..	..	..	..	1226	..
Liphook	..	..	..	..	..	..	1032	..	..	..	..	..	..	..	11 2	..	..	..	..	1132	..	..	..	..	12 2	..	..	..	..	1232	..
Liss	..	..	..	..	..	..	1039	..	..	..	..	..	..	..	11 9	..	..	..	..	1139	..	..	..	..	12 9	..	..	..	..	1239	..
Petersfield 180d	..	..	..	..	..	..	1044	..	..	..	..	..	..	..	1114	..	..	..	..	1144	..	..	..	..	1214	..	..	..	..	1244	..
Rowlands Castle	..	..	..	..	..	..	1056	..	..	..	..	..	..	..	1126	..	..	..	..	1156	..	..	..	..	1226	..	..	..	..	1256	..
Havant **239**, 272	..	..	..	..	..	..	11 1	..	..	..	11 5	..	..	..	1131	..	..	..	..	12 1	..	..	12 5	..	1231	..	..	..	..	1 1	..
Bedhampton Halt	..	..	..	..	..	..	11 3	..	..	..	..	..	..	..	1133	..	..	..	..	12 3	..	..	..	..	1233	..	..	..	..	1 3	..
Fratton 239	..	..	..	..	..	..	1111	..	..	..	..	..	..	..	1141	..	..	..	..	1211	..	..	..	..	1241	..	..	..	..	1 11	..
Portsmouth & S'thsea	..	..	..	1045	..	1050	1114	..	..	..	..	1120	..	..	1144	..	..	1145	1150	1214	..	..	..	1220	1244	..	..	1245	1250	1 14	..
" Harbour arr.	..	..	..	1050	..	1055	..	..	..	..	1120	1125	..	..	..	..	..	1150	1155	..	..	..	1220	1225	..	..	..	1250	1255	..	..
Ryde Pier 1129 (Boat) "	..	..	..	1145	..	1145	..	..	..	..	1215	1205	..	..	..	..	..	1245	1245	..	..	..	1 15	1 5	..	..	..	1 45	1 45	..	..

Waterloo,	S RC	mrn RC	mrn	aft	mrn	S RC	aft S	S RC	aft	aft	aft S	S RC	aft S	aft RC	aft	aft E	aft		S RC	aft S	S RC	aft	aft S	aft	S RC	aft S	aft RC	aft	aft	aft	S RC	aft S	S RC
LONDON .... dep.	1145	1150	1154	..	1157	1215	1217	1220	..	1227	1239	1245	1247	1250	..	1254	1257	..	1 15	1 17	1 20	..	1 24	1 27	1 45	1 47	1 50	..	1 54	1 57	2 15	2 17	2 20
Surbiton	..	..	..	..	1213	..	..	..	..	1243	..	..	..	..	..	..	1 13	..	..	..	..	..	..	1 43	..	..	..	..	..	2 13	..	..	..
Esher, for Sandown Park	..	..	..	..	1217	..	..	..	..	1247	..	..	..	..	..	..	1 17	..	..	..	..	..	..	1 47	..	..	..	..	..	2 17	..	..	..
Hersham	..	..	..	..	1220	..	..	..	..	1250	..	..	..	..	..	..	1 20	..	..	..	..	..	..	1 50	..	..	..	..	..	2 20	..	..	..
Walton-on-Thames	..	..	..	..	1223	..	1238	..	..	1253	..	..	1 8	..	..	..	1 23	..	..	1 38	..	..	..	1 53	..	2 8	..	..	..	2 23	..	2 38	..
Weybridge **A**	..	..	..	..	1227	..	1242	..	..	1257	..	..	1 12	..	..	..	1 27	..	..	1 42	..	..	..	1 57	..	2 12	..	..	..	2 27	..	2 42	..
West Weybridge.	..	..	..	..	1230	..	..	..	..	1 0	..	..	..	..	..	..	1 30	..	..	..	..	..	..	2 0	..	..	..	..	..	2 30	..	..	..
Byfleet **B**	..	..	..	..	1233	..	1246	..	..	1 3	..	..	1 16	..	..	..	1 33	..	..	1 46	..	..	..	2 3	..	2 16	..	..	..	2 33	..	2 46	..
Woking **C**	..	..	1225	..	1238	..	1251	..	..	1 8	1 10	..	1 21	..	..	1 25	1 38	..	..	1 51	..	..	1 55	2 8	..	2 21	..	..	2 25	2 38	..	2 51	..
Worplesdon	..	..	..	..	1243	..	..	..	..	1 13	..	..	..	..	..	..	1 43	..	..	..	..	..	..	2 13	..	..	..	..	..	2 43	..	..	..
Guildford 192, 271, 290, 292 arr.	..	1225	..	..	1250	..	..	1255	..	1 20	..	..	..	1 25	..	..	1 50	..	..	..	1 55	..	..	2 20	..	..	2 25	..	..	2 50	..	..	2 55
Guildford dep.	..	1226	..	1231	..	..	..	1256	1 1	..	..	..	..	1 26	1 31	..	..	..	..	..	1 56	2 0	..	..	..	..	2 26	2 31	..	..	..	..	2 56
Farncombe	..	..	..	1236	..	..	..	..	1 6	..	..	..	..	..	1 36	..	..	..	..	..	..	2 6	..	..	..	..	..	2 36	..	..	..	..	..
Godalming	..	..	..	1239	..	..	..	1 3	1 9	..	..	..	..	..	1 39	..	..	..	..	..	2 5	2 9	..	..	..	..	..	2 39	..	..	..	..	3 5
Milford	..	..	..	1244	..	..	..	..	1 14	..	..	..	..	..	1 44	..	..	..	..	..	..	2 14	..	..	..	..	..	2 44	..	..	..	..	..
Witley, for Chiddingfold	..	..	..	1248	..	..	..	..	1 18	..	..	..	..	..	1 48	..	..	..	..	..	..	2 18	..	..	..	..	..	2 48	..	..	..	..	..
Haslemere **D**	..	1245	..	1256	..	..	..	1 15	1 26	..	..	..	..	1 45	1 56	..	..	..	..	..	2 18	2 26	..	..	..	..	2 45	2 56	..	..	..	..	3 18
Liphook	..	..	..	1 2	..	..	..	..	1 32	..	..	..	..	..	2 2	..	..	..	..	..	..	2 32	..	..	..	..	..	3 2	..	..	..	..	..
Liss	..	..	..	1 9	..	..	..	..	1 39	..	..	..	..	..	2 9	..	..	..	..	..	..	2 39	..	..	..	..	..	3 9	..	..	..	..	..
Petersfield 180d	..	..	..	1 14	..	..	..	1 31	1 44	..	..	..	..	..	2 14	..	..	..	..	..	2 33	2 44	..	..	..	..	..	3 14	..	..	..	..	3 33
Rowlands Castle	..	..	..	1 26	..	..	..	..	1 56	..	..	..	..	..	2 26	..	..	..	..	..	..	2 56	..	..	..	..	..	3 26	..	..	..	..	..
Havant **239**, 272	1 5	..	..	1 31	..	..	..	1 48	2 1	..	..	2 5	..	2S12	2 31	..	..	..	..	..	2 48	3 1	..	..	3 5	..	..	3 31	..	..	..	..	3 48
Bedhampton Halt	..	..	..	1 33	..	..	..	..	2 3	..	..	..	..	..	2 33	..	..	..	..	..	..	3 3	..	..	..	..	..	3 33	..	..	..	..	..
Fratton 239	..	..	..	1 41	..	..	..	..	2 11	..	..	..	..	2S20	2 41	..	..	..	..	..	..	3 11	..	..	..	..	3S19	3 41	..	..	..	..	..
Portsmouth & S'thsea.	..	1 20	..	1 44	..	1 45	..	1 59	2 14	..	..	..	..	2F20	2 44	..	..	..	2 45	..	2 59	3 14	..	..	..	..	3 20	3 44	..	..	3 45	..	3 59
" Harbour .. arr.	1 20	1 25	..	..	..	1 50	..	2 5	..	..	..	2 20	..	2F25	..	..	..	..	2 50	..	3 5	..	..	..	3 20	..	3 25	..	..	..	3 50	..	4 5
Ryde Pier 1129 (Boat) "	2 15	2 5	..	..	..	2 45	..	2 45	..	..	..	3 15	..	3 5	..	..	..	..	3 45	..	3 45	..	..	..	4 15	..	4 5	..	..	..	4 45	..	4 45

The Art Deco interior of the buffet on a 4 BUF introduced for the 'Portsmouth No. 2 Electrification Scheme' of 1938 – the route via Arundel and Chichester. In later years these often found their way on to the Portsmouth Direct. By contrast, the 4 RES interiors were very conventional. (NRM 1348/86)

niceties to be observed. The headcode for a Harbour train was 8, with 7 for trains terminating at Portsmouth & Southsea. The Alton line stock, also used for the Portsmouth stopping trains, consisted of two-car units designated 2 BIL without corridor connections and with only one carriage having a corridor.

The new service consisted of an hourly fast train stopping at Guildford, Haslemere and Portsmouth & Southsea, although later many trains stopped at either Havant or Woking, as did many peak period extras, with a half-hourly stopping train that ran fast to Surbiton and divided into Portsmouth & Southsea and Alton portions at Woking.

The service was accelerated, with the fast trains taking 95 minutes compared to the 2 hours of the steam trains, the difference in performance compared to the Brighton fasts being partly accounted for by the number of stops and also by the steep gradients on the line which were of little consequence to the electric trains. The Portsmouth direct had not enjoyed a particularly good service before electrification, with just four fast trains a day, and these struggled with the gradients on the line, but electrification meant that on a summer Saturday there were four fast trains every hour!

In retrospect, it seems strange that such a major city as Portsmouth should have suffered such a poor service for so long, for in addition to being the largest city on the south coast, it also had the extensive Royal Dockyard and many other naval facilities. It was additionally the quickest route for passengers travelling to Gosport and even Fareham, using the steam launches across the harbour. It was the main port for travellers taking a ferry to the Isle of Wight, with those from Portsmouth to Ryde having the advantage that they also were the shortest and quickest route to the island's main resorts at Ryde, Sandown, Shanklin and Ventnor, and it had its own resort at Southsea. This history of neglect ended in July 1937, and was put to rest completely the following year with the 'Portsmouth No. 2 Electrification Scheme' taking the old LBSCR line through Horsham, Arundel and Chichester.

The decision to electrify railways has not always been universally popular, despite the benefits which have led to the term 'sparks effect' being applied to the traffic growth generated by electrification. Landowners and farmers in West Sussex objected strongly to the 'Portsmouth No. 2 Electrification Scheme', concerned about the dangers to people and livestock. A deputation went to meet the Southern directors, and questions were even raised in the House of Commons. Suggestions were made that the third rail should be boxed in, which was quite impractical, or that the current should only be on when a train was about to pass, which was almost as bad, or that certain sections of line should have overhead conductor wires. The Southern's management pointed out that adequate fencing was always used, and that the only people at risk were those who trespassed on the line.

Work on this scheme which required 165 track miles of electrification was well advanced when the Portsmouth Direct electrification was inaugurated. Incidental works were again considerable, with additional sidings electrified at New Cross gate and carriage sheds with a carriage washer erected at Streatham Hill, the Slade Green workshops were extended, and a new carriage shed was built at Littlehampton. Almost inevitably, platform lengthening was necessary at Sutton, Dorking North, where the Down bay became a loop, Pulborough, Arundel, Littlehampton and Chichester, Barnham and Bognor Regis, as well as to a lesser extent at many of the small halts along the coastal stretch of this route. There was a further extension of colour light signalling. One of the most costly items was the rebuilding of the bridge over the River Arun at Ford in Sussex, which had originally been built with lifting spans to allow ships to pass under. Although the bridge had only been used rarely, its modification still needed parliamentary approval. The line had to be closed for the weekend of 23–25 April 1938 to enable the new spans to be lifted into position. An electricity substation at South Stoke near Arundel had to be built on 50 ft concrete piles sunk into the Arun Marshes to enable it to remain above flood level.

Trial trains started in May 1938, and in June there were a number of specials between London Bridge and Bognor Regis. The new services started on 3 July 1938, using further examples of the 4 COR sets built for the original Portsmouth electrification, plus a variation on these known as 4 BUF with a buffet car manned initially by the Pullman Car Company, and painted in a new lighter shade of green. In addition, the service was diverted from London Bridge to Victoria, with London Bridge being used only for rush-hour extras.

The service was less frequent than that on the Brighton and Portsmouth lines, with an hourly departure from Victoria. The front section was for Portsmouth Harbour and the rear section for Bognor Regis with the buffet car. Trains were initially divided at Barnham, but over the years this varied and sometimes the trains were divided at Arundel. Journey time to Portsmouth Harbour was 2 hours 12 minutes, and to Bognor 1 hour 42 minutes. A new coastal electric service was introduced at the same time, with two trains an hour between Brighton and Portsmouth and one an hour from Brighton to Littlehampton and Bognor, and this was amalgamated with the existing West Worthing service so that there were now six trains an hour running west from Brighton, with three of them terminating at West Worthing. In addition, the Victoria–West Worthing service was extended to Littlehampton, and trains from Waterloo to Dorking North extended to Holmwood, with one of them running on to Horsham. The extra service provision was slightly less than on previous electrification schemes, at around 95 per cent, but revenue still rose by 13 per cent in the first six months of operation.

A far smaller scheme involved the electrification of the line to Reading, with much of the route already being covered by earlier schemes, so that just 88 track miles were involved. In a sense, while the actual electrification to Reading itself was new, those from Ascot to Ash Vale and Aldershot and Guildford were infilling between existing schemes. Although platforms were lengthened at a number of stations, the new length was just 540 ft rather than the 820 ft favoured on the main lines. Trial trains were operated from 30 October 1938, with a formal opening on 30 December, and the new services commencing on 1 January 1939. The new service was not strictly suburban, but the pattern of services reflected suburban practice, possibly in order to find paths through such congested spots as Richmond, with a peak period service every 20 minutes and half-hourly off-peak. Trains usually ran fast between Waterloo and Staines, and divided at Ascot, with the front section continuing to Reading and the rear to Guildford via Camberley and Aldershot, where the unit had to reverse. The overall journey time to Reading was 75 minutes, somewhat slower than on the GWR. The increase in frequencies was around 85 per cent.

The final electrification scheme, again an extension of existing schemes, before the outbreak of the Second World War was to Gillingham and Maidstone. This was slightly more

Even with the addition of trains between Chichester and Portsmouth (middle), the important Brighton–Portsmouth service in 1922 (top) was less frequent than that in 1938, when, although this timetable extract only shows the period up to 8.33 am, a luncheon car was no longer viable with the improved timings. *(Bradshaw)*

extensive than the Thames Valley route at 117 track miles. Incidental works were extremely heavy, with many clearances having to be eased to allow 9 ft-wide carriages, platform extensions at Holborn Viaduct and additional roads electrified at Cannon Street, while a new station was needed at Swanley where the Gillingham and Maidstone East lines divided. A carriage shed was erected at Gillingham with a carriage washer. In some senses this extension made far less sense than pressing ahead with the Sevenoaks to Hastings scheme, since the route was still planned to carry many steam-hauled trains and the role of the electric trains was seen mainly as collecting traffic from intermediate stations. In addition to the passenger service, the route also carried a considerable volume, at least by Southern Railway standards, of goods trains, which at this time were still steam-hauled. An oddity was the construction of platforms for a station at Lullingstone, where a site for a proposed new airport for London had been identified, but this was never progressed with, probably due to the outbreak of the Second World War, and the platforms were later removed.

Trial running commenced in May 1939, and there was an official opening on 30 June, when the directors and senior officers of the Southern Railway travelled from Charing

The result of Walker's leadership. Guildford at 9.30 on an August morning in 1939. On the left is a 4 SUB operating on the Guildford 'New Line' to Waterloo via Cobham. In the centre is an Up Portsmouth fast via Woking headed by a 4 COR, with another 4 COR or a 4 RES completing the train. On the right is a 2 BIL, introduced for the Portsmouth stopping services but also, as in this case, used on the newly electrified line from Guildford to Waterloo via Aldershot and Ascot. *(NRM Box 512)*

Cross to meet the mayors of Maidstone, Chatham and Gillingham. The new service was introduced on 2 July 1939. There was an hourly service from Victoria, stopping only at Bromley South and at Swanley, where the trains would divide, with the front portion running fast to Otford and then all stations to Maidstone East, while the rear portion continued all stations to Gillingham. Timings were 65 minutes to Maidstone East, 63 minutes to Gillingham. There were additional trains during peak periods to and from Holborn Viaduct. Now that the electric network had become so extensive, new opportunities for electric trains were opened up, and it was possible to operate special summer excursion trains from Gillingham to Portsmouth via London Bridge, Epsom, Effingham Junction and Guildford.

This marked the end of one of the most ambitious electrification schemes ever, and certainly the most extensive at the time, giving the Southern the world's largest suburban electric railway network. The increase in frequencies that accompanied electrification is almost beyond belief. At Waterloo, for example, off-peak services had gone from just two main-line departures an hour in the steam era to twenty-one, and during the peak from four to twenty-nine, while on Sundays they had gone from one to eighteen. On the busy Central Section at Victoria, off-peak departures had gone from one an hour hauled by steam to eighteen, and in the peak from two to twenty-eight.

The annual report and accounts for the Southern Railway for 1938 provide some interesting information on the running of a railway. During that year 46.7 million miles had been worked by steam at a total cost of £3,079,000, while 37.47 million miles had been worked by electric at a total cost of £1,642,000. Wages for the steam mileage amounted to £1,668,000, but for the electric mileage were just £327,000. Electricity itself was expensive, costing £1,190,000 against £1,295,000 for coal and water, but obviously this was more than offset by greater labour productivity. The volume of stores used was also less for the electric trains, at £10,000 against £60,000 for steam, but this may have been affected by the fact that the electric trains were on average much newer. The high volume of shunting movements for steam trains has already been mentioned, but for the electric trains only 123,000 miles out of more than 37 million were down to empty working or shunting.

The Southern had taken the few isolated electric services of the LSWR and LBSCR and created a network of 1,759 track miles, with 3,040 motor, trailer, restaurant and Pullman cars on its electric trains, with a total of 176,905 seats, against 3,618 steam passenger carriages with a total of 185,339 seats.

Chapter Seven

Steam Twilight

Even on the Southern Railway, with its passion for electrification, the age of steam was far from over. At first, electrification was seen as being suitable only for suburban services. There was much logic in this. Electric trains showed their greatest advantage over steam on services with frequent calls at stations, because one of the great weaknesses of steam was poor acceleration. Even when main-line electrification came about, on services such as the non-stop London and Brighton expresses, the new electric trains showed no real improvement over the steam expresses they replaced, although punctuality may have been better.

Steam was also seen as the ideal medium for goods trains, and on occasions whenever a locomotive was needed, since at first it was believed that electric locomotives would be unable to cope with gaps in the conductor rail. Some intensive work was involved in overcoming this problem and the first electric locomotives did not enter trial service until during the Second World War (see Appendix V).

The policy of 'cascading' equipment meant that in relegating elderly steam locomotives and rolling stock to the less busy lines, capital costs were kept down. This was especially important on lines with a high seasonal variation in traffic, such as those on the Isle of

A two-car articulated push-pull unit at Queenborough waits to depart for Leysdown. *(HRMS AER803)*

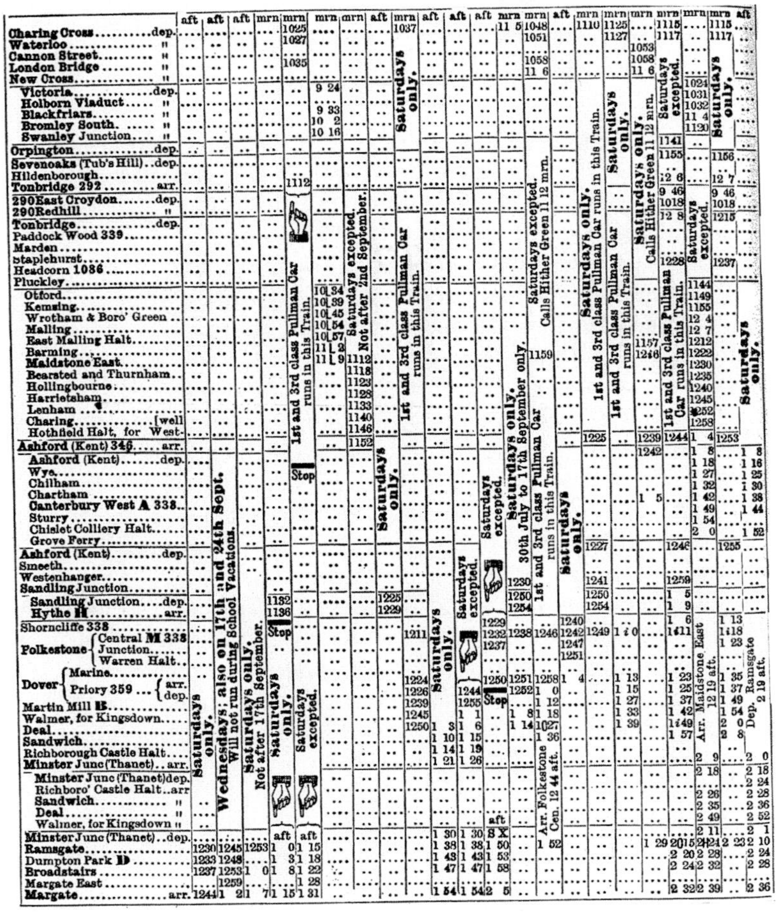

Timetable (top): Charing Cross to Dover and branches — SECR main line

Mls	Station																	
	Charing Cross ....dep.				7 26		9 15		9 50		9 53	1040	115	11 38		1122		
	Waterloo Junction ..... "				7 28				9 52									
3	Cannon Street .... "	3 40	5 20 6 45		8 29	8 25	9 39		9 57		1045	1045	10 8 1046	11 7		1127 1157		
1¼	London Bridge .... "	3 43	5 25 6 50	7 37 4 8	8 29	9 39		9 45						11 4				
—	Victoria ....dep.													1057				
—	Holborn Viaduct ...... "													1059				
—	St. Paul's .... "													1117				
—	Herne Hill .... "											1015		1135	12 4			
5	New Cross	5 35 6 58	7 40	8 32		10 4					1015		1135	12 4				
5½	St. John's	5 42 7 46	46	8 39		9 58		1011				1118		1143 1210				
7	Hither Green	5 50 7 97	51	8 44		10 3		1018						1148 1214				
9	Grove Park			8 48				1010						1153 1222				
10½	Elmstead Woods	5 57 197	57	8 52		1010		1014						1157 1225				
11½	Chislehurst	6 7 7 7	8	9 0		1020		1020						12 3 1234				
13½	Orpington	6 207	36	9 9														
15½	Chelsfield	6 27 7 44		9 15								1046						
16½	Knockholt	6 32 7 50		9 20								1053						
20½	Dunton Green 254 ..		9 30									1058						
22	Sevenoaks (Tub's Hill)	4 19	6 44 8 1	9 35 1010		11 0						1117 1128						
27	Hildenborough	4 34	6 50 8 8															
29½	Tonbridge Junc 242 ..	4 58	7 10 8 33		1024		1120					1142						
34½	242 Tunbridge Wells arr.		8 40 1025				1112		1240 1245			1240						
62	242 Bexhill-on-Sea .. "	6 0	8 40 1030				1112		1215			1234						
62½	242 Hastings .... "			9 16	1018		11 4					1115						
—	Tonbridge Junction ..dep.	4 39	6 55 8 11			1024	1120 1136			1142 1147			1239 1 48					
343	Paddock Wood 237 {arr.	4 48	7 4 8 20		1033													
	{dep.	4 51	7 9 8 25		1036													
39½	Marden		7 18 8 32		1042													
41½	Staplehurst		7 26 8 39		1055													
45½	Headcorn 273	9 36	7 35 8 47		11 4													
50½	Pluckley		7 47 8 59															
56	Ashford 238,241,247 "	5 27	8 0 9 11	9 51	1050		1116 1120 1136					1239 1 48						
82½	247 Hastings ....arr.		9 15		1155								1 24					
70½	238 Canterbury West "		8 57		1129				1212				2 16					
86½	238 Sandwich ..... "		9 45		1229								2 27					
90½	238 Deal .... "		9 52		1236								2 40					
92½	238 Walmer .... "		10 2		1245								2 51					
86	238 Ramsgate Town .. "		9 48		1229				1239 1239				2 18					
90	238 Margate Sands .. "	3 cl. 9 48			1221				1251 1251				2 18					
—	Ashford ....dep.	5 35 8 20	9 55	1055		1123 1140			1145 1147			1252						
60½	Smeeth	8 28										1 12 13						
64½	Westenhanger	8 37		11 8								1 2 21						
65½	Sandling Junction 256	5 50 8 42	10 7	1112		1135 1152		1157		1230		1 5 2 27						
69½	Shorncliffe Camp 245	6 7 8 52		1120		1144 12 0				1248		1 15 2 32						
70	Folkestone (Central) ..				1129		1149		12 6				1 20 2 32						
71	" (Junction)	6 24 9 3		1018	1132		12 7		12 8				1 26 2 38						
—	Dover (Marine) ....arr.				1032	1146													
76½	Dover (Harbour) 234..	6 45 9 25				1212 1230		1230 1230				1 10 1 45						
77½	" (Priory)	6 53 9 30					1241		1241 1241				1 15					
82½	Martin Mill	9 41				1227 1249		1249 1249				1 25 2 8						
85	Walmer, for Kingsdown	9 48				1232 1256		1256 1256				1 30 2 13						
86½	Deal 233 ....arr.	9 53				1242							1 40 2 27					
91	Sandwich 239	10 3																

Timetable (bottom, July 1938): Charing Cross to Dover / Margate

Stations (in order): Charing Cross — Waterloo — Cannon Street — London Bridge — New Cross — Victoria — Holborn Viaduct — Blackfriars — Bromley South — Swanley Junction — Orpington — Sevenoaks (Tub's Hill) — Hildenborough — Tonbridge 292 — East Croydon 290 — Redhill 290 — Tonbridge — Paddock Wood 339 — Marden — Staplehurst — Headcorn 1086 — Pluckley — Otford — Kemsing — Wrotham & Boro' Green — Malling — East Malling Halt — Barming — Maidstone East — Bearsted and Thurnham — Hollingbourne — Harrietsham — Lenham — Charing — Hothfield Halt, for West... — Ashford (Kent) 346 — Wye — Chilham — Chartham — Canterbury West 338 — Sturry — Chislet Colliery Halt — Grove Ferry — Ashford (Kent) — Smeeth — Westenhanger — Sandling Junction — Hythe — Shorncliffe 338 — Folkestone (Central / Junction / Warren Halt) — Dover (Marine / Priory 359) — Martin Mill — Walmer, for Kingsdown — Deal — Sandwich — Richborough Castle Halt — Minster Junc (Thanet) — Ramsgate — Dumpton Park — Broadstairs — Margate East — Margate

The old SECR main line to Dover was not electrified, but even so the July 1938 (bottom) schedule showed a marked improvement over that for 1922. There were more trains and they were faster, with the best taking less than 2 hours to Dover. What the timetable doesn't show is that corridor rolling stock would also have become the norm. (*Bradshaw*)

Wight, where it would also have been impossible to use, say, London suburban stock for summer Saturday peak traffic. Nevertheless, many services worked by steam also enjoyed an increase in frequency during the Southern's reign, with the summer daily service between Ryde and Ventnor, for example, rising from twenty-nine trains in 1931 to thirty-eight in 1936.

Yet there can be little doubt that the Southern Railway had, by the early 1930s, decided that steam had a limited future. Walker may have dreamt of an all-electric railway, but his successors planned a railway that was largely electric accompanied by the substantial use of diesel-electric and even some diesel-mechanical motive power. Diesel would be used on those routes unable to justify electrification, and for stopping freight workings so that the many small goods sidings at country and suburban stations would not need to be electrified.

Even when the end of steam could be foreseen, the timescale was such that new steam locomotives were still needed. The history of steam on the Southern Railway can be divided into the two periods presided over by its two chief mechanical engineers, Richard Maunsell and his successor Oliver Bulleid. Maunsell had great difficulty in obtaining approval for the large Pacific locomotives he felt were essential. Civil engineers objected that the track, bridges and viaducts were not sufficiently strong, and as we can see in the survey of accidents that there was indeed much wrong with the track, especially on the former SECR lines, though much of the LBSCR track was far from satisfactory. By the time Bulleid took over, much had been done to improve matters, but even he had to compromise, producing lighter Pacifics to accompany the 'Merchant Navy' class.

The Maunsell Era

Maunsell's period at the SECR must have been extremely frustrating for him, since the First World War intervened and limited what he could achieve. The need for standardisation and improvement was most marked on the SECR, taking over as it had done in a 'mini-grouping' the locomotive stock of two impoverished companies, yet having to operate substantial continental expresses and handle heavy commuter traffic. He achieved much in modifications to the existing locomotive stock, but only two new classes could be introduced because of wartime restrictions on materials and the shortage of manpower before the real grouping came into being.

The first Maunsell design was the 'N' class 2–6–0, built at Ashford and the first of which appeared in 1917, with another eleven following by the end of 1922, while the class continued to be produced by the Southern. There were two versions of the 'N' class, the original having two cylinders and 5 ft 6 in wheels, while the later version, the 'N1', had three cylinders. These were good mixed-traffic locomotives. The basic design was retained for a 2–6–4T with 6 ft diameter wheels intended for passenger services, which was effectively the prototype for the Southern's 'K' class, more usually known as the 'River' class, although redesignated the 'U' class after rebuilding as tender locomotives.

Becoming the first CME of the new Southern Railway must have been a welcome relief for Maunsell as he was given the opportunity to make his mark on a railway company, freed from the restrictions of wartime. It was soon clear that the Southern was indeed desperately short of modern locomotives capable of handling express passenger trains, especially as the trains were becoming heavier as standards of comfort improved and the new management team was anxious to accelerate schedules.

The two routes for which new and more powerful locomotives were required were the longer-distance services out of Waterloo and those to the Channel ports, and it was the latter that received attention first. The SECR had used its most modern locomotives on trains between Charing Cross and Folkestone and Dover, with Wainwright's 1914 4–4–0 'L' class managing the 69½ miles to Folkestone in 80 minutes. However, this was going to be difficult to maintain with the introduction of corridor carriages and an intermediate stop. Such was the sense of urgency that Maunsell had to modify the 'L' class rather than

Class 'U1' renumbered 31816 heads a Birmingham to Brighton train at Clapham Junction in 1949. *(HRMS AER200)*

'K10' class locomotive No. 345 waiting at Eastleigh to take a train to Fareham and Portsmouth in 1947. *(HRMS ABS914)*

A 'Lord Nelson' class 4–6–0 at London Bridge alongside clear signs of substantial electrification in 1933. *(HRMS AAE734)*

produce an all-new design. This involved raising boiler pressure, improving the blast arrangements, using smaller cylinders and increasing valve travel to create the 'L1' class, built by North British. To save time and money, as many 'L' class components as possible were used. The class was a success, maintaining the 80 minute schedule and capable of hauling trains of up to 320 tons, as against 225 tons for the original 'L' class.

The same practice was adopted as a stopgap measure for services out of Waterloo, where the most powerful and up-to-date locomotives were Urie's 4–6–0 'N15' class. These also benefited from redesigned valve gear and improved blast arrangements, while both the North British Locomotive Company and Eastleigh works built additional locomotives as the 'King Arthur' class. The 'King Arthurs' were an immediate success and their use was not confined to the Western Section, with many of them working to the Channel ports, and a batch built with six-wheeled rather than LSWR-style eight-wheeled tenders for use on the Central Section. Unfortunately though, their time on the Central Section was short as main-line electrification took over. A 5 ft 7 in small-wheeled version of the 'N15' was designated 'S15', while Urie's 'H15' also remained in production.

Maunsell's first completely new design for the Southern was again for the boat trains, and again was a 4–6–0 design, this time the four-cylinder 'Lord Nelson' class, capable of working a 500 ton train. When they first appeared in 1926, the 'Lord Nelsons' were the most powerful locomotives on Britain's railways, with a nominal tractive effort of 33,500 lb. The drive on these locomotives was divided between the first and second coupled axles, and the cranks were set to provide eight beats per revolution. Wheel diameter was an impressive 6 ft 7 in, and this was retained after experiments with 6 ft 3 in wheels on *Lord Hood* to see if performance on steeply graded routes was improved showed that there was little benefit to be had from the smaller diameter. A number of other experiments with crank angles and with special blastpipes and a double chimney, the last two features on *Lord Collingwood*, were attempted to improve performance, but although *Lord Collingwood* did indeed offer a much-improved performance, it was at the cost of higher fuel consumption. Bulleid continued trials with the 'Lord Nelson' class after he took over from Maunsell, comparing the Kylchap blastpipe with a Lemaitre blastpipe allied to a large-diameter chimney, and when the latter proved to be much more effective, a programme of replacement was introduced and completed by October 1939. The 'Lord Nelson' class worked well on both the Eastern and Western sections, putting in fine performances on both the Exeter and Bournemouth lines.

Meanwhile, Maunsell had turned his attention to the more difficult main lines, such as that between Tonbridge and Hastings, with tight curvatures and loading gauge limitations. The result was a new three-cylinder 4–4–0 design using a boiler adapted from that of the 'King Arthur' class – the 'Schools' class, named after leading public schools. The first example appeared from Eastleigh in 1930, and with a nominal tractive effort of 25,130 lb was the most powerful 4–4–0 on Britain's railways. Once again, Maunsell had produced a locomotive that was at home working anywhere on the Southern, capable of speeds of almost 80 mph and able to work trains of almost 400 tons.

Less successful was Maunsell's 'Z' class 0–8–0T shunter, which first appeared at Brighton in 1929. There was nothing wrong with the 'Z' class, but they were built in small numbers as the need for such locomotives was limited, so that by 1937 only eight had been built. It was at this time that Maunsell introduced his first diesel-electric shunters, and trials soon showed that the diesel-electrics were more economical.

'Schools' class 4–4–0 V30913 *Christ's Hospital* at Salisbury on a Waterloo–Plymouth express, and a long way from home since her shed plate, 74B, indicates Ramsgate! *(HRMS AEN616)*

A final Maunsell design was the 'Q' class, not to be confused with the utility 'Q1', but this design overlapped between the two CMEs, and was seen into service by Bulleid in 1938 after Maunsell had retired owing to ill health. It was that relative rarity, an 0–6–0 tender locomotive for freight work.

In addition to rebuilding the 'River' class, Maunsell also rebuilt the Baltic tanks as 4–6–0 tender locomotives, designated 'N15x' but more usually known as the 'Remembrance' class, even though the rest were named after famous engineers. As the designation indicates, in performance they were classed as similar to the 'King Arthur' class.

The Bulleid Era

Oliver Bulleid arrived on the Southern railway in 1937, determined to give the company the 4–6–2 Pacific locomotives that it needed and which had become the standard for express work on both the LMS and LNER. It takes time to design a brand-new locomotive class, and in any case, as with Maunsell before him, much of his early work was confined to improving the performance of existing classes, as shown above. Wartime meant stringent state control of what could and could not be built, and indeed of the allocation of materials, while skilled manpower became increasingly short and productive capacity was often redirected to war production. Realising that some new locomotives would be needed, two official designs were sanctioned, and almost everything else was banned.

It has often been wondered just how, in such conditions, Bulleid was able to build his 'Merchant Navy' class locomotives. In fact, he had gone against the trend for larger coupled

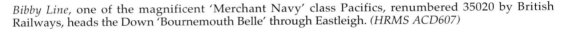

Bibby Line, one of the magnificent 'Merchant Navy' class Pacifics, renumbered 35020 by British Railways, heads the Down 'Bournemouth Belle' through Eastleigh. *(HRMS ACD607)*

wheels for high-stepping express locomotives and chosen a wheel diameter of 6 ft 2 in, allowing him to argue that these were general-purpose locomotives, express passenger locomotive construction having been banned. The first of the class appeared during the dark days of 1941, marking a break with all previous designs and using an 'air-smoothed' exterior design rather than the streamlining that had been so popular with the LNER and LMS immediately before the war. The valve gear was unconventional, with a chain drive running through an oil bath, while there were three cylinders with the relatively small size of 18 in by 24 in. The new locomotives were a massive step-up in power, with a 47 per cent increase on the grate area compared with the 'Lord Nelson' class and a 38 per cent increase in heating surface, allied to the highest boiler pressure so far on any production express

Miles from Ashford		mrn	mrn	mrn	mrn	mrn	mrn	mrn	aft	mrn	aft	aft	aft	aft	aft	aft	aft	aft	aft Wednesdays and Fridays.	aft Saturdays only.	aft Tuesdays only. One class only.
	222 Charing Cross....dep.							9 15		11 0			1c25		4 30			7 18			
	222 Waterloo Junc. .. "																				
	222 Cannon Street.... "	3 40			5 20																
	222 London Bridge.... "	3 43			5 25			9 23		11 7					4 37			7 26			
	240 Victoria.......... "												2e12					7 15			
–	Ashford ....dep.	6 55			8 10			11 3		1246			4 5		6 10			9 20			
5¼	Ham St. and Orlestone.....	7 3			8 19			1112		1255			4 14		6 19			9 29			
8½	Appledore	7 9			8 27			1118		1 1			4 20		6 25			9 36			
—	Appledore ....dep.	7 14				9 55		1124		1 15			4 26		6 35		8 15	9 42			
11	Brookland	7 19				10 0		1128		1 21			4 31		6 41		8 20	9 47			
15¼	Lydd ....arr.	7 28				10 9		1137		1 32			4 40		6 50		8 29	9 56			
—	Lydd ....dep.	7 36		8 25		1011		1139		1 42		2 55	4 41		6 52				9 57		
19½	New Romney *....arr.	7 44		8 35		1019		1148		1 52		3 3	4 49		7 0				10 5		
—	Lydd ....dep.		7 30							2 13							8c32			10 0	
19½	Dungeness..........arr.		7 42				m		m	2 25	m			m		m	8c44			1012	
15¼	Rye..........................				8 42		9 30	1130	1237	1 13	2 40		4 32	5 15	6 39	8 0		9 48			1135
17¼	Winchelsea ¶..............				8 51		9 35	1136	1241	1 20	2 45		4 39	5 20	6 46	8 5		9 55			
	[illegible]						[illegible]	[illegible]	1 10	1 35	3 11		4 55	5 49	7 4	8 34		1010			

Miles from Ashford		mrn	mrn	mrn	mrn	mrn	mrn	mrn	mrn	mrn SO	mrn	mrn SX	mrn	noon SO	aft	aft	aft	aft	aft SO	aft	aft SX	aft SX	aft SO	aft
	322 Charing Cross..dep.			7‡8		7 24	7 24	9 15		9 55		11 15	11 15	12 0		1U15	1 15		2 18	2S025	3 0	3 0	3 0	
	322 Waterloo ...... "			7‡10		7 26	7 26	9 17				11 17	11 17			1U17	1 17			2S027	3 3	3 3	3 3	
	322 Cannon Street.. "		5 8	7‡11									10S053			1S03	1S03		1 38					
	322 London Bridge. "		5 12	7 22		7 30	7 30						10 58			12H15	12§15		1 48	2S034	3 10	3 10	3 10	
	322 Victoria........ "	3∥0		6 44							9 10		10SX24				12S025		1 15	12L44	2 55	2 55	2 54	
—	Ashford (Kent) .....dep.	5 40	8 0	9 10		9 42	9 55	1048		1130	1155	12 55	1 10	1 30		2 30	2 52		3 40	4 15	4 38	4 55	4 55	
5¼	Ham Street & Orlestone..	5 48	8 8			9 50		1056				1 3	1 18								4 46			
8¼	Appledore..................	5 54	8 13			9 58	10 7	11 2		1141		1 9	1 24	1 42	1 54	2 46	3 3		3 52	4 27	4 51	5 7	5 7	
—	Appledore.........dep.	5 56	8 20			9 59		1111		1142		1 10		1 43		2 47			3 53		4 52		5 15	
11	Brookland	6 3	8 26			10 5		1118		1148		1 16		1 49		2 53			3 59		4 58		5 20	
15½	Lydd Town	6 15	8 35			10 14		1127		1158		1 25		1 59		3 2			4 9		5 7		5 29	
18¼	Lydd-on-Sea H..	6 40	8 42			10 20		1135		12 6		1 34		2 6		3 10			4 15		5 15		5 35	
20¼	Greatstone-on-Sea	6 46	8 47			10 25		1140		1212		1 43		2 13		3 17			4 22		5 20		5 40	
22	New Romney L...arr.	6 51	8 52			10 30		1145		1217		1 48		2 18		3 22			4 27		5 25		5 45	
15¼	Rye........................		8 25	9 31	9 50		1018	1114	1137		1215		1 37		2 5		3 14	4 10		4 38		5 18	5 18	6 20
17¼	Winchelsea		8 30		9 54				1141		1220				2 10		3 19	4 14		4 43		5 23	5 23	6 24
19¼	Snailham Halt............				10 0				1147						2 16			4 20						6 30
21¼	Doleham Halt .....[Halt		8 38		10 5				1152						2 21			4 24						6 35
22¾	Three Oaks & Guestling		8 42		1010				1157						2 26			4 29						6 40
25¼	Ore........................		8 48		1016				12 4						2 33			4 36				5 36	5 36	6 48
26¼	Hastings 240, 343..arr.		8 52	9 49	1020		1036	1131	12 8		1236		1 54		2 37		3H35	4 40		4 59		5 40	5 40	6 52

Down.	Week Days—*Continued* aft	aft	aft SX	aft SO	aft	aft
322 Charing Cross..dep	4S030		5 31	6 15		7 30
322 Waterloo ...... "	4S033		5 33	6 17		7 32
322 Cannon Street.. "	5SX0		6 18			
322 London Bridge. "	4S040	4SX42	5 45	5 44		7 40
322 Victoria........ "	3SX50	4 50	5 28		5Y50	7 33
Ashford (Kent) .....dep.	6 10	6 54	7 40	7 45	8 59	9 42
Ham Street & Orlestone..	6 18					9 50
Appledore................	6 24	7 6	7 51	7 56		9 56
Appledore.........dep.	6 32		8 4	8 4		10 6
Brookland	6 38		8 10	8 10		10 12
Lydd Town	6 47		8 19	8 19		10 24
Lydd-on-Sea H........	6 55		8 27	8 27		10 31
Greatstone-on-Sea.....	7 0		8 32	8 32		10 36
New Romney L...arr.	7 4		8 37	8 37		10 41
Rye.......................	6 37	7 17	8 4	8 9	9 19	10 11
Winchelsea			8 9	8 14		10 16
Snailham Halt..........			8 15	8 20		
Doleham Halt .....[Halt			8 20	8 25		
Three Oaks & Guestling			8 25	8 30		
Ore......................		7 32	8 31	8 36		10 32
Hastings 240, 343..arr.		7 36	8 35	8 40	9 36	10 37

Ashford–Hastings has been something of a backwater until recent years, when the Channel Tunnel has provided additional traffic to and from Ashford, but here too the 1922 timetable (top) was inferior to that of 1938, although in the latter case it is worth noting that even-interval services did not seem to reach out this far from London. *(Bradshaw)*

locomotive, giving a nominal tractive power of 37,500 lb. The reason for so much innovation was the need to observe weight restrictions on many Southern routes, allied to a shortage of space within the resulting design.

One of the most significant changes had nothing to do with the locomotive as such, but was the introduction of a new numbering system, alphanumeric numbering with three coupled axles denoted by the use of the letter C, followed by a new locomotive number, so that Bulleid's Pacifics became 21Cxxx.

The 'Merchant Navy' class introduced new standards of driver comfort and gave the Southern a massive step-change in locomotive power, but mechanically they required considerable attention. Oil leaks during service were one problem, the valve gear rapidly getting out of adjustment and the chain gear stretched. Nevertheless, Bulleid persisted with the novel features and retained them when he introduced his lighter-weight 'West Country' and 'Battle of Britain' classes, starting in 1945.

Meanwhile, Maunsell's 'Q' class had proved successful and the increased volumes of freight being carried on the Southern meant that more were needed. Even with wartime restrictions, Bulleid could have built more of the same, but instead decided to modify the design in an attempt to produce more power from a locomotive of the same weight. The cylinder dimensions of the 'Q' were retained, but his new 'Q1' class had an increased boiler pressure and again the grate area and heating area were increased, using a firebox based on that of the 'Lord Nelson' class. The new arrangements naturally increased the weight, so a true utility look was conveyed by the simplest possible boiler casing and the absence of running plate and splashers. In a word, the 'Q1' was ugly!

Bulleid's desire for novelty next found full reign with the 'Leader' class, an 0–6–6–0T locomotive with a driving cab at each end which looked like a steam engine in the shell of an electric or diesel locomotive. The first did not appear until after nationalisation, and it failed to impress, for while the driver was able to sit in the front in reasonable comfort, the fireman was located in the middle between the boiler and tender and was almost fully encased, so that heat was a problem. A few trial runs of the prototype saw five locomotives still under construction cancelled.

In common with the other railway companies, to help alleviate the wartime shortage of locomotives, the Southern also received its share of a batch of US-built tank engines, mainly for shunting, although these required considerable modification before they could run on Southern metals.

Chapter Eight

Closures, New Lines and Junctions

There is a popular misconception that railway closures have been a comparatively modern phenomenon, with many laying the blame at the feet of a certain Dr, later Lord, Beeching, a former chairman of Imperial Chemical Industries. In fact the pace of line closures had accelerated after nationalisation, with all but two of the lines in the Isle of Wight, for example, closed by the mid-1950s, but railway lines were closed even before this by the old railway companies.

In any discussion of line closures, two points must be borne in mind. The first of these is that many of the lines constructed were over-optimistic and had little chance of paying their way, as railways became the exciting new opportunities of the day, and in fact we have had a recent reminder of how this can occur in the so-called 'Dot.Com' stockmarket boom at the turn of the twenty-first century. The difficulties were also compounded when too many railway companies were promoted to cater for the same market, and a good example of this was the ruinous competition and 'me too' planning and marketing of the SER and LCDR that prevented a truly viable and healthy railway to develop.

The second point is that the railways arrived at a time when inland transport was painfully slow and primitive. The canals had marked a revolution in transport, cutting the prices of bulk goods and raw materials in particular and bringing a previously unknown degree of reliability to movement, but they were slow. Travel by road was faster, but not that much, expensive and uncomfortable, with even the best mail and stagecoaches prey to snow and mud in the winter months, and running over rock hard and dusty tracks in the summer. It followed that railways found a ready market even on the shortest routes, and indeed these were the basis of many a successful railway since few people travelled any great distance, and it was common for people seldom to leave the village in which they were born. People would catch the early trains if only to travel a mile or two. This was why small islands, including those much smaller than the Isle of Wight, such as Jersey, for example, had two railway companies. There were even plans for a railway on smaller Guernsey, although reality took a grip and the island remained content with its one short stretch of tramway.

The problem was that as soon as the trams came, such short routes were vulnerable to a mode of transport that was cheaper and came much closer to the doorstep and the destination of many travellers. Once the trams were electrified, they were often much faster than many local trains. On the busier routes, this was a spur to electrification, but on the quieter ones, the temptation was to consider closure. Better roads and road surfaces were also accompanied by the spread of bus services after the First World War, and the motor bus was even less expensive and more flexible than the tram.

The upshot of both these factors meant that some places were ridiculously over-served. A prime example in the Southern Railway's territory was Midhurst, a very attractive small town served by the LSWR from Petersfield and by the LBSCR from both Chichester and Pulborough. With three railway routes and two stations, it was not surprising that the SR closed the old LSWR station. In fact, especially after electrification of the Portsmouth Direct,

The small Isle of Wight network has all the hallmarks of a set of branch lines, but the 'main line' between Ryde and Ventnor could carry a service of suburban intensity on a summer Saturday. Even on a summer weekday (middle and lower) it was very busy in July 1938 – certainly far more so than in 1922 – and the trains were heavier as well. *(Bradshaw)*

it was quicker to drive to Haslemere and catch a fast train to Waterloo than take the local trains to any of the main lines, despite the fact that even today the drive, which is certainly attractive, can by no means be described as fast.

All these problems were in addition to those that can occur when a market changes because of industrial decline or depopulation.

It might even be worth considering an alternative argument, that the railway companies were often too slow to consider closure. As we can see elsewhere, even under the shadow of imminent nationalisation, the Southern's directors were still anxious to maintain and, as

The LSWR station at Midhurst was closed in 1925 as part of a post-grouping rationalisation. *(HRMS ACD828)*

far as they could under postwar shortages, develop their railway. There was certainly also a considerable reluctance, even a failure, to consider rationalisation after the grouping. One would also have thought that with such a considerable investment in local bus companies across the south of England, there would have been more enthusiasm for rationalisation. Perhaps the Southern's experience with electrification tempted many senior railwaymen to believe that somewhere there might one day be a solution to the problem of the rural railways, for after all, they would have been aware of the GWR's pioneering work with railcars.

Either way, nothing can detract from the great work done on modernising the railway with the electrification programme in particular, and the small number of genuinely new lines also built showed that the railway was being remodelled to reflect changing traffic patterns and cover suburban development. As the chapter on London's termini also showed, remodelling and fresh track layouts were often necessary to accommodate increased traffic and eliminate bottlenecks, and here too the Southern and its predecessors were great exponents of the flying junction and the dive under, and were well ahead of the highway engineers in these respects.

The Southern was also mindful of ways of keeping loss-making lines open by cutting costs. A good example was in its treatment of the Somerset & Dorset, a line much enthused over by the railway buffs, but not used sufficiently by the passenger and in any case running through some of the least densely populated parts of the south-west. After grouping, the line was worked jointly by the Southern and the London Midland Scottish, but it was not until 1929 that the two companies ended the anomaly of the line being

The Southern's sole narrow-gauge railway was the short-lived Lynton & Barnstaple in north Devon. Here is No. 759 *Yeo*. *(HRMS AAC932)*

worked as a separate entity. The equipment was divided and credited to the Somerset & Dorset Joint Committee at cost. The Southern took over track maintenance and the LMS took over responsibility for locomotives, allowing Highbridge works to be closed, while carriages were divided between the two companies, reflecting an earlier and similar arrangement for goods wagons between the pre-grouping LSWR and Midland Railway, dating from 1914. The changes took effect in 1930, and the impact can be judged by the fact that the closure of Highbridge works alone cut 300 jobs.

Line Closures

Prior to the grouping, about 400 miles of railway had been closed in the British Isles, mainly because of First World War economy measures, but in fact few lines were reopened after closure. Between the beginning of 1923 and the end of 1947, a further 1,650 miles were closed.

Typical of the wartime closures was the so-called East Southsea branch, which was built by an independent company and ran for just 1¼ miles from Fratton to Southsea. Opened on 1 July 1885, it was initially worked by the LSWR, and then jointly from 1886 with the LBSCR. How anyone could have imagined such a line being viable even in 1885 is beyond belief, but electrification of the tramways in 1908 meant that the service was unattractive – it was in any case far better to take the tram to Portsmouth town station and catch a faster train. It was closed within days – although the exact date is not clear – of the First World War breaking out and never reopened, until closure was finally officially authorised in 1923.

The Southern Railway instigated a small number of line closures, of which perhaps the most spectacular was that of the 19¼ mile-long narrow-gauge Lynton & Barnstaple Railway, when a complete route serving a sparsely populated area of north Devon was abandoned. The Southern had purchased the LBR in 1922 in advance of grouping, which makes closure all the more difficult to understand. The LBR dated only from 1898 and had been built to a 1 ft 11½ in gauge. Opened amid great public enthusiasm, construction had been far more costly than the promoters had anticipated, although the projected lower costs of construction had been one reason for choosing a narrow gauge, and it enjoyed little traffic except in summer, when even then it seems to have existed for the enthusiast market. That the shareholders did not do well from the deal can be judged from the fact that the line cost £129,000 to build and equip, while the Southern bought it for £39,267. The Southern did its best to improve the service and publicise the line, but eventually in 1935 had to admit defeat, having gone through the rigorous closure procedure. Most commentators believe that had the line survived in the postwar period, it might have benefited from the growing railway preservation movement, and certainly it would have been well placed to attract tourists in the postwar world of paid holidays. Of course, preserved lines depend heavily on a mass of unpaid and enthusiastic labour.

The Lynton & Barnstaple figures show just how difficult it could be to make money from a railway, even if using a narrow gauge cut costs considerably. The grouping reflected state intervention on a massive scale, something that is not always appreciated today. A Railways Amalgamation Tribunal forced the four groups to accept companies that they did not want, and for which no sane businessman would make an offer. The Southern Railway was forced to accept the liabilities of three bankrupt companies, the Lee-on-the-Solent, the Brighton & Dyke and the Freshwater, Yarmouth & Newport, although the last-named was to survive into nationalisation, possibly because of its contribution to such successful ventures as the cross-island train, 'The Tourist'.

The resort of Lee-on-the-Solent, more usually referred to as Lee-on-Solent, or just 'Lee', had potential as a dormitory for nearby Gosport and Fareham or, for those prepared to travel further, Portsmouth or even Southampton. A light railway was opened from Fort Brockhurst on the line from Fareham to Gosport on 12 May 1894. A contractor worked the line until the LSWR took over operations in 1909, although the previous year costs had totalled £1,102 against receipts of £702! The line meant that passengers for Fareham and Gosport had to change trains at Fort Brockhurst, and further changes were necessary to reach Portsmouth or Southampton, while the advent of bus services meant that these were not only cheaper, but more direct and as a result quicker. The Southern closed the line to passengers from 1 January 1931, and to freight from 28 September 1935. All one can say is that it might have had some minor value in wartime with troop trains for Browndown Camp and for HMS *Daedalus*, the Royal Naval Air Station at Lee, which was also used as a holding camp when the training barracks at HMS *St Vincent* was full to overflowing, but these would have been short journeys, and again a bus, or for servicemen, the back of a lorry, would have been quicker.

Another branch off the Fareham to Gosport line had run to Stokes Bay, and had been the first route to the Isle of Wight, with a direct train-ferry link using a specially built pier. This was the route favoured by Queen Victoria and Prince Albert on their journeys to and from Osborne House. It was closed during the First World War and never reopened.

Brighton had one 'suburban' branch line, running off the Brighton to Lewes, or 'East Coast', line for almost 1½ miles to Kemp Town, with a fourteen-arch viaduct and a tunnel of just over 1,000 yds. There was just one intermediate station at Lewes Road. The line was immediately vulnerable to competition from trams and buses, and it is surprising that the line, opened in 1869, survived as late as 1933, when passenger services were withdrawn on 2 January, although the branch was still used for goods traffic. The line was never electrified, but the tunnel was to prove invaluable during the Second World War.

The Brighton & Dyke line was opened on 1 September 1887 and ran for 3½ miles from Dyke Junction, just west of Hove, to the beauty spot of Devil's Dyke, a climb with gradients of 1 in 40 or more to a height of 400 ft. The LBSCR had worked the line and on a fine day in the holidays, it could be very busy, although expensive to work. The final day of operation was 31 December 1938. The view from an open-top bus was always likely to be better than staring from a railway carriage window with the view obscured by smoke and steam as a tank engine struggled to reach the end of the line.

Rather more promising on paper was the Basingstoke & Alton, a light railway that cut across the rural northern part of Hampshire, but Alton was, and remains, a small country town and the countryside in between was sparsely populated, so while the line offered a short cut to the main line to Exeter, traffic was never heavy and it never made a profit. It closed during the First World War from 1 January 1917. Apparently very reluctantly, the Southern reopened the line on 18 August 1924, but it soon realised its mistake and obtained authorisation to close the line on 12 September 1932 to passengers, and to freight on 1 June 1936. Its sole claim to fame was as the scene for the comedy film *Oh! Mr Porter*.

Midhurst could never justify three railway lines, and when all traffic was concentrated on the LBSCR station in 1925, the location was still inconvenient for the town. Passenger services were withdrawn between Midhurst and Chichester from 7 July 1935, but the other services to Petersfield and Pulborough survived through to the days of British Railways.

A good example of a line being made redundant by changes in the pattern of the railways occurred with the branch to Ringwood. As already mentioned, Bournemouth was at first bypassed by the railway when the LSWR got through to Poole, then regarded as being far more important. The line through Ringwood provided Bournemouth's first link with the railway in 1870, but the line was difficult to work, and still far from the direct link that the now fast-growing resort deserved. The opening of a cut-off between Brockenhurst and Christchurch immediately undermined the viability of the line between Ringwood and Bournemouth, which was closed to passengers and freight from 30 September 1935.

The distinction of being the earliest steam railway in the south of England belongs to the Canterbury & Whitstable, opened in 1830 and just 6 miles long, with an extremely low tunnel that could only be worked in later years by locomotives with a specially cut-down chimney. At one time it had been worked by stationary engines, but the SER, which took it over in 1844, reverted to locomotives. It was closed to passengers from 1 December 1931, although it survived for goods traffic until after nationalisation.

New Lines

The Southern inherited a number of improvements put in hand by its predecessors, including many delayed by the First World War. While Waterloo was the best example of a significant major improvement late in the history of one of the pre-grouping companies, there were a number of others.

Farthest west of the improvements was the new line running some 20 miles from Halwill Junction to Torrington. Halwill was the junction where the lines to Bude and Padstow parted. Authorised in 1914, the line was to be constructed for a North Cornwall & Devon Railway, but war intervened and work started on 30 June 1922, with the line opening on 27 July 1925 and leased to the Southern. There were seven intermediate stations and halts, but after reasonable passenger traffic in its early years, the line failed to live up to the expectations of its promoters and was expensive to work with many gradients. Its value lay in the heavy china clay and lignite freight traffic originating around Meeth.

One line that was to see its full freight potential many years after the Southern was no more was the branch from the Southampton–Bournemouth line to Fawley. Again, this was a project that had been delayed by the First World War. The area was close to Southampton but had been bypassed in the original phase of railway construction, largely because the quickest and shortest route to Southampton from the dormitory town of Hythe was by ferry. The original company for the line, the Totton, Hythe & Fawley Light Railway Company, was merged into the Southern Railway, which laid a single track from a point just west of Totton station, with stations at Marchwood and Hythe, and sidings at Hythe, with a siding at Fawley for the Agwy Petroleum works and for Calshott flying-boat station. The line was worked by token as a single block. The passenger service was from Southampton Docks station through Southampton West (now Central). Postwar the line became freight-only for the large Esso refinery at Fawley. Had plans for a tunnel to the Isle of Wight progressed, a tunnel from near Fawley to Cowes would have been a far more hopeful prospect than that of the Lymington branch to Yarmouth.

Another project that had been delayed, although one suspects not so much by the war as by uncertainty and the sometimes slow expansion of the underground system, was a line between Wimbledon and Sutton. This had been authorised in 1910 for the Metropolitan District Railway, with Wimbledon as the southernmost of the three branches of the District. As originally conceived, the line would have been a continuation of the District. The project was revived in 1923 because the Southern was anxious about further extensions of the City & South London tube beyond Morden, and it was agreed that the tube would not be extended and that the Southern would build the new line. Work started in 1927, opening as far as South Merton on 6 July 1929 and Sutton on 5 January 1930, providing a convenient link between the London Section and Central Section. Six new stations were provided on the line, including one at St Helier where the London County Council was building a vast new housing estate for 10,000 people, and this was the only station to have a goods yard, doubtless for household coal traffic. Electrified from the outset, the line cost £1 million and required a high embankment and twenty-four bridges to carry it over the many roads in the area. The double track ended on the opposite side of Wimbledon from the District platforms, and instead of connecting with the underground system linked with a line originally worked jointly by the LSWR and LBSCR to Streatham Junction, and services operated over the line between Holborn Viaduct and West Croydon.

An ambitious scheme to create a new seaside resort and dormitory town at Alhallows on the north Kent coast across the Thames estuary from Southend-on-Sea caused the Southern to build a single-track 1¾ mile branch line off its Gravesend–Port Victoria line. After special excursions on 14 May 1932, the line opened on 16 May. It was steam-worked from the outset, with a regular service to and from Gravesend but with a few peak period trains to and from London. It was not electrified when the third rail was extended east from Gravesend in 1939.

The spread of the London suburbs between the wars, with three-bedroom semi-detached houses being built by speculative builders for as little as £200, was a driving force in the extension of the Southern's network. One area enjoying such development was Chessington in Surrey, and the Southern decided to build a 4¼-mile branch off the line from Raynes Park to Epsom at Motspur Park. The new line was mainly either in cutting or on embankment as the countryside was undulating, while the heavy clay subsoil also required the extensive use of dry filling material, mainly taken from London slum clearance. The terminus, Chessington South, was in a cutting and had a goods yard as well as a number of unusual features, such as an island platform, possibly because the original plan was that the line should continue to Leatherhead, and a 6 in concrete floor under 8 in of ballast. Electrified from the outset, the line opened as far as Tolworth on 29 May 1938 and to Chessington South on 28 May 1939. A major traffic generator for the line was Chessington Zoo, providing a useful two-way traffic flow on weekdays, and keeping the line busy on Sundays and holidays.

Some of the new lines reflected the way in which the railway had grown. At Ramsgate the SER and LCDR had separate termini, and the SECR had other priorities when it took over management from its two cash-strapped predecessors in 1899. It was left to the Southern to rationalise the situation, building a new bypass line 1½ miles long between St Lawrence on the former SER line and just south of Broadstairs on the former LCDR route, with two stations on the new line, one being a single new Ramsgate station and the other at Dumpton Park. The two termini were closed, as was the SER Ramsgate–Margate line, made redundant by the new line and the station at Margate Sands. The new line and its stations opened on 2 July 1926.

The SECR had achieved some connections between its former routes, and the Southern made further improvements with two short curves at Lewisham, opened on 7 July 1929. The first curve assisted the progress of goods trains to Hither Green marshalling yard from the LMS and LNER, while the second put Lewisham Junction station (later renamed Lewisham) on a loop off the main line between St Johns and Hither Green, allowing more suburban services to be routed through the station.

Junctions

The concept of flyovers and burrowing junctions, or dive unders, on the railways of the south of England long pre-dated their use by highway engineers. The first seems to have been on the London & Croydon Railway in 1845, when the company's atmospheric line crossed over the ordinary line at Norwood. This was followed by the start of what was to become a complex set of flying junctions at Norwood Junction in 1857, when an additional LBSCR line crossed the Up and Down main lines to reach the West Croydon branch.

The Southern inherited this valuable legacy from its predecessors, with a total of twenty-five flying junctions or dive unders. Its main contribution was a flyover at Wimbledon carrying the Up local line over the main lines so that there would be no interference between main-line and suburban trains at Waterloo. This was opened in 1936. The following year saw a flyover opened at Worting Junction, near Basingstoke, eliminating conflicting movements and increasing traffic capacity at the point where the line to Exeter diverged from that to Southampton. This meant that the original main line from London to Southampton, the start of the LSWR, had but three flat junctions throughout the 80 miles, at Woking for the Portsmouth line, at Winchester where the line from Alton joined the main line, and at Eastleigh where the lines to Romsey and Fareham left the main line. Unfortunately, of all the junctions south of Clapham, that at Woking was the busiest and the one most in need of a flying junction or a dive under.

Chapter Nine

'ACE' and the 'Belles'

While so often thought of as a commuter railway, lacking the speed and flair of the expresses on the Great Western, the London & North Eastern and even the London Midland Scottish, the Southern had if anything more than its fair share of named expresses. Although the term 'commuter' had still to be imported from the United States, the Southern was what would now be described as a commuter railway, and the titled expresses didn't neglect this market, with the most obvious example being the 'Southern Belle', especially after it became the all-electric 'Brighton Belle'. Many also think of the Southern as being the holiday railway, something that the company's advertising did much to encourage, and for the holidaymaker and business traveller alike, there was a wonderful selection of named expresses. Who could not be attracted by a train with the title of the 'Atlantic Coast Express', for example? There were also some unofficial names, including the rather less exciting 'Invalids Express' assigned to certain workings between Ryde and Ventnor. Then, of course, there were the expresses linking the metropolis with the ferries and ocean liners, and most intriguing of all today, in an era in which through UK– continental railway travel is now commonplace, the 'Night Ferry', carrying the passenger without changing trains all the way from London to Paris.

Another 'modern' idea is that of feeding passengers into airports by train, but the Southern did this as well as early as 1937 with what must have seemed to be a logical extension of the boat train, the flying-boat train! That, however, was an unofficial title for a very official working.

The Southern did not keep its titled trains to itself, as there were several examples of through running with other companies, although compared to the 'Night Ferry', these must have seemed very ordinary indeed. The inter-company trains did at least mean that Southern locomotives and rolling stock wandered some distance beyond Southern metals, in contrast to the specially built Wagons Lits stock used on the 'Night Ferry', while the Southern hosted locomotives and rolling stock from other companies, notably the Great Western and LMS.

Reasons of space mean that it is not really practical to give a history of such inter-company trains as the 'Pines Express', operating between Manchester and Bournemouth, or the 'Sunny South Express', that ran between Liverpool and Eastbourne. In considering titled trains, specials such as 'Excursion' or descriptive terms such as 'Limited' or 'Mail' are generally rejected, although this does cause problems with titles such as 'Brighton Belle' or 'Night Ferry'. Purists also reject informal titles, but it can surely be argued that these gain a certain credibility through constant use. In fact, early Bradshaws did include a number of titled trains that were descriptive, and also justified their status with accelerated timings, and by 1877 there were already several of these, mainly mail trains.

The Titled Train

The first titled train in the south of England arrived almost by accident. It wasn't a railway-man's idea at all, but that of a hotelier! Nor was it introduced by one of the smart, well-heeled and progressive companies such as the GWR was to become, and as the LBSC and Midland Railway already were. It was the humble and poverty-stricken South Eastern

Railway that introduced the first named railway train in the British Isles when, on 22 December 1876, it launched the 'Granville Special Express'. The promoter of this train was the new owner of the Granville Hotel at Ramsgate, although at the time it proclaimed its address as being in the rather more up-market sounding St Lawrence-on-Sea. Anxious to develop the winter weekend market, the hotelier started advertising in *The Times* in December 1876 that there would be a 'First Class Special Private Express' running from Charing Cross to Ramsgate every Friday from 22 December onwards, leaving London at 3.45 pm and arriving at Ramsgate at 6 pm, with passengers from the City of London able to depart from Cannon Street at 3.50 pm. This first working was obviously aimed at the Christmas market, since the return was not until 27 December, when it left Ramsgate at 8.30 am to arrive at Charing Cross at 10.45 am. The return fare was 30s and the train could be used by non-residents since the advertising mentioned an allowance of 12s 6d against the hotel bill for those hotel guests using the express.

The 'Granville Special Express' afterwards settled down to a Friday afternoon Down, Monday morning Up existence. It also developed into a two-class train, and by the following summer was also serving Margate. Its impact was such that the rival London, Chatham & Dover Railway also introduced its own competitor, the 'Granville Express', but this was in the nature of the ruinous 'me too' competition between these two companies until they finally settled on a joint working arrangement as the South Eastern & Chatham Railway. The 'Granvilles' were relatively short-lived, being dropped in 1880 and then revived again in 1884. As for the SECR, all titles were dropped abruptly in 1905, but suddenly in 1921 the title 'Granville Express' reappeared. The LBSCR continued with its named trains right up to the grouping, but alone among the three larger companies, the LSWR never bestowed any titles on its trains, despite operating the longest-distance services.

Our interest centres around the titled trains operated by the Southern Railway, and these follow in alphabetical order. Many of the Southern Railway's named trains were Pullmans, not only because of the relative prosperity of the area throughout the twentieth century, but because the journey times were often well-suited to Pullman service, with at-seat meals and no time for more than a single sitting, which otherwise would have favoured a conventional dining car.

ACE – The Atlantic Coast Express

While the Southern Railway's management philosophy was largely based on that of the LSWR, a more imaginative and publicity-conscious stance evolved soon after the grouping, with its first manifestation being the decision to introduce names for the company's express locomotives. The logical next step was to introduce named trains. At that time the main departures from Waterloo to the south-west of England were at 10 am, serving Bude and Padstow; 11 am, serving Ilfracombe and Plymouth; and noon, serving Exmouth, Sidmouth and Seaton. The decision was taken that the 10 am should be the 'North Cornwall Express', while the midday train would be the 'East Devon Express'. It was proposed that the 11 am should become the 'Devonian Express', but this failed to catch the imagination at the company's headquarters at Waterloo and a competition for a new name appeared in the July 1925 issue of *The Southern Railway Magazine*. The competition was won by Guard Rowland of Waterloo who was first with the suggestion 'Atlantic Coast Express', for which he was awarded the then useful sum of three guineas, somewhat more than a week's basic pay, while three other employees received a 'King Arthur' locomotive paperweight for having made the same suggestion.

The new train appeared in the timetables for the first time on 19 July 1926, no mean achievement given that operations had been adversely affected by the General Strike and that coal miners continued their dispute for some time afterwards. Strangely, because of major timetable changes, the names for the 10 am and 12 noon were never introduced, and unusually, with the exception of the 'Brighton Belle', the name of 'Atlantic Coast Express'

The 'Atlantic Coast Express' benefited from both Bulleid's locomotives and his later rolling stock, showing the wide-body design in its main-line form in this restaurant car at Clapham Junction. *(HRMS AER301)*

A feature of the 'Atlantic Coast Express' postwar was its so-called tavern-cars, which carried the theme so far as to have 'pub' names, in this case *The Green Man*, and a livery that was meant to convey a pub theme. *(HRMS AER302)*

was applied to more than one departure! The main train was, as originally planned, the 11 am to Ilfracombe and Plymouth, dividing at Exeter, but the name was also carried by the new 11.10 am to Bude and Padstow, which were at least, unlike Plymouth, on the 'Atlantic Coast' of north Cornwall. The main train ran non-stop to Salisbury and offered connections at Barnstaple for Lynton using the narrow-gauge Lynton & Barnstaple, and the front portion eventually reached Ilfracombe at 4.24 pm. The rear portion reached Plymouth at 4.29, having taken the inland route via Okehampton. Meanwhile, the second train had followed at a slightly more leisurely pace, and eventually reached Padstow at 5.41 pm, having been anything but an express for much of the distance from Exeter. The Bude portion was detached at Halwill Junction, reaching Bude at 4.42 pm. *En route*, the second train had also detached a portion at Yeovil Junction for Sidmouth, reached at 3.24 pm, and Exmouth, at 4 pm. Over the years other portions were detached, often serving relatively small resorts, and attached to the scheduled local train that would otherwise have provided a connection.

If running two trains with the same name was complicated enough on weekdays, Saturday, which was very much the day for starting and finishing a holiday at the time, saw no fewer than four trains. Although only two held the title officially, there were times when Waterloo would credit the other trains with the title – the marketing opportunity of a prestige train must have been too good to let slip by! The 11 am departure ran on Saturdays, but with a slightly later arrival at Plymouth than on weekdays, while the name was also carried by the 10.25 am departure to Padstow, arriving at 4.35 pm, and Bude at 3.37 pm. There was also a 10.35 am departure to Ilfracombe, which arrived at 4 pm, while the Saturday 11.10 am ran unnamed to Sidmouth and Exmouth.

In the opposite direction, there were departures from the country termini which combined at Exeter, where the name was allocated to the 12.04 pm and 12.32 pm from Queen Street to Waterloo, which the former reached at 3.39 pm.

Winter schedules allowed the train to be a conventional single departure in each direction, albeit with many more divisions, but the consistent pattern, summer and winter, was that the main portion was that for Ilfracombe.

Initially the train used existing rolling stock, unlike many of the later named trains on the Southern. It was not until May 1928 that the first new rolling stock appeared, with the arrival of the first of six sets each consisting of a first-class kitchen car and a third-class dining saloon. The train must have been a drain on the rolling stock requirement since its multi-portion working meant a preponderance of brake composite coaches, each division requiring first- and third-class accommodation, each with smoking and non-smoking compartments. Catering facilities on many of the trains were scheduled to be detached at Exeter, although there are photographs of Padstow station with the catering units present.

Over the years before the outbreak of the Second World War, a number of changes were made to the schedule and to the composition of the train, with stops added or deleted, mainly with the objective of accelerating the Waterloo–Salisbury schedule, which by 1936 saw the fastest running at that time on the Southern with an average speed of 58.5 mph, the 80 mile journey taking just 86 minutes. The winter single train just before the war had ten carriages, and starting from the locomotive these were five corridor brake composites, each with six compartments, including one each of first-class smoking and non-smoking, and two each of third-class smoking and non-smoking, which would be sent through to Ilfracombe, Torrington, Plymouth, Padstow and Bude. These were followed by the catering set of a first-class kitchen car and third-class restaurant car, normally detached at Exeter, and finally, three more corridor brake composites for Exmouth, Sidmouth and Seaton. For the passenger, there was always the nagging fear that one might be in the wrong section, especially if one had left one's compartment to visit the restaurant car for lunch – an attractive option given the departure times! In the summer, with up to four trains, the brake composites were each joined by as many as three corridor carriages, giving a more normal appearance to the trains, which usually had ten or twelve carriages in total.

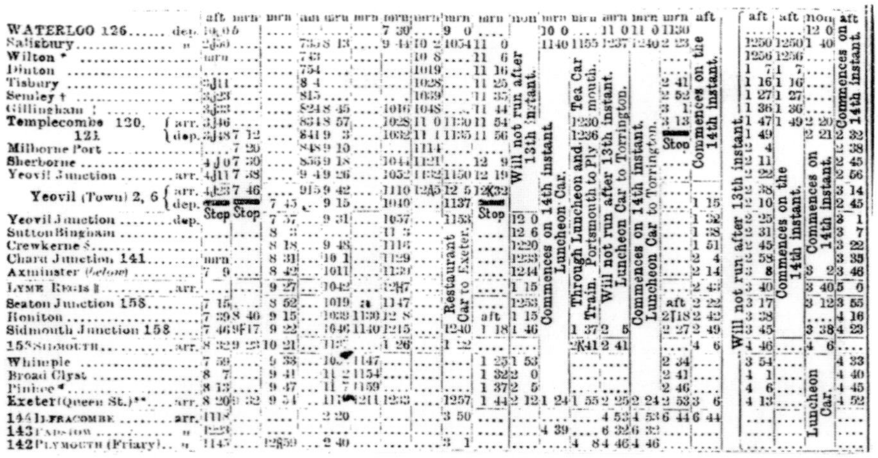

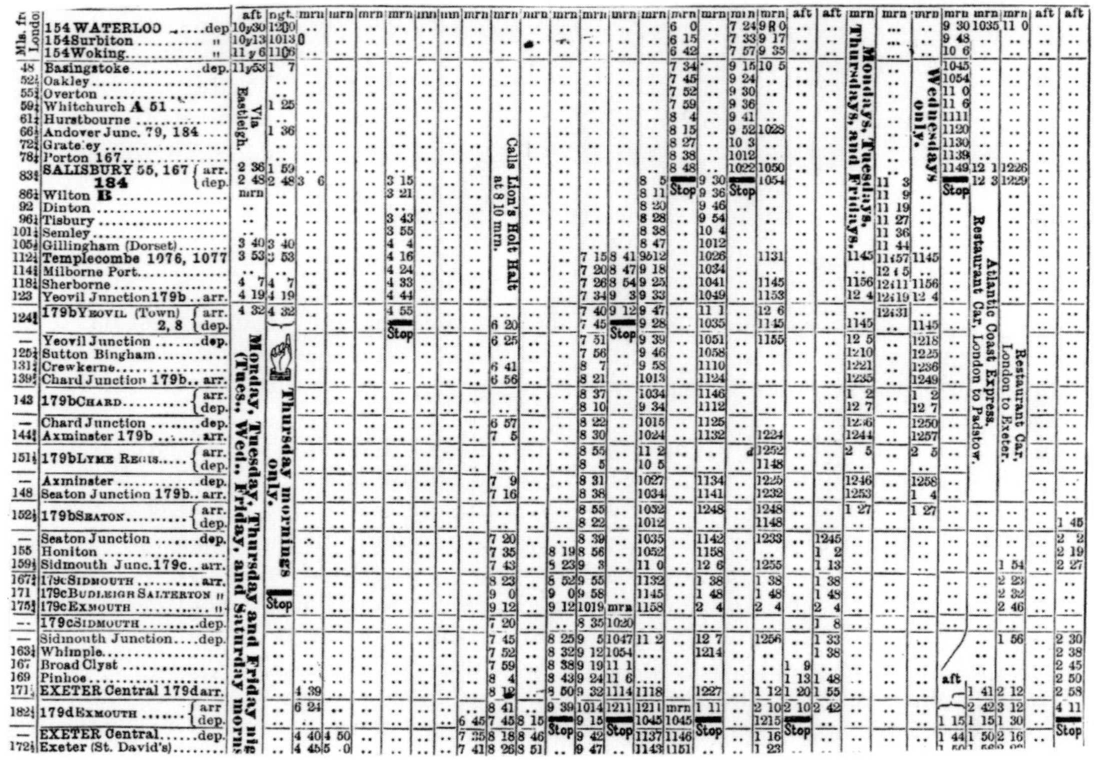

	aft	mrn	mrn			am	mrn	mrn								aft	aft	noon	aft
WATERLOO 126 ..... dep.	10 06				7 30		9 0			10 0		11 0	11 0	1130				12 0	
Salisbury .... "	2 50			7 58 18		9 44	10 2	1054	11 0		1140	1155	1237	1240	12 12		1250	1250	1 40
Wilton * .... turn				7 43			10 8		11 6								1256	1256	
Dinton				7 54			1019		11 16								1 7	1 7	
Tisbury	3 11			8 4			1028		11 25								1 16	1 16	
Semley †	3 23			8 15			1039		11 35								1 27	1 27	
Gillingham ‡	3 33			8 24	8 45		1016	1048	11 44								1 36	1 36	
Templecombe 120 { arr.	3 46			8 34	8 57		1028	11 0	1120	11 56							1 47	1 49	
121 { dep.	3	87	12		8 41	9		1032	11 4	1135							1 49		
Milborne Port		7 29			8 48	9 10			11 14								1 57		
Sherborne	4	07	50		8 59	18		1041	1121	12 9							2 8		
Yeovil Junction ...... arr.	4	17	48		9 49	36		1052	1152	1150	12 19						2 18		
Yeovil (Town) 2, 6 { arr.	4	57	46		9	59	42		1110	1245	12 5	1258					2 28		
{ dep.	Stop	Stop		7	45	9	15		1040		1137						2 38		
Yeovil Junction .... dep.				7	45	9	31		1057		1153	Stop					2 48		
Sutton Bingham				8					11 5								2 56		
Crewkerne				8 18		9 48			1116								3 7		
Chard Junction 141 ...	mrn			8 31		10 1			1129								3 20		
Axminster (below) ...	7 9			8 42		1011			1139								3 30		
LYME REGIS ‡ .... arr.				9 27			1042		1247								3 40	4 05	6
Seaton Junction 158 .. arr.	7 15		3 52			1019	2a	1147									3 40	3 123	5
Honiton	7 29	3 46	9 15			1028	1130	12 8									3 50		
Sidmouth Junction 158 ..	7 46	3 57	17	9 22			1016	1140	1215		1240	1 18	1 46				3 57		
158 SIDMOUTH .... arr.	8 32	9	10 21			112		1 26									4 6		
Whimple	7 59		9 33		105	1147			1 23	1 53							4 33		
Broad Clyst	8 7		9 41		11 2	1154			1 322	0							4 41		
Pinhoe ‡	8 12		9 47		11 7	1159			1 372	5							4 46		
Exeter (Queen St.)* ... arr.	8 20	32	9 54		1115	12 3	1235	1257	1 442	121	241	552	252	243	533	6	4 52		
144 ILFRACOMBE .... arr.	111		2 20			3 50			4 532	536	446	44							
143 PADSTOW	1253							4 39		6 326	32								
142 PLYMOUTH (Friary) ..	1143	1250	2 40			3 1			4 84	464	46								

Mls. fm London			aft	ngt	mrn	turn	mrn	mrn	mrn	mrn	mrn	mrn	mrn	mrn	mrn	mrn	mrn	mrn	mrn	mrn	aft	aft			mrn	mrn	mrn		mrn	mrn	mrn	aft	aft
154	WATERLOO .... dep	10y30	1200											6 0		7 249	R 0			9 30	1035	11 0		
154	Surbiton .... "	10y13	1013	0										6 15		7 339	17		9 48		
154	Woking .... "	11y 6	110	0										6 42		7 579	35		10 6		
48	Basingstoke .... dep	11y53	1 7										7 34		9 15	10 5		1045		
52½	Oakley												7 45		9 24		1054		
55½	Overton												7 52		9 30		11 0		
59½	Whitchurch A 51 ..		1 25										7 59		9 36		11 6		
61½	Hurstbourne		1 36										8 4		9 41		1111		
66½	Andover Junc. 79, 184											8 15		9 52	1028		1120		
72½	Grateley												8 27		10 3		1130		
78½	Porton 167												8 38		1012		1139		
83½	SALISBURY 55, 167 { arr.	2 36	1 59										8 48		1022	1050		1149	12 1	1226
184 { dep.	2 48	2 48	3 6		3 15					8 5	9 30	Stop	1054		11 3	12 3	1229
86½	Wilton B	mrn			3 21					8 11	9 36	Stop		11 9		
92	Dinton								8 20	9 46			11 19		
96½	Tisbury			3 43					8 28	9 54			11 27		
101½	Semley			3 55					8 38	10 4			11 36		
105½	Gillingham (Dorset)	3 40	3 40		4 4					8 47	1012			11 44		
112½	Templecombe 1076, 1077	3 53	3 53		4 16			7 15	8 41	9	512	1025		1131		1145		1157	1145
114½	Milborne Port			4 24			7 20	8 47	9 18	1034			12 45		
118½	Sherborne	4 7	4 7		4 33			7 26	8 54	9 25	1041		1145		1156		1211 1156		
123	Yeovil Junction 179b .. arr.	4 19	4 19		4 44			7 34	9	9 31	1049		1153		12 4	1219 12 4		
124½	179b YEOVIL (Town) { arr.	4 32	4 32		4 55		6 20	7 40 9	129	9 47	11 1		12 6		1231	1145		
2, 8 { dep.			Stop		7 45	9	28	1035	1145		1145		
—	Yeovil Junction .... dep.					6 20	7 51	9 39	1051	1155		12 5		1218		
126½	Sutton Bingham					7 56	9 46	1058		1210		1225		
131½	Crewkerne				6 41	8 1	9 55	1110		1221		1236		
139½	Chard Junction 179b ...				6 56	8 21	1013	1124		1235		1249		
143	179b CHARD { arr.					8 37	1034	1146		1 2		1 2		
{ dep.					8 10	9 34	1112		12 46		12 7		
—	Chard Junction .... dep.			6 57	8 22	1015	1125		12 46		1250		
144½	Axminster 179b .... arr.			7 5	8 30	1024	1132	1224		1244		1257		
151½	179b LYME REGIS { arr.				8 55	11 2		d1252			
{ dep.				8 5	10 5		1148		2 5		2 5		
—	Axminster			7 9	8 31	1027	1134	1225		1246		1258		
148	Seaton Junction 179b .. arr.			7 16	8 38	1034	1141	1232		1253		1 4		
152½	179b SEATON { arr.				8 55	1032	1248		1248		1 27		1 27						1 45
{ dep.				8 22	1012	1148			
—	Seaton Junction ...... dep.			7 20	8 39	1035	1142	1233		1245			2 12
155	Honiton			7 35	8 19	8 56	1052	1158		1 2			2 19
159½	Sidmouth Junc. 179c .. arr.			7 43	5 23	9 11	11 0	12 6	1255	1 13		1 54	2 27
167½	179c SIDMOUTH .... arr.			8 23	5 52	9 55	1132	1 38	1 38		2 23
171	179c BUDLEIGH SALTERTON "			9 0	9 58	1145	1 48	1 48		2 35
175½	179c EXMOUTH "			9 12	9 12	1019	mrn	1153	2 4	2 4		2 46
—	179c SIDMOUTH .... dep.			7 20		4 8		2 1	
—	Sidmouth Junction .... dep.			7 45	8 25	9 51	1047	11 2	12 7	1256	1 33		1 56	2 30
163½	Whimple			7 52	8 32	9 12	1054		1214	1 38			2 38
167	Broad Clyst			7 59	8 38	9 19	11 1		1 9			2 45
169	Pinhoe			8 4	8 43	9 24	11 6		1 13			2 50
171½	EXETER Central 179d arr.		4 39	8 1	8 50	9 32	1114	1118	1227	1 12	1 20	1 55		aft	1 41	2 12	2 58
182½	179d EXMOUTH { arr.		6 24		8 41			2 10	2 10	2 42		1 51	15	1 30	4 11
{ dep.				6 45	7 45	8 15	9 15	1045	1045	mrn	11	1215		
—	EXETER Central .... dep.		4 40	4 50		7 35	8 48	8 15	9 42	1137	1146	Stop	1 16	Stop		1 44	1 50	2 16	Stop
172½	Exeter (St. David's) .. "		4 45	5 0		7 41	8 26	8 51	9 47	1143	1151		1 23

In 1938 (bottom) there were more trains to Exeter by 11 am than there had been in 1922 by noon, although inevitably on this steam-hauled route the intermediate stopping services were at a leisurely pace. On this timetable only the 10.35 carries the 'Atlantic Coast Express' label, but it was occasionally applied to other departures around the same time, as it suited Waterloo's marketing plans. (Bradshaw)

Wartime saw the title dropped and the train given an earlier departure along with many more stops and often more carriages, leaving even the best of the Southern steam loco-motives struggling, so that it was no longer an express. Worst of all, with sixteen or more carriages, the train often had to be assembled outside Waterloo, having started as two portions on adjoining platforms, and at most stops, unless passengers could be marshalled in the right portion of the train, two stops had to be made so that everyone could board or

An aerial view of the end of the Southern's westward extension into Cornwall at Padstow, with the 'Atlantic Coast Express' rolling stock prominent. *(HRMS AES531)*

alight. This cumbersome procedure, intended to save fuel and make the best use of the available locomotives and rolling stock, was not unique to the 'Atlantic Coast Express', or indeed to the Southern, but instead was one of the many unattractive features of wartime travel by train.

It was not possible to return the train to the summer timetable for 1945, which did see many other improvements in services, and sadly no attempt was made to reinstate the train in 1946, so it was not until 6 October 1947, with the start of the winter timetable, that the 'Atlantic Coast Express' reappeared. The delay seems all the less excusable since summer 1947 had seen the introduction of a brand-new titled train, the 'Devon Belle'. However, it is true that there were shortages of rolling stock, and schedules were by no means back to peacetime frequencies or journey times, owing to wartime damage, the arrears of maintenance and the use of inferior coal, with supplies still not fully meeting demand. When revived, the wartime 10.50 am departure time was maintained, and arrivals continued to be later, with examples including Ilfracombe reached at 4.36 pm after a spell as a local all-stations train, and Plymouth at 4.55 pm. Post-nationalisation, 'ACE' continued, and was used in the locomotive exchange trials to see which of the Big Four companies' locomotives was best suited to the new railway. In due course, special rolling stock that had originated as a Southern Railway design, with Bulleid wide-bodied tavern cars decorated inside and out in some vague resemblance of a West Country pub, appeared, hauled by Bulleid's beautiful Pacifics, but in the longer term the train was fated. Overlap between companies was too much for the neat and tidy minds of the bureaucrats, and Waterloo had to surrender its Devon and Cornwall services to Paddington, ignoring the connections from the major cities of the south coast made possible by a line running through Woking and Salisbury. The number of possible destinations also suffered a dramatic reduction as the era of branch-line closures really began to bite. The 'ACE' trains disappeared at the end of summer 1964.

'Bournemouth Belle'

The 'Bournemouth Belle' was introduced at a time when the Southern Railway's appetite for luxury trains was at its peak, and it must have been a confident company indeed that could think of an all-Pullman train at a time when the economy was in a poor state, since the country took almost a decade to recover from the effects of the Great Depression. The old LSWR had provided Pullman cars on the Bournemouth route before the First World War, but afterwards had been content to serve the route with conventional restaurant cars.

Introduced for the summer 1931 timetable, the new train was scheduled to operate from Waterloo to Southampton and Bournemouth, where it divided and sent five carriages onwards to call at Poole, Wareham, Dorchester and Weymouth, while the other five ran the short distance to Bournemouth West, which was the terminus for the entire train on Sundays. Starting on Sunday 5 July 1931, the ten carriages consisted of first-class *Flora*, *Montana* and *Aurelia* and seven numbered but unnamed third-class cars, with four of the latter newly built for the service, giving 74 first-class and 240 third-class seats. As was the practice with Pullman trains, a supplement was payable, which varied between 1s 6d third-class Waterloo–Southampton and 4s first-class between Waterloo and Weymouth. While not as fast as the 'Bournemouth Limited', the 'Belle' was no slouch, despite the weight of the Pullman cars with their six-wheeled bogies, leaving Waterloo at 10.30 am to arrive at Southampton in 89 minutes for 80 miles, and taking just 2 hours 9 minutes to Bournemouth Central. In the Up direction, the train left Bournemouth Central at 5.10 pm and reached Waterloo at 7.18 pm. Initially the train was hauled by the 'King Arthur' class, but later workings became the preserve of the 'Lord Nelson' class.

Originally, the Southern had planned to run the train only during the summer months, but it was so popular that it was decided to retain Sunday workings throughout the year. Less profitable was the operation west of Bournemouth, and by 1932 it was decided that all trains would terminate at Bournemouth West. Despite the distance to Bournemouth, the luxury of the train and the supplementary fares, the day-tripper market was significant, and in 1932 this led to the evening return journey being put back to arrive at Waterloo at 8.30 pm, allowing a longer stay at Bournemouth, with an even later return in summer 1934 of 9.40 pm. By this time it seems clear that the Southern's confidence had been fully justified, but no one seems to have settled on a suitable time for the Up train and this varied between timetable issues. From 1 January 1936 the train became daily throughout the year, and six months later a two-hour Waterloo–Bournemouth schedule became standard, only slightly slower than the 'Atlantic Coast Express' at 54 mph end-to-end, largely owing to the call at Southampton. Sunday arrivals at Waterloo finally settled on 8.45 pm until the train was withdrawn for the duration of the Second World War on 10 September 1939.

It was an indication of the train's success and its reputation among what must have been a strong regular clientele that there was relatively little delay in reinstating it after the war ended. Starting on 7 October 1946, a full ten cars were available, including the first-class *Philomel*, *Lydia* and *Rosemary*, so that 66 seats were provided in first class, with another 236 third-class seats in the two brakes and five parlour/kitchen cars. Several of these cars had been refurbished ready for the service. The big difference was in the motive power, with a powerful 'Merchant Navy'-class locomotive, No. 21C18 *British India*, on the first postwar run. Leaving Waterloo at 12.30 pm, the train reached Southampton Central at 1.57 and Bournemouth Central at 2.35, before proceeding to Bournemouth West, where it arrived at 2.46. Station calls were just 2 minutes each. The return from Bournemouth West was at 7.15, reaching Waterloo at 9.25 pm. Given the operating problems of the day, and the weight of the train, this was a reasonably good schedule. The basic supplement in third class was just 3s.

Many have ascribed the Southern's enthusiasm for the reinstatement of its luxury train to a desire to sweep away austerity and boost national morale, and certainly this was a time when morale needed a boost. No less important, bringing Pullman cars out of storage helped to ease the critical rolling stock shortage at a difficult time, while for the traveller,

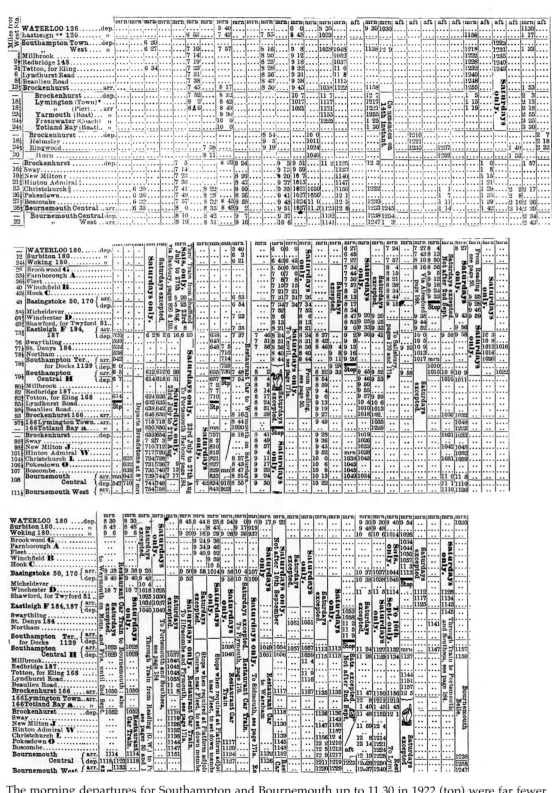

The morning departures for Southampton and Bournemouth up to 11.30 in 1922 (top) were far fewer than those in 1938 up to 10.30, when the 'Bournemouth Belle' managed the 108 miles to Bournemouth Central in just over 2 hours, including a stop at Southampton. *(Bradshaw)*

opulent accommodation and a reserved seat were an attractive proposition at a time when far too many trains were overcrowded and still making extra stops. Perhaps too the Southern Railway's management was forward-looking enough to appreciate that unless something was done quickly to cater for the top end of its market, many would be lured away by the motor car and the aeroplane.

Given this forward thinking, it seems strange that for the following summer timetable, the train reached Waterloo at 6.45 pm, giving just 2 hours in Bournemouth and putting an end to the day-tripper market. This may have reflected overwhelming demand from other users, but for the longer term it was short-sighted, breaking the concept of a luxurious day return to an up-market resort, with luncheon on the Down train and dinner on the Up train at attractive times for both meals. The only positive note was the acceleration to a 2 hour end-to-end schedule.

The train survived nationalisation, but initially with 5 minutes being added to the schedules in 1948, and remained until 1963, before further decelerations were reintroduced to allow for delays due to engineering works as electrification of the Bournemouth line pressed ahead. No attempt was made to continue the train after electrification, even though diesel-electric motive power had made an appearance latterly. The schedules also prevented any reinstatement of the day-tripper market. No doubt the bean counters of the nationalised railway placed more emphasis on saving wages with a 2 hour lay-over at Bournemouth than in growing the market!

'Bournemouth Limited'

Bournemouth was a relatively new resort at the beginning of the twentieth century, but one that had grown rapidly. Even before the outbreak of the First World War, the best trains managed the non-stop journey to Waterloo in just 2 hours, although timekeeping could be erratic on what was, for the period, a tight schedule. As soon as the war was over, pressure grew for the reinstatement of this service. A fast service between Bournemouth and Waterloo could be justified by virtue of the fact that most trains reaching Bournemouth continued to Poole, itself a not inconsiderable traffic generator, Dorchester and Weymouth.

Despite all of this, the pressures on the new company were great, and it had inherited a very mixed collection of assets, and almost immediately entered the years of the General Strike and the Depression, so it was not until 1929 that the summer schedule could accommodate the wishes of the people of Bournemouth. Two trains in each direction were accelerated using the still relatively new 'King Arthur' class locomotives and rather older corridor stock with a restaurant car. The trains were the 7.30 am from Weymouth, which left Bournemouth Central at 8.43, and then made a call at Southampton, before reaching Waterloo at 11.00, and the 4.30 pm Down. Faster still were the 10.30 am from Waterloo and the 5.15 pm from Bournemouth Central, which shaved 15 minutes off the best existing schedule to provide a flat 2 hour timing, and for which the title 'Bournemouth Limited' was coined. The name was not without meaning, because to keep to the exacting timings the formation had to be fixed at ten carriages, with the dining car, a composite and two corridor brake thirds providing the Weymouth portion, while the Swanage portion consisted of just a corridor brake third and corridor composite, leaving the remaining four carriages, a corridor first, a corridor third and two corridor brake thirds, to proceed to Bournemouth West. Only the portion for Bournemouth West was favoured with the 'Bournemouth Limited' roofboards.

The new service started on 8 July 1929, after a preview trip the previous Wednesday. From time to time the Southern succumbed to the temptation to add extra carriages, including an extra dining car, and it seems that timekeeping was not always all that might have been expected. Even so, in 1934 the summer timetable provided a 3 hour timing between Weymouth and Waterloo. Other changes included diverting the restaurant car to the Bournemouth West portion. In 1935 the times between Bournemouth and Waterloo were trimmed to cut 2 minutes off the 2 hour schedule. The service also benefited when the newer 'Schools' class locomotives were cascaded from Fratton to Bournemouth following the Portsmouth electrification, allowing the weight of the typical train to be raised from 330 tons to 365 tons, yet still managing an improvement in timekeeping. Other minor improvements sought to provide a better service from Swanage, offering the choice of a cross-platform connection at Wareham instead of an earlier departure on the Swanage portion that stopped at all stations, but this also added extra minutes to the Weymouth portion.

The outbreak of the Second World War meant the end of the train, which almost immediately lost its name, and while it could still be traced in the timetable, inevitably wartime conditions meant that extra stops were added and timings much extended. Nevertheless, even before the outbreak of war, there was a luxury rival for the more affluent market, the 'Bournemouth Belle'.

'Brighton Belle'

The 'Brighton Belle' was simply a renaming of the 'Southern Belle', taking over that train's still-new electric Pullman multiple units on Friday 29 June 1934, and riding on the back of the publicity associated on that day with the opening at the Sussex resort of what was then the world's largest covered seawater bathing pool. When the 11.00 am arrived at Brighton, it was formally renamed by the mayor, who then went off to open the new swimming pool. As with the 'Southern Belle', two 5 BEL units were used, with a third unit in reserve for maintenance.

These were the days when large crowds, few of whom would have regarded themselves as enthusiasts, would turn up for a railway event, such as the naming ceremony for the 'Brighton Belle', at Brighton, of course! *(NRM 57/98)*

The new service continued to work on the 'Southern Belle' timings until the outbreak of war in September 1939, when the name was dropped. For a while the Pullman units were dispersed to work in tandem with ordinary Brighton express stock, until all Pullman services were finally withdrawn in May 1942. Before this, set 3052 had been damaged by enemy action when caught in an air raid at Victoria at 10.30 pm on 9 October 1940.

A return to full Pullman working was not possible until the damaged unit had been repaired, but from 6 May 1946 there was a reversion to the practice of the early war years of running hybrid unnamed trains with the two undamaged units supporting a conventional non-Pullman set, usually a 6 PAN. On 6 October 1947 the damaged unit was repaired and back in service, and the 'Brighton Belle' returned to the timetables. The only difference with the pre-war timetable was that there was just one return working on a Sunday, at 11.00 am down and 5.25 pm up. After nationalisation, the summer 1948 timetable saw the full pre-war timetable reinstated. In later years the train was to operate four return journeys, and even accelerate to a 55 minute timing with the arrival of new electric multiple units, the 4 CIG and 4 BIG, to the Brighton line after the 'Brighton Belle's standard 6 PUL and 6 PAN contemporaries were withdrawn. By that time, of course, the 'Belle' offered the only Pullman cars in the south, and all good things came to an end when, on Sunday 30 April 1972, the service operated for the last time, despite intense pressure from regular travellers who included many famous stars of stage and screen, and for whom the 11 pm from Victoria seems to have been a substitute for the Green Room!

Channel Island and French Boat Trains

The London & South Western Railway had originally acquired Southampton Docks, and set about developing this new asset with an enthusiasm that was only surpassed by the Southern Railway. There were two types of passenger service from Southampton, the railway-operated packet service to France and the Channel Islands, and the deep-sea ocean liners, which here have been grouped under the 'Ocean Liner Expresses'.

Given the enthusiasm for the docks and even for the connecting air services of the so-called 'Flying-Boat Train', it seems strange that the boat trains were simply referred to in the working timetables as the 'Continental Express', and it was not until after nationalisation that named trains for specific routes and ships appeared.

'City Limited'

Another train inherited from the LBSC, the 'City Limited' was very much a commuter train, although the term 'commuter' was not in use at the time. In many ways, the title was misleading, since it operated to and from London Bridge, on the wrong side of the River Thames from the City of London, but it was aimed fairly and squarely at the 'City' market, running its clientele non-stop from Brighton to London, and home again in the evening. The train originated in a service that actually did run to and from Cannon Street, comfortably within the City of London, in 1867, and although operated for less than a year and never named, this service has been credited with having the title unofficially. The train first appeared officially in the timetables on 7 February 1921, taking over from a train that had departed Brighton at 8.45 am and was re-timed as the 'City Limited', departing at 8.48 am and reaching London Bridge at 9.50. In the Down direction, it departed from London Bridge at 5 pm and ran non-stop to Brighton in an hour. The service did not operate on Sundays, and the afternoon service operated Monday to Friday only.

Initally, there were no refreshment facilities on the train, although a special rake of wide carriages with 'balloon' rather than the still-common clerestory roofs was used, and these were also unusual in having recessed doors. There was first- and third-class accommodation in a mixture of open saloons and compartments. For a year from 14 July 1924, the Up schedule was reduced to an hour, but this must have been over-optimistic as on 13 July 1925 the original schedule was reintroduced. Motive power was provided by the

LSBC 'L' class 4–6–2Ts, including the famous First World War memorial locomotive *Remembrance*.

Late in 1925, an eleven-carriage set of corridor stock, numbered 471, was completed at Lancing for the train, with 312 first-class and 192 third-class seats in seven first-class, one third, a composite and two third-class brakes. In spring 1926 one of the first-class carriages was replaced by the Pullman *Princess Patricia*, allowing the timetable to advertise the service as a 'First Class Pullman Breakfast' in the Up direction, and a 'First Class Pullman Tea' in the Down direction. A further attempt to cut the Up timing to an hour came on 9 July 1928, with an 8.45 am departure from Brighton, and this remained until the train was officially withdrawn on 31 December 1932.

Withdrawal came about because of electrification, as the Southern did not intend to abandon its 'City' customers, possibly because many of them were probably shareholders. The Southern built three special six-carriage electric multiple units designated 6 CIT, numbered 2041–3. Usually with two coupled together, they had a high proportion of first-class seats, including the Pullmans *Gwladys*, *Olive* and *Ethel*, so that in twelve carriages there were 276 first-class and 244 third-class seats. While the name of 'City Limited' lingered on among railwaymen and the regulars for the new service, the title was dropped completely for the Up service, although by an oversight it remained in the timetable for the Down service until July 1934. After this, the service appears to have steadily declined, with fewer first-class seats and longer timings in the years immediately preceding the Second World War.

'City Expresses'

On 1 July 1896 the LCDR introduced the 'City Express to the Kent Coast', which left Holborn Viaduct at 6.10 pm, called at St Paul's at 6.12, and then ran non-stop to Westgate-on-Sea, where it arrived at 6.45, reaching Margate at 6.51, Broadstairs at 7 pm and Ramsgate at 7.05. As with the 'Cliftonville Express', a portion was slipped at Faversham which reached Ramsgate 20 minutes after the main train. An Up working was not introduced until 6 June 1898, departing on Mondays from Ramsgate at 7.45 am and eventually arriving at St Paul's at 9.48. This service became a weekday service the following month, before becoming a Mondays-only service again in the winter. Numerous amendments were made to the service over the next few years before the title was dropped in 1905.

On 11 July 1921 the title 'City Express' was applied to a number of existing trains in the SECR timetable, including two Up trains, one of which proudly announced that it did not carry luggage!

By the time the Southern Railway inherited these trains, Pullman cars had been added to the rakes of several of them, while there were also Saturday-only Down services shortly after 1 pm. In February 1923 there was a morning Up 'City Express' leaving Ramsgate Harbour at 7.05 am, reaching Cannon Street at 9.20, with another train leaving Margate at 8.03 to arrive in London at 10.08, as well as two Up workings by the 'Thanet Express'. Pullman cars had also spread to a number of unnamed trains. The service reached its best performance in July 1926, when the first 'City Express' departure was the 7.30 am from Ramsgate Harbour, which reached Cannon Street at 9.24, but by January 1927 this had to be eased to a more practical 7.26 departure. That summer saw the various 'City Express' titles dropped.

'Cliftonville Express'

Originating with a summer weekday service in 1894 that survived from July to September and ran from Holborn Viaduct to Ramsgate Harbour in the Down direction only, the 'Cliftonville Express' service was reinstated in 1911, after more than six years without a named train on the SECR. The service ran from Victoria to Ramsgate Harbour. Inevitably, the train was dropped during the First World War, and its return was delayed by the coal miners' strike of 1921.

The 'Cliftonville Express' recommenced operations on 11 July 1921, leaving Victoria at 9.00 am and reaching Margate West at 10.35, Broadstairs at 10.47 and Ramsgate Harbour at 10.55. Meanwhile, a portion had been slipped at Faversham to provide a stopping service which also eventually reached Ramsgate Harbour at 11.21. In the Up direction, the train left Ramsgate Harbour at 5 pm and arrived at Victoria at 6.58. The service operated daily throughout the summer, but on winter Sundays operated in the Up direction only, when it was combined with the 'Thanet Pullman Limited'. A first-class Pullman tea car was added to weekday Up services in February 1922. That summer, the train returned to full daily service, but the departure from Victoria was advanced to 8.45 am, and timings were accelerated so that it reached Margate West at 10.17, Broadstairs at 10.30 and Ramsgate Harbour at 10.36, where the slip portion caught up at 11.01. Unusually, the train differed in each direction, with the Down train consisting of a three-carriage set accompanied by two third-class compartment carriages, and the slip portion including a three-coach set and a slip brake composite. The Up train included two brake thirds, a lavatory third (still something of a luxury on the SECR, whose customers were expected to have strong bladders), another three thirds, three composites and the Pullman, with only the lavatory third having a corridor.

Grouping saw little immediate change, with the Sunday service for the 1922/23 winter similar to that of the previous winter, and this was repeated for 1923/24. That summer the Down train was put back to 9.06 am, losing the slip portion and calling at Faversham, Margate West and Broadstairs to reach Ramsgate Harbour at 11.10, except on Saturday when it left at 8.50. The return train left at 5.05 pm, but omitted the call at Faversham, and also lost the Pullman car on Sundays, and eventually reached Victoria at 7 pm, except on Saturdays when it was 12 minutes later and Sundays when it arrived at 7.07. Thereafter, the timetable was varied with every seasonal change, including a Dover portion for the Down train during the winter of 1925/26. For summer 1927 the title was dropped, although the service continued.

This was most definitely not one of the Southern Railway's luxury trains, having developed out of a plan for a service to the Thanet coast that was both fast and cheap.

'Devon Belle'

In an attempt to blow away postwar austerity, and make use of stored Pullman carriages, for the summer timetable in 1947 the Southern Railway launched a new titled train between Waterloo and Devon, the 'Devon Belle'. The opportunity was also taken to reintroduce seat reservations, generally still suspended for ordinary trains as many wartime restrictions lingered on into peacetime. The absence of reservations in a period of rolling stock shortages was a cause of considerable discomfort for passengers on longer journeys. Despite shortages of materials, it proved possible to convert two Pullman carriages into observation cars at Preston Park, Brighton, fitting these with just twenty-seven seats, each designed to be comfortable for a short period and ensure a steady turnover of custom for the bar at the other end of the coach. Two complete sets of Pullman cars were provided, with the train departing from Waterloo on Fridays, Saturdays and Sundays at noon, and dividing at Exeter Central with one portion going forward to Plymouth, reached at 5.36 pm and the other to Ilfracombe, reached at 5.32 pm. Pullman supplementary fares were charged, varying from 3s 6d third class Waterloo to Exeter to 8s first class Waterloo to Ilfracombe. The Up train left Plymouth at 11.30 am and Ilfracombe at noon, reaching Waterloo at 5.20 pm.

The Southern lacked water troughs for its locomotives, and the limited water capacity of the 'Merchant Navy' class meant that a non-stop run from Waterloo to Exeter was impossible, so locomotives had to be changed at Wilton South and then again at Exeter, where a lighter weight 'West Country' or 'Battle of Britain' Pacific took over because of the weight restrictions on the Southern lines in the south-west. The train having divided at Exeter, the smaller Pacifics were capable of a sparkling performance, especially on the Plymouth section where they were hauling just four carriages.

'West Country' class 21C101 *Exeter* at Exeter St David's with the 'Devon Belle'. Bulleid introduced an unusual numbering system for his Pacifics. *(HRMS AET006)*

The Plymouth portion would have a Pullman third parlour car with 36 seats, a first-class kitchen car with 22 seats, a third-class kitchen with 36 seats and a third-class brake with 30 seats. The Ilfracombe portion had a first parlour car with 24 seats and two first kitchen cars with 22 seats each, as well as a third parlour car with 42 seats, two third-class kitchens, one with 30 and the other with 36 seats, a third-class brake and the observation car.

The train was an immediate success, so that by August, ten carriages were rostered for the Ilfracombe section, giving the 'Merchant Navy' locomotives used between Waterloo and Exeter the demanding task of hauling a fourteen-carriage train. The following year, an additional Down service was added on Thursdays and a balancing Up service on Mondays. By this time the railways had been nationalised and weekday seat reservations had been reintroduced, so that some of the appeal of the train had gone, with the Plymouth portion abandoned. Despite plans to withdraw the service in 1952, the 'Devon Belle' lingered on until September 1954, when it was withdrawn for the winter, but not reinstated for the 1955 summer season. The reintroduction of the 'Atlantic Coast Express' also undermined much of its *raison d'être*.

'East & West Through Train'

This was the predecessor of 'The Tourist', which connected east Wight with west Wight.

'Eastbourne Sunday Limited'

The LBSC had operated an 'Eastbourne Pullman Limited' before the First World War, and with the addition of some ordinary third-class accommodation on Sundays this became the

'Eastbourne Sunday Limited' in 1913. After being suspended during the First World War, the train was reintroduced on 4 December 1921, but with both classes of Pullman stock and no ordinary carriages. Departure from Victoria was at 10.45 am and from Eastbourne at 6.45 pm, with a 90-minute non-stop timing in each direction. Under Southern management, the timings were reduced to 85 minutes in October 1923, and then to 80 minutes on 1 January 1933. The number of cars varied between five and nine, and in 1933 the ex-'Southern Belle' steam-hauled Pullmans (only eight years old) took over the service. Locomotive power varied, and at first included the 'B4x' 4–4–0s, but these were later replaced by 'King Arthurs' or 'L1' 2 4–4–0s, and then by 'Schools' class locomotives.

The train disappeared on electrification in 1935, although a hint of what might have been came after nationalisation, when a 'Brighton Belle' unit was used to provide an unnamed Eastbourne return working on Sundays for a period of about nine years.

The 'Flying-Boat Train'

When the Empire Air Mail Scheme was inaugurated in 1937, the Southern found another opportunity with what became popularly known as the 'Flying-Boat Train', a name that was used in a magazine article on the service. The famous Short Empire flying-boats could only accommodate around twenty-four passengers apiece, so the term 'train' remained something of an unofficial term. The reality was that the regular 8.30 am departure from Waterloo to Southampton and Bournemouth was strengthened twice a week by one or two Pullman carriages and a brake, with roof boards on the carriages proclaiming 'Imperial Airways Empire Services', and these vehicles were detached from the train at Southampton Central, and shunted to No. 50 Berth in the docks, where the passengers transferred to fast motor launches to be taken to the flying-boat terminus just off Hythe. The twice-weekly flights to Australia via India and to Africa left on the same day and about the same time to make the railway service worthwhile. Waterloo to flying-boat took just 3 hours, and passengers were accompanied by the Imperial Airways flight clerk, who had to handle passenger documentation and prepare the manifest for the air mail and freight en route.

After the completion of a new London terminus near Victoria for Imperial Airways, which became the British Overseas Airways Corporation on its merger with the original British Airways in 1940, the service switched to Victoria and ran to Poole, from where transatlantic flying-boat services operated, mainly for VIP passengers.

'Golden Arrow'

Undoubtedly one of the most famous named trains anywhere, the name originated with the decision to provide a network of overnight Wagons Lits and daytime Pullman services throughout Europe. This was an Anglo-French venture with a ferry link between Dover and Calais. In France, the Paris–Calais Pullman boat train was known as *La Flèche d'Or*, but the all-first-class Pullman train introduced between London and Dover in July 1926 was at first unnamed. It was not until 15 May 1929 that the name was adopted, following with the introduction of a specially commissioned cross-Channel steamer for the service, the TSS *Canterbury*, built by William Denny at Dumbarton. The train left Victoria at 11.10 am and reached Dover Marine non-stop at 12.35, with a 12.55 sailing and eventual arrival in Paris Nord at 5.35 pm. In the reverse direction, passengers left Paris at 12 noon, reached Calais at 3.10, left Dover at 4.57 and reached Victoria at 6.35. All of this was just £5 single, including reservations and supplements. Heavy luggage could be collected and delivered for a small additional fee, which also covered Customs inspection arranged by the Southern Railway and, on the London-bound journey, delivery was promised within the London area during the evening of arrival. The Pullman cars were initially hauled by 'Lord Nelson' class locomotives. One of these, *Sir Richard Grenville* (E853), managed to derail itself while running through Kent House station on the Up journey on 23 January 1930. It damaged a quarter of a mile of track and safely rerailed itself without the driver or fireman noticing.

The palatial dining room on the *Canterbury* – a not altogether successful posed shot! *(NRM BTC-collection 1434/63)*

This was an event that spoke volumes about the quality of ride on some of the Southern's metals, especially on the Eastern Section!

The concept of a luxury train between London and Paris, then as now the main European business route and the main leisure route, seemed to be the key to success. Yet the early 1930s saw a further bout of recession and, although not immediately appreciated, the situation may have been aggravated by growing competition from the air, which the Southern admitted in later years was affecting its continental traffic, especially at the upper end. For international traffic the recession was worsened by the devaluation of sterling, which made any travel outside the sterling area much more expensive. The result was that with effect from 15 May 1931 the sea crossings of the 11 am 'Golden Arrow' were combined with those for the 11.15 departure from Victoria to the continent, although to maintain some semblance of a better service, the 11.15 was advanced by 30 minutes to 10.45, so that at least the premium traffic had a shorter through journey time. This change was accompanied by a reduction in the through first-class Pullman fare to £4 12s 6d. A year later, worse was to follow, with the two trains combined so that the 'Golden Arrow' became an ordinary continental boat train with ordinary first- and third-class passengers, as well as a reduced number of Pullman cars. This radical move highlights the gravity of the situation, for traffic had not simply fallen, it had plummeted, from an annual average during the late 1920s of 1,500,000 to just 975,000 in 1932. Even when recovery came, it was nothing like complete, with the 1933–5 average rising to just 1,125,000, a fall of 25 per cent over a period of ten years. Given the limited capacity of the airliners of the day and the poor frequency of flights compared to those of today, air competition alone certainly could not be blamed for a slump of this level.

The original concept of the 'Golden Arrow'/'*Flèche d'Or*' had been on a grand scale with scant regard for costs, and this was all the more marked on the French side. The 'Golden Arrow' made what by today's demanding standards would be regarded as insufficient use of a single rake of very well-appointed rolling stock; the '*Flèche d'Or*' made even less use of two such rakes. From 6 October 1935 the answer was to advance the timing of the Paris departure to 10.30 and divert the service via Boulogne, so that a single set of Pullman cars would now suffice for the '*Flèche d'Or*', although these would have to make a hasty and non-revenue earning run from Boulogne to Calais to collect the Paris-bound passengers afterwards! This must have affected the reliability of the London to Paris operation, and it also meant that the *Canterbury* only appeared on one leg of the service each day. Some hint of exclusiveness was revived in November 1938, with an extensive renovation of the eight ordinary first- and third-class carriages, which were also painted in a new shade of olive green, or 'Dover' as it was known initially to the Southern, with four 'Lord Nelson' class locomotives painted to match. By this time there were just four Pullman cars on the train. The service at this stage seemed to be fated, for within a year of the new look being introduced to the ordinary rolling stock, the service was abandoned when the port of Dover was closed to civilian traffic on 4 September 1939, the day after the Second World War started.

Nevertheless, the 'Golden Arrow' was the first luxury train to make a reappearance after the war ended, resuming on 15 April 1946. Some observers of the railway scene postwar have described the reintroduction in terms of a 'single-handed attempt to dispel postwar austerity', but the timetable told a tale of track, especially in France, that had been affected by enemy attack, wartime traffic demands and neglect because of shortages of materials and skilled labour. The new timings involved a 10 am departure from Victoria, with a slightly longer journey to reach Dover at 11.40, while it took from 2.47 to 6.45 to travel from Calais to Paris Nord. In the return direction, the train left Paris Nord at 11.35 and reached Calais at 3.30. Departure from Dover was at 6.50 pm, with a 8.30 arrival at Victoria. An innovation was that the 'Golden Arrow' now offered third-class Pullman accommodation, but since this was not reciprocated on the French side, these passengers had to travel non-Pullman second class in France. The French train also continued to be a mixture of ordinary and Pullman stock, but the Southern reverted to running a second train for the non-Pullman passengers. A more practical innovation on the British side was the introduction of the 'Merchant Navy' class Pacifics to the service. *Canterbury* resumed her service as the ferry for the 'Golden Arrow' service, but carrying all classes of passenger, and for a short period she was the only ship to make regular daily sailings between Dover and Calais. She was also the first ship in the Southern fleet to be fitted with radar. The use of a single platform at Victoria, No. 6, for the first time now meant that the barrier could be suitably embellished. For the first time too, the locomotives received the 'plunging' golden arrow emblem on the smokebox doors, below which were flown small Union Flags and Tricolours from just above the buffer beam.

That winter, another packet, *Invicta*, launched in 1939 but taken up by the Admiralty and not 'demobbed' until after the war, took over from the *Canterbury*. The French adopted the British practice of separate trains for Pullman and ordinary passengers, while in May 1947 both the British and French trains became all-first-class Pullman again. Timings also improved, with a departure from London at 9 am giving a 5.50 arrival at Paris, while a noon departure from Paris resulted in arrival in London at 7 pm.

After nationalisation, the train survived, receiving a new set of Pullmans for the Festival of Britain, and at one stage being pulled by 'Britannia' class locomotives. Eventually, as with the later years of the 'Brighton Belle', the Pullmans were repainted in the British Rail colours of blue and pale grey, for which they were never designed, and the service was finally withdrawn on 30 September 1972.

'Granville Express'

On 11 July 1921, after an interval of almost twenty years, the 'Granville Express' was reintroduced as a weekday service, with an Up departure from Ramsgate Harbour at 10 am, with calls at Broadstairs, Margate West, Westgate-on-Sea and Sittingbourne, reaching Victoria at 12.08. The Down train left the London terminus at 3.15, and only called at Margate West and Broadstairs before arriving at Ramsgate Harbour at 5.07. For a supplement of 2s, first-class travellers had the luxury of a Pullman car, which was described, perhaps rather disappointingly, as a buffet car for the Up train and a tea car for the Down service. In 1922 the Sittingbourne call was removed, allowing arrival at Victoria to be 3 minutes earlier. The Pullman car apart, the train was hardly the last word in luxury, as the other rolling stock included three non-corridor carriages, two compartment thirds and a composite.

Under Southern management the Sittingbourne call was reinstated in 1923, with the Down service taking an extra 10 minutes on Saturdays, but dropped again the following summer, when the Saturday Down train lost its title. A number of minor timetable changes followed over the next couple of years before the title was dropped for good for the summer 1927 timetable, although the actual departures remained as standard anonymous trains.

'Night Ferry'

Unique in British railway history, this was the first train to carry its passengers from London to Paris, and vice versa, without the need to change – although claims that one could go to sleep in one city and wake up in the other were probably wide of the mark! It was also the train that the author found, at least twice, people refused to believe existed, losing him what could have been an enjoyable and profitable magazine commission on the second occasion!

Train ferries were not new, with the first in Britain completed in 1849, while a later one had operated from Langstone Harbour to Bembridge on the Isle of Wight. Over the years there were a number of proposals for train ferries across the English Channel, while the concept of a Channel Tunnel surfaced from time to time, having originally first been mooted as early as 1802. Given the great drive and bold innovation of the Victorians, it seems strange that nothing happened to produce a train ferry for the Channel for many

A relatively rare shot of a locomotive with 'Night Ferry' rolling stock, in this case 'Battle of Britain' class 21C156 *Croydon*. (*NRM Cawston Collection SR145*)

years, although the lack of enthusiasm for a tunnel was justified by fears over national security.

The possibility of a through train between London and Paris was first aired on 27 November 1930, when Sir Herbert Walker told his fellow directors of a proposal for a train ferry between Dover and Boulogne, while the following month he advised them that the French were planning a ferry for goods traffic. The French intended to operate between Calais and Richborough, a suburb of Sandwich in Kent that had been used as a port for the BEF during the First World War. The Southern wanted any ferry to use Boulogne in France, and anywhere but Richborough in England. The Southern's objection to Richborough was that it would form an isolated part of the operation, but the French saw it as attractive as it had handled military goods train ferries during the war. Nevertheless, it was the Southern Railway view that prevailed at first and in 1931 the two railways settled on Dover–Boulogne, while the Southern undertook to invest in the necessary shipping. Even so, with cross-Channel traffic moving towards recession, it was only the threat by the French to introduce a Calais–Harwich service that forced the Southern's directors to act in November 1932, and the following month as a compromise it was agreed that the French port should be Dunkirk. The threat of a Calais–Harwich service seems to have been a strange one to make, since this would have involved a most roundabout railway and steamer journey.

Three ships were ordered from Swan Hunter on the Tyne, all named after crossing points on the River Thames. These were the *Twickenham Ferry, Hampton Ferry* and *Shepperton Ferry*, all 359 ft in length, although the beam varied between 62 ft 10 in and 63 ft 9 in, so that the tonnage also varied between 2,839 and 2,996. Maximum speed for these coal-fired ships was 16½ knots. The train decks had two tracks running from the stern, with two sidings branching out, and provided accommodation for twelve sleeping cars. Below the train deck there was also a smaller deck for motor vehicles. Delays in getting the special dock ready at Dover meant that the ships were delivered in 1934 and 1935, but had to be laid up until October 1936. The ships themselves proved to be unsteady during sea trials, requiring heavy permanent ballasting, with more than 200 tons of discarded railway track concreted over and taking up part of the lower deck intended for motor vehicles. French pride, and no doubt trade union intransigence, meant that the crew of a French ferry due to be replaced by the new ships be transferred to one of the vessels, so on 22 September 1936 *Twickenham Ferry* was transferred to the French flag.

The *Wagons Lits* rolling stock was specially constructed to meet the British loading gauge, which required them to be lower and narrower than usual. Each of the twelve carriages had nine compartments with upper and lower berths, with four of the compartments having inter-connecting doors to convert into four-berth compartments. The doors at each end of the carriages were inward opening. The carriages were all fitted with securing rings, allowing them to be chained to the deck of the ferry. Three guard's vans with baggage accommodation were built by the Southern and painted to match the blue passenger rolling stock, while the French Nord railway modified a dozen of its existing four-wheel vans to a similar pattern. There were also another 100 vans and 50 wagons built by the Southern for international freight use.

Given the time spent on preparations, the start of the 'Night Ferry' was an anticlimax. On 5 October 1936 the 11 pm departure from Victoria had its carriages shunted on to the *Hampton Ferry*. Once aboard, the twenty-five passengers got out and went to their cabins, while the carriages were shunted off and twenty-six freight wagons loaded. At 2 the following morning the ship sailed for Dunkirk, while the *Twickenham Ferry* brought thirty-seven passengers in the opposite direction, as well as four empty *Wagons Lits* sleeping cars, three of which were intended for public display at the Southern's main London termini, while the fourth was retained at Dover for crew training.

Official inauguration ceremonies often bear little relationship to the start of a service, but the 'Night Ferry' inauguration was an extreme example of this! On Monday 12 October 1936 the French ambassador reached Dover Marine at 10.23 am on a special train. The VIPs

The train deck of the 'Night Ferry' ship is certainly an uncommon sight, yet photographs of it are rare. These are goods wagons on the deck of the *Twickenham Ferry*. While great care was taken to shunt carriages gently and quietly on to and off the ferries, nothing could be done to quieten the essential shackling of the rolling stock to the decks. *(NRM BTC-collection 691/9/65)*

and guests then embarked on *Hampton Ferry*, so that the ambassador could wave a green flag to signal the shunting of four sleeping cars on to the ship. The party then left the ship so that the ambassador could make his way to the pump house and press a bell push to open the dock gates, and at 11.55 the *Hampton Ferry* set off for Calais. Many of the party went with her, and disembarked to travel to Paris for a special celebratory dinner, at which Sir Herbert Walker was invested as a Commander of the *Légion d'Honneur*, while the *Hampton Ferry* then made her way along the French coast to unload the sleeping cars at Dunkirk. Far more realistic was the return journey that night of the 189 VIPs and guests who actually used the 'Night Ferry' service, sailing on the *Twickenham Ferry*. It is maintained that this was the only occasion when all twelve cars were used on the train. Arriving at Dover on 13 October, the ship was damaged as she reversed on to the link span, and then the last sleeping car off the ship was derailed, possibly by the damage to the ship, leaving Walker and some other VIPs to be transferred to another carriage. They could at least count themselves lucky that the whole operation hadn't been affected by the first car being derailed! The undamaged eleven cars were taken to London by two trains, one hauled by a 'Schools' class and the other by a 'Lord Nelson' class, with the former including a Pullman and a number of ordinary carriages.

The regular public service commenced on 14 October from London, and 15 October from Paris. Trains left Victoria each evening at 10, travelling via Dover Marine to be shunted from there to the ferry berth, from which the ship, or 'boat' as the landlubbers at the Southern Railway would always have it, sailed at 12.35, reaching Dunkirk at 4.30. Departure from Dunkirk was at 5.10, with arrival at Paris Nord at 8.55. In the reverse direction, trains left Paris at 9.50 and reached the ship at 1.30, with the sailing at 2 am to arrive at Dover at 6 am. Leaving the ship at 6.39, London Victoria was reached at 8.30. To justify the service, ordinary carriages were always attached to the trains. The all-inclusive sleeping car rate, including a gratuity for the conductor, was £4 19s 6d single, £9 4s return first class, and £3 16s 6d single, £7 2s return second class. The class structure reflected continental practice, where three classes were normally provided, but not on Pullman or Wagons Lits services. The first-class fare compared favourably with that for the 'Golden Arrow', for an operation that must have been considerably more expensive.

The operation was beset with problems. It took time to secure the rolling stock and more time to reverse the process, while the state of the tide could affect the time it took to enter and leave the dock. The 'Lord Nelson' class locomotives found the trains difficult, and double-heading by 'D1' or 'L1' classes was more common. The ships were all found to have problems with their bow rudders. Then there were the inevitable problems in keeping time during the winter storms, so much so that by 1 December 1936 the arrival time at Victoria was put back to 9.05 am. At least the decision had also been taken to provide a Pullman car on the British leg of the service, providing supper for early arrivals at Victoria on London departures, or breakfast on the way inwards, rather than the continental breakfast that was the best the *Wagons Lits* conductor could manage. Unaccustomed to international trains, British Customs refused to conduct examinations on the trains, so a separate third-class Pullman also had to be introduced to serve breakfast to those passengers travelling in the ordinary carriages.

Those with experience of being on a passenger train while being coupled or uncoupled, and shunted, may well doubt the claim that the 'Night Ferry' passenger could go to bed in London and wake up in Paris. In fact, those who experienced travel on the 'Night Ferry' maintain that the shunting itself was indeed quiet and gentle on both sides of the Channel – the problem lay with the noise created by shackling and unshackling the carriages to the deck of the ship! One or two also noted that passengers were locked into the carriages for the crossing, which made them feel uneasy in case of a collision since they risked being trapped. Fortunately, on the one occasion that the train ferry did suffer a collision in fog, during the early hours of the morning of 28 May 1937, the damage was not serious, although the ferry and the London-bound train were both delayed.

Unlike most of the other titled trains, the 'Night Ferry' was suspended after the services of 25/26 August 1939, a week before the outbreak of the Second World War.

The value of the train ferries to the British Army meant that the 'Night Ferry' could not be reinstated quickly once hostilities ended, and there was further delay while the ships were refitted, including conversion to oil-burning. There were also only nine *Wagons Lits* cars left. It is not clear whether the three missing cars were lost at Paris or London, and whether they were bombed or perhaps taken by the military as accommodation in Europe. Time was running out for the Southern. It was hoped that the through service would start on 1 December 1947, but the French were having a railway strike, and it was not until the night of 14/15 December that operations started, with the welcome addition of a 'Battle of Britain' class steam locomotive for the Victoria to Dover leg. The following night the outbound ferry was badly delayed at Dunkirk as another ferry was trapped behind the dock gates, with a corresponding late arrival in Paris.

The 'Night Ferry' survived nationalisation, although it must have been a drain on the finances of both British Railways and the SNCF. In its usual way, BR subjected the service to death by a thousand cuts, reducing breakfast custom with a too early arrival at Victoria, and then taking off the breakfast car. Towards the end, after electrification of the lines to the Kent coast, BR also put the foot passengers on a separate electric multiple unit, running two trains instead of one. It might have been expected that the Channel Tunnel would have been the death knell for the 'Night Ferry', but when the end did come it was for a far more mundane reason – the service was abandoned after the departures of 31 October 1980 so that space on the ferries could be allocated completely to freight traffic.

'Ocean Liner Express'

In addition to the development of services to the Channel Islands and France, the Southern Railway's development of Southampton Docks saw the port emerge as the pre-eminent liner port for the United Kingdom, as gradually services were moved from Liverpool and London to the south coast. The Southern started work on a new Ocean Terminal, making use of space freed in the old docks by the new Western Docks developed between the wars, but wartime intervened and the project could not be completed until after nationalisation. Growth was helped by the ability of liners from the Netherlands and France to call at the port en route, but it also had its own transatlantic services by Cunard and United States

Lines, and its African services by Union Castle, later operated jointly with Safmarine. The period between the two world wars was the heyday of the large ocean liners, but it was not until after the opening of the new Ocean Terminal in the old docks in 1950 that named trains for the various shipping lines began to make an appearance, commencing in 1952.

The 'Southern Belle'

The Victoria to Brighton 'Southern Belle' was inherited by the Southern Railway, a legacy of the LBSC, which had introduced this, the first daily all-Pullman train in the British Isles, on 1 November 1908. It was the successor to the 'Brighton Limited', a service inaugurated in January 1899, some years after the company had introduced its first Pullman cars. The service had been suspended both for the First World War and again for most of 1921 as a result of the coal miners' strike in the spring.

An unusual feature of the 'Southern Belle' was that this was not a once-daily train, but one that ran twice a day in each direction. On weekdays both classes of traveller were catered for, but on Sundays the train was first class only. Despite the limited motive power available and the weight of the Pullman cars, the journey was completed non-stop in exactly one hour, and on a Sunday the day-tripper could spend 9½ hours at the Sussex resort. The Southern added some new Pullman cars to the original American cars, and introduced the 'King Arthur' class steam locomotives to the train, which frequently comprised ten or more Pullman cars. The final steam-hauled run of the 'Southern Belle' was on 31 December 1932, when it arrived 1¼ minutes early, and had it not been for signal checks might have managed the trip in 55 minutes.

The next day, the new all-electric Pullman service was introduced, with the Pullman motor coaches the heaviest to run on British lines at 62 tons apiece, and also long by the standards of the day at 68 ft 8¾ in over the buffers. The other innovation was the increase in the schedule to three return journeys daily, leaving London Victoria at 11 am, 3 pm (not Sundays) and 7 pm, and Brighton at 1.25 (not Sundays), 5.25 and 9.25. In between these timings, an hourly schedule was maintained by ordinary express stock, which, of course, included individual Pullman cars. All of the London to Brighton non-stops continued the best times of the steam services, with a flat hour end-to-end, but the working timetable showed 58 minutes in an attempt to maintain high levels of punctuality. The service was advertised as 'The finest train in Britain!'

The 'Southern Belle' did not remain an electric train for long, as it was soon superseded by the 'Brighton Belle', and last ran under its old name on 28 June 1934.

'Thanet Express/Pullman Limited'

Although there was a 'Thanet Express' from 1886 to 1905, and the title was revived in 1912 for a brief period, the title was reinstated on 11 July 1921 for no fewer than four trains. Unlike the 'City Express', these were not trains for the commuter, and not necessarily worthy of the title 'express'. The first departed Victoria at 11.30 am and included a first-class 'Pullman Luncheon Car', for which a supplement of 2s was charged, arriving at Whitstable Town at 12.52 and then stopping at most stations to Ramsgate Harbour, where it arrived at 1.49. This service survived only until October. A later departure was the 7 pm from Victoria, also with Pullman, that reached Ramsgate Harbour at 9.14. Both trains used rebuilt 4–4–0 express locomotives, and rolling stock was mainly without gangways or corridors except for the Pullman and a couple of lavatory brake thirds, as well as a 'picnic' saloon. This service lasted until 1927.

There were also two Up services, including a departure from Ramsgate Harbour at 3 pm that reached Victoria at 5.03, with a first-class 'Pullman Tea Car' that continued until March 1922, when it was dropped, until being reinstated that summer for Mondays, Fridays and Saturdays only. It survived in this form for 1923 and 1924, but was withdrawn in 1926. The only morning service was the 7.42 from Ramsgate Harbour, which had a 'Pullman Breakfast

As far away from the West Country as one could get on Southern metals, unrebuilt No. 34031 *Torrington* heads the 'Thanet Belle' through Wandsworth Road. *(HRMS AER204)*

Car' and reached Cannon Street at 9.30, but this must have been too exacting a timetable as departure times were advanced by 2 minutes later that year, and arrival at Cannon Street put back by 2 minutes. Between June 1922 and July 1923 it became a Monday-only working, leaving Margate West at 7.43 and reaching Cannon Street at 9.32, but it still retained the title. Under the Southern, the rolling stock was improved and timings altered, and although the title was finally abandoned for all of the 'Thanet Express' trains in 1927, it was only after having introduced yet another train with the title, the 5.05 pm from Holborn Viaduct, in 1923, and also having given the name to the 'City Express' leaving Cannon Street at 1.20 pm on Saturdays.

Meanwhile, a Sundays-only 'Thanet Pullman Limited' had been introduced on 10 July 1921, leaving Victoria at 10.10 and calling at Margate West and Broadstairs to reach Ramsgate Harbour shortly before noon. The return train started at 5.30, and arrived at Victoria at 7.15. This was clearly an attempt to capture the day-tripper market and utilise rolling stock off-peak, with a fare of £1 4s single and £2 2s return first class, including the Pullman supplements. Only 124 passengers could be carried in six first-class cars. As already mentioned, winter Sunday Up workings were combined with those of the 'Cliftonville Express', and the train survived until 1928, slightly longer than some of its contemporaries. Under Southern management, fares were cut to 17s and £1 4s, and the departure of the Up train put back to 7 pm, although in later years this was advanced by 10 minutes or so.

As part of its planning for the postwar railway, the Southern prepared for a 'Thanet Belle' to complement the services to Bournemouth and Brighton, but this did not appear until after nationalisation.

'The Tourist'

One of the Southern Railway's great successes was in creating a cohesive railway network on the Isle of Wight for the first time. The small island had no fewer than three railway companies, while the line from Ryde Esplanade to St John's had been owned jointly by the LSWR and LBSCR, bringing the total to five!

To stimulate railway travel by visitors to the island, the Southern had introduced a weekly ticket which had been a great success. In an attempt to further stimulate traffic, it was decided to introduce an 'East and West Through Train' linking the main holiday resorts, and this ran for the first time during summer 1932. The train ran every day except Saturdays, when all available rolling stock was required for the heavy traffic caused by visitors arriving and departing. At first the train started at Shanklin, and called only at Sandown, Merstone Junction, Newport, Carisbrooke and Yarmouth on its run to Freshwater. A former IWCR railcar was rebuilt as a third-class observation car, and there were five other carriages, all non-corridor, but including both first- and third-class accommodation. The total of six carriages was the limit for the railways on the island, and indeed apart from the 'East and West Through Train' such a number of carriages was only to be found on the busy route between Ryde and Ventnor. The through train covered the metals of all three of the island railway companies, and used an 'E1' tank between Shanklin and Newport, with an 'A1x' between Newport and Freshwater.

The success of the service was immediate – hardly surprising given the poor and winding state of the island's roads, many of which were unmetalled. For the summer of 1933 the service was increased to three trains daily, and the original departure was extended back to Ventnor and given the official title of 'The Tourist', with each carriage given a nameboard with the title in gold letters on a red background. This was the island's first named train, and the only official one! There was also an untitled through train between Ryde and Freshwater, the first since 1913.

The summer of 1934 saw the train pulled by an 'O2' tank engine throughout its entire journey, while the stops at Merstone Junction and Carisbrooke were dropped. The train left Ventnor at 9.55 am, and called at Wroxall, possibly to allow a train to pass in the opposite direction, Shanklin, Sandown, Newport and Yarmouth, before arriving at Freshwater at 11.12. In the opposite direction the train left Freshwater at 5.20 pm and arrived at Ventnor at 6.46. Over one week in the summer, a total of 2,700 passengers travelled on 'The Tourist'. The observation coach was joined by an ex-LBSCR invalid saloon, with a first-class observation compartment and a large open third section.

Postwar, the service was quickly reinstated on 7 May 1945, possibly because the only special rolling stock needed was the two observation cars. In some ways the early reinstatement was surprising, since the Ventnor line had just three out of its pre-war four trains an hour, but with fuel and vehicle shortages still affecting bus services, the east–west through link must have been well used. Nevertheless, the service was doomed, as after nationalisation the emphasis moved to closing as many of the island railways as possible, with the Newport–Freshwater line being one of the first to go in 1953, followed by that between Sandown and Newport just three years later.

Chapter Ten

Selling the Southern

From the start, much emphasis was placed on promoting the railway. The wider introduction of named trains was just one aspect of this. The railway companies promoted themselves individually, especially with what might be described as destination advertising, but they also operated collectively when it was sensible to do so. This apparent lack of competition seems strange today, but was perfectly acceptable in the period between the two world wars, for a major objective of the grouping was to minimise competition between the railway companies.

There were several examples of collaboration between the 'Big Four'. Obviously, this extended to lobbying to resist growing cries for nationalisation, but it also covered the marketing of railway services abroad. In Paris, new offices were opened for the *Chemins de Fer Britannique* at 12 Boulevard de la Madeleine. A photograph of this dignified setting appeared in *The Southern Railway Magazine*. A similar venture was operated in the United States in the drive for tourist traffic, with offices in a skyscraper for 'Associated British Railways Inc' at 551 Fifth Avenue, New York.

At home, leisure traffic was important for the railways, although holiday entitlements were, for most of the population, far less generous than today. Then, as now, leisure traffic filled off-peak trains and the viability of any transport undertaking, regardless of the mode, is fixed by its off-peak business rather than its peak business, for which a substantial investment in rolling stock and infrastructure is often necessary, and which is often only fully utilised for a few hours each day, and then not on every day of the week.

Holiday Traffic

No railway had a greater interest in holiday traffic than the Southern, with its continental services and the long chain of resorts stretching from north Kent round to south Devon and across the peninsula to north Cornwall. Individual railway workers were seen as having an important role to play in promoting use of the railway, and so inevitably *The Southern Railway Magazine* readers were treated to regular features that were meant to improve their performance, and not just in increasing sales. For example, competitions were held to see just how many shunting movements might be needed to sort out a particular traffic problem.

A regular feature for some time consisted of 'Selling Southern', and looked at means of improving business. A ticket inspector who had produced blackboard notices advertising services and special offers was rewarded – the magazine declined to say by how much – and shown with two samples of his work in the magazine. The tone of the features was often very worthy, perhaps ponderous and even pompous by today's standards, even when asking the reader how many salesmen 'were not truly salesmen at all but simply "order takers", and a sad reflection on the sales manager who had sent them to see prospective clients'.

Advertising was an important part of marketing the railway, and with so much advertising space readily and freely available at the stations, it is not surprising that poster campaigns were very much to the fore in promoting railways. The most famous of the Southern posters was among its first, in 1925, showing a small boy carrying a suitcase and talking to the driver of one of the Urie 4–6–0s at the end of a platform at Waterloo, and

Frequencies increased every time the Southern extended electrification, often doubling the service, and this young man is prepared to wait a whole hour for his beloved. (*NRM 1339/86*)

saying 'For Holidays I always go Southern 'cos it's the Sunshine Line' (*sic*). It was based on a photograph offered to the publicity department of the former LSWR and on which the locomotive tender was doctored, not very convincingly by modern standards, so that the first letters of 'Southern' could just be seen. The problem was that no one could identify the boy, and a framed copy of the poster was offered as a reward in the hunt for the child. This rather miserly offer by modern standards resulted in a number of children being brought forward by hopeful and opportunistic parents who failed to realise that the photograph had not been taken recently, and in the end the youngster was discovered to have been Wilfred Witt, the son of a former employee who had emigrated to Canada. The poster eventually evolved to become 'IM TAKING AN EARLY HOLIDAY COS I KNOW SUMMER COMES SOONEST IN THE SOUTH' (*sic*).

SOUTHERN RAILWAY

BRUSSELS - COLOGNE
BERLIN - VIENNA

by *Short Sea Routes*

All Services run Daily (Sundays included) in each direction, except where otherwise shown.

VIA DOVER-OSTEND.

Outwards	1, 2, & 3 Cl.	1 & 2 Cl. Lux	1, 2, & 3 Cl.	1 & 2 Cl. Lux	1 & 2 Cl. Lux	1, 2, & 3 Cl.	1, 2 & 3 Class	1, 2, & 3 Cl.	1, 2, & 3 Cl.
LONDON dp (Victoria)	am	am 11D0	am 10H30	pm 3 K0	pm 3 L0	pm 3 K0	pm 3 0	pm	pm 11N0
(Can'n S) dp	9E20	pm	pm				am 12 18	8 P0	am
Brussels arr	..	6 0	6 18	1036	(A)	1036		..	7 40
	pm			am	am	am	6 0	am	am
Cologne ,,	10 0	9 35	10 35	1 46	1 23	2 36		8 49	1146
							2 Cl. 1,2,3Cl.		
	am	am	am				pm pm	pm pm	
Berlin... ,,	7 14	7 14	7 52	8 32	..	..	12B25 4 13	5 40 8R18	
(Fried.)				pm pm					
Vienna.. ,,	..	..	..	..	3 14	7 30	.. ..	.. ..	

VIA DOVER-CALAIS, FOLKESTONE-BOULOGNE & DOVER-DUNKERQUE.

Outwards	1, 2, & 3 Cl.	1 & 2 Cl. Lux	1 & 2 Cl. Lux	1, 2, & 3 Cl.	1 & 2 Cl. Lux	1 & 2 Cl.	1, 2 & 3 Cl.
LONDON dp (Victoria)	am 1100	pm 2 0	pm 2 0	pm 2 0	pm 2 0	pm 4 30	pm 10 0
		pm					am
Brussels ar.	6 55	(A)	8 26	9 55	(F)	..	9G17
			am	am			pm
Cologne ,,	..	..	1 45	6 0	..	..	1 49
				pm			
Berlin.. ,,	..	..	8 32	4 13	..	..	1033
(Fried.)							
Vienna. ,,	..	3 14	..	..	5 14	1013	..

A—Tues., Thurs. and Sats. only from London.   B—Fast Railcar from Cologne; supplement payable.
C—3rd Class passengers dep. 10 30 a.m.   D—10 30 a.m. on Sats. to Sept. 10.   E—Sats. to Sept. 10.
F—Mons., Weds., and Fris. only from London.   G—Change at Lille (2 & 3 Cl. train).
H—Passengers for Cologne and beyond leave Cannon St. at 9 20 a.m. on Sats. to Sept. 10.
K—On Sats. to Sept. 10 passengers for Cologne and beyond leave Victoria at 2 30 p.m.
L—On Sats. to Sept. 10 passengers leave Victoria at 2 30 p.m.   N—From London every night to Sept. 18.
P—Fris. to Sept. 2.   R—Potsdamer Bhf.

For all information as to Services, Fares, etc., see the Continental Handbook, obtainable at Southern Railway Stations, or apply Continental Enquiry Office, Victoria Station, London, S.W.1, and any Travel Agency.

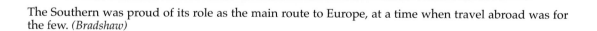

The Southern was proud of its role as the main route to Europe, at a time when travel abroad was for the few. *(Bradshaw)*

One of the most famous Southern posters was that featuring a professional model, Harry Tilbury, an actor from Lancashire who portrayed 'Sunny South Sam', supposedly 'a cheery and typical Southern Railway guard', because the actor was regarded as being the 'friendly type of person to whom people would like to write about their holidays'. The persona was used in connection with a series of advertisements for cheap fares and excursions, as well as for a campaign running 'Why Do They Call Me Sunny South Sam? Because – The Sun Shines Most on the SOUTHERN Coast'. Unfortunately the original actor died just two months after the first posters were issued in 1930, and they all had to be removed.

Nevertheless, a successor was found, and the campaign was also used to promote the Southern's holiday brochures, *Hints for Holidays* and *Sands across the Sea*.

In competition for the scant holiday savings of the inter-war worker, it was not always sweetness and light between the railway companies. The LNER launched a campaign in 1939 encouraging the public To 'Meet the Sun on the East Coast', which caused the Southern to launch a poster campaign using Meteorological Office records to prove that twenty-six out of the thirty-two sunniest resorts were served by the company. These were followed by one featuring a barograph chart in which the South Coast was featured as a wavy line.

Given the vast investment in electrification, the commuter was not neglected, although the term was not in use in the UK at the time. Peak period traffic in the outer suburbs and on the main-line electrification schemes was not at this stage so heavy that it had a devastating impact on railway finances, although this was already certainly a problem on many of the inner suburban routes, which is one reason why the Southern management hoped to be able to use the trains on these routes on excursions to the coast off-peak once the main lines were given the third rail. Posters exhorted would-be travellers to 'Live in Kent and be content' and 'Live in Surrey free from worry', while developers were able to offer discounted season tickets to purchasers of property served by the Southern. There was no such similar campaign for Sussex – no doubt suitable alliteration would have been difficult!

As today, advertising could be divided between that intended to market the railway and that intended to reassure the customer. In the former case, it is strange to see a pre-war advertisement for the 'Golden Arrow' complete with a plunging arrow and a fine colour illustration of the train, but without the famous arrow symbol adorning the front of the smokebox – a postwar innovation. Another advertisement, entitled 'The Viaduct', and showing a Pullman, probably the 'Southern Belle', still in the days of steam on what looks like a representation of Balcombe Viaduct, informs the public that the Southern Railway is spending a quarter of a million pounds strengthening bridges and viaducts throughout the system for heavier and faster trains. Advertisements for cheap day tickets for shopping rubbed shoulders with advertisements sponsored jointly by the four main-line companies encouraging the would-be passenger to 'Take your dog with you by rail', subtitled 'Return tickets at single rate', though this came with the proviso in brackets, 'At owner's risk'. In the latter case, there was the reassuring message that water could be obtained for dogs at refreshment rooms or from a member of staff. Less reassuring were advertisements for insurance for luggage that might get lost or pilfered! These were the days when luggage could be sent in advance, a civilised arrangement that spared the passenger the trouble of carrying heavy cases, although porters were very much in evidence at all stations, especially the main termini, and also avoided cluttering up trains with luggage. It must have been an uneconomic arrangement overall, and only worked when every town and even many villages had their own parcels office at the local station, as it disappeared after nationalisation, along with the porters!

Devaluation

Amid all the signs of hope and enterprise, there were many problems to contend with. The devaluation of sterling led to falling travel to the continent, which became a much more expensive destination, so that there were 21,300 fewer cross-Channel journeys in 1930 compared with 1929. That year the Southern made a profit of £1,169,000 and ferries a further £197,000, with £63,000 from docks, £60,000 from hotels, £30,000 for local collection and delivery services, and £3,000 from the various investments in road transport.

By 1933 passenger receipts had risen to £14,510,000, an increase of £268,000 over the previous year, but freight continued to suffer from the effects of the recession and fell further. That same year, 'summer tickets' had been introduced to attract additional traffic

SOUTHERN RAILWAY.
OFFICERS.

GENERAL MANAGER—
Gilbert S. Szlumper, C.B.E. (Waterloo).
Telegraphic Address—
General Manager, Waterloo Station, London.

ASSISTANT GENERAL MANAGER—
J. B. Elliot (Waterloo).

SECRETARY—
Major L. F. S. Dawes (Waterloo).
Telegraphic Address—
Secretary Waterloo Station, London.

SOLICITOR—
H. L. Smedley, M.C. (Waterloo).
Telegraphic Address—
Solicitor, Waterloo Station, London.

JOINT ACCOUNTANTS—
R. G. Davidson } (Waterloo).
A. Howie
Telegraphic Address—
Accountants Waterloo Station, London.

TRAFFIC MANAGER—
E. J. Missenden, O.B.E. (Waterloo).
Telegraphic Address—
Missenden, Waterloo, Rail, London.

CHIEF ENGINEER—
G. Ellson, O.B.E. (Waterloo).
Telegraphic Address—
Engineer Waterloo Station, London.

CHIEF MECHANICAL ENGINEER—
O. V. Bulleid (Waterloo).
Telegraphic Address—
Locomotive, Waterloo Station, London.

DOCKS AND MARINE MANAGER—
R. P. Biddle (Southampton).
Telegraphic Address—
Foremost, Southampton.

SURVEYOR and ESTATE AGENT—
A. Endicott, M.B.E., F.S.I.,
Victoria Station, London, S.W.1,
Telegraphic Address—
Estate Agent, Southern Railway, Victoria Station, London.

> *Telephone No. Waterloo 5100*
> *(Private Telephone Exchange connecting*
> *General Offices and Terminal Stations*
> *in London).*

THE SOUTHERN RAILWAY

serves the wonderful Holiday resorts of the South and South West of England with Pullman and Restaurant Car Express Trains throughout the year. It operates the

World's Largest Suburban Electric System;

and by means of its eight routes and luxurious fleet of steamers to all parts, it is

The "Key to the Continent."

It owns and manages the magnificent
SOUTHAMPTON DOCKS.

'Key to the Continent' – another example of Southern pride, and so too were the suburban system and Southampton Docks. All this was achieved in fifteen years, before war and nationalisation brought an end to it. *(Bradshaw)*

Train Ferry to the Continent
LONDON—PARIS

THROUGH SLEEPING CARS
(1st and 2nd Class)
WITHOUT CHANGE EN ROUTE
via
DOVER — DUNKERQUE
EVERY NIGHT IN EACH DIRECTION.

TRAIN FERRY STEAMERS:—
"TWICKENHAM FERRY," "HAMPTON FERRY," "SHEPPERTON FERRY"

		p.m.		**p.m.**
LONDON (Victoria) ... ... dep.	10 0	PARIS (Nord) ... ... dep.	9.50
		a.m.		**a.m.**
Dover Marine ... ... arr.	11 36	Dunkerque (Ferry Berth) ... { arr.	1.30
	a.m.	{ dep.	2.0
Dover (Ferry Berth) ... ... dep.	12 35	Dover (Ferry Berth) ... ... arr.	6 15
Dunkerque (Ferry Berth) ... { arr.	4.30	Dover Marine ... ... dep.	7 20
{ dep.	5.15		
PARIS (Nord) ... ... arr.	9.0	LONDON (Victoria) ... ... arr.	9 10

Restaurant Car, London to Dover and vice versa.   Buffet Car, Dunkerque to Paris and back.

Customs and Passport Examinations in the Train.

For Tickets and full information apply to :—
CONTINENTAL ENQUIRY OFFICE
VICTORIA STATION, LONDON, S.W. 1, or to any S.R. Travel Agency.
SOUTHERN RAILWAY

Advertisement and timings for the 'Night Ferry', wisely proclaiming 'Without change en route' rather than 'Go to sleep in London and wake up in Paris'! (*Bradshaw*) and also to counter road competition from the increasingly refined and comfortable motor coaches. The summer tickets were returns at a fare of 1*d* per mile, and offered a one-third reduction on the Southern's standard long-distance fares. The summer tickets helped finally to stem a decline in traffic, and indeed reverse it, but only slightly.

Passenger traffic continued to climb through the mid-1930s, but freight remained down. The 1935 figure showed passenger revenue at £15,626,000, up £462,000 on 1934 and £760,000 on 1933, no doubt due mainly to the 'sparks effect' of advancing electrification rather than to any publicity coup. Electrification continued almost up to the outbreak of the Second World War, with the completion of the 'Portsmouth No. 2 Electrification Scheme' from Victoria to Portsmouth via Arundel and Chichester in 1938, and of the Thames Valley lines and those to Maidstone in 1939. Air travel continued to be blamed for the loss of first-class travellers between England and France. Nevertheless, by 1936 travel to the continent was again rising, in part owing to the introduction late in the year of the 'Night Ferry'. This rise continued through to 1938, aided further by the devaluation of the French franc. It was at this time that the Southern decided to keep its feet firmly on the ground and get out of aviation.

The 1938 AGM was told that capital expenditure in 1937 had been £2,351,000, of which £972,000 had been for completion of the 'Portsmouth No. 1 Electrification Scheme' and the start of the 'Portsmouth No. 2 Electrification Scheme', and for electrification from Ascot to Aldershot and Guildford.

An idea of the passenger growth enjoyed by the Southern comes from figures quoted by the then Traffic Manager Eustace Missenden at the opening of the new line to Chessington as far as Tolworth in May 1938. Traffic at the company's London termini had grown by 42 per cent over the previous ten years. The Southern Railway's route mileage of 2,200 miles carried 378 million passengers in 1937, whereas in 1936 the combined totals for all railways in the United States had been 490 million passengers on just under 242,000 route miles.

Chapter Eleven

Shipping Services

All of the main constituent Southern companies were heavily engaged in shipping, mainly cross-Channel, but the LSWR had also developed services to the Channel Islands from Southampton. At first these Channel Island services competed with those operated by the GWR from Weymouth, until the two companies agreed to pool their resources in 1899. Together, the LSWR and LBSCR operated ferry services from Portsmouth to the Isle of Wight, using Ryde as the port, while the LSWR had its own service from Lymington, on a branch off the main line to Bournemouth, to Yarmouth, a small port in what is usually known as West Wight, and in Freshwater, Yarmouth & Newport Railway territory before the grouping.

Some of the Southern's initiatives on cross-Channel shipping seem to have been influenced by whether or not construction of a Channel Tunnel seemed imminent, and it was the dropping of such a proposal that was instrumental in the creation of the 'Night Ferry' through sleepers from London to Paris. It is often forgotten today that there was also a proposal for a tunnel to the Isle of Wight, not taking the most obvious and direct route, between Portsmouth and Ryde, which would also have linked places with the highest population at each end, but from a point in the New Forest just north of Lymington to Yarmouth. This approach would also have meant an awkward entry to Newport, with the need to reverse trains going on to Ryde or Sandown. It is possible that this route was favoured over Portsmouth–Ryde because of likely Admiralty objections to a tunnel under the approaches to Portsmouth Harbour, even if it had been possible to route the mainland approach to the tunnel over the former Southsea branch.

The cross-Channel shipping services of the constituent companies varied. Those of the SECR were what today would be described as the short crossings, Dover and Folkestone to Boulogne being typical, while those of the LSWR were longer crossings, best overnight, from Southampton to Le Havre and St Malo. The LBSCR operation between Newhaven and Dieppe fitted in between. At around 4 hours it was a trifle too short for a decent overnight crossing, but it could be a tedious day crossing, especially in bad weather.

Bad weather on the other hand was the saviour of the ferry services, as pre-Second World War air services were notoriously unreliable, and even postwar, until the advent of blind landing equipment in the early 1970s, fog was a far more serious threat to the airlines than to the ferries.

The SECR had operated an overnight service to Calais via Dover, but this was withdrawn by the Southern during 1923, and Dover remained without a night service until the start of the 'Night Ferry'.

Across the Channel

One of the first actions by the Southern on its shorter cross-Channel services was to concentrate the railway connections, the boat trains, on Victoria, and this was done as early as autumn 1923. Cross-Channel passenger traffic was far less heavy than today, and so services on the short sea routes departed Dover just four times daily, at 9.05 and 11 am, and 2 and 4.30 pm. Passengers must have been grateful for the SECR's foresight in building the new Dover Marine station which eased the transfer between train and ship, for even with

Passengers on the luxury 'Golden Arrow' Pullman had their own ship, the *Canterbury*, indicating that prestige was far more important at times even to the Southern than high utilisation. Here she departs from Dover. *(NRM BTC-collection 305/59)*

the traffic levels of the day the former LCDR pier station would have been inadequate. The situation was less comfortable at Folkestone, where the harbour station's platform was not lengthened from 308 ft to 700 ft until 1938, with additional roofing and a covered footbridge. While the SECR had put in junctions near Bickley between the SER and LCDR main lines to the Channel ports, it was left to the Southern to instigate a programme of bridge strengthening to allow larger and more powerful locomotives to be used on the heavy continental boat trains. This bore fruit as early as 1925, when 'King Arthur' class locomotives were able to work trains through Tonbridge and Ashford to Folkestone and Dover, while the following year they could also use the alternative route via Swanley and Maidstone, and the old 'Brighton' route to Newhaven for Dieppe.

In 1929 the most luxurious route ever across the Channel was introduced with the all-Pullman 'Golden Arrow' and its French counterpart the 'Flèche d'Or', linked by their own ferry, the specially built *Canterbury*. The 'Night Ferry' was introduced in late 1936, intended as a response both to the decision not to proceed with a Channel Tunnel and to growing airline competition, which even at that time was making its mark on railway revenues, and most especially at the upper end of the market, as one might have expected. As covered elsewhere, this also spurred the Southern to become interested in air transport, and to do so in several different ways by taking an interest in providing stations for airports and even trains for air travellers, as well as becoming involved in air transport directly.

The Southern's fleet of cross-Channel ferries, or more properly 'packet steamers', on grouping totalled twenty-one, while there were also twenty-five smaller vessels, some of which would have been engaged in the Isle of Wight traffic.

As on the railways, at sea the Southern soon proved to be a moderniser. In 1925 two new ships were introduced to the short crossings between Dover and Calais and Folkestone and Boulogne. These were *Isle of Thanet* and *Maid of Kent*, both around 2,700 tons, and in 1929 these were joined by the slightly larger *Canterbury*, at 2,910 tons, built as an all-first-class ship for the 'Golden Arrow' service. This was an extravagance, given both the small number of passengers carried in what was for the day a substantial ship, and the poor rate of utilisation with just one return trip daily, compared with up to four return trips by modern vessels. Undaunted by this waste of capital and manpower, the Southern ordered an even larger ship for the service, *Invicta*, at 4,178 tons. At least she was intended to carry passengers of both classes, but when she was delivered in 1939 she was immediately taken up for war service.

Hampton Ferry at Dover in 1937 waiting for foot passengers, although a goods wagon can be seen on the train deck at the stern. *(HRMS AAD129)*

The longer Newhaven–Dieppe route was not neglected, receiving two ships, the *Worthing*, at 2,294 tons and with a capacity of 1,288 passengers, in 1928, and *Brighton*, slightly larger and holding 1,450 passengers, in 1933. Meanwhile, the even longer services from Southampton had received the *Dinard* and *St Briac* in 1924.

The Southern was responsible for much innovation, but this did not really extend to service for the motorist. When a purpose-built ship, the *Autocarrier*, was introduced to the Dover–Calais service on 31 March 1931, cars still had to be lifted aboard by cranes and manhandled to their parking positions. It was service like this that led Captain Townsend, whose car had been damaged while being craned aboard a ship and to whom the Southern offered no compensation, to form his own competing company. The actual sailing time was only a little longer than today at 1 hour 45 minutes, although again only one return trip was made daily, with passengers paying a single fare of 10s, while taking a car across the Channel cost between £1 17s 6d and £5, depending on the length. The only concession to the needs of the cars was that they were all carried under cover, but just thirty-five could be carried, along with 120 passengers.

The concept of 'drive-on/drive-off' for motorists did not come until the advent of the three ferries for the 'Night Ferry' service, which are described in Chapter Eight, and which could carry between twenty-five and thirty cars on a special 'garage' deck. These ships, coming just five years after the *Autocarrier*, made the ship obsolete immediately, though she remained in service.

Meanwhile, the accolade of the fastest London to Paris railway service had passed to the 11 am 'Golden Arrow' departure each day, which by 7.30 pm could see the traveller between the two capitals in 6 hours 35 minutes, while a connection was also provided at Calais for those travelling to Brussels. For those with more time, the journey from London to Paris via Southampton and Le Havre meant a 9 pm departure from Waterloo with a 10.15 arrival in Paris the following morning. In between these timings came the service via

Newhaven and Dieppe, which at least did offer the opportunity of Pullman travel on the 10 am from Victoria, arriving in Paris at 5.58. For the overnight traveller via Newhaven and Dieppe, departure was from Victoria at 8.20 with an arrival in Paris at 5.23, although passengers could stay in their carriages until 7.30 am. The route offered three classes of accommodation on the ship and the French trains, and the early arrival in Paris was recommended for those seeking early-morning departures from the French capital 'to all parts of the Continent'.

In 1930/31 the Southern provided three new ships for the Channel Island services from Southampton.

The Southern also provided boat trains for other packet companies, not surprisingly since many of them were not competitors. For example, the Batavier Line operated from Gravesend to Rotterdam, and in 1930 a typical schedule allowed the traveller to leave Victoria at 6.10 and arrive at Gravesend Pier at 7.02 pm, with the steamer sailing just 10 minutes later, and arriving at Rotterdam at 8 the following morning. It was still possible at this time to embark on the Rotterdam sailing in London, and on the return crossing, passengers disembarking at Gravesend could leave their luggage aboard for collection when the ship berthed in London. Arrangements at the Dutch end seem to have been less accommodating, with the ferry berth a 10 minute taxi ride from the nearest station.

It is sad that after nationalisation the cross-Channel services from Southampton were gradually run down and then abandoned. That a market existed for these services was soon proven as private enterprise quickly appeared on the scene, with the Norwegian Thorensen concern, which later merged with Townsend, and the Anglo-French Normandy Ferries providing services to Cherbourg and Le Havre, before eventually these moved to Portsmouth, where commercial port space appeared with the contraction of the Royal Navy and which offered a shorter and faster access to the Channel.

The Isle of Wight Services

At the time of the grouping the main service between Portsmouth Harbour and Ryde Pier Head was covered by five ferries, all paddle-steamers, that had been owned jointly by the LSWR and LBSCR. These were the *Duchess of Albany*, *Duchess of Fife*, *Duchess of Kent*, *Duchess of Norfolk* and *Princess Margaret*; all had been built between 1889 and 1911. The first move was to repaint their white funnels with black-topped buff. Since none of these ships was exactly new, a steady stream of new vessels appeared for the services to the Isle of Wight. An additional vessel, the paddle-steamer *Shanklin*, entered service in 1924, and was followed by *Merstone* and *Portsdown* in 1928, replacing *Duchess of Albany* and *Princess Margaret*, then by the *Southsea* and *Whippingham* in 1930. These ferries had a speed of 16 knots and each was capable of accommodating 1,100 passengers. They were also used for cruises around the island and for excursions up Southampton Water to view the ocean liners in the docks. They replaced the *Duchess of Fife* and *Duchess of Norfolk*. The sole remaining pre-grouping 'paddler', *Duchess of Kent*, was replaced in 1934 by the *Sandown*, slightly smaller than the *Southsea*, and capable of carrying 900 passengers. She was joined by a sister ship, *Ryde*, in 1939.

The Lymington–Yarmouth service on grouping was worked by the small LSWR paddle-steamers *Lymington* and *Solent II*, built in 1893 and 1902 respectively, and they were joined by the *Freshwater* in 1927. Cars could be carried on this route, but they were towed by barges behind the paddle-steamers, and most of the car traffic at this time was carried between Southampton and Cowes by a competitor, the Southampton, Isle of Wight and South of England Royal Mail Steam Packet Company, more usually known by the shorter title of 'Red Funnel Steamers'. The Southern couldn't ignore this market and started to look for a suitable spot to operate a car ferry service between Portsmouth and Ryde, but none was available, mainly owing to tidal problems, but eventually a suitable location was found at Fishbourne, in Wootton Creek, a few miles to the west of Ryde, while the ideal landing at

The Southern's shipping services included the short crossings from Portsmouth to Ryde, and here is the paddle-steamer *Ryde*. Naming the ships after Isle of Wight towns is once supposed to have confused an elderly passenger who thought the names were in fact destinations, and let several sailings go by as a result! In common with many Southern ships, it had an active war service as a minesweeper. *(NRM BTC-collection 493/67)*

Portsmouth was found on a slipway at Broad Street near Old Portsmouth. In 1928, the new service was inaugurated with two new drive-on double-ended ferries, *Fishbourne* and *Wootton*. So successful was the new service that these two ships were joined by a third, the *Hilsea*, in 1930.

It soon became clear that the facilities offered for cars between Lymington and Yarmouth were no longer satisfactory, and that something similar to the Portsmouth–Fishbourne ferries was needed. This did not arrive until 1938, in the form of the ferry *Lymington*, although on this route motorists and their passengers were joined by ordinary foot passengers.

Chapter Twelve

Road Transport and Feeder Services

The 'Big Four' railway companies were active in pressing for regulation of road transport and this eventually arrived with the passing into law of the Road Traffic Act 1930. It can be debated whether the new law was overly protectionist to the railways, and whether or not similar relief could have been gained by ending the restrictions of the common carrier arrangement, forcing the railways to accept all traffic regardless of its profitability, or the cheap workmen's tickets, although these at least did have the merit of extending the start of the morning peak, allowing more journeys to be worked by the available rolling stock. The Act did much to preserve the route structures of established bus and coach operators from pirates, but made the development of new services difficult if the railways objected, and the appearance of new operators for bus services became a rare event indeed. Road haulage was also put into a straitjacket, and it became difficult for businesses with their own vehicles carrying their own goods in one direction to offset their costs by carrying goods for someone else on the return journey.

The railway companies did, of course, have substantial fleets of motor vehicles themselves, mainly for collection and delivery work and attached to stations and goods yards. Overall, between 1929 and 1939, the number of Southern lorries and vans rose from 278 vehicles to 757. The largest were a few tractors, with just four having a 10 ton haulage capacity in 1939 and another seven capable of 15 tons. The big growth area was in so-called mechanical horses, largely because these were extremely manoeuvrable, effectively operating as three-wheeled articulated tractors, and in 1939 the Southern had 105 of these with a 6 ton capacity, and another 255 of 3 tons, as well as 41 6 ton conventional articulated vehicles. There were also three horseboxes.

Once they were allowed to own bus companies, the railways went on a spending spree, buying or taking shareholdings in many of them. By 1930 the Southern owned Southern Vectis in the Isle of Wight and Southern National in Dorset. In both cases the 'Southern' in the title appeared on the acquisition, and the companies adopted the green livery of the Southern. In the case of Southern Vectis, the company's vehicles had been painted in an unusual livery of blue and red, and before the takeover had been operating as Dobson Brothers, trading as Vectis, while Southern National marked the break-up of the old National Steam Omnibus concern. The Southern also had a stake in Aldershot & District, the Devon General Omnibus and Touring Company, East Kent Road Car, Hants & Dorset Motor Services, Maidstone & District Motor Services, Southdown Motor Services, Thames Valley Traction and Wilts & Dorset Motor Services. Shares were held in the parcels carrier Carter Patterson and in Pickfords, the removals company.

The temptation to invest in bus services was understandable. The railways had long seen buses as providing economical feeders to railway stations, especially those inconveniently situated for the towns that they were supposed to serve. Bus services could also link railway stations, as happened between Farnham and Haslemere stations in Surrey, where a bus route linked the two towns for the LSWR and survived to become part of the Aldershot & District network as their No. 19 route.

There was nothing unique or even British about this move, but because of the early restrictions on the railway's operating buses, there were few 'railway' buses as such on the lines of those operated in, say, the Netherlands or Spain. In Ireland, both the Londonderry & Lough Swilly Railway and the County Donegal Railway survived as cross-border bus operators long after their trains had been withdrawn. Some commentators have criticised the railways for not integrating their services with those of the associated bus companies, as happened in many European countries where the state took a more active interest in transport. This is an interesting debating point. There can be no doubt that many people who would happily travel by train turn up their noses at the humble bus, while it is also the case that buses are cheaper to operate per mile and left to their own devices reflect this in their fares. In the London Passenger Transport Area, for example, after the formation of London Transport bus travellers probably paid more than the true cost of their travel, and users of the underground paid less.

One of the best examples of how 'integration' can adversely affect the cost of travel comes from the Isle of Wight, post-nationalisation, when both the railways and Southern Vectis were in state ownership. By this time, the direct route from Sandown to Newport had been closed and to travel between the two, passengers had to go via Ryde St John's. In *The Great Isle of Wight Train Robbery*, R.E. Burroughs recounts how a traveller discovered that the day return fare from Ventnor to Haven Street, on the line between Ryde and Newport, was 4s 9d, but that to Newport, 4 miles further on, was only 4s 6d. Tongue firmly in cheek, he enquired at the booking office just how much further he had to travel before it was free, and was told that 'the fares are tied up with those of the bus company'.

Romney, Hythe & Dymchurch

The Southern did not confine itself to bus feeders, and the most notable example of its support for other railways providing feeder services was in its backing for the Romney, Hythe & Dymchurch Light Railway, a narrow-gauge line that brought railway travel to Romney Marsh in Kent, an area over which building a standard-gauge line would have been impractical because of the weight of the locomotives and rolling stock.

Enthusiasts for narrow-gauge railways are accustomed to the layman regarding these as 'toy' railways, doubtless because they can also be found in many pleasure parks, and are usually at pains to point out that the railway concerned is a real railway. This is easy to do with the Welsh narrow-gauge railways, with their history not in passenger work but in the necessary but more mundane work of moving goods such as slate, for example. They even look different from main-line railways. The RHDLR was an exception, for it looked like a toy railway, and still does, and it was established to carry passengers, not goods. The locomotives have always been scaled down copies of main-line and US locomotives rather than something distinctive as in Wales, or, for that matter, on the Lynton & Barnstaple. This problem probably arose from the fact that it was the brainchild of Captain J.P. Howey, a motor racing driver who also enjoyed driving steam locomotives.

The Romney, Hythe & Dymchurch Light Railway was established by a Light Railway Order of 1926 authorising the construction of a double line of 15 in gauge for 8 miles between Hythe and New Romney, and was opened on 26 July 1927. A success from the beginning, it became a favourite with tourists and an attraction in its own right, so that in 1929 a 7 mile extension opened between New Romney and Dungeness lighthouse, with a long turning loop. During the Second World War it was closed to the public on 30 June 1940 and commandeered by the military and used to move troops along this vital section of coast where, it was feared, an invasion might start. It suffered considerable wartime damage, but still managed to reopen on 2 March 1946 between Hythe and New Romney, while the Dungeness extension reopened the following year.

Despite this, the postwar history was by no means as happy as the early years, with the line eventually facing closure until rescued by the preservation movement.

Light Railways

In Sussex and Kent, the Southern enjoyed a small number of railway feeders operated as light railways and in independent ownership, some of them reflecting the involvement of Lieutenant-Colonel H.F. Stephens. These did not constitute a single railway, still less a network, but a number of individual lines each with its own differing characteristics, with possibly the only one in common being the cheapness with which they were built and operated. Most of the other 'independent' lines across the south had been operated on behalf of the owners by the Southern's predecessor companies, with the only other substantial group of true independents being on the Isle of Wight.

From his head office in Tonbridge, Stephens managed the Kent & East Sussex Railway and the Hundred of Manhood & Selsey Tramways, but earlier he had been engineer for the Rye & Camber Tramways. A fourth line was the East Kent (Light) Railway.

The Kent & East Sussex had its origins in proposals to provide a railway connection for Tenterden. Originally, a branch had been proposed from Cranbrook as early as 1864, but nothing happened until the Rother Valley (Light) Railway was formed in 1896 and then authorised under the provisions of the new Light Railways Act 1896. This line ran from Robertsbridge to Tenterden and opened to goods traffic on 29 March 1900, with passenger services starting on 2 April. The line was extended to Tenterden Town on 15 April 1903, and a 9½ mile extension to Headcorn from Tenterden Town opened on 15 May 1905, by which time the name had been changed to the Kent & East Sussex Light Railway. The extension proved to be a mistake, running at a loss after 1924 while the original line managed to remain profitable until 1930. It went into receivership in 1932, after Stephens died, but was rescued by W.H. Austen, and continued to be managed from Tonbridge along with the Hundred of Manhood & Selsey. The Kent & East Sussex Light Railway survived to become part of British Railways, after which its fate was sealed.

The Rye & Camber Tramways Company had originally used Stephens as engineer when it was incorporated in 1895. The line ran from Rye to Camber Golf Links, where a ferry took passengers on to the village of Rye Harbour on a 3 ft gauge track, and opened on 13 July 1895. An extension to Camber Sands, ½ mile further on, opened on 13 July 1908. Two steam locomotives and two carriages provided the sum total of the line's equipment, but a petrol locomotive was obtained before winter services ceased in 1925, and the line managed a seasonal existence until 1939. After the evacuation at Dunkirk, the line was requisitioned by the military, but was not returned to public service after the war.

The Hundred of Manhood & Selsey Tramways system was actually built without parliamentary powers and used its own station at Chichester, from which a line extended 7¾ miles to Selsey, opened on 27 August 1897, with an extension to Selsey Beach opening on 1 August 1898. Described as being operated 'in the most primitive manner', it survived until 19 January 1935.

Another significant light railway was established to serve the growing coalfields of Kent. This was the East Kent (Light) Railway, linking the Canterbury–Minster and Canterbury–Dover lines, authorised in 1911 and parts of which were carrying coal a year later. The 10¼ mile line opened to passenger and coal traffic on 16 October 1916, and was soon carrying a worthwhile volume of traffic, including coal from the pits at Wingham and Tilmanstone. The company operating the latter colliery was anxious to develop the port of Richborough, effectively a suburb of Sandwich, that had been used by the military during the First World War. A branch opened to Sandwich Road in 1925 and was extended to Richborough in 1928, but coal exports were disappointing and passenger services, which had used a single carriage, were withdrawn on 1 November, while only occasional coal workings followed after that. Tilmanstone continued to produce coal but Wingham was run down, leaving the railway to struggle on until nationalisation in 1948, after which the end was rapid, with passenger services withdrawn on 30 October and goods trains ceasing shortly afterwards, except for the short stretch between Tilmanstone and Shepherd's Well.

Chapter Thirteen

Air Services and Airports

If the railways were interested in the 'doorstep to destination' business of the humble motor bus, the Southern was also very interested in the more grandiose and at the time highly futuristic business of aviation. Powers were obtained to allow the Southern to own airlines and operate aircraft.

'We have arrived at an understanding with Imperial Airways as we are entitled to do in accordance with the powers we obtained last year,' the Chairman told those present at the AGM in 1930. 'The companies mutually recognise each other's natural desire to develop their own services, and the two companies agree to be mutually helpful in through bookings, display of literature and other matters.

'The Southern Railway have acquired a shareholding interest, but not a controlling interest in Imperial Airways, and the Southern Railway have agreed that should they wish to run air services under the new powers which I have mentioned, such air services will be operated by Imperial Airways.

'Both companies feel that this understanding is a mutually beneficial arrangement and will avoid wasteful and unnecessary competition between the two companies in air transport.'

The reason for this interest in aviation was not hard to find. The Southern Railway had found that it was becoming increasingly vulnerable to competition from the airlines on its services to the continent. This was serious enough to encourage the company to take a keen interest in aviation, not least because the impact was felt most at the upper end of the market. The 'Golden Arrow' traveller was far more likely to fly than the traveller in third class. In addition, it was clear that the increasingly reliable aeroplane could offer many new connections and short cuts for the more affluent traveller.

As early as 1929, Parliament had granted the railways the powers to operate air services, and that year the Southern became a shareholder in the new airline, Imperial Airways, created by the government in 1924 from four small airlines. Some believe that the directors seriously considered buying the airline, but this seems unlikely since its powers restricted its area of operations. However, during the mid-1930s, with a growing network of air services of its own, the company did approach Imperial Airways with an offer to merge the Southern's air services with Imperial's short-haul routes. The deal stumbled on the question of the price that the railway might pay for the routes from London to Paris and Brussels, which Imperial would then operate on its behalf, even though the airline was later discovered to have been keen to get rid of them.

Initially the Southern hesitated to establish an airline of its own, but entered into an agreement with Spartan Airlines to provide an air service from London to Cowes in the Isle of Wight, a destination not served by the Southern's own steamers. Spartan had started operating on the route in 1933, flying from Heston to the west of London, but under the arrangement with the Southern, the London terminus was moved to the new airport at Croydon, and the railway company took a 50 per cent share of revenue and expenses, subject to a maximum expenditure on each flight of £5 18s. There was no suggestion that the Southern Railway should become a shareholder. It was anticipated that there would be a small loss on the first year's operations.

Railway Air Services aircraft included the de Havilland Dragon Rapide biplane, one of which is seen here loading cargo. (*NRM 494/93*)

Railway Air Services

When the post-grouping railways found themselves with new challenges, they tended to act in concert, and on 21 March 1934 Railway Air Services was formed, with each of the 'Big Four' railway companies having a director on its board and with the involvement of Coast Lines, a coastal shipping operator later acquired by P&O, and the support of Imperial Airways. The Southern and the Great Western then established a joint service operated by RAS linking Birmingham, Bristol, Southampton and Cowes, which started on 30 July 1934 and competed with the services of the Midland & South Western Junction Railway. Later that year, on 12 December, the Southern Railway and the GWR started negotiations over an investment in Channel Islands Airways, an enterprise set up to expand the operations of the airline that had established a route to Jersey in 1933. It was not only the Anglo-French market that the Southern wanted to protect. The negotiations would initially have seen the two railway companies each acquire a third of the airline's capital, but were stalled because the airline was using a beach landing site, which the Southern's directors regarded as unorthodox, something that had been proved on one occasion when the converted motor coach used as a booking office failed to start and was overtaken by the incoming tide! In 1937 Jersey Airport, sometimes referred to as 'States Airport', opened on an inland site well above the high tide mark, and the two railway companies went ahead with their investment, taking 16½ per cent each, the remainder being split equally between the founder, Walter Thurgood, and Whitehall Securities.

Channel Islands Airways operated in competition with Channel Air Ferries, founded on 8 May 1936 by the businessman Sir Hugo Cunliffe-Owen, chairman of British American Tobacco, and Captain Gordon Olley, a former Imperial Airways pilot and later that airline's charter manager, and operated as part of the Olley Air Services group. By this time the Southern had already got its first 'airport station'. The unattractively named Bungalow Town Halt on the line between Brighton and Worthing had been closed when the line was electrified in 1933. On 1 July 1935 it was resurrected as Shoreham Airport, ready for the new RAS service across country to Bristol and Birmingham. Channel Air Ferries had established itself at Shoreham, using the airport as its main base, and agreed to operate the airport.

The RAS service from the Midlands to the Isle of Wight was extended in 1935 from Birmingham to Liverpool at its northern end and from Southampton to Portsmouth and Shoreham in the south, and changed again the following year with Gloucester served on request and Manchester added to the northern end of the route, while on the Isle of Wight, Ryde was added to the network.

The joint service with Spartan reverted to Heston as the London terminal in 1935, but moved again in 1936, this time to Gatwick Airport, although the original pre-war airport was on the opposite side of the A23 London to Brighton road from the present airport, and was served by the Southern station at Tinsley Green, from which a subway led to the airport terminal building, known today as the 'beehive'. Nearby, another station served the then Gatwick racecourse, and this was the one developed postwar to serve the new London Gatwick Airport.

Despite the tinkering with the London terminal, the venture with Spartan Airlines failed to pay and was withdrawn in 1936. There was competition, even for the sparse pickings on what must have been a highly seasonal route, from Portsmouth, Southsea and Isle of Wight Aviation, and when the Portsmouth Direct was electrified in 1937 the airline adjusted its timetables to connect with the new service. The airline also operated from the Isle of Wight to Shoreham.

Competition seems to have been anathema to the SR. The 1938 AGM was told that an arrangement had been reached between Southern Airways and Great Western Airways with Channel Air Ferries to eliminate competition. Even so, air transport had lost a further £5,000 in 1937.

There were also problems with the services of RAS, whose other routes were incurring losses that the Southern and Great Western found unacceptable since they were outside their geographical areas. The consequence was that in December 1938, both companies withdrew and set up their own airline, Great Western & Southern Airlines, to operate the RAS services in the west of England and along the south coast, while services were introduced from Croydon to Dieppe and to Le Touquet, later to be used for the 'Silver Arrow' rail–air–rail service between London Victoria and Paris by British United Airways, as well as to Luxembourg.

Airports

The Southern's interest in aviation was comprehensive, remarkably so for the period, with a keen desire to have airports with attendant stations established within its area of operations. In the mid-1930s it took an option on what it regarded as a potential aerodrome site at Lullingstone in Kent, just above the railway tunnel at Eynsford, which was seen as the best site for a new airport for London, and the decision seemed to have been vindicated when, on 17 March 1937, Imperial Airways told a House of Commons Select Committee that this was to be its new airport for London. The site was described to shareholders as being on top of a hill and outside the fog area. When first announced, the SR had no intention of developing the site itself, and was prepared to pass the site on at no profit to

During the early days of flight, weight was extremely critical in small aircraft, and so passengers had to be weighed as well as their luggage. This is at Croydon. (*NRM LMS7143*)

anyone who would develop it, suggesting, oddly for this bastion of private enterprise, that airports should be developed by the state 'like roads'. Had the development gone ahead, special trains would have been run to the airport from Victoria, with an underground station providing access to the passenger terminal. In fact, the Southern built a temporary station near to the airport site in anticipation of moving workmen to and from the construction site, and this appeared in the working sheets after its completion on 2 April 1939, although no trains were scheduled to stop there. However, there was no indication by this time of an airport being built, and instead the authorities were considering improvements at Croydon.

As might have been expected, the services to the Channel Islands were far more successful, and the SR and GWR both increased their shareholding in June 1939, by which time the airline was operating from London, Shoreham, Southampton and Exeter. The airline maintained its services until June 1940, and the company remained in existence throughout the war, with the two railway companies taking outright control in June 1943. Services resumed in 1946.

The 1945 AGM again referred to aviation, but this was before that year's general election returned a Labour government, one committed to nationalisation of all road, rail and air transport. The Southern might have seen one war end, but it now had a battle on its hands. The lack of any mention of this prospect at the 1945 AGM, held as usual in the first quarter of the year and with victory in Europe in sight, was no doubt down to the assumption that Churchill, having led the country to victory in wartime, would lead the Conservative Party to victory at the polls.

Postwar, the government formed a nationalised airline out of the European operations of the British Overseas Airways Corporation and two RAF transport squadrons, British European Airways, and this took over all domestic air services on 1 April 1947. Subsequently, private enterprise could only operate air services on a charter basis, or as 'associates' of the two state airline corporations.

Chapter Fourteen

Accidents

Even today, with modern signalling having the ability to stop trains that run past a signal set at danger, accidents still happen, and there are those who have made the point in the railway press that some at least of the accidents in recent years would not have been prevented by even the most modern systems. It is not surprising, therefore, going back more than half a century and beyond, that the Southern Railway had its share of accidents. In addition, the standard of track and ballasting inherited by the railway was not of the best, especially on the former SECR routes, but probably at no point could the Southern claim to match the best standards of the Great Western or the London & North Eastern.

In any examination of safety, it has to be accepted that luck sometimes plays an important part. Many accidents are not caused by a single failure of personnel or equipment, but more usually by a combination of factors that come into play at the same time. It is also the case that circumstances can play a part in the outcome, so that a simple derailment is made more serious if it does not occur on plain track but close to points, or if the derailed rolling stock should happen to hit a lineside structure, such as a bridge support or a building. The railway carriages of the day had bodies that were often constructed almost entirely of timber, or at best with steel frames and steel sheet metal, but with much wood still in evidence. These were mounted on a separate underframe, and provided little protection for the occupants compared to modern all-metal monocoque construction.

That luck plays a part will already have been noted in Chapter Eight, where the accident to the steamer carrying the sleeping cars of the 'Night Ferry' in May 1937 is mentioned. Had the collision, which took place in fog, been more severe, many of those aboard could have been killed, and most at risk would have been the passengers locked in the sleeping cars. So much progress in safety comes about not by careful planning with due thought to the consequences, but through bitter experience. Today, of course, passengers are not allowed on the vehicle decks of ferries while at sea.

The Loss of the *Caesarea*

Inevitably, a book such as this concentrates on the railway, but the post-grouping railways were to become what would today be described as 'multi-modal' transport operators. Indeed, they could even be described as such from the beginning since they inherited their predecessors' shipping interests, road delivery vehicles and, of course, ports.

The first serious accident to befall the new Southern Railway was not to a train but to one of the company's ships, the *Caesarea*, employed on services from Southampton to the Channel Islands. The *Caesarea* left St Helier on Jersey for Southampton shortly after 7.15 am on a foggy Saturday 7 July 1923. Claimed by one contemporary report to be 'one of the most popular boats on the Channel Islands service', she was commanded by Captain Smith, Commodore of the Southern Railway fleet, and on the day in question carried 373 passengers, probably a full load or close to it, as it was a summer Saturday.

Shortly after the *Caesarea*'s departure, another vessel, the *Alberta*, arrived, but hardly was she safely berthed alongside than a ship's siren could be heard. Her crew hastily lowered the ship's boats, while ashore, a rumour is thought to have started that the *Caesarea* had struck a rock in St Aubin's Bay. It soon transpired that in making way for the *Alberta* in the fog, the *Caesarea* had struck the Four Reef, near Noirmont Point. Water started to flood aboard and, realising that the ship must be badly holed, Captain Smith tried to turn and head back to St Helier, while the ship's wireless operator signalled to the GWR vessel *Reindeer*, asking her to stand by while this was attempted. No ship of the day had radar and the Channel Island waters have always been notorious for their many rocks and reefs, often combined with very strong currents, and so it was hardly surprising that, by now low in the water, the *Caesarea* struck the Oyster Rock shortly before entering harbour. Meanwhile, another GWR steamer, the *Gazelle*, inbound for St Helier, appeared, and the *Reindeer* requested that the *Gazelle* should stand by the stricken *Caesarea* so that she could continue on her passage to Guernsey and Weymouth. By this time, the *Caesarea*'s stern was low in the water, and she grounded. Her own crew, helped by those of the *Alberta* and the *Gazelle*, started to land the passengers, followed by the mails and their luggage. No one was hurt, although it appears that much of the luggage, when brought ashore, was 'the worse for immersion', and the passengers were able to continue their passage to Southampton aboard the *Alberta*.

Sevenoaks

The first serious accident on the Southern Railway involved a steam-hauled passenger service at Sevenoaks and the causes were inherited from the old SECR companies. Habitually, track had been ballasted using shingle from the beach at Dungeness, even on the main lines. The problem with this material was that beach shingle consisted of rounded smooth stones that lacked the stability of granite chippings and, worse still, became decidedly greasy after heavy rain. The track had in any case suffered excessive wear from the use of the heavier 'King Arthur' class locomotives on the Channel expresses. Coupled with this, the 2–6–4T tank engines of the 'K' class tended to roll uncomfortably, largely due to the effect of water surging in the tanks whenever oscillation occurred, and this feature was obviously aggravated when travelling over an unstable formation, where subsequent investigation found one rail on the curve had become super-elevated in places. On 24 August 1927 the 5 pm express from Cannon Street to Dover started to roll dangerously while travelling at 55 mph between Dunton Green and Sevenoaks. The train included a Pullman car and this became so much out of line as a result of the locomotive's rolling as it rounded a bend and the poor track that it struck the central pier of the bridge at Shoreham Lane and became jammed across the track, leaving the following carriages to pile up behind it, with the result that thirteen people were killed and another sixty-one injured.

The accident at Sevenoaks resulted in a fundamental reassessment of the way in which the Southern handled its track maintenance, and also had implications for the future of the 'K' class. The class had been involved in three previous incidents on the Eastern Section and Gilbert Szlumper, the assistant general manager, immediately ordered that the 'K's were to remain on shed until an investigation had been completed. Maunsell maintained that the locomotives were safe and stable on good track, while Ellson, who had taken over as civil engineer from Szlumper's father shortly before the accident, maintained that there was nothing wrong with the track. It was left to Walker, neither a civil nor a mechanical engineer, to arbitrate. He reminded his colleagues that people had lost their lives on their railway. He confirmed Szlumper's decision to keep the locomotives out of traffic, told Maunsell that it might be wise to consider converting the entire class to tender locomotives, and asked Ellson to prepare an estimate of the cost of re-ballasting the entire boat train route between London and Dover.

Trials with the 'K' class at 83 mph were conducted by Sir Nigel Gresley on the LNER main line between St Neots and Huntingdon, when the locomotives were found to be perfectly stable. For comparison, running on the south-western main line between Woking and Walton-on-Thames produced severe rolling at 70 mph. There had also been problems with the class on the South Central Section, which used shingle ballast on ash foundations. The problems had been recognised before the accident, and had led the assistant divisional engineer for the South Eastern to identify bad spots on his lines for improvement, but this had been shelved by his superior as too costly. The result was that the class was converted to tender locomotives while a programme of ballasting with Meldon stone was instituted throughout the two wayward sections. Particular attention was paid to soft spots which were blanketed to stop the track pumping up and down with passing trains.

The Southern's board of directors paid their regrets to the victims of the accident, while doctors who had attended the scene were reimbursed, for these were pre-National Health Service days, and a donation amounting to twice the recorded treatment costs was given to Sevenoaks and Holmesdale Hospital, with an expression of the board's gratitude. Due tribute was also paid to those of the Southern's own employees who had assisted at the scene, and especially to those trained in first-aid work.

Accidents on the Electric

The 1928 extension of the Central Section electrification was to suffer worse than the teething problems that dogged its first few weeks. The service was still new when, on 9 July, a serious accident occurred at London Bridge. As so often happens, the accident followed a day of disruption starting with a power failure in the morning and a points failure later on in the day. By early evening services had still not recovered. A passenger steam locomotive, 'B2x' class 4–4–0 No. B210, running tender first, was put on to a road on the north side of the signal-box to do some shunting before running light to New Cross Gate sheds. The driver saw a colour light signal on the Down local change to green, and ignoring the ground signalling controlling the exit from his line, moved off, running into the side of the leading motor coach of the Down 7.22 pm to Epsom Downs as it emerged from the other side of the signal-box and for which the Down local had been set. One passenger was killed and another died later from the injuries suffered, while another nine were injured, five of them very seriously. The locomotive and two carriages of the train were derailed and services were not back to normal until late the following day. The subsequent enquiry heard that the new signals were difficult to understand, but did not make any recommendations.

A more serious accident occurred in thick fog on 2 April 1937 at Battersea Park with ten deaths and as many as eighty people injured. At 8.02 the 7.30 am from London Bridge to Victoria via Tulse Hill was waiting at the Up local home signal for the 7.37 from London Bridge via the south London line to leave, when it was run into by the 7.31 from Coulsdon North, a train not scheduled to stop at Battersea Park and which, as a consequence, was travelling at around 35 mph. The driver of the 7.31 saw the earlier train when he was about 50 yd away, but did not have time to stop. In the resulting collision, the bodies of both the leading carriage of the 7.31 and the rear carriage of the waiting 7.30 were torn from their underframes. Miraculously, the driver of the 7.31 was uninjured, although badly shocked. The guard of the 7.30 was among those killed. Fortunately, neither train had been crowded and no other trains were involved because of prompt action by the signal staff, who cut off the current and summoned help. The lines were cleared and normal traffic resumed at 4.30 that afternoon.

In the subsequent enquiry, the inspecting officer found that the accident was due to human error by a signalman. A new signalman had been rostered for duty at Battersea Park Junction that morning. He had been an experienced relief signalman and had been given three weeks' supervised training before being allowed to work the box single-handed for the first time that morning. While the 7.30 was standing at the Up local home signal, he was offered the 7.31 from Coulsdon North by Pouparts Junction, but could not accept it since lock and block was in operation. For some reason he appears to have thought that the equipment had failed, and broke the seal to allow him to give the 'line clear' to Pouparts

Junction, who then allowed the 7.31 to continue. The inspecting officer recommended that a track circuit be provided in the rear of the Up local home signal and that the seals on the lock and block apparatus be replaced by padlocks with the keys held by a person other than the signalman, and that because of the pressure on this section, automatic colour light signalling should be installed as soon as possible. The first of these recommendations was already in hand and the last was under consideration before the accident.

Wartime

In peacetime the Southern was a passenger railway, but in wartime goods trains had priority over everything other than troop trains and ambulance trains. On 4 November 1942 there was thick fog before daybreak and the usual blackout restrictions were in force. The 5.34 am from London Bridge to Epsom was standing at Waddon station and could not be passed on to Wallington because shunting was in progress. The delay to the train was so long that, in accordance with the rule book, the guard made his way to the signal-box. While he was there, both he and the signalman heard the 6.15 from West Croydon to Holborn Viaduct approaching, but neither could do anything to prevent the ensuing collision in which the 6.15's motorman and a passenger were killed. Even in wartime, attention still had to be paid to safety, and at the official enquiry the signalman at West Croydon South box maintained that he had received the 'all clear' from Waddon on the Sykes lock-and-block instrument. The implication was that the signalman at Waddon had freed the instrument using his release key in the belief that the 5.34 had departed, but he denied doing so and it seems unlikely that this would have happened with the train's guard present. The inspecting officer suggested installing a system that required signalmen to cooperate – quite how this could be done was never resolved.

An Unhappy Ending to the Southern

The postwar railway suffered from three major accidents between the end of the Second World War and nationalisation.

On 24 October 1947 the 7.33 am from Haywards Heath to London Bridge was held on the Up main by signals at Purley Oaks in thick fog for around 8 minutes, before continuing its journey running at between 15 and 20 mph. As the train approached South Croydon Junction at around 8.37, the 8.04 from Tattenham Corner, running at 40 mph, ran into the back of it, causing severe damage to the rear coach of the 7.33 and so damaging its own front coach that accident investigators could not discover whether the motorman had been able to apply the brake or not. The disruption to services caused by the thick fog meant that both trains were packed, with about eight hundred passengers on the first train and a thousand on the second. The driver of the second train and thirty-one passengers were killed, with another fifty-eight people injured.

The porter signalman at Purley Oaks admitted responsibility for the accident. This was the first time he had worked the box in thick fog. It seems that he could not see the 7.33 standing in the station because of the thick fog, and advised Purley North signal-box that it was 'out of section' when the signalman there telephoned. Once again a signalman assumed that the Sykes lock-and-block instrument was out of action and he then accepted the 8.04 by using his release key. The acceptance of the 7.33 by South Croydon Junction was then taken by the signalman at Purley Oaks to apply to the 8.04, even though he had not offered it to them, and he pulled off all of his signals, giving the 8.04 a clear road. A last chance to save the situation occurred as the 7.33 tripped a rail treadle that changed the indication on the Sykes instrument to 'locked', but the porter signalman again regarded this as a failure of the instrument and against the regulations manipulated the instrument to return it to show 'free'. The inspecting officer felt that the accident was caused by the porter signalman's inexperience, forgetfulness and his ready acceptance of irregular working. This was an accident that could have been prevented had colour light signalling been in use on this stretch of track.

On 6 November, again in thick fog, two accidents occurred on the same day. The first of these was at Motspur Park, where the 4.45 pm from Holmwood to Waterloo ran into the second coach of the 5.16 from Waterloo to Chessington South as it crossed to the Chessington branch, killing four passengers and injuring another twelve, as well as the motorman of the 4.45. At the enquiry, the motorman maintained that the Motspur Park outer and inner distant signals were at caution. He approached the outer home signal slowly, but he saw a fogman showing a green light. He did not see any lights on the Chessington train and was not aware of its presence until the collision. The fogman admitted that he had not gone up the signal to check its position, but had instead relied on the sound of it rising or falling as an indication of whether he should put down or take up his detonators. The inspector laid the blame fully on the fogman, but observed that the accident might have been avoided had there been a ground-based repeater or a co-acting detonator placer.

A couple of hours later the second accident happened at Herne Hill at around 7.30 pm, again in very thick fog with extremely poor visibility. The 5.15 from Ramsgate to Victoria, hauled by a 2–6–0 tender locomotive with two vans and nine corridor carriages, was checked by signals at West Dulwich, after which it should have stopped at the home signals at Herne Hill to allow the 6.54 from Holborn Viaduct to West Croydon to cross its path to take the line to Tulse Hill. Instead, the Ramsgate train failed to stop and struck the electric train, again as it was crossing the junction, badly damaging the first two carriages as it forced them across the Up line and to the edge of the viaduct. Fortunately it did not breach the retaining wall, otherwise the casualties would have been far worse than one passenger killed and nine injured. The enquiry heard that visibility was almost nil, but on this occasion the fogman at the home signals did attempt to catch the attention of the enginemen as the locomotive passed, but this particular locomotive had right-hand drive and the driver was depending on his fireman, who was inexperienced in main-line working in fog, to keep a good lookout in addition to his other duties. Even so, all might have been well as the guard of the Ramsgate train had seen the fogman, but only made a partial brake application when a full application would have stopped the train in time.

Now in his eightieth and last year, Sir Herbert Walker nevertheless found time to drop a line to his old public relations man, John Elliott, by now running the Southern, offering his sympathy after the last of these accidents. Always supportive and never anything other than realistic, Walker wrote on 7 November from the Devonshire Club:

> My dear John
> You have had damnably bad luck! But don't let it worry you. Now that there have been the series of three mishaps, we must all hope there will be no more. These things will happen. Whatever precautions are taken! Cheer up: give my very best compliments to your wife.

It is not only the superstitious who believe that bad luck comes in runs of three! This apparent fatalism with regard to accidents may seem strange to people today who believe that every accident can be safeguarded against, but we live in a different era, that of the compensation culture.

Chapter Fifteen

Railways at War

There are several aspects of the history of the Southern Railway during the Second World War. First of all, there was the heavy damage inflicted on the system, its rolling stock and personnel by the war, with heavy bombing for a full year from mid-1940, until the demands of Operation Barbarossa, the German invasion of the Soviet Union, at last provided some relief, but even after this there were still periods of bombing, including a 'mini-blitz' and the so-called 'Baedeker Raids', before the advent of the V1 and V2 missiles or flying bombs. Then there were the demands placed on the system, which handled the despatch of the British Expeditionary Force to France as its predecessors had done at the outset of the First World War, and the dispersal of schoolchildren in the evacuation away from the major cities, as well as the heavy strain placed on the railways at the time of Dunkirk, when hundreds of thousands of British and allied soldiers were lifted off the beaches. Dunkirk and the evacuation of the Channel Islands saw the Southern's fleet of ferries playing an important role, and ships were lost. The Southern was once again hard at it following the invasion of Normandy.

In between Dunkirk and the Normandy landings, the Southern was under intense pressure supplying industry and the armed forces, providing many troop trains often at extremely short notice, suffering a shortage of personnel as many volunteered to join the armed forces, and a shortage of spares and equipment for maintenance as so much had to be diverted to the war effort. Many of the Southern Railway's ferries and packets were also 'taken up from trade', as the saying goes, and pressed into the war effort. The regular passengers suffered as services were reduced, and trains lengthened to the extent that they often had to make two stops at a station so that passengers could alight or board. Some trains had to load in two portions at the terminus, with the first portion being pulled out and then reversing on to the second portion so that they could be coupled together. Routine maintenance and renewal of track and signals took second place to repairing bomb damage so that services could be restored. Railway workshops were often diverted to wartime production.

Even this is not the complete picture of wartime on the railways. Once the Germans had occupied Europe from Norway to Brittany, the North Sea and the English Channel became virtually unusable by merchant shipping, and this at a time when coastal shipping was still an extremely important part of the UK's transport system, especially for bulk goods such as coal and iron ore. The risk of attack by E-boats or U-boats, or from the air, or of ships being lost to mines, meant that even a convoy system could not guarantee safety. The burden of moving the displaced cargoes fell fully on the railways, adding to their existing problems. Added to this, the main ports for unloading convoys were in the west of Great Britain, increasing traffic again, as access to ports on the East Coast became extremely difficult.

There were also problems of administration, with key personnel evacuated to areas where it was hoped that they could continue with their work uninterrupted by heavy bombing. There was an economic and political side to this as well, as the railways were taken into state control, with the state taking all of the receipts and allocating what it regarded as a suitable sum to each of the four main-line railway companies and London Transport on a predetermined basis. The inclusion of the London Passenger Transport Board in the scheme was opposed by the Big Four railway companies, who believed that

Blackout brought operating difficulties and finding one's train must have been especially difficult at a large terminus such as Waterloo, shown here. (*NRM 1155/6/63*)

passenger traffic would slump in wartime, and that as the only all-passenger operator, London Transport would become a liability for the others. It certainly meant that the allocated funds would have to be spread around more thinly.

The state also decided what resources could be made available in terms of raw materials and manufacturing capacity to keep the railways running. This was not nationalisation in the true sense of the word, but it was a bureaucratic straitjacket, although it must be remembered that the control of raw materials and manufacturing capacity applied to the entire economy and not just the railways.

None of this, of course, can give a real impression of what it must have been like operating a railway in the blackout, or of the problems of individual railwaymen and women having to report for work after a broken night's sleep in a crowded air-raid shelter, or of coming off a night shift to find that their home had been destroyed, and perhaps family members and neighbours killed. The efficient working of a railway requires skill and experience, but under wartime conditions most adults had to be available for either the armed forces or prepared to be directed to essential war work, and as skilled men volunteered or were conscripted into the armed forces, many of their places were taken by women, who did cope extremely well. Indeed, many historians believe that one factor in the defeat of Germany was that the Germans were reluctant to mobilise the civilian population and instead relied too heavily on slave labour and people conscripted from the occupied territories or Vichy France.

Wartime meant shortages of everything, except demand. The shortages were soon seen, as *The Southern Railway Magazine* was no longer published monthly from the beginning of

The Channel Islands packet, SS *Isle of Jersey*, seen on war service as a hospital ship. (*NRM 366/69*)

1941, but on alternate months, until the issue of September 1944, when monthly publication resumed.

In the meantime, the Southern had played a major role in taking the British Expeditionary Force to France, and then, after Dunkirk, bringing them back, along with French, Dutch, Belgian and Polish troops all escaping the German advance, with long trains taking them from the Channel ports to barracks throughout Great Britain. A few days before the Dunkirk evacuation ended, the Luftwaffe bombed and sank *Maid of Kent* and *Brighton* in a French port, despite the fact that these two Southern Railway vessels were both clearly marked with red crosses to show that they were hospital ships. Three more of the Southern's fleet were lost during the evacuation.

Communities and businesses started collections and events to raise funds to buy aircraft for the RAF, and the Southern also ran one of these 'Spitfire Funds'. A small plaque next to the cockpit proclaimed the company's involvement and the aircraft was named *Southern Spitfire*. Needless to say, this appeared in a report with a photograph in *The Southern Railway Magazine*.

Evacuation and Emergency Measures

After the false hopes raised by resolution of the Munich Crisis of 1938, it soon became clear that war was more of a probability than a possibility. Preparations were made by the railway companies, although they were not helped by threatened industrial action, which was only averted at the last moment. On virtually the eve of war, evacuation of children and many others, including their teachers and expectant and nursing mothers, started to get them away from London and other major cities, especially those judged to be likely targets. The pressure on the Southern and other railways was such that during the four

The flying bombs brought about a further evacuation late in the war. These are schoolchildren waiting for a train to take them outside the danger zone at Surbiton on 11 July 1944. (*NRM 1155/36/63*)

days of the operation, from 1 to 4 September 1939, only a skeleton service could be provided for the public outside the rush hours.

The order to begin the evacuation was given on 31 August. The threatened areas were seen as London and many of the surrounding areas which had important factories or docks, the Medway area, and Southampton, Portsmouth and Gosport. Children assembled at their schools and from there either walked or were taken by bus to the station allocated to them, with many having to use suburban stations either because of convenience or because the London termini could not handle all of them. In the case of the Southern, the pressure on the London termini was spread by also using Richmond, Wimbledon and New Cross Gate. Even so, in London alone, 5,895 buses were required to move 345,812 passengers to the stations. The Southern Railway was not unique in handling this traffic, but did account for a substantial proportion of it, providing seventy-five trains a day to carry evacuees from south and south-east areas of London to Kent and Sussex, a total of more than 138,000 passengers.

Even while the evacuation from London was in full swing, twenty-seven trains a day were moving children from the Medway towns to safer parts of Kent, including the young occupants of the Borstal prison near Rochester. Another 127 trains took some 30,000 people from Southampton and Gosport to the more remote parts of Hampshire and to adjoining Dorset and Wiltshire, and later in September, a further eighteen trains were run from these two towns and from Portsmouth.

The railways also had to arrange thirty-four ambulance trains for the partial evacuation of hospitals in these areas, while later all hospitals within 20 miles of the south coast were also partially evacuated. These measures were not just to remove patients to places of greater safety, but to free beds for the bombing when it came, and also to empty hospitals near the coast in case of an invasion.

Other preparations were also put in hand, with air-raid notices displayed in the compartments of trains on the Eastern Section, judged most likely to be affected because of its proximity to Europe, and at Victoria the station lights were replaced by blue lights. The blackout was enforced from 2 September, and the next day Britain and France were at war with Germany.

Meanwhile, the Ministry of War Transport, as the Ministry of Transport had become, moved quickly to seize control of the railways on 1 September, using powers granted under the Defence Regulations Act 1939. The minister operated through a Railway Executive Committee, which included the general managers of the four main-line railways, including Gilbert Szlumper of the Southern. The London termini were seen as likely targets in wartime, so the Southern evacuated as many of its administrative personnel as possible to the outskirts, with the headquarters sent to a mansion near Dorking, to which a large number of outbuildings had been added as offices.

Gilbert Szlumper later transferred to the War Office as Director-General of Transportation, a compliment to his abilities, and his place as general manager was taken by Eustace Missenden, who had been traffic manager, with John Elliot, a former journalist who had handled the Southern's publicity, as his deputy.

Despite the haste to grab control of the railways, there was considerable delay in finalising the means of working. The system of state control meant that the railways effectively became contractors to the government, with all revenue passing to the government which then allocated a shareout of a pool, which was set at a guaranteed £40 million. The Southern share of the pool was fixed at 16 per cent, the same as for the GWR, while the LPTB received 11 per cent, the LMS 34 per cent and the LNER 23 per cent. These percentages were based on the average net revenues for the companies and LPTB in the three years 1935–7, which the government regarded as the standard revenue for each company. Once the guaranteed £40 million had been paid, any balance was allocated to the five train operators on the same percentage terms up to a maximum of £3.5 million. After this, the arrangements became complicated, since if there was a further balance, the revenue over a total of £43.5 million would be divided equally between the government and the pool until the pool total reached £56 million. At this stage, if the revenue share allocated to any of the companies then exceeded its standard revenue, the excess would be shared out proportionately among the other companies.

Costs of maintenance and renewals had to be standardised, while the cost of restoring war damage would be met up to a total of £10 million in a full year. Privately owned wagons were also requisitioned by the Ministry of War Transport, and the individual companies had to meet the costs and revenue attributed to the wagon owners out of their share of the revenue pool.

This was a 'take it or leave it' type of agreement, with the government leaking threats of nationalisation if the companies failed to agree, although these were officially denied. The years in question had not been good ones for the British economy, although 1938 had been worse and the railways had had to work hard to get the government to recognise this. The difficult economic conditions that had prevailed for almost all of the inter-war period had meant that the railway companies had never achieved the revenues anticipated by the Railways Act 1921, the measure that authorised the grouping. The best that can be said for the deal was that the government was anxious to avoid inflationary pay claims from railway employees, and no doubt anxious to ensure that it did not play a part in war profiteering since it was likely to be its own single biggest customer, but the inescapable fact was that the railways were having their revenues more or less fixed while costs were bound to rise as they struggled to meet increased demands. Placing an upper limit on the cost of making good war damage was another instance of either political expediency to keep the unions and Labour

Party quiet in the wartime coalition government, or simple naivety since normal insurance measures were not available in wartime.

Initially, excursion and cheap day tickets were withdrawn, but day tickets were reintroduced on 9 October, although with tighter conditions attached that meant that they were not available before 10 am and could not be used on trains departing from London between 4 and 7 pm Monday to Friday.

There had been much rehearsal of all of this over the previous year or so. Railwaymen had practised working in blackout conditions, which meant that no lights could be shown externally, with all windows screened, while station platforms could only be lit by blue lights or, as there were still many lit by gas, specially shaded gas lamps, and drivers and motormen had to pull up their trains beside oil lamps placed on the platform as markers. Steam locomotives had canvas draped between the engine cab and tender to hide the light of their fires, while the side windows that had appeared on the more modern locomotives were blanked out. The colour light signals of which the Southern was so proud and which raised railway safety were now a danger and a marked disadvantage because they were so visible, and long hoods had to be fitted over them as a priority so that they could not be seen from the air, although this did not prevent some extensions of colour light signalling being completed early in 1940 around Richmond and Clapham Junction, since the equipment had already been manufactured and was not suitable for any other application. Shades were also fitted to guards' lamps. The route indicators on the front of electric trains were also shaded blue at first, but these later reverted to white. One of the more extreme measures was that trains initially ran at night without lights, but later shaded lights were introduced.

Wartime acted as a spur to extending loudspeaker announcements to stations, and while initially station name signs were no longer lit, those under station canopies were allowed to be illuminated later provided that they were swung round at right angles to the platform. Those stations that had had their names painted on the canopies to help airmen with their navigation had them blanked out. A final safety measure at stations was the removal of glass from roofs and canopies, essential since even a small bomb could create so many shards of broken glass as to be an effective anti-personnel weapon.

Drastic Cuts

After the evacuation was over, services returned to normal, but only briefly, for on 11 September drastic cuts were imposed on train services, meaning great hardship for passengers since, although the late-holiday and day-tripper traffic had virtually disappeared, normal business travel was still at pre-war levels, especially with large numbers of people commuting to their offices in the City. Some large companies had dispersed, especially those with strategic importance such as the shipping lines, but it was not possible for everyone to do so, for apart from business considerations, the number of suitable venues outside London and other major cities was limited. The usual 20 minute suburban frequencies were cut to half-hourly, while off-peak and Sunday services became hourly. A number of services were cancelled completely, including London Bridge– Streatham Hill and Holborn Viaduct–Herne Hill–Orpington. Not only did this lead to unacceptable levels of overcrowding with many passengers left behind, it also meant that station dwell times were extended as passengers struggled to alight from or board trains. After the uproar that followed, normal services were reinstated on weekdays from 18 September.

Nevertheless, this was simply a temporary reinstatement and indicated nothing more than that the blanket reductions of 11 September had not been properly thought out. Wartime conditions meant that services had to be reduced, both to save personnel, fuel and wear and tear and to make trains and paths available for the military. Reductions in passenger services followed on 16 October, although on this occasion better allowances were made for peak period travel. Off-peak, most main-line services lost their hourly trains, to be replaced by a service every 2 hours, often running to extended timings. Some, as on the Waterloo to Portsmouth service, on which an additional stop at Woking was introduced for the 'fast' trains, called at more stations.

Cannon Street was closed between 10 am and 4 pm Monday to Friday and after 7.30 pm on weekdays, as well as closing all day on Sunday. Services were suspended between Holborn Viaduct and Dartford via Nunhead, and between London Bridge and Streatham Hill and Victoria to Beckenham Junction, with only a peak period service on Waterloo–Putney–Wimbledon and to Addiscombe. On the Eastern and Central sections a number of stations lost their off-peak direct services. On the busy Brighton line, the only non-stop trains were in the rush hours, and their journey times were extended in some cases. Off-peak, there were just three trains an hour on the Brighton line, less than half the pre-war service, as through services to Worthing and Littlehampton were only available at peak periods. Waterloo to Reading became a tedious stopping service after a call at Richmond, and the Alton line lost its rush-hour extras. There were also reductions in catering arrangements, with Pullman and most buffet cars being withdrawn and the restaurant car service ceasing on the Portsmouth Direct. Once again, off-peak suburban services were hourly, although the busy line from Charing Cross to Bexleyheath and Sidcup remained half-hourly. On some lines, such as the south London, services were curtailed late in the evening, but others had special late services running after midnight for the benefit of shift workers.

These cutbacks must have once again aroused some public reaction and been regarded as too severe, for on 1 January 1940, Pullman cars reappeared, as did pantry cars, and there was an increase in the number of buffet cars, while restaurant service resumed on the Portsmouth Direct. A number of services were also reinstated during peak hours, as were some of the cancelled rush-hour extra trains.

Limiting a railway service has some disadvantages, especially during bad weather when the frequent passage of trains and movement of signals and points can help to stop icing. Late January saw exceptionally severe weather which froze the conductor rails and, having started on a Sunday when only a limited service was operating, also froze many trains in the sidings. Communications were disrupted as the railway telegraph wires were brought down. On the more exposed routes, steam locomotives had to push or pull the electric multiple units through the worst affected lengths of track. Accustomed to the Southern's normal quiet efficiency, passengers suffered the worst disruption many had seen.

Dunkirk

The 1940 Whitsun holiday was cancelled by the government since the Germans were sweeping through the Low Countries and into France. This ultimately led to the evacuation of the British Expeditionary Force from Dunkirk, along with many French troops and some from Belgium as well.

By the time of Dunkirk, six of the Southern Railway's cross-Channel packets and the Channel Island ferry *Isle of Guernsey* were already working as hospital ships, while another eight, including *Autocarrier* and *Canterbury*, had been taken up from trade and were in service as military transports. Early on 29 May, the *Brittany* was also requisitioned by the government and warning given that two more ships might be wanted, but by noon the situation was such that 'all available Southern Railway steamers of 1,000 tons gross with a range of 150 miles are required for immediate Government service'. Nine ships were quickly handed over, including four Isle of Wight ferries, of which two were car ferries with low open vehicle decks and certainly not best suited to a squall in the English Channel.

The Southern had already lost two ships by this time. On 23 May the *Maid of Kent*, clearly marked as a hospital ship and crowded with wounded soldiers, sank in the harbour at Dieppe after being hit by five bombs. That same day *Brighton*, again marked as a hospital ship, was also bombed and sunk.

On 30 May *Lorina* and *Normannia*, operating as military transports, were both sunk at Dunkirk, although the crew of the latter were all saved and reached England. Another hospital ship, the *Paris*, was bombed on 2 June and the damage was such that she had to be abandoned.

It was the small Isle of Wight paddle-steamer, *Whippingham*, that took the record for the number of men rescued from Dunkirk, carrying 2,700 men on 4 June.

During the rest of the war, another seven Southern Railway vessels were lost to enemy action. The ships did not simply operate as military transports, with some of the Isle of Wight paddle-steamers serving as minesweepers, although their work was usually close to home in the Solent.

Meanwhile, ashore in England, the Southern Railway was already hard at work handling special trains, many of them sent south by other companies, to get the soldiers away from the Channel ports. At 5 pm on 26 May, the code-word 'Dynamo' was sent to the railways, warning them that the evacuation was due to start. The operation ran from 27 May to 4 June, and the difficulty of organising it was made worse by the sudden realisation on the part of the authorities that a second evacuation was needed of many children moved from London, but who were now too close for comfort to German airfields. Neither the railways nor the military knew how many men to expect from Dunkirk – in the end more than 338,000 were carried. This of necessity meant massive disruption to ordinary services, with even the slimmed-down wartime timetable suspended in many cases. Worst affected were the services from Tonbridge to Redhill, and Redhill to Guildford and Reading, an all-important cross-country route bypassing the London area for those being taken to Wales, the West Country and the Midlands. All of the usual passenger trains along the Tonbridge–Reading lines were suspended and replacement bus services provided, which must have resulted in greatly extended journey times given the meandering nature of the A25.

While the whole exercise has been seen since the war as a masterpiece of organisation and improvisation, the evacuation took place in an atmosphere of chaos. No one knew how many troops would arrive or when, and certainly they had no idea of how many were fit and how many were wounded, and still less of where to send them when they did arrive. The chaos was such that trains were turned round at Dover and sent off before the authorities had any idea where they could send the rescued troops, so often drivers were instructed to 'Stop at Guildford and ask where you are going to'.

Volunteers tried to ensure that the arriving troops were given tea and something to eat, as well as a card so that they could write home to let their families know that they were safe. A collection at one station to provide food and drink for the troops, organised by the stationmaster's wife, raised more than £1,000 from passengers and from people who had been drawn to the station by the continuous flood of the heavily laden troop trains. Inevitably, everything was under unforeseen pressure. One example was that at some stations used as refreshment stops, there weren't enough cups: tins had to be used as improvised cups, and just before a train left from a refreshment stop, the order was given for these to be thrown out so that the volunteers could wash them ready for the next train.

Exceptional circumstances demand exceptional measures, and the railway companies quickly agreed among themselves to provide a large pool of carriages. The GWR provided sufficient for 40 trains, the LMS 44, the LNER 47 and the Southern 55, making 186 trains with a total of almost 2,000 carriages. The Southern's total implied great hardship for many of its regular passengers on the non-electrified routes, as the electric trains could not reach the Channel ports. The railways did not know how many journeys would need to be made by these trains and at the outset just where the troops would land, but Dover filled 327 trains, Ramsgate 82, Margate 75 troop trains plus another 25 ambulance trains, while Folkestone had the surprisingly low figure of 64 trains. Sheerness handled 17 trains while there were also a small number of men landed at Newhaven and even a few at Southampton, a considerable distance from the main evacuation scene. The busiest days were 1 June and 4 June, with as many as 60 vessels alongside at Dover at any one time on the latter day. The entire operation was achieved by having holding points for empty trains at Faversham, Margate, Queenborough and Ramsgate, although at one time the system became so congested that four trains had to be held as far away as Willesden. Possibly the railways managed so well because they were used to the demand for special trains caused by major sporting events, but one general was heard to wish that the army 'could operate with as few written instructions as the Southern Railway does!'

The big bottleneck in this system, not surprisingly, was Redhill, where trains travelling from Tonbridge towards Guildford had to reverse across a completely flat junction which also had a heavy traffic of Brighton line semi-fast and stopping trains. This was not the only problem, since at one stage this station, with just three platform faces, ran short of water, not usually required for its customary service of electric trains with only the relatively infrequent cross-country trains worked by steam at this stage. Another problem soon surfaced, for by 4 June the station had accumulated 300 tons of ashes! Despite the awkward layout for such traffic, 80 per cent of the Dunkirk trains passed through Redhill, and most trains took no longer than 4 minutes to change locomotives and reverse, with the record being 2½ minutes. This was no easy task, as second locomotives had to be waiting ready for every train from the Kent coast, while others were waiting for empty trains returning to the coast. Locomotives needing coaling had to be sent as light engines to Earlswood or even Three Bridges, as Redhill's limited facilities were soon overwhelmed and then exhausted.

The Channel Islands

Dunkirk was one consequence of the German invasion of France, and the next was the realisation that the Channel Islands could not be held. For the first nine months of war, these islands had been a haven of tranquillity, although RAF and Fleet Air Arm units had been based there, and life had continued as before, including the use of the railway ships to bring the potato harvest to England. Some of the local hoteliers were even expecting holidaymakers to arrive that summer.

Realising that the Channel Islands would be almost impossible to defend and supply once France fell to the Germans, an evacuation was put in hand by the authorities. On 19 June the British government declared the islands to be a demilitarised zone, and the RAF and Fleet Air Arm units returned home, and voluntary evacuation was offered to women and children as well as to those men willing to volunteer to join the armed forces. Five Southern Railway cargo steamers were used in the evacuation, taking 8,000 people from Jersey, 17,000 from the smaller island of Guernsey and 1,500 from Alderney. These ships were hardly well suited to the purpose, although temporary shelter was provided, and the small fleet struggled to take so many people to England between 17 and 28 June. Alderney was completely evacuated, Sark almost completely, but while many on the two largest islands decided to leave, others stayed put. Then there were those who left it too late.

After the evacuation, the Southern Railway agreed with the authorities that the company's ships would continue operating even after the evacuation ended, so that life on the Channel Islands could continue as usual. This was not necessarily a wise move, since it was inconceivable that life would not be disrupted, and certainly any shipping attempting to reach the islands would be very vulnerable. It seems incredible that the Southern Railway was expected by the government to maintain its regular services in such circumstances, even though the service was much reduced owing to wartime restrictions, uncertainty and the requisition by the military of so many ships, many of which, as we have seen, had already been lost.

On 27 June the regular packet vessel the *Isle of Sark* left Southampton for Jersey and Guernsey with more than 250 passengers, making the overnight passage to arrive at Jersey at 6.30 the following morning, where she was seen, but not attacked, by a German aircraft. The service also carried passengers between the islands, so that when the *Isle of Sark* reached Guernsey at 12.30 on 28 June, she had 454 passengers on board, many of whom were to continue to Southampton. However, a lot of the passengers took the opportunity to go ashore for the afternoon as the return trip was again to be an overnight passage. At 7 pm, as passengers were embarking, three German aircraft attacked, bombing the pier, while the ship's AA armament – an old 12-pounder and four Lewis guns – went into action. But as additional aircraft attacked, more than fifty people ashore were killed and a number of small craft sunk, although the *Isle of Sark* herself was undamaged. The master was ordered to sail as soon as the tide permitted, but he held back until 10 pm and reached Southampton safely the following morning with 647 passengers. This was the last British ship to leave the Channel Islands, which then had to endure almost five years of German occupation.

The Southern Railway's decision to continue services, doubtless taken under government pressure, contrasts with the action of the directors of one of the main coastal and short sea shipping companies, the General Steam Navigation Company. The company had seen some of its ships taken over by the Germans and employees interned when they were caught in German ports on the outbreak of the First World War, and so it moved during the final days of peace to ensure that no ships and no employees were likely to be caught in German ports. The same measures were put in hand for those in the Low Countries once the advance westwards started. The result for the Southern Railway by contrast was that, when the Germans did arrive, a number of the company's employees were caught and interned. At the 1941 AGM, the Chairman drew attention to this and said that special provision had been made by the company for the wives and children of these employees.

In the Front Line

The rapid German advance westwards had changed everything. At the outset many had believed that the Second World War would see the same long-drawn-out tussle on French soil that had marked the First World War. Now the authorities found themselves in the embarrassing situation that some of the original areas chosen to send evacuees to were no longer safe. A further evacuation was necessary, moving children from Kent (and, for that matter, Essex and Suffolk as well) westwards. This started as early as 19 May 1940, using sixteen special trains to carry 8,000 children from the three most threatened counties. On 2 June, in the midst of the Dunkirk evacuation, 48,000 children were moved from towns on the East Coast in seventy trains. Ten days later, on 12 June, the move of 100,000 London children to Berkshire, Somerset, the south-west and Wales started, and continued until 18 June. The Southern's share of this exodus was to carry 42,391 children in eighty-four trains from Waterloo, Vauxhall, Clapham Junction and a number of suburban stations. As with the original evacuation, many parents changed their minds at the last minute and kept their children, so that a train from Vauxhall to North Cornwall intended for 600 passengers only carried 417 children and thirty-two adults.

As the Battle of Britain raged, hop-pickers in Kent were offered the opportunity to travel westwards rather than return to London, and this required another fifteen trains for 8,000 people. In the autumn a further evacuation was organised from London for 13,500 women and children, demanding twenty-three trains. As the length of journey increased and the winter weather set in, the authorities asked the Southern if they could provide hot meals on the trains – a tall order since, with the exception of Pullman trains, normally only a fraction of the usual number of travellers on a train required hot meals – but this was done on condition that the escorts for the children helped with serving and washing up, and all for 1s.

Some idea of the effect of the war on the civilian population on the Kent coast can be illustrated in Dover having a pre-war population of around 40,000, which had reduced to around 23,000 after Dunkirk. Of course, some of these people may have moved not because the town was vulnerable, but because the ending of the cross-Channel ferries would have meant that many jobs were no longer available and the labour would have been directed elsewhere, while the crews of the Channel packets would have often followed their ships as they went over to war work.

As the Battle of Britain turned to the Blitz, with London bombed every night bar one for sixty-seven nights, a scheme was drawn up to evacuate 746,000 people from certain parts of the south coast and east coast during early summer 1941. The plans were prepared in great secrecy to avoid panic, but they called for 988 trains to be used and for the operation to be completed in just four days. Fortunately, it was not necessary.

The threat of invasion faded away and the blitz also eased after the German invasion of the Soviet Union. Even so, even after D-Day there were other threats to contend with. In 1944 the appearance of the flying bombs meant yet another evacuation, although at first this was unofficial. Many left on ordinary services, but the authorities once again sanctioned an official evacuation of children and mothers with young children, and 200,000 people were moved from London and the south coast on special trains. This was a more difficult evacuation than the earlier ones, largely because previous evacuations had been carried out in anticipation of attack, but the latest evacuation was carried out under attack. It was also carried out while the Southern especially was busy moving reinforcements and supplies to support the fighting in France, and, of course, it was using a system that had suffered four years of wartime attack and neglect.

Restrictions

Throughout the war years there was an almost constant trimming of services to reduce fuel consumption and eliminate under-used train miles. Shoreham Airport Halt closed on 15 July 1940, while on 6 January 1941 Crystal Palace High Level lost its direct services and was worked by a shuttle from Nunhead, before being closed on 1 May 1944. Waterloo–East Putney–Wimbledon ended altogether on 5 May. On 1 January 1942 Bishopstone Beach Halt was closed.

At the same time, the changing traffic patterns created by wartime saw a new halt opened at Hilsea, close to Portsmouth Airport, to meet the needs of war workers. On 11 October 1942 a spur was opened at Crayford from the Sidcup loop to the north Kent line. Another halt was opened at Longcross, between Virginia Water and Sunningdale, on 3 May 1943, and one was also opened at Upper Halliford, near Shepperton, on 1 May 1944.

In addition to trimming services, as the war progressed other restrictions were applied. On 6 October 1941, under the directions of the Minister of War Transport, all suburban trains became third class only. The reasons for the move were practical, the idea being not only to make the best use of all accommodation on the reduced number of trains, but also to recognise the difficulty in finding the right class of accommodation in a hurry during the blackout. To drive the point home, carpets were removed from first-class compartments and the first-class indications on the compartment doors painted out, while timetables and departure indicators described trains as 'Third Class Only'. After the withdrawal of first-class accommodation, blackout or not, regular travellers seemed to be able to find their way to the superior leg and elbow room and plusher upholstery of the former first-class compartments, so that these soon became shabby with intensive use. While main-line trains retained first-class accommodation, on 22 May 1942 they lost all catering facilities on the electrified lines, although some service was maintained on the steam-hauled services because of the longer distances involved. The Pullman cars were all taken out of the sets and stored, as were the buffet cars on the 4 BUF sets. Restaurant and pantry cars, because of their higher seating capacity, remained in the sets, but with the catering areas locked out of use. Later that same year, many suburban electric multiple units were lengthened from three to four carriages by the simple expedient of breaking up the trailer sets and inserting an additional trailer in the motor sets. This eliminated some shunting and the time and manpower needed to insert extra sets at peak periods, and also provided extra accommodation when a single set was being operated.

It now became important to discourage unnecessary travel. The lack of sporting events and the fact that the coastal resorts had their beaches wrapped in barbed wire meant that normal leisure pursuits were not available. Again on the instructions of the Minister of War Transport, on 5 October 1942 off-peak cheap returns were scrapped, leaving seasons as the only 'cheap', or discounted, tickets. Evidence of the impact of the economy measures came at a conference on fuel in 1944, which showed that in each of the last two years before the war, the Southern had operated 220 million car miles and used 530 million units of electricity, while its reduced wartime service was using 164 million car miles and 409 million units. This gives little idea of the impact of the service on the traveller, since the 'reduced' wartime service included a substantial number of troop trains. The wartime service also seemed to use slightly more power per car mile than the peacetime service, possibly due to extra stops. In an attempt to economise on electricity, coasting marks were sited for stopping trains, and while there were no such marks for non-stop trains, an unofficial system of 'on' and 'off' points was established. Heating was another area in which fuel could be saved, so the pre-war system of switching on full heat on main-line trains between October and April when the temperature fell below 48°F at any one of a number of monitoring points, and half-heat when the temperature fell below 55°F, was reduced to having full heat when the temperature fell below 45°F and half-heat when it fell below 50°F between November and March.

Shortages of skilled staff in the workshops and the conversion of many of these to war production, as well as shortages of materials, meant that the intervals between routine overhauls were extended. Overall, the Southern lost 9,000 men to the armed forces, and these were replaced by 8,000 women.

Nevertheless, the pressure on the Southern railway was such that not all production and innovation could be abandoned. To get the most out of the electrified lines, the first of two electric locomotives, mothballed on the outbreak of war, was completed and ready for trials in 1941, and a second was completed in 1943; more details of these are in Appendix III. The railway also received the first of the 0–6–0 'Q1' class tender utility locomotives. These were an ugly creation but still showed evidence of Bulleid's design and were used mainly for goods trains. The Southern also received a token number of US-built tank engines after these had been modified to run on British lines. Earlier, wartime restrictions also failed to stop Oliver Bulleid building the first of his magnificent Pacifics, the 'Merchant Navy' class and the smaller 'West Country' and 'Battle of Britain' classes. The only oddity was that the 'Merchant Navy' class locomotives were too heavy to take boat trains into the docks at Southampton, but postwar they were to excel on Channel boat trains and, not surprisingly, the first was named *Channel Packet*.

Helping the War Effort

The Southern played an important role in the concentration of personnel, equipment and supplies in preparation for the D-Day landings in Normandy. The planning also affected the Southern's traffic in another way, as added to the normal wartime restrictions, from 2 April 1944 visitors were banned from the south coast, and this also meant that a number of main-line services were suspended. The restrictions were eased after the landings.

Southampton Docks played a major role during the preparations for D-Day, with many of the landing ships loaded there, while the Western Section was heavily used by goods trains moving equipment and supplies to the docks. One small branch line station, Dunbridge, near Romsey, gives a good indication of the impact on the railways of the run-up to D-Day. In June 1938 this small station had handled 182 goods wagons, but in June 1944 it handled 5,246! New sidings had to be built just for the landings at both Micheldever and Brockenhurst. Military passenger traffic was also heavy, with Southampton handling 364,350 British troops between D-Day and VE Day, as well as 2,165,883 American troops and 310,113 prisoners of war. Lymington had its slipways doubled so that two tank landing craft could be loaded at the same time, while Littlehampton handled ammunition and Newhaven was used as an embarkation port for troops.

Railway workshops were heavily committed to wartime production, with Eastleigh Works producing, among other things, guns. (*NRM 1350/86*)

Newhaven had closed in July 1940, but reopened the following year to handle coal brought by coastal shipping mainly from south Wales. In fact, while the North Sea and Straits of Dover were closed to normal merchant shipping movements, coal shipments by sea increased between south Wales and the SR ports of Southampton, Newhaven, Fremington, Cowes and Highbridge from their pre-war level of 37,500 tons to a peak of 111,200 tons in 1943.

The 'Rhino' pontoon sections of the famous Mulberry Harbours for the landings were built in the King George V graving dock at Southampton, just one of many contributions to the war effort, with many of the workshops turned over to war production as part of the 'shadow' factory network, often building components for armaments manufacturers, especially at Eastleigh and Ashford. The pressures of wartime saw Brighton works back in production, building thirty locomotives in 1943, while personnel rose from 253 men in 1939 to 755 men and 214 women working full-time and 38 working part-time by the end of 1943. One of the orders handled by Ashford works was the construction in 1941 of a thousand open 13-ton freight wagons for the USSR, despatched in sections to the Middle East and reaching their destination through Persia. The works also built bridge components for the LMS and parts for howitzers. Eastleigh built bomb trolleys, parts for aircraft and also for

Matilda tanks, as well as complete landing craft and tailplanes for Horsa troop-carrying gliders. Lancing built stampings for gun breech mechanisms, ambulance trains and wagons.

The marine workshops at Southampton handled repairs and refits to 184 warships, 723 merchant ships and maintenance of water ambulances. Those at Newhaven handled 603 warships, 140 merchant ships, ten hospital carriers and twenty-one RAF high-speed launches. The workshops at Dover, with their Southern Railway personnel, were taken over by the Admiralty on 1 July 1940 and retained until 31 January 1945, keeping warships based at the port in fighting condition.

Some idea of the Southern Railway's contribution to the war effort in terms of railway operations alone can be gathered from the number of special trains for the government handled by the company between 3 September 1939 and 8 May 1945:

Troop trains: 30,890
Troops carried: 9,367,886
Goods trains: 35,360
PoW trains (June 1944–May 1945): 1,127
PoWs carried: 582,005
Ambulance trains: 1,797
Passengers on ambulance trains: 408,051 (including medical staff)
BEF leave trains, 1940: 1,429 with 142,021 personnel
BEF leave trains, January–May 1945: 1,746 with 845,940 personnel

By 6 December 1944 the launching sites for the German V-weapons had been overrun, and the Germans no longer had fuel to mount any other form of attack, so evacuees were officially encouraged to return. While there was an initial surge before Christmas, on this occasion the flow homewards was far steadier, increasing after 8 May 1945.

Chapter Sixteen

Railways under Attack

The wartime railways had to continue to serve the nation and provide numerous special trains of one kind or another amid heavy aerial bombardment. In any modern war the transport system is one of the most important targets, for it not only allows the swift reinforcement of the front line, but also conveys essential supplies, raw materials and, of course, fuel. As war threatened, the Southern's directors and senior management were concerned over whether the electrified lines would cope with the heavy punishment of a bombing campaign, but the deciding factor was whether trains could run at all. The electric trains could run wherever steam trains could, with the added advantage of not needing to find turntables, or coaling and watering facilities. They also had the advantage, as we have already seen, of not leaving large quantities of ash to be removed.

The Southern suffered the severe disadvantage that of the 'Big Four' it was closest to the enemy's airfields and operating in what was regarded as a prime invasion area. Although spared the massive industrial conurbations of the Midlands and the north of England, or central Scotland, it did have three major naval bases at Chatham, Portsmouth and Plymouth, as well as a less important one at Portland, the ports of London and Southampton, and a substantial proportion of the RAF's fighter stations within its area, as well as being more heavily exposed to the plight of the capital than any other railway. It also served the area chosen for the massive build-up of men, equipment and supplies for the Normandy landings.

Blitzed!

The enemy air attacks followed the fall of France and at first were concentrated on British airfields as the Luftwaffe attempted to wipe out the RAF. The first impact on the Southern was as early as 19 June 1940, when bombs destroyed the engineering works at Redbridge, near Southampton, and destroyed a large quantity of sleepers. On 10 July a train was bombed near Newhaven, killing the driver and injuring the guard. Then on 16 August 1940 a bomb blocked two lines at Malden and killed railwaymen and passengers. This type of incident was to become commonplace as the blitz on London and other major cities got under way, effectively lasting from September 1940 until May 1941.

Between 24 August 1940 and 10 May 1941 there were raids on some part of the Southern network for 250 out of the 252 days. One of the most serious incidents occurred on 7 September 1940, when a high-explosive bomb hit the approaches to Waterloo, penetrating the brick viaduct before exploding and causing so much damaged that the station had to be closed. Despite the railway's own resources being reinforced by those of the army, the station could not be reopened until 19 September, and then only partially with just two roads available for traffic. Operations returned to normal on 1 October. The running of so much of the approaches to the London termini over viaducts was a serious weakness, with those between Blackfriars and Loughborough Junction damaged in two places by bombs during the blitz, and the line to Herne Hill from Loughborough Junction hit twice, with the overbridge carrying the south London line and Catford loop having a narrow escape. The Southern's own power station at Durnsford Road was hit by another high-explosive bomb on 12 October, destroying one of the chimneys and part of the boiler house, so that the

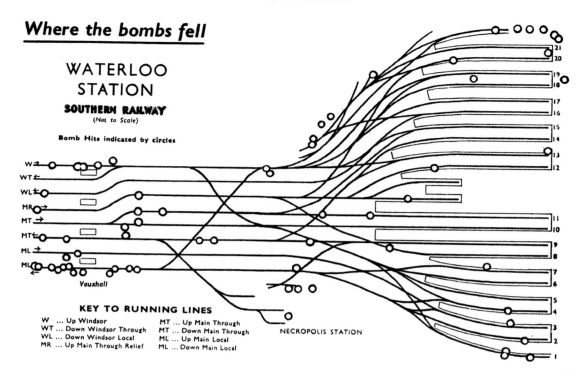

Where the bombs fell

WATERLOO STATION

SOUTHERN RAILWAY

(Not to Scale)

Bomb Hits indicated by circles

Vauxhall

KEY TO RUNNING LINES

W ... Up Windsor	MT ... Up Main Through
WT ... Down Windsor Through	MT ... Down Main Through
WL ... Down Windsor Local	ML ... Up Main Local
MR ... Up Main Through Relief	ML ... Down Main Local

NECROPOLIS STATION

'Where the bombs fell' – Waterloo. *(Southern Railway)*

station's generating capacity was cut by half. The repairs included erecting a new 100 ft-high steel chimney, and weren't complete until 12 February 1941. In the meantime, a parachute mine landed next to the signal cabin at London Bridge on 12 December but did not explode and, as mentioned in Chapter Two, the signalmen continued working while a naval bomb disposal team defused it. London Bridge was less lucky the next time, as the so-called 'fire raid' on the night of 29/30 December saw the station buildings gutted and the southern side of the Central Section station badly damaged. That night, Waterloo also had to close again for a time because of incendiary bombs.

At the height of the blitz, one train arriving from Ramsgate at Charing Cross had been driven through heavy bombing, and at times the two enginemen had been forced to stop and leave their cab to lie flat on their faces to avoid being injured by shrapnel. As they approached Charing Cross an oil bomb landed in their tender, but they managed to put it out using the engine hose.

A further major raid on the night of 16/17 April 1941 saw a landmine fall on the original section of the Hungerford Bridge, while incendiary bombs started fires inside Charing Cross station itself, damaging buildings, platforms and rolling stock. The landmine was welded to the third rail but failed to explode, and fortunately a fire started in the bridge timbers was put out just 10 ft away from it. Downstream there was far worse, as another high-explosive bomb destroyed the bridge across Southwark Street on the approaches to Blackfriars and Holborn Viaduct, and knocked out the Blackfriars signal cabin. Once again, the Southern's own resources were reinforced by the military, but it took fifteen days to restore two roads, and a new bridge was not completed until 9 October 1942. A temporary signalling arrangement had to be installed.

The final raid on the night of 10/11 May was one of the worst. Waterloo was damaged by high-explosive bombs while incendiaries started a major fire after they penetrated into a spirits store in the arches beneath the terminus. Cannon Street also suffered from bombs

Portsmouth Harbour station after the air raid that marooned trains and cut the station off from the rest of the Southern network. (*NRM 792/68*)

and incendiaries, and the locomotive that tried to rescue a van train by pulling it out from under the blazing roof on to the bridge was itself struck by a bomb. Holborn Viaduct was gutted by fires started by incendiary bombs and could not be used until 1 June. At Elephant & Castle, the island platform and Up local platform were burnt out, and a temporary Up main platform had to be provided before the station could reopen on 1 September.

Driver L. Stainer of Bricklayers' Arms recalled of the night of 10/11 May:[1]

We stopped the engine at Borough Market and the Fireman put out incendiaries. On arriving at Cannon Street, Platform 6, bombs began to drop, then the aspect signal lights all went out, and then some bombs dropped outside the station, bringing clouds of dust.

A fire had then started at the side of the station, and it rained bombs and there seemed to be no stopping. The fires were then like huge torches and there were thousands of sparks.

The smoke from the fires blacked out the moon, and fires seemed to be everywhere, and then the station roof caught alight.

To save the trains catching fire, two engines coupled together, No. 934 and No. 1541, pulled out of Platform 8 on to the bridge. We stopped twenty yards ahead of the other train, and then, after about ten minutes we ducked down on the footplate. We counted three bombs, the last one was terrific and very close. There was a terrific explosion and our engine seemed to roll; at first we thought our train had been hit. The debris flew in all directions – we were very lucky. My fireman said at the time, 'Look out – we are going in the drink', and I said, 'I thought my back week had come.'

We looked round, and found that the bomb had made a direct hit on the boiler of No. 934 engine, and it had also blasted our train, and turned part of the train over on its side.

My fireman and myself went to see where the driver and fireman were, and I am pleased to say that they had got off the engine in time.

'Then, looking around, we found our train had caught fire, and the fireman with buckets of water tried to put same out, but it was impossible as a strong wind was blowing up the Thames, and the fire got the master.

I uncoupled my engine from the train, and drew back about two yards, and secured the engine, and then crossed to the west of the bridge until dawn, watching the fires. It was just like as if Hell had been let loose.

Fortunately, no one was injured and Driver Stainer paid tribute to the coolness of the station staff at Cannon Street.

The worst-affected parts of the Southern Railway network were, naturally enough, all on the approaches to the London termini, and of these the most bombs and parachute mines per route mile were on the 2¼ miles between Waterloo and Queens Road, with no fewer than ninety-two 'incidents', as the authorities rather coyly described them. Charing Cross and Cannon Street to New Cross and New Cross Gate, 5½ route miles, recorded 123 incidents, and the 4½ route miles from Holborn Viaduct to Herne Hill suffered sixty-two incidents.

London was not alone in receiving the attentions of the Luftwaffe. At Portsmouth, both Portsmouth & Southsea station and Portsmouth Harbour suffered severe damage from bombing, with considerable loss of rolling stock, including electric multiple units. On the night of 11/12 January 1941, a train, including 4 COR sets, was hit while at platform 4 at Portsmouth Harbour, with the viaduct breached leaving the train marooned. It was not lifted out by cranes until September 1946.

Tunnels and Caves

Keeping rolling stock as safe as possible was a major consideration. The one place that was ideal for this was Kemp Town Tunnel at Brighton, although still used by goods trains after passenger trains had been withdrawn. The tunnel was first used to stable electric stock for a trial three weeks in October 1941, but the practice then became regular and continued until May 1944. The electric multiple units were shunted into and out of the tunnel by steam locomotives. At Bournemouth West the station was kept open all night so that rolling stock could be moved to safety at short notice.

Trains weren't the only residents of caves at night. At Dover the number of casualties during the shelling of the port and town was kept relatively low because the remaining residents spent much of their time in the caves beneath the famous white cliffs. At Chislehurst in Kent the caves provided a natural air-raid shelter, and many people would 'commute' by train to Chislehurst each evening to seek shelter.

Uniquely, at Dover, the main threat came not from bombs but from relentless shelling across the Dover Straits. Between three and four thousand shells landed on Dover and the surrounding area between 1940 and 1944, with another 1,800 falling into the harbour or offshore, as against 464 bombs, three parachute mines and three flying bombs. During the final days of the heavy shelling, on 13 September 1944, a shell scored a direct hit on the Priory station – the station for the town as opposed to ferry travellers – with several people killed and many more injured.

Travel by sea was extremely limited in wartime, with few routes open. One that remained operational with a skeleton service was that between Portsmouth and Ryde on the Isle of Wight. Early in the morning of 20 September 1941, the paddle-steamer *Portsdown* was lost after she struck a mine, with eight of her crew of eleven killed along with twelve passengers. One of the survivors was the lookout man, called Jupe. He reported:

The railways were a prime target during the months of the blitz on Britain. This is the carriage shed at Clapham Junction after a direct hit during the night of 8/9 September 1940. (*NRM 498/67*)

We left Portsmouth Harbour Pier at 4 am and I took up my position as look-out in the bows of the *Portsdown*. After we had cleared the outer harbour Channel buoys I reported this to Captain Chandler on the bridge and the vessel was then rounded up to go through the swashway to continue our journey to Ryde. About a minute after this, and before the vessel had completed her alteration of course, I heard a sort of scraping noise along the port side of the ship, and then, after what must have been a few seconds, there was a terrific explosion. At this moment I was looking out across the port bow and I was thrown into the sea. When I came to the surface I grasped a piece of floating wood and swam to the after port sponson, when I climbed on board and assisted in getting out the life boats, both of which were lowered and loaded with passengers.[2]

Another seventeen passengers were rescued by a boat launched by the Royal Navy.

Once the blitz was over, the Luftwaffe still mounted many 'hit and run' raids, usually at targets on the south coast. On 25 May 1943, during a raid on Brighton a bomb passed through a house and bounced over the garden wall to explode against one of the 70 ft-high piers of the London Road viaduct, bringing down two spans. It took fifteen days to effect temporary repairs and the damage was not completely repaired for four months. In the meantime, passengers between Brighton and Lewes had to make a lengthy diversion via Haywards Heath, although extra trains were operated between Haywards Heath and Lewes for their benefit.

Strafing and Flying Bombs

Trains were a tempting target for German fighter pilots on a strafing attack. On one occasion, a fine calm summer's evening, a train was approaching Deal on its run from

Ramsgate to Dover when six German fighters dived out of the sky, deliberately aiming at the locomotive footplate. The crew drew into what shelter they could find, and then at the last moment slammed on the brakes, hoping to make the Germans miss their target and meanwhile jump down on to the track to save themselves. As they jumped, it was clear that the driver had been hit, and that the fireman was now in charge. The fireman was wounded in the arm, thigh, leg and foot, and as he staggered towards the guard he fainted. Fortunately, the guard had been trained in first aid and was able to use a tourniquet for the fireman's arm, where an artery had been severed, and saved his life. Royal Marines stationed nearby provided assistance, putting out the fire and helping to rescue passengers from the burning train. A light engine came off a train at Deal station and, having obtained permission for wrong-line working, pulled the crippled train back to Walmer.

This was just one of many similar incidents, and in one case, when a Guildford to Horsham train was attacked near Bramley, just a few miles south of Guildford, the fireman was the only person on the train not to be injured, while seven passengers were killed.

Any feeling that the return of Allied forces to France meant that the war was ending was soon dispelled when the flying bomb campaign began in summer 1944. The arrival of a V1 near Haywards Heath is thought to have been the first. On 17 June a V1 hit a goods train on a bridge between Elephant & Castle and Loughborough Junction. The next day, another wrecked 100 ft of the southern end of Hungerford Bridge, and while restricted working resumed on 20 June, full normal working could not resume until 4 December. Further damage occurred at Victoria, Eastern Section, to the terminal platforms at Wimbledon normally used by the District Line, and to Charlton, Falconwood and Forest Hill stations. A bridge on the Quarry Line at Merstham was damaged, shifting its girders, and the main lines at Bricklayers' Arms Junction were cut. The bridge carrying the Catford loop over the south London line at Peckham Rye was so badly damaged by a V1 landing alongside on 12 July that it had to be demolished and replaced, giving the Southern's engineers a massive problem since the bridge also carried high-tension cables from the distribution room at Lewisham. The temporary bridge was ready for normal services to resume on 23 July. Another 'near miss' wrecked the signal cabin at Tulse Hill and damaged an underbridge, leading to diversions and cancellations until a temporary signal-box could be brought into use and the bridge repaired on 27 August.

The flying bombs stopped at the end of August, only to be followed by the V2 rockets, against which there could be no defence and no warning, as winter approached. The colour light signalling on the Up side of Hampton Court Junction was put out of action on 2 November, but normal working was restored by 4 November. On 5 November, at Bermondsey, the bridge carrying the Up main and local lines and south London lines over Southwark Park Road was hit and collapsed into the road. Again, a temporary bridge had to be provided, and normal working was reinstated late on 14 November. In the meantime, trains had to be cancelled or diverted. A block of flats at Deptford owned by the Southern Railway which accommodated railwaymen and their families was hit by a V2 in March 1945, with a quarter of the flats demolished and fifty-one people killed.

Conventional bombing had stopped by this time, and restrictions on lighting on trains and at stations were eased from October 1944. Station nameboards started to be reinstated in the normal positions. The blackout ended on 23 April 1945. Germany surrendered on 8 May.

All in all, the Southern alone had seen 14 bridges demolished, another 42 seriously damaged and 143 less seriously damaged. Incidents per 100 route miles on the Southern tell the story, with 170 incidents per 100 route miles compared to 33 on the GWR, 29 on the LMS and just 28 on the LNER, despite the latter's lines in Essex and East Anglia, and up the East Coast. There were 3,637 incidents on the Southern's 2,135 route miles, whereas the LMS had 1,939 incidents on 6,672 route miles.

1. and 2.   *War on the Line*, Southern Railway, London, 1946.

Chapter Seventeen

Deliverance and Nationalisation

'Victory – and Deliverance' was the message across the front of the May 1945 issue of *The Southern Railway Magazine*, and for the only time in its history, blue ink was used instead of the usual black.

Naturally, wartime restrictions had meant that *The Southern Railway Magazine* had become less newsy, not so much because of the shortage of paper and the halved issues, but because of security concerns. Even on 15 January 1945, when the first continental boat train left London, there was no mention in the report of which of the London termini it used, or which of the Channel ports it operated to. The locomotive was mentioned as being No. 2038, and referred to as *Portland Bill*. Nevertheless, throughout the previous year, the Southern had been looking forward to the end of the war, and like many, it seemed to believe that victory might even be possible in 1944. That year's AGM returned to aviation, but mainly in connection with its potential for growing the railway business, with new stations mentioned for the airports at Gatwick and Shoreham.

The euphoria at the end of hostilities was short-lived. It would be some time before those serving in the armed forces could be released, and while the war had ended in Europe with German surrender on 8 May, it was still raging in the Far East, and at the time no one knew when Japanese surrender would come. Indeed, a massive build-up of forces for an invasion was regarded as the most likely next step. For the railways, the return of peace meant that many of the wartime problems lingered on. The railways were all in a far worse state than in 1939. The Southern in particular had taken heavy punishment during the war, and in 1945 revealed that its most bombed stretch of track had been that between Waterloo and Queens Road. There were massive arrears of maintenance and renewal of track, signalling and rolling stock, but the Southern was soon to discover that it would not receive even its normal peacetime allocation of materials, let alone that regarded as essential to make good war damage.

Worse still, within a couple of months, as war still raged in the Far East, there was a general election that produced a landslide victory for the Labour Party. The new government was fully committed to the nationalisation of transport, and with a Commons majority that meant it was unstoppable.

Reversing the Cuts

Nevertheless, the Southern Railway still had to be run, and run as well as possible given the constraints under which it was still labouring.

The reduced demand for troop trains and other government charters, coupled with an easing of travel restrictions, meant that additional trains were soon required, and it was clear that the public were keen to enjoy their holidays that summer after six years of doing without. On 16 June the Southern reintroduced a limited number of trains, providing an extra two daily between Waterloo and Portsmouth Harbour, while between Victoria and Brighton there were an extra six, increasing to an extra nine on Saturdays. Other electrified main lines saw an additional train daily, with some having two additional trains on Saturdays. In case these trains tempted the public into wanderlust, it was explained that the

A post-nationalisation shot, with No. 30567 heading a goods train at Feltham. *(HRMS ABS703)*

state of the trains and track and the general shortage of labour and materials for repairs would mean that there would not be sufficient trains to provide a service of peacetime standards. Yet on Saturday 28 July 1945 the main concourse at Victoria was packed solid with people, as indeed were the trains that could be run, including one to Brighton and another to Eastbourne comprised of suburban stock. None of this should have been surprising, for after all, even the civilian population had been through a lengthy war with little in the way of break or recreation, while leisure pursuits were curtailed by the demands of shift work, long hours and by such spare-time activities as service in the Home Guard or as air-raid wardens.

The end of the war with Japan was not announced until midnight on 14 August, and as a result many people did not hear the broadcast that the 15 and 16 August would be public holidays. The result for the railways was that on the morning of 15 August, most people travelled to work as usual and then almost immediately went home again, by which time an off-peak service was operating. Nevertheless, the Southern managed to run some extra trains, including a number on its main-line services.

It was not until 1 October that anything like a pre-war service of trains could be reinstated. The Portsmouth Direct again had an hourly fast train, albeit leaving Waterloo at a quarter to the hour, while there were once again the half-hourly stopping trains shared with the Alton line and dividing at Woking. Evening services were less frequent than pre-war, with a gap in the fast service at 7.45 to allow for the displacement caused by the additional trains required for the evening peak, and last trains were earlier than in 1939. The Brighton line revived its non-stop trains taking just an hour, but with some gaps in the service during the afternoon. Sunday services were also improved. The Christmas Day and Boxing Day services had usually operated on Sunday schedules, but in 1945 the Christmas Day service was reduced after 1 pm as a result of complaints by drivers that a substantial number of them would have to work both days, rather than work on one day and take the other off.

During this still bleak period, with the Southern electrification programme well and truly on hold, the one bright spot was the commissioning of a new signal cabin at Tulse Hill on 1 July 1945.

A former LBSCR locomotive, classified C2X and numbered 32528 by British Railways. *(HRMS ABS419)*

The start of the new year saw further enhancements to the service, with restaurant cars reintroduced on ten trains between Waterloo and Portsmouth Harbour on 7 January 1946, and twenty-four trains from Victoria and another six from London Bridge with buffet or pantry cars reinstated. Further trains received catering from 1 March, and on 4 March services to Crystal Palace High Level were reinstated with a shuttle service to and from Nunhead.

However, the winter period had seen many trains heavily overcrowded, and punctuality fell far short of the pre-war standard, forcing the Southern to resort to a poster campaign and press advertisements to explain its position. A good example of the impact of war was that in January 1946, the 2¼ route miles between Waterloo and Queens Road had no fewer than four severe speed restrictions, three to 15 mph and one to just 10 mph. Needless to say, the poor state of the track was also reflected in the state of the rolling stock, with frequent breakdowns, while on the Eastern Section at Victoria the number and poor regularity of military leave specials had an impact on the normal services. In December 1945 the electric trains, at one time noted for their punctuality, had an average delay of 5 minutes.

The chairman raised these matters at the 1946 Annual General Meeting, held in March. He told the shareholders that the restoration of normal services could not be done quickly, owing to the shortage of materials and of men, with only a quarter of Southern personnel serving with the armed forces having been released by that time. The railway was still running 570 special trains for the government every week, and long-distance traffic was up 480 per cent compared with 1939, yet the quantity of electric rolling stock available was down by 3½ per cent. While a considerable mileage of track had been renewed in 1945, in 1946 it was also hoped to renew damaged bridges and stations. On a more hopeful note, the chairman also talked of further electrification and explained that the 1935 loans from the government for electrification could now be repaid, even though repayment was not due until 1952.

The management, many of them soldiering on beyond their usual retirement age while they waited for colleagues to be released from military service, turned its attention to improving the railway as it was, and by July 1946 electric trains were suffering an average delay of just one minute.

Naturally, the Southern also had to meet public demand for its services, which increased as the pattern of peacetime life re-established itself. In 1946 race meetings were once again allowed, and these were especially well attended at bank holidays. Derby Day at Epsom on 5 June saw twenty-six trains run between Victoria and Epsom Downs between 9 am and noon, with a further eighteen between Charing Cross and Tattenham Corner, five from Cannon Street and eleven from London Bridge over the same period.

On 6 May Pullman cars returned to the Central Section, although the 'Brighton Belle' was not officially reinstated. However, at least one of its multiple units was used with a 6 PUL set on certain trains. In August there were further reinstatements of rush-hour suburban services scrapped under wartime restrictions, including trains from Holborn Viaduct and Blackfriars to Dartford via Nunhead, doubtless helped by the commissioning of a new signal cabin at Blackfriars and the restoration of colour light signalling. The signal cabin at Elephant & Castle was never restored, however. Further steps towards normal peacetime running were made throughout the autumn as abandoned services were reinstated and the frequency of trains increased.

Electrification

Even while battling for the company's survival in the face of the government's commitment to nationalisation, the Southern Railway was looking ahead and planning further electrification and, after a visit by a delegation to the United States in November 1946, also announced that lines that were not to be electrified would be converted to diesel-electric traction. The extension of the third rail from Sevenoaks to Hastings had been prevented by

Branch-line locomotives seldom have names, but one marked exception was the Isle of Wight, where all of the locomotives were named after towns and villages on the island, where train services on the line between Ryde and Ventnor operated at suburban frequencies on busy summer weekends. This is 02 No. 18 *Ningwood* at Ryde St Johns with a Ventnor train – very much a Victorian railway atmosphere despite nationalisation. *(HRMS AES509)*

BY DAY!

THE FAMOUS
"GOLDEN ARROW" PULLMAN SERVICE
BETWEEN
LONDON AND PARIS
Via
DOVER-CALAIS SHORT SEA ROUTE

Daily (Suns. included) in each direction

Sea crossing by S.R. Steamer "INVICTA"
Comfortable Private Cabins and Cabines-de-Luxe

BY NIGHT!

COMMENCING DECEMBER 1st, 1947,

Re-introduction of THROUGH SLEEPING CAR SERVICE, LONDON to PARIS (via Train Ferry) DOVER-DUNKERQUE ROUTE

Ferry Steamers:
"HAMPTON FERRY"
"SHEPPERTON FERRY"
"TWICKENHAM FERRY"

Entirely reconditioned and redecorated throughout

SLEEP YOUR WAY TO PARIS—NO CHANGE EN ROUTE

**For Time-table of Services, Tickets, Reservations, etc., apply to
CONTINENTAL ENQUIRY OFFICE, Southern Railway,
VICTORIA STATION, LONDON, S.W.1,
or Travel Agencies.**

Postwar optimism, as the Southern proclaims the return of the 'Night Ferry', but an industrial dispute on French railways delayed the start until little more than a fortnight before nationalisation. Note the slogan, 'SR – The Key to the Continent'. *(Southern Railway)*

the war, but by 1946 this seemed to have slipped down the list of priorities and was fourth, as can be seen below, on the new 'wish list' announced by the Southern. Nevertheless, it was also announced that all lines east of Portsmouth would be steadily converted to electric or diesel-electric traction.

The order of priorities was:

1   Gillingham–Faversham–Ramsgate, Faversham–Dover
2   Sevenoaks–Tonbridge–Ashford–Folkestone–Dover–Deal–Ramsgate
3   Maidstone East–Ashford, Maidstone West–Paddock Wood, Ashford–Canterbury West–Ramsgate
4   Tonbridge–West St Leonards, Crowhurst–Bexhill West
5   Christ's Hospital–Steyning–Shoreham-by-Sea
6   South Croydon–Oxted–East Grinstead–Horsted Keynes

This was an ambitious plan, estimated to cost £15 million, which by today's standards, even allowing for inflation, seems like an incredible bargain. It is also worth noting that the lines mentioned include some that have since been closed, and the question is what would have happened had these lines enjoyed the benefits of electrification and the increased frequency of services as well as savings in costs that accompanied the third rail? Typical of the Southern, the directors planned to have this programme completed by 1955, provided that labour and materials were available, which was not something that could be taken for granted in postwar Britain, where rationing by one means or another was to remain in force until 1954 and priority was being accorded to social issues rather than important investment in industry and the national infrastructure. This was a period of planning and state direction and intervention, hardly conducive to ambitious business planning.

The plan was that the Eastern Section would have some 70 per cent of its passenger mileage worked by electric multiple unit trains in the now well-proven Southern fashion, but electric locomotives had also proved themselves viable by this time, and these would work the continental boat trains and the principal through freight services, while diesel-electric trains, presumably also in multiple unit form for the passenger services, would work the non-electrified routes, and diesel-electric traction would also be used for stopping freight services and for shunting. Given the massive closure of goods yards at stations, and not just small country stations, that later occurred, this showed a continued commitment to local freight, which even at this time must have been uneconomic. On the other hand, it can be argued that this was not the best means of moving freight, that it would have been unsuitable for today's concept of 'just in time' stock control, and that the space used for the goods yards was probably better utilised for commuter car parking.

In the end, Kent coast electrification did not come until 1959 for north Kent, with the rest following in 1962, but this still left Hastings with only an electric service via Eastbourne, something that was not to be rectified until many years later.

The next announcement from the Southern was that colour light signalling was to be further extended from Battersea Park and Bricklayers' Arms to East Croydon and Coulsdon North. The official government reaction to these ambitious plans for modernisation and improvement was to publish the Transport Bill, promising widespread nationalisation of not just the railways, but also of canals and long-distance haulage, in December 1946. Separate legislation covered air transport, with the successor to Imperial Airways, the British Overseas Airways Corporation (BOAC), and the new British European Airways (BEA), to be state-controlled to ensure a market for the British aircraft industry.

The Final Year

Having been suitably discouraged by the political elite, the Southern Railway had to make the best of the year left to it. The outlook was not good, with continued shortages of men

SOUTHERN RAILWAY

TRAVEL
TO THE
CONTINENT
BY
S.R. ROUTES
Via

DOVER-CALAIS (Daily Service)
FOLKESTONE-CALAIS (Daily Service)
DOVER-OSTEND (Daily Service)
NEWHAVEN-DIEPPE (Daily Service)
DOVER-DUNKERQUE (Nightly from Dec. 1st)
SOUTHAMPTON-HAVRE (Mon. Nights)

"GOLDEN ARROW" PULLMAN SERVICE, LONDON-PARIS BY DAY, and commencing December 1st, 1947, LONDON-PARIS Sleeping Car Service BY NIGHT

Joint Service to the Channel Islands (Jersey and Guernsey) by S.R. and G.W.R. Routes

For all information, apply
CONTINENTAL ENQUIRY OFFICE, SOUTHERN RAILWAY,
VICTORIA STATION, LONDON, S.W.1,
or any Travel Agency.

THE KEY TO THE CONTINENT
S R

The 'Golden Arrow' and 'Night Ferry', together attempting to dispel austerity, provided that the traveller could obtain enough foreign currency! *(Southern Railway)*

After nationalisation even the smallest locomotives had to be renumbered. This is 0–4–0ST No. 30458 at Guildford shed. *(HRMS ABS507)*

and materials. Starting in January 1947, a spell of exceptionally severe weather swept across the country. Heavy snowfalls were accompanied by strong gales and in between the periods of calm were marked by freezing fog. The Southern reacted by introducing de-icing trains, with elderly trailer carriages modified to spread a thin film of warm oil on the third rail, sent on a tour of the electrified lines. This worked up to a point in keeping lines open, provided that the interval between trains was not too long. Nevertheless, services were affected both by the bad weather and by the looming shortage of coal. Bad weather kept miners away from work, and the coal that was brought to the surface was often frozen at the pit head and difficult to load. The colliers bringing the coal that could be loaded to London and the ports on the south coast were kept in port or delayed by the strong gales. By early February the Southern had enough coal for just one week, including coal for its own power station, and the government was forced to act, introducing curbs on the use of electricity by industry. Starting on 5 February, cuts were enforced on many suburban services, followed on 11 February by a further round of cuts, while still more followed on 15 February. Worse was to follow. During the severe gale of 4 March, heavy rain washed the de-icing oil from the third rail, then turned to a blizzard, and the resulting precipitation froze, causing massive disruption. The 4.25 pm non-stop from Brighton to Victoria took more than eight hours! Throughout the country, many train drivers stopped their trains at stations while waiting for the weather to improve.

If these severe conditions were not bad enough, the massive freeze continued until 8 March, when a thaw started, augmented by heavy rain on 10 March. The Portsmouth Direct, notoriously prone to earth slips, was hit between Petersfield and Rowlands Castle, and the section was reduced to single-line working. The line to Sidcup flooded at Mottingham.

The Brighton line was also badly affected, as heavy rain caused chalk falls on the approaches to both the Quarry and Merstham tunnels early on 13 March, blocking the former line and leaving the other with just one line clear. The hard-pressed control staff had to introduce widespread cancellations and diversions, including the substitution of a steam train via Oxted for the busy 5.45 pm from London Bridge to Eastbourne. It took until 17 March to clear the mess, by which time the heavy rain had caused the fallen chalk to become sticky, damaging the track and the ballast, and its removal had to be followed by extensive reballasting.

Elsewhere, the line between Windsor and Staines was flooded, and the line between Eynsford and Shoreham in Kent was also closed by chalk falls. It took until the end of March before trains could operate normally, and even then the service was still massively reduced by the fuel shortages.

The Annual General Meeting in March 1947 was a far from happy occasion, with all too little good news to report and nationalisation now uncomfortably close.

As always, the chairman reported on the progress made during the year, but had to admit that efforts to reinstate the network to the condition it had enjoyed in 1938 were being hampered by a shortage of materials and of labour, all encouraged by strict government controls. The fuel crisis had also set back progress. Even so, sixty-five stations had been renovated and 30 acres of glass in the roofs of the termini and other main stations replaced. The first stage of repairs to Portsmouth Harbour had enabled three of the five platforms to be returned to use. Despite the shortage of steel, 127 carriages had been built for electric trains in 1946, as well as the first of a new series of carriages for the steam-hauled services to Southampton, Bournemouth and the south-west. The permanent way department had renewed 153 miles of track, but further efforts were being hampered by the shortage of sleepers. Before the onslaught of the winter months, the Southern had managed to get 84 per cent of its pre-war services running, and during the morning and evening peaks a full pre-war service had been reinstated. No less creditable, by the middle of the year the efforts made to improve punctuality had resulted in 94 per cent of passenger trains running on time or within 5 minutes of their scheduled arrival. However, it should be pointed out that this was partly because the overall journey times on many lines had had to be extended to take into account the poor condition of much of the track and many line structures.

The last year was also marred by an industrial dispute, no doubt the workers feeling that the railway would soon be 'theirs'. This is not an unreasonable assessment of their attitudes since the establishment of the Railway Executive disappointed many trade unionists because it was dominated by railway managers! They had clearly expected some form of workers' control.

The industrial dispute had its origins in an incident that occurred the previous October, when a motorman had passed a colour light signal at red between Waterloo East, as Waterloo Junction had become, and London Bridge, although he had managed to stop behind the preceding train. An internal disciplinary hearing applied the lenient punishment of a one-day suspension from duty, and he appealed against this on the grounds that the signal had actually shown 'caution' and that colour light signals were not infallible. The management decided that the original punishment must stand and that he would be suspended from duty for Saturday 22 March 1947. On that day, against union advice, 175 motormen on the Eastern Section struck, causing all services from Charing Cross and Cannon Street to be suspended.

While the Southern had many schemes for future improvement in hand, including a joint venture with the LMS for a diesel-electric locomotive, the last significant advance before nationalisation was the introduction of electric services to the boat train station at Newhaven on 16 July 1947.

Nationalisation

Nationalisation was not a new concept. It had been mooted, as far as the railways were concerned, since the early days of steam power. On the continent railways were already owned by the state or had a state interest, while as early as 1838 the Duke of Wellington had argued for state intervention to prevent the railway companies exploiting their monopoly

An ex-LSWR composite carriage, C12N, still in service in 1955, thirty-two years after the South Western ceased operation. (*HRMS ACA509*)

power. A plan for state purchase was published as early as 1843 in William Galt's book *Railway Reform*. This led to Gladstone's Regulation Act of 1844, which gave the government the option, from 1865 onwards, to purchase any railway company authorised thereafter. A later edition of Galt's book published in 1865 continued to press for nationalisation, not on doctrinaire grounds as with the Labour Party and the trade unions, but in the interests of the country. A Royal Commission considered the matter in 1865, but decided that nothing needed to be done. The first British experience of nationalisation came in 1868, with the nationalisation of the hitherto privately owned and fragmented telegraph system. This was to prove successful and when the benefits of an integrated telegraph system became apparent, they fuelled the pressure for nationalisation of the railways.

While many doubted that nationalisation could be a practical proposition, others had attempted to see how it could work. The trade unions favoured state ownership as early as 1894, while early in the twentieth century nationalisation became official Labour Party policy. A Liberal government appointed a Royal Commission to consider the question in 1913, but the First World War intervened before it could conclude its work. Wartime government control of the railways, nevertheless, pointed the way to greater state intervention if not outright control, and this was reflected in the postwar plans to group the railways into four large companies, each with what amounted to a regional monopoly, and with few opportunities for competition. The mainly Conservative governments of the inter-war years managed to bury the question, although the London Passenger Transport Board was a further step towards state control of public transport in 1933, as in some ways had been the restrictions on the road transport sector first introduced in the Transport Act of 1930. However, it could be argued that it would have been better to have removed many of the conditions imposed by Parliament on the railways.

The Railway Companies Association mounted a fierce defence of its members' interests, but to no avail. Labour had an overwhelming majority and was committed to nationalisation.

Lord Anson, one of the 4–6–0 'Lord Nelson' class locomotives, imbibing at Basingstoke shortly after nationalisation, and not looking too well cared for despite having been repainted at such an early stage. *(HRMS ACM323)*

Labour in 1945 was determined to nationalise almost all transport, including bus companies, canals, road haulage and airlines, although shipping companies seemed to slip the net and, like ports, were only included if owned by the railways. Coal mining and the steel industry were other candidates, along with gas and electricity supply and generation. In the case of the railways, shareholders were granted British Transport Stock in return for their shares, with the value of the latter being assessed as the average value of railway shares over the six months prior to the general election or the price immediately before the publication of the Transport Bill, whichever was the higher, with the value of the shares and interest at 3 per cent guaranteed by the Treasury. The interest was to be a charge on the revenues of the new British Transport Commission, which would operate the railways through a management team known as the Railways Executive. Wagons belonging to private owners were simply purchased on the basis of a simple valuation formula, but this was in many ways a red herring since the main owners were the coal mines, which were also on Labour's shopping list.

Naturally, the threat of nationalisation was the main point to be made by the Chairman, Colonel Gore-Browne, at the 1946 AGM. 'Do they think that the public will have a better and a cheaper service?' he asked those present. 'Do they think that the wage-earning and the salaried staffs of the Main Line Railway Companies will be better off? . . . I challenge the nationalisers to prove their case. I accept the challenge to prove that public interest can best be served by private ownership of the Southern Railway.'

But Labour had a massive majority and intended to use it. Logic had no place in the argument. Ignoring the evidence of the extensive pre-war modernisation and the heavy investment in electrification, among other things, the Chancellor of the Exchequer

'H' class No. 31530 following British Railways renumbering in 1949. Although the locomotive is still in Southern livery, these carriages have already been repainted in carmine and cream. However, the Southern Region was for a long time a bastion for green carriages. *(HRMS AAM300)*

described the railways as a 'very poor bag of physical assets'. This hurtful insult was disproved in debate. The railways were war-battered, but so too was the rest of the country.

Nevertheless, the battle was lost and defeat was clear by the time of the 1947 AGM.

The Southern's directors and senior management had continued to plan as if nothing was going to change, and some angry shareholders wanted to know why. After all, every penny spent on modernisation was money that could have been paid in dividends, and a gift to the future owner of the railways. They got their answer from the chairman.

'Now may I turn to the record of last year and to the plans which we have in view. Some . . . have asked "Why as things are now, have you made any plans? Is not your only duty to protect your stockholders' interests?" We feel it necessary to take a wider view. We have always regarded your undertaking as a service to the public . . . the Chancellor of the Exchequer who described the railways as "a very poor bag of physical assets" will in our case be agreeably surprised.'

Such a poor bag of assets that the Isle of Wight continued to operate Victorian locomotives and rolling stock right up to 1966, when these were replaced by elderly rolling stock dating from the 1930s and withdrawn from the London Underground, and this replacement stock was substituted by 1938 tube stock that still operates in the twenty-first century!

Chapter Eighteen

What Might Have Been

Could the Southern Railway have completed its postwar electrification schemes by 1955? Would it have become an all-electric system? What would have been the fate of the many branch lines that were axed in the postwar period, and the many more cut by Beeching? Would the Southern have made a major investment in air transport?

We shall never really know.

To take the questions in order, it is extremely unlikely that the massive planned electrification in Kent, plus the infilling in Sussex, would have been completed on time, given the tight controls on materials applied by the postwar Labour government, although completion by 1959 might well have been a possibility. It also seems possible that electrification would have reached Bournemouth many years earlier than was the case, and indeed that the line through to Weymouth might have been electrified by the early 1960s, although this would have depended on the cooperation of the GWR. The operation of the boat trains through the streets of the town to the harbour might well have persuaded even the Southern to limit electrification as far as Bournemouth or Poole, initially using electric locomotives to haul the trains, and then diesel-electric traction to the final destination. If

Concern over certain aspects of the Bulleid Pacific designs led to most of them being rebuilt. Here is 'West Country' class No. 34098 *Templecombe* attracting the attention of the photographers as she heads an Up Channel Islands express through Upwey & Broadwey. *(HRMS ACM934)*

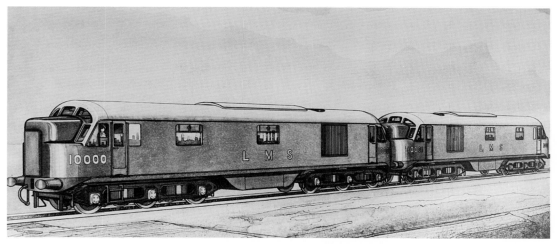

Collaboration between the railway companies was far from unusual, and this was a postwar joint project by the Southern and the LMS for diesel-electric locomotives for the non-electrified lines and stopping goods trains. *(NRM Brighton-collection B245)*

this hybrid solution was accepted there, then the same practice would have seen electrification extended to Exeter, with onward traction again by diesel-electric. Given the interest in diesel-electric traction and the proposal for a locomotive design to be developed jointly with the LMS, the Southern's partner on the Somerset & Dorset line, it is difficult to believe that the entire Southern would ever have become an all-electric railway.

On the other hand, given the Southern Railway's commitment, even determination, to keep as much of the system intact as possible, it does seem unlikely that branch line closures would have been as drastic as they have been. One suspects that much would have been done to improve productivity and reduce costs as an alternative to closure, for after all, even though many argue that the nationalised railway was the low-cost leader among nationalised railways in Europe, no less a railwayman than Gerald Fiennes has argued, in *I Tried to Run a Railway*, that many branch lines could have been retained and could have survived if everything had been done to ensure low-cost operation.

Yet, even with the utmost optimism, it is hard to believe that the Meon Valley line could have survived, or the Ventnor West and Bembridge branches, and while the line between Uckfield and Lewes almost certainly would have survived, along with that between Alton and Winchester, those to Midhurst might well have been closed, or at least thinned out, with perhaps just Petersfield–Midhurst surviving to provide connections to Portsmouth and London. Places such as Horsted Keynes and Uckfield could have stayed on the railway map, and possibly Cranleigh as well, but would Budleigh Salterton have joined them?

Some further reduction in the branch-line network seems inevitable, especially in north Cornwall, and there might even have been some rationalisation of other routes as well, although Exeter would almost certainly have had a far better service than today to Waterloo.

Of course, the problem is that the position of the railways began to change considerably after nationalisation. The railway companies were saddled with a common carrier obligation that demanded that they carried any goods traffic offered regardless of its profitability, which became an anachronism as road haulage adapted to providing cheaper and more efficient transport. The ending of this freed up the railways to get rid of their costly and uneconomic stopping freight trains and paved the way for fast freight between major marshalling yards or to and from the container ports, as well as the 'merry-go-round' trains shuttling coal between the pithead or coal terminal and the power stations.

Even before the war, pressure on peak period suburban services forced Bulleid to look at ways of squeezing more passengers into the same number of carriages. Postwar, and post-nationalisation, his 'double deck' suburban units appeared, although both normally worked together as one train to and from Charing Cross. The inter-leaved upper decks really meant that these were half-decks rather than true double-deck trains. (NRM 548/83)

The cramped lower deck, with the steps to the upper deck in the foreground. Note the lack of luggage racks, with the upper deck seating occupying the available space. Upstairs, ventilation was a problem. (NRM 58/98)

It seems likely that the Southern would have invested heavily in road haulage postwar, since it already had a stake in Pickfords and Carter Patterson, as well as its interest in bus companies. That could have been the way forward, and it could also have ensured greater coordination of road haulage and railway goods traffic, with the railways undertaking the 'trunk' element of the journey.

The Southern would have been to the fore in developing airport stations and links to airports, and would certainly have been anxious to ensure that the railway link to London's Heathrow Airport ran from Waterloo, or possibly Victoria, rather than Paddington. Indeed, it seems likely that a railway line into the airport would have come much earlier, even

Intended to combine the advantages of steam-power, such as a lower unsprung weight, and of diesel or electric locomotive design, the 'Leader' class proved uncomfortable for the fireman, and only the first prototype went on trials while the rest were cancelled. (*Kevin Robertson*)

before the Piccadilly Line extension, and it might not be too fanciful to suggest that the railway link could have been built to the airport at the same time as the construction of the modern terminals started.

A strong involvement in air transport could have followed, if this industry had not been subjected to so much state control, especially to the Channel Islands and to the nearer continent. It is even possible that the domestic and European route network of the old British United Airways and its subsidiaries would have given us an idea of just what could have been achieved.

It also seems likely that Oliver Bulleid would have remained as CME for far longer, with all that entailed for innovation and experiment, but would the traffic people have allowed him to persist with his double-deck trains with their extended station dwell times? It seems unlikely, but perhaps lessons would have been taken from the type of trains run on the District Line, and sliding door trains with extra standing room would have become more widespread earlier on the inner suburban routes. The Southern directors and senior management also seem to have been no 'stay-at-homes', maintaining a close awareness of progress in France and the United States, so perhaps we might have seen continental-style 'bi-levels', double-deck trains with upper and lower saloons, and, more importantly, double deck trains that worked. The choice would have been one of extending station platforms with its implications for changing track layouts and signalling, and sometimes lineside structures as well, or of raising bridges and tunnels, unless of course, the track could have been lowered without affecting ride quality or risking flooding.

What would have happened? An interesting thought.

Appendix I

Locomotive Headcodes

The Southern used two train identification systems, that of headcodes using white discs during the day for locomotives, with lamps at night, and numbers or letters for electric multiple units, with the latter system serving passengers as well as signalmen.

The limited number of positions available for headcodes meant that the same headcodes had to be repeated for different routes, and often these were fairly short so that a locomotive might have to change its headcodes as it passed over different sections of track. Typical of a short-distance headcode would be empty stock or light-engine workings between, say, Fratton and either Portsmouth & Southsea or Portsmouth Harbour stations. The longest distance covered without a change of headcode was from Waterloo or Nine Elms to Plymouth. Headcodes would differentiate between a standard train between Waterloo and Southampton and a boat train, and would also differ according to the route, whether it was direct via Woking and Basingstoke, or in the case of boat trains, whether it ran into the docks via Millbrook for the new West Docks or via Northam into the old docks and the new Ocean Terminal. On the other hand, not only was it usual to use the same headcode for Waterloo and Nine Elms, or Victoria and Stewarts Lane, or Victoria and Battersea Yard, or London Bridge and Bricklayers' Arms, but in some cases the same headcode would be used for Victoria or Holborn.

The system was egalitarian. A titled express, such as the 'Atlantic Coast Express', would carry the same headcode as a more modest train on the same route.

Fortunately the Southern Railway system was large enough to ensure that there was no risk of two identical headcodes appearing on the same section. As the electric network grew in size, similar problems occurred, and were solved in the same way, even after nationalisation saw two-digit numeral codes for electric trains, simply because the second number usually indicated the stopping pattern while the first provided the destination.

Space does not permit a full list of headcodes, but the main ones were indicated by one or two discs, or lamps, and these are given. Three disc or lamp headcodes were normally reserved for race specials, although the regular exceptions to this were the Brighton–Plymouth and Brighton–Bournemouth through services, and they also seem to have been used on empty stock workings from Waterloo and Nine Elms to stations west of Salisbury. Four disc or lamp headcodes were reserved for Royal Specials, and standardised throughout the entire British railway network.

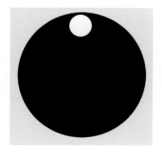

Victoria and Dover via Chatham
Loughborough Sidings to Holborn
Ashford and Hastings
Reading and Margate via Redhill
Eastleigh and Bulford via Chandlers Ford and Andover
Southampton Terminus, and Brockenhurst and Weymouth via
    Wimborne
Weymouth, Portland and Easton
Plymouth Friary and Tavistock

Woking and Reading via Virginia Water West Curve
Exeter Central and Ilfracombe
Bodmin and Wadebridge
Petersfield and Midhurst
Exeter Central and Exmouth
Ryde Pierhead, Esplanade or St Johns and Ventnor
Newport and Freshwater

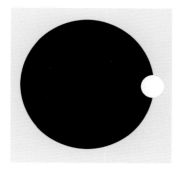

London Bridge or Bricklayers' Arms and Portsmouth via
    Quarry Line and Horsham
Via Mid-Kent Line and Beckenham Junction
Ashford and Eastbourne Direct
Waterloo or Nine Elms and Southampton Terminus via
    Woking (*not* boat trains)
Willesden and Feltham Yard via Gunnersbury
Waterloo or Nine Elms and Windsor via Twickenham
Southampton Central to Lymington
Yeovil Junction and Yeovil Town
Seaton Junction and Seaton
Barnstaple Junction and Torrington
Halwill and Bude

One of the numerous 2–6–0 'U' class, in this case No. 1614, heads a Down local to Salisbury between Woking and Basingstoke in 1945. *(HRMS AAA806)*

London Bridge or Bricklayers' Arms and Brighton via
     Quarry Line
Tonbridge and Brighton via Eridge
Hastings via Mid-Kent Line, Oxted, Crowhurst Junction
     and Tonbridge
Dunton Green and Westerham
Ashford and Margate via Canterbury West
Lydd branch
Canterbury West and Whitstable Harbour
Sandling Junction and Hythe
Folkestone Junction and Folkestone Harbour
Crowhurst and Bexhill
Swanley Junction and Gravesend West Street
Sittingbourne and Sheerness
Queenborough and Leysdown
Deal and Kearney
Gravesend Junction and Alhallows on Sea or Port Victoria
All stations to Feltham except via Mortlake
Weymouth and Portland Easton goods
Bournemouth West and Brockenhurst via Wimborne
Brading to Bembridge
Newport and Sandown

Ryde Pier from the Esplanade station, with the pier tramway in the background. The tramway consisted of two two-car petrol railcars, usually with a flat trailer for baggage and each confined to its own track. *(Kershaw Collection, HRMS ACM427)*

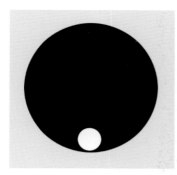

Victoria or Battersea Yard and Brighton via Redhill
Oxted and Eastbourne via Eridge
London Bridge and New Cross Gate via Bricklayers' Arms
Horsham and Brighton
Brookwood and Bisley Camp
Alton and Fareham
Bentley and Bordon
Salisbury and Bulford
Axminster and Lyme Regis
Tipton St John's and Exmouth
Wareham and Swanage
Brockenhurst and Lymington Pier
Bere Alston and Callington

Oxted and Tunbridge Wells via East Grinstead High Level
Pulborough, Midhurst and Chichester
Havant and Hayling Island
London Bridge and Bricklayers' Arms
Tonbridge and Maidstone West
Ashford (Kent) and Dover via Minster and Deal
Elham Valley Line
Stewarts Lane to Victoria
Southampton Docks and Nine Elms via Woking fruit or
    vegetable train
Light engines to Nine Elms
Newport and Cowes to Ryde Pierhead, Esplanade or St Johns

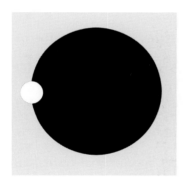

London Bridge or Bricklayers' Arms and Dover or Ramsgate
    via East Croydon, Oxted and Tonbridge
Tonbridge and Hawkhurst
Battersea Yard and Kensington
Waterloo or Nine Elms and Reading via Twickenham
Willesden and Feltham Yard via Kew East Junction
Exeter Central and Sidmouth
Plymouth Friary and Turnchapel
Eastleigh or Southampton and Fawley
Bournemouth Central and Brockenhurst via Wimborne
Torrington and Halwill

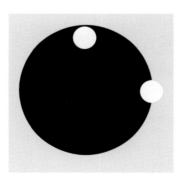

Victoria or Battersea Yard and Portsmouth via Quarry Line
    and Horsham
Via Maidstone East Line to Victoria or Holborn
Waterloo or Nine Elms and Southampton Docks via
    Brentford, Chertsey and Woking

'H15' No. 483 on an Up West of England express in 1945. *(HRMS AAA801)*

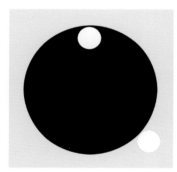

London Bridge or Bricklayers' Arms and Eastbourne or
    Hastings via Quarry Line
Victoria or West London Line and Ramsgate via Herne Hill
    or Catford Loop
London Bridge or Bricklayers' Arms and Hastings via
    Chislehurst and Tunbridge Wells Central
West London Line to East Croydon via Crystal Palace Low
    Level
Waterloo and Southampton Docks special boat trains via
    Northam
Waterloo and Southampton West Docks special boat trains
    via Milbrook
Southampton and Andover via Redbridge

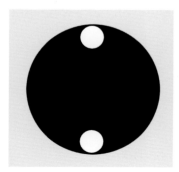

Victoria or Battersea Yard and Eastbourne or Hastings via
    Quarry Line
London and Hither Green sidings
Victoria and Folkestone Harbour or Dover Marine via
    Swanley, Otford and Tonbridge
Waterloo or Nine Elms and Plymouth
Bournemouth Central and Dorchester goods
Battersea Yard and Brent via New Kew Junction
Southampton Terminus and Portsmouth Harbour via Netley

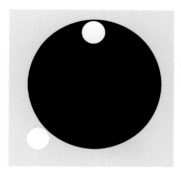

London Bridge or Bricklayers' Arms and Portsmouth via Redhill and Horsham

Victoria or Battersea Yard and Norwood Yard via Crystal Palace Low Level

London Bridge and New Cross Gate to Eardley sidings via Peckham Rye

Deptford Wharf and New Cross Gate

London Bridge or Bricklayers' Arms and Folkestone or Dover via Chislehurst, Tonbridge and Ashford

Dover and Margate via Deal and Minster Loop

Waterloo and Southampton West Docks special boat trains via Milbrook

Victoria or Battersea Yard and Portsmouth via Redhill and Horsham

Via Dartford Loop

Victoria or Holborn and Hastings via Orpington Loop and Tunbridge Wells Central

London Bridge or Bricklayers' Arms and Guildford via Leatherhead and Effingham Junction

Waterloo or Nine Elms and Southampton Terminus via Alton

Salisbury and Bournemouth West via Wimborne

Fareham and Gosport

Ballast trains to Meldon Quarry from Exeter Central and stations westward

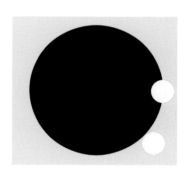

Victoria or Battersea Yard and Portsmouth via Mitcham Junction

London Bridge or Bricklayers' Arms and Eastbourne or Hastings via Redhill

Victoria, Stewarts Lane or Holborn Viaduct to north Kent via Nunhead

Nine Elms and Feltham Yard via Mortlake

Exeter Central to Nine Elms market goods and fish

Down main-line goods terminating at Woking

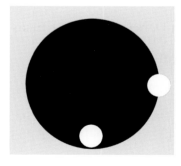

London Bridge or Bricklayers' Arms and Brighton via Redhill

Oxted and Brighton via East Grinstead Low Level and Lewes

Three Bridges and Tunbridge Wells West

West London Line to Norwood Yard via Thornton Heath

Victoria or Holborn Viaduct to Dover via Nunhead and Maidstone East

Parcels and empty stock workings Waterloo to Clapham Junction (Kensington sidings)

Feltham Yard and Neasden via Kew East Junction

Portsmouth Harbour or Portsmouth & Southsea to Fratton Locomotive Depot

Exeter Central and Exmouth Junction

Bournemouth West to Dorchester

Southampton and Salisbury via Redbridge

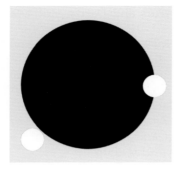

London Bridge and Portsmouth via Mitcham Junction

London Bridge, Oxted and Tunbridge Wells via Hever

Oxted and Lewes or Seaford or Eastbourne via Keymer Junction, changing to code 5 or 21 at Lewes

London Bridge or Bricklayers' Arms and Dover via Chislehurst Loop and Maidstone East

Waterloo or Nine Elms and Brockenhurst or Bournemouth West via Sway

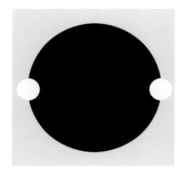

Via Bexley Heath Line

Victoria, Stewarts Lane or Holborn Viaduct via Nunhead and Bexley Heath

Oxted and Brighton via Haywards Heath

Waterloo or Nine Elms and Reading via Hounslow Loop

Trains terminating at Portsmouth & Southsea, with trains from Salisbury displaying code 17 to Eastleigh

Exeter Central and Padstow

Light engines, Bournemouth Central or Bournemouth West to Bournemouth Central, via triangle to turn

Light engines, Eastleigh Locomotive Depot to Portsmouth & Southsea

Light engines, to Guildford Locomotive Depot via Woking

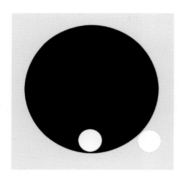

London Bridge or Bricklayers' Arms and Portsmouth via West Croydon

Victoria or Battersea Yard and Eastbourne or Hastings via Redhill

Oxted and Brighton via Eridge

London Bridge or Bricklayers' Arms and Ramsgate via Tonbridge and Canterbury West

Waterloo or Nine Elms and Woking via Richmond and Chertsey

Milk and empty trains to Clapham Junction via Byfleet curve and Richmond

Bembridge to Brading

London Bridge or Bricklayers' Arms and Tonbridge or Reading via East Croydon and Redhill

Tonbridge and Reading

Brighton and Hove via Preston Park spur

Three Bridges and Eridge

London Bridge or Bricklayers' Arms and Gillingham, Faversham, Ramsgate or Dover, via Chislehurst Loop and Chatham

Victoria or Holborn and Folkestone or Dover via Orpington Loop, Tonbridge and Ashford

Empty stock and light engines, Waterloo or Nine Elms and Clapham Junction

Passenger trains, Bournemouth Central and Weymouth

Ryde Pierhead, Esplanade or St Johns and Newport and Cowes

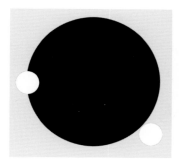

London Bridge or Bricklayers' Arms and Dover, Ramsgate or
   Hastings via Chislehurst, Swanley, Otford and Sevenoaks.
Victoria, Oxted and Tunbridge Wells West via Hever
Holborn and Ramsgate via Herne Hill or Catford Loop
Southampton and Andover via Eastleigh
Light engines and trains terminating at Clapham Junction
   from stations westward
Light engines or empty stock workings running around the
   triangle at Bournemouth West to turn

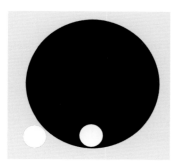

Victoria or Battersea Yard and Brighton via Quarry Line
London Bridge or New Cross Gate and Norwood Yard
Tunbridge Wells West and Eastbourne
Victoria or Holborn and Ramsgate, Dover or Hastings via
   Nunhead and Tonbridge
Waterloo or Nine Elms and Southampton Docks via East
   Putney
Horsham and Guildford
Salisbury and Portsmouth Harbour via Eastleigh
Portsmouth & Southsea to Salisbury via Eastleigh

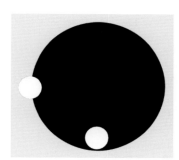

London Bridge or Bricklayers' Arms and North Kent Line via
   Greenwich
Victoria, Stewarts Lane or Holborn to Ramsgate via
   Nunhead, Chislehurst and Chatham
Portsmouth & Southsea to Salisbury via Redbridge
Via Streatham spur
Feltham Yard and Brent via Kew East Junction
Clapham Junction and Kensington

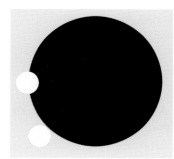

Victoria and Newhaven Harbour
Victoria or Holborn to Ramsgate via Nunhead and Maidstone
   East
Waterloo or Nine Elms and Portsmouth via Woking and
   Havant
Light engines to Feltham Locomotive Depot
Light engines to and from stations west of Basingstoke to
   Eastleigh Locomotive Depot

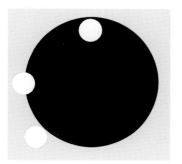

Brighton and Bournemouth

Appendix II

Station Name Changes Post-Grouping

The new railway company initially had problems with station names, not only because there was more than one Ashford, Gillingham or Shoreham, for example, but also the overlap between the railway companies meant that some towns, such as Dorking, had two stations. Before grouping, it was possible to describe the station by its company name, but the continuation of this practice was clearly not in the spirit of the grouping.

By spring 1923 the directors of the Southern Railway had decided on revised names to avoid confusion, and published this in *The Southern Railway Magazine*.

Stations on Different Routes having Identical Names

Station	Section	New Designation
Ashford	SECR	Ashford (Kent)
	LSWR	Ashford (Middlesex)
Bexhill	SECR	Bexhill
	LBSCR	Bexhill Central
Boxhill	SECR	Deepdene
	LBSCR	Boxhill & Burford Bridge
Dorking	SECR	Dorking Town
	LBSCR	Dorking North
Ewell	LBSCR	Ewell East
	LSWR	Ewell West
Gillingham	SECR	Gillingham (Kent)
	LSWR	Gillingham (Dorset)
London Road	LSWR	London Road, Guildford
	LSBCR	London Road, Brighton
New Cross	SECR	New Cross
	LBSCR	New Cross Gate
Penge	SECR	Penge East
	LBSCR	Penge West
Tunbridge Wells	SECR	Tunbridge Wells Central
	LBSCR	Tunbridge Wells

Stations on Different Routes having Similar Names

Station	Section	New Designation
Aldershot North Camp & South Farnborough	SECR	Aldershot North
Farnborough (for Frimley)	SECR	Farnborough North
Blackwater & Camberley	SECR	Blackwater (Hants)
Blackwater	IoWR	Blackwater (IoW)
Coulsdon & Cane Hill	SECR	Coulsdon East
Coulsdon & Smitham Downs	LBSCR	Coulsdon West

Chipstead & Banstead Downs	SECR	Chipstead
Banstead & Burgh Heath	LBSCR	Banstead & Burgh Heath
Ford	LSWR	Ford (Devon)
Ford Junction	LBSCR	Ford (Sussex)
Shoreham	SECR	Shoreham (Kent)
Shoreham-by-Sea	LBSCR	Shoreham-by-Sea

Source: *The Southern Railway Magazine*, April 1923.

Locomotives Inherited by the Southern Railway in 1923

Inevitably, the Southern started life with the steam locomotives operated by the pre-grouping companies, many of which were to survive Southern ownership and into nationalisation, with a few, mainly on the Isle of Wight, lasting until the end of steam in 1967. Others were disposed of fairly quickly. The longevity of many pre-grouping locomotives is surprising, considering that the companies operating in the south-east were impoverished, a factor borne out by the fact that only the LSWR contributed any 4–6–0s to the new company.

Wheels	Pre-Gr	Date	Class	CME[†]	No. Op
0–4–0T	LSWR	1891	B4	Adams	20
0–4–0T	LSWR	1908	K14	Drumm	5
0–4–0T	LSWR	1913*	C14	Drumm	3
0–4–2T	LBSC	1873	D1	Stroud	107
0–4–2T	LBSC	1910	D1x	Stroud	1
0–4–4T	LCDR	1884	A	Kirtley	18

A 'D15' class locomotive heads an unidentified passenger train in 1931. *(HRMS AAM430)*

Wheels	Pre-Gr	Date	Class	CME[†]	No. Op
0–4–4T	LCDR	1884	A1	Kirtley	12
0–4–4T	LCDR	1884	A2	Kirtley	6
0–4–4T	LBSC	1892	D3	Billin	2
0–4–4T	LBSC	1909	D3x	Billin	34
0–4–4T	LSWR	1888	F6	Adams	30
0–4–4T	LSWR	1888	T1	Adams	20
0–4–4T	SECR	1904	H	Wainwr	66
0–4–4T	LSWR	1897	M7	Drumm	55
0–4–4T	LSWR	1897	X14	Drumm	50
0–4–4T	LSWR	1889	O2	Adams	60
0–4–4T	SER	1881	Q	Stirling	32
0–4–4T	SECR	1903	Q1	Wainwr	46
0–4–4T	LCDR	1891	R	Kirtley	18
0–4–4T	SECR	1900	R1	Wainwr	15
0–6–0T	LBSC	1872	A1	Stroud	7
0–6–0T	LBSC	1872	A1x	Stroud	15
0–6–0T	LBSC	1874	E1	Stroud	61
0–6–0T	LBSC	1911	E1x	Billin	1
0–6–0T	LBSC	1913	E2	Billin	10
0–6–0T	LSWR	1894	G6	Adams	34
0–6–0T	SECR	1909	P	Wainwr	8
0–6–0T	SER	1888	R	Stirling	11
0–6–0T	SECR	1910	R1	Wainwr	13
0–6–0T	LCDR	1879	T	Kirtley	10
0–6–0T	FY&N	1876	–	Stroud	1 [1]
0–6–0T	IoWC	1872	–	Stroud	4 [1]
0–6–0T	LSWR	1907	–	Hawth	1 [2]
0–6–0ST	SECR	1917	S**	Mauns	1
0–6–0ST	LSWR	1876	0330	Beattie	20
0–6–0ST	FY&N	1902	–	Mann	1
0–6–2T	LBSC	1891	E3	Billin	17
0–6–2T	LBSC	1897	E4	Billin	70
0–6–2T	LBSC	1909	E4x	Billin	4
0–6–2T	LBSC	1902	E5	Billin	26
0–6–2T	LBSC	1911	E5x	Billin	4
0–6–2T	LBSC	1904	E6	Billin	10
0–6–2T	LBSC	1911	E6x	Billin	2
0–6–2T	LSWR	1907	–	Hawth	2 [2]
2–4–0T	IoW	1864	–	Beyer	7
2–4–0T	IoWC	1876	–	Beyer	4
2–4–0WT	LSWR	1874	0329	Beattie	3
4–2–4T	LSWR	1899	F9	Drumm	1 [3]
4–4–0T	IoWC	1890	–	Black	1
2–4–0T	L&B	1890	–	Baldw	1 [4]
2–6–2T	L&B	1897	–	Mann	3 [4]
2–6–4T	SECR	1917	K	Mauns	1
4–4–2T	LBSC	1906	I1/I1x	Marsh	20
4–4–2T	LBSC	1907	I2	Marsh	10
4–4–2T	LBSC	1907	I3	Marsh	27
4–4–2T	LBSC	1908	I4	Marsh	5
4–4–2T	LSWR	1883	046	Adams	7 [5]
4–4–2T	LSWR	1882	0415	Adams	48
4–6–2T	LSWR	1921	H16	Urie	5
4–6–2T	LBSC	1910	J1	Marsh	1
4–6–2T	LBSC	1912	J2	Marsh	1
4–6–4T	LBSC	1914	L	Billin	7
4–8–0T	LSWR	1921	G16	Urie	4
0–4–2	LSWR	1887	A12/04	Adams	90
0–4–2	LBSC	1882	B1	Stroud	26
0–6–0	LCDR	1877	B1	Kirtley	2
0–6–0	LCDR	1891	B2	Kirtley	6
0–6–0	SECR	1900	C	Wainwr	108
0–6–0	LBSC	1882	C1	Stroud	1
0–6–0	LBSC	1893	C2	Billin	24
0–6–0	LBSC	1902	C2x	Billin	31
0–6–0	LBSC	1906	C3	Marsh	10
0–6–0	SER	1878	O	Stirling	31
0–6–0	SER	1903	O1	Wainwr	56
0–6–0	LSWR	1897	700	Drumm	30

No. 759 *Yeo* again, calling at Lynton for Lynmouth at what might be described as the 'country' end of the line. *(HRMS AAC127)*

Wheels	Pre-Gr	Date	Class	CME[†]	No. Op
0–6–0	LSWR	1872	0273	Beattie	6
0–6–0	LSWR	1874	0302	Beattie	15
0–6–0	LSWR	1881	0395	Adams	20
2–6–0	LBSC	1913	K	Billin	17
2–6–0	SECR	1922	N/N1	Mauns	16
4–4–0	SER	1898	B	Stirling	4
4–4–0	SER	1910	B1	Stirling	25
4–4–0	LBSC	1895	B2x	Marsh	25
4–4–0	LBSC	1899	B4	Billin	31
4–4–0	LBSC	1922	B4x	Billin	2
4–4–0	LSWR	1898	C8	Drumm	10
4–4–0	SECR	1901	D	Wainwr	41
4–4–0	SECR	1921	D1	Mauns	10
4–4–0	LSWR	1912	D15	Drumm	10
4–4–0	SECR	1905	E	Wainwr	15
4–4–0	SECR	1919	E1	Mauns	11
4–4–0	SECR	1883	F	Stirling	12
4–4–0	SECR	1903	F1	Wainwr	75
4–4–0	SECR	1899	G	Pickers	5[(6)]
4–4–0	LSWR	1901	K10	Drumm	40
4–4–0	SECR	1914	L	Wa/Ma	22
4–4–0	LSWR	1903	L11	Drumm	40
4–4–0	LSWR	1904	L12	Drumm	20
4–4–0	LCDR	1880	M1	Kirtley	1
4–4–0	LCDR	1880	M2	Kirtley	1
4–4–0	LCDR	1880	M3	Kirtley	26
4–4–0	LSWR	1903	S11	Drumm	10
4–4–0	LSWR	1892	T3	Adams	20
4–4–0	LSWR	1895	T6	Adams	10
4–4–0	LSWR	1897	T7	Drumm	1
4–4–0	LSWR	1901	E10	Drumm	5
4–4–0	LSWR	1899	T9	Drumm	66
4–4–0	LSWR	1890	X2	Adams	20
4–4–0	LSWR	1895	X6	Adams	10
4–4–0	LSWR	1880	0135	Adams	3

'H15' No. 30488 heads a down 'Ocean Liner Express' through Clapham Junction. *(HRMS AER333)*

Wheels	Pre-Gr	Date	Class	CME[†]	No. Op
4–4–0	LSWR	1879	0380	Adams	8
4–4–0	LSWR	1883	0445	Adams	12
4–4–0	LSWR	1884	0460	Adams	21
4–2–2–0	LSWR	1897	T7	Drumm	1
4–2–2–0	LSWR	1901	E10	Drumm	5
4–4–2	LBSC	1905	H1	Marsh	5
4–4–2	LBSC	1911	H2	Marsh	6
4–6–0	LSWR	1913	H15	Urie	16
4–6–0	LSWR	1908	G14	Drumm	5
4–6–0	LSWR	1918	N15	Urie	20
4–6–0	LSWR	1910	P14	Drumm	5
4–6–0	LSWR	1920	S15	Urie	20
4–6–0	LSWR	1911	T14	Drumm	10

Notes to Table:

CME[†] Chief Mechanical Engineer or Builder (the smaller companies normally bought from the independent locomotive manufacturers)

* Originally built in 1906 as 2–2–0T rail motor engines

** Rebuild of SECR class 0–6–0

[1] Ex-LSBC 'Terriers'

[2] Originally built for Plymouth, Devonport & South Western Junction Railway

[3] Inspection saloon

[4] 2 ft gauge

[5] Originally built in 1879 as 4–4–0T; rebuilt 1883

[6] Originally built by Neilson, Reid for Great North of Scotland Railway to a design by Pickersgill, but taken over by SECR

Chief Mechanical Engineers and Builders – abbreviations used:

Beyer – Beyer, Peacock
Billin – L. Billington
Black – Black, Hawthorn
Drumm – Drummond
Hawth – Hawthorn, Leslie
Mann – Manning, Wardle
Mauns – Maunsell
Pickers – Pickersgill
Stroud – Stroudley
Wainwr – Wainwright
Wa/Ma – Wainwright & Maunsell

Nicknames

Many of the classes of steam locomotives acquired nicknames over the years, which must have confused the newcomer to a depot. One can imagine the confusion on being told to phone another depot to say that a 'Bulldog' was not available, and that all that could be provided was a 'Grasshopper'. These seem to be names generally recognised by the LSWR people at least, although no doubt locomotives that were known to be unreliable or troublesome in any way also had their own individual nicknames!

Camelback: The 0127 class shunting tanks had the water tank located over the boiler, giving the appearance of a camel's back.

Black Motor: Some confusion was apparent on this name applied to the 0127 class goods engines, but opinions differed over whether this was a criticism of the engine or as a compliment to the increasingly common motor car!

Grasshopper: The small Drummond 329 class mixed-traffic locomotives acquired this name, but how and when has been lost in the mists of time.

Jumbo: When the Adams 0396 class entered service in 1888, they were regarded as the most powerful engines of their day, and their arrival also coincided with that of the famous elephant Jumbo at the London Zoo.

Bulldog: The Drummond 415 class express engines had a bold aspect to the front of the boiler that gave a fanciful resemblance to a bulldog, although the name is also attributed to a driver who bred bulldogs!

Rocket: Very small passenger tanks used on motor-rail units, which were supposed to resemble Stephenson's famous *Rocket*, at least in the minds of some railwaymen!

Jubilee: Mixed-traffic engines of 527 class built in the year of Queen Victoria's Jubilee.

Double Breaster: The mixed-traffic Drummond 448 class were supposed to be so exposed that the unfortunate driver would have to wear two double-breasted overcoats.

Appendix IV

Southern Railway Locomotives

Initially, the Southern Railway absorbed the existing locomotive numbers of its constituent companies by the simple expedient of prefixing the numbers with a letter showing the company of origin, with 'E' for the LSWR; 'B' for the LBSCR and 'A' for the SECR. This was a strange choice, since the use of 'W', 'C' and 'E' respectively would have tied in with the main-line sectional structure, albeit that 'W' would have stood for both the Western Section and London (West), which extended to what must have been the very outermost suburbs of Portsmouth and Southampton.

Since the system was introduced virtually overnight in a wide number of locomotive depots throughout the Southern Railway's area, it can be imagined that application varied considerably. Standing looking at a front buffer beam, the letter was on the left replacing the original 'No', while on other positions the letter might prefix the number or be above it. Almost ten years later, in 1931, a different system was adopted, and in many ways this pointed the way in which the 'Big Four' locomotives were to be treated on nationalisation, with the Western Section locomotive numbers unchanged other than for the dropping of the 'E' prefix, while Central Section locomotives also dropped the prefix and had 2000 added to their number, with 1000 added for Eastern Section locomotives. This was a far neater system and would have been no more difficult to introduce than the original system of prefixes. More to the point, it allowed the use of letters to indicate to which of the locomotive works engines were allocated for heavy maintenance: This was far more logical, with 'A' for Ashford; 'B' for Brighton, and 'E' for Eastleigh. Inevitably, a certain amount of rationalisation still had to take place as locomotives were moved around in the interests of efficiency, and this meant that similar locomotives from different sections found themselves with different works allocations. Maunsell's 'Z' class 0–8–0Ts were allocated to Eastleigh for maintenance rather than Ashford, losing their 'A' code, but also retained their original numbers, 950–95, as these fitted comfortably into the Western Section system.

While the old LSWR had not been noted for a locomotive naming policy, under the new regime matters changed completely, with the Western Section taking the lead. This may have been down to Maunsell's influence as first Chief Mechanical Engineer, since he had introduced the practice in the closing years of the SECR, or it may have been that the presence of so many named locomotives from the constituent companies, including the minor ones, encouraged the process. It also fitted very neatly with Walker's eye for publicity. Since individual first-class Pullman cars also carried names, it would have seemed odd if the mighty express locomotive heading the named train with its named carriages carried nothing more than a number. The locomotive naming policy did much to identify areas, communities and institutions with the Southern.

Eventually a complicated system of numbering was introduced. This was really down to Bulleid's term as CME, and originated with his 'Merchant Navy', 'West Country' and 'Battle of Britain' classes. The first numeral gave the number of leading axles, the second the number of trailing axles, followed by a letter indicating the number of driving axles, with 'A' for one, 'B' for two and 'C' for three, and finally, a third numeral gave the actual locomotive number.

To complicate matters even more, further letters were painted on Western Section locomotives to indicate their power classification, using the letters A to K, with A for the most powerful and J for the least, with K for tank engines other than the powerful 0–8–0T 'G16' and 4–6–2T 'H16'. These letters were painted on the side of the frame close to the front buffer beam, and were to be found as:

A – 'G16', 'H15', 'H16', 'N15', 'Q1', 'S15', 'V' and 'Lord Nelsons'
B – 'Q', 'T14'
C – 700
D – 'D15', 'L12'
E – 'S11'
F – 'K10', 'L11'
G – 0395
H – 'T9'
I –' T3', 'X6'
J – 'A12'
K – Tank engines other than 'G16', 'H16'

Oddly, given the interest in naming locomotives, when the 'River' class was rebuilt from 2–6–4T tanks to 2–6–0 tender engines following the Sevenoaks derailment, they lost their names. Since the construction spread over the amalgamation, the names were not confined to rivers in the Eastern Section.

While the small tank engines operating on the Isle of Wight were all named, to the delight of visitors and enthusiasts alike, as were the humble shunters in the railway-owned docks, notably Southampton, a large number of locomotives remained nameless. The numbers below reflect changing policy, most notably with the 'C' prefix accorded the wartime utility 'Q1' class.

'Merchant Navy' class No. 35030 *Elder Dempster Lines*, seen here at Stewart's Lane, gets ready to head the 'Night Ferry' in 1950. *(HRMS ACN008)*

Numbering of unnamed classes

Class	Wheels	Nos
L1	4–4–0	753–9, 782–9
N	2–6–0	A823–75, 1400–1414
N1	2–6–0	A876–880
Q	0–6–0	530–539
Q1	0–6–0	C1–C40
S15	4–6–0	823–37
U	2–6–0	A610–39
U1	2–6–0	A891–900, 1901–1910
W	2–6–4T	1911–15
Z	0–8–0T	950–957

'River' class before rebuilding

A790 *River Avon*
A791 *River Adur*
A792 *River Arun*
A793 *River Ouse*
A794 *River Rother*
A795 *River Medway*
A796 *River Stour*

A797 *River Mole*
A798 *River Wey*
A799 *River Test*
A800 *River Cray*
A801 *River Darenth*
A802 *River Cuckmere*
A803 *River Itchen*

A804 *River Tamar*
A805 *River Camel*
A806 *River Torridge*
A807 *River Axe*
A808 *River Char*
A809 *River Dart*
A890 *River Frome*

'N15', later named the 'King Arthur' class:

Built at Eastleigh by the Southern Railway
448 *Sir Tristam*
449 *Sir Torre*
450 *Sir Kay*
451 *Sir Lamorak*
452 *Sir Meliagrance*

453 *King Arthur*
454 *Queen Guinevere*
455 *Sir Lancelot*
456 *Sir Galahad*
457 *Sir Bedivere*

Built under Urie
736 *Excalibur*
737 *King Uther*
738 *King Pellinore*
739 *King Leodegrance*
740 *Merlin*
741 *Joyous Gard*
742 *Camelot*
743 *Lyonnesse*
744 *Maid of Astolat*
745 *Tintagel*

746 *Pendragon*
747 *Elaine*
748 *Vivien*
749 *Iseult*
750 *Morgan le Fay*
751 *Etarre*
752 *Linette*
753 *Melisande*
754 *The Green Knight*
755 *The Red Knight*

Built by the North British Locomotive Co.
763 *Sir Bors de Ganis*
764 *Sir Gawain*
765 *Sir Gareth*
766 *Sir Geraint*
767 *Sir Valence*
768 *Sir Balin*
769 *Sir Balan*

770 *Sir Prianius*
771 *Sir Sagramore*
772 *Sir Percival*
773 *Sir Lavaine*
774 *Sir Agravaine*
776 *Sir Galagars*
777 *Sir Lamiel*
778 *Sir Pelleas*

'King Arthur' class 'N15' No. 30741 *Joyous Gard* at Eastleigh after nationalisation. Note the multiple jet blastpipes and large-diameter chimney. *(HRMS AEW512)*

779 *Sir Colgrevance*
780 *Sir Persant*
781 *Sir Aglovale*
782 *Sir Brian*
783 *Sir Gillemere*
784 *Sir Nerovens*
785 *Sir Mador de la Porte*

786 *Sir Lionel*
787 *Sir Menadeuke*
788 *Sir Urre of the Mount*
789 *Sir Guy*
790 *Sir Villiars*
791 *Sir Uwaine*
792 *Sir Hervis de Revel*

793* *Sir Ontzlake*
794* *Sir Ector de Maris*
795* *Sir Dinadon*
796* *Sir Dodinas le Savage*
797* *Sir Blamor de Ganis*
798* *Sir Hectimere*
799* *Sir Ironside*
800* *Sir Meleaaus de Lile*
801* *Sir Durnore*
803* *Sir Harry le Fise Lake*
804* *Sir Cador of Cornwall*
805* *Sir Constantine*
806* *Sir Galleron*

* Six-wheel tenders

'Lord Nelson' class

850 *Lord Nelson*
851 *Sir Francis Drake*
852 *Sir Walter Raleigh*
853 *Sir Richard Grenville*
854 *Howard of Effingham*
855 *Robert Blake*
856 *Lord St Vincent*
857 *Lord Howe*

858 *Lord Duncan*
859 *Lord Hood*
860 *Lord Hawke*
861 *Lord Anson*
862 *Lord Collingwood*
863 *Lord Rodney*
864 *Sir Martin Frobisher*
865 *Sir John Hawkins*

'Schools' class (V)

900 *Eton*
901 *Winchester*
902 *Wellington*
903 *Charterhouse*
904 *Lancing*
905 *Tonbridge*
906 *Sherborne*
907 *Dulwich*
908 *Westminster*
909 *St Pauls*
910 *Merchant Taylors*
911 *Dover*
912 *Downside*
913 *Christ's Hospital*
914 *Eastbourne*
915 *Brighton*
916 *Whitgift*
917 *Ardingly*
918 *Hurstpierpoint*
919 *Harrow*

920 *Rugby*
921 *Shrewsbury*
922 *Marlborough*
923 *Bradfield*
924 *Haileybury*
925 *Cheltenham*
926 *Repton*
927 *Clifton*
928 *Stowe*
929 *Malvern*
930 *Radley*
931 *King's Wimbledon*
932 *Blundells*
933 *King's Canterbury*
934 *St Lawrence*
935 *Sevenoaks*
936 *Cranleigh*
937 *Epsom*
938 *St Olave's*
939 *Leatherhead*

'N15X' 'Remembrance' class

2327 *Trevithick*
2328 *Hackworth*
2329 *Stephenson*
2330 *Cudworth*

2331 *Beattie*
2332 *Stroudley*
2333 *Remembrance*

One of the famous 'Schools' class locomotives, No. 936 *Cranleigh*, at Hither Green on the Eastern Section in 1947. *(HRMS AAG306)*

Unrebuilt 'Battle of Britain' class No. 34067 *Tangmere*, with the more logical but much less descriptive BR numbering system, heads a train of mixed Maunsell and Bulleid rolling stock past BR Mk I carriages at Ashford. *(HRMS AEV902)*

'H1' class

2037 *Selsey Bill*
2038 *Portland Bill*
2039 *Hartland Point*

2040 *St Catherine's Point*
2041 *Peverill Point*

'H2' class

2421 *South Foreland*
2422 *North Foreland*
2423 *The Needles*

2424 *Beachy Head*
2425 *Trevose Head*
2426 *St Alban's Head*

'Isle of Wight' locomotives

1* *Medina*
2* *Yarmouth*
3* *Ryde*
4* *Wroxall*
8** *Freshwater*
11** *Newport*
13** *Carisbrooke*
14 *Fishbourne*
15 *Cowes*
16 *Ventnor*
17 *Seaview*
18 *Ningwood*
19 *Osborne*
20 *Shanklin*

21 *Sandown*
22 *Brading*
23 *Totland*
24 *Calbourne*
25 *Godshill*
26 *Whitwell*
27 *Merstone*
28 *Ashey*
29 *Alverstone*
30 *Shorwell*
31 *Chale*
32 *Bonchurch*
33 *Bembridge*

*E1 **A1X; otherwise all 02

'King Arthur' class 'N15' No. 30778 *Sir Pelleas* takes an Up Folkestone express through Headcorn. *(HRMS AEW321)*

'B4' class dock engines

81 *Jersey*
85 *Alderney*
86 *Havre*
89 *Trouville*
90 *Caen*
93 *St Malo*

95 *Honfleur*
96 *Normandy*
97 *Brittany*
98 *Cherbourg*
101 *Dinan*
102 *Granville*

147 *Dinard*
176 *Guernsey*
734* *Clausentum*
3458* *Ironside*

* 0458 class, 0–4–0T acquired on purchase of Southampton Docks in 1892

There was also a small number of locomotives that were unclassed but named. These were 756 *A.S. Harris*, 0–6–0T; 757 *Earl of Mount Edgecombe*, and 758 *Lord St Levan*, both 0–6–2Ts, all acquired from the Plymouth, Devonport & South Western Junction Railway; and 949 *Hecate*, from the Kent & East Sussex Railway.

'Merchant Navy' class

21C1 *Channel Packet*
21C2 *Union Castle*
21C3 *Royal Mail*
21C4 *Cunard White Star*
21C5 *Canadian Pacific*
21C6 *Peninsular & Oriental SN Co.*
21C7 *Aberdeen Commonwealth*
21C8 *Shaw Savill*
21C9 *Orient Line*
21C10 *Blue Star*

21C11 *General Steam Navigation Co.*
21C12 *United States Line*
21C13 *Blue Funnel*
21C14 *Netherlands Line*
21C15 *Rotterdam Lloyd*
21C16 *Elders & Fyffes*
21C17 *Belgian Marine*
21C18 *British India Line*
21C19 *French Line CGT*
21C20 *Bibby Line*

After nationalisation, in addition to renumbering these locomotives, BR also built another ten members of the class.

Not exactly what the authorities meant by utility locomotives were Bulleid's famous Pacifics, including 'Battle of Britain' class No. 34082 *615 Squadron*, here seen under British Railways ownership but still in Southern Railway colours, at Waterloo. *(HRMS AAM534)*

'West Country' class

21C101 *Exeter*
21C102 *Salisbury*
21C103 *Plymouth*
21C104 *Yeovil*
21C105 *Barnstaple*
21C106 *Bude*
21C107 *Wadebridge*
21C108 *Padstow*
21C109 *Lyme Regis*
21C110 *Sidmouth*
21C111 *Tavistock*
21C112 *Launceston*
21C113 *Okehampton*
21C114 *Budleigh Salterton*
21C115 *Exmouth*
21C116 *Bodmin*
21C117 *Ilfracombe*
21C118 *Axminster*
21C119 *Bideford*
21C120 *Seaton*
21C121 *Dartmoor*
21C122 *Exmoor*
21C123 *Blackmoor Vale*
21C124 *Tamar Valley*

21C125 *Whimple*
21C126 *Yes Tor*
21C127 *Taw Valley*
21C128 *Eddystone*
21C129 *Lundy*
21C130 *Watersmeet*
21C131 *Torrington*
21C132 *Camelford*
21C133 *Chard*
21C134 *Honiton*
21C135 *Shaftesbury*
21C136 *Westward Ho!*
21C137 *Clovelly*
21C138 *Lynton*
21C139 *Boscastle*
21C140 *Crewkerne*
21C141 *Wilton*
21C142 *Dorchester*
21C143 *Coombe Martin*
21C144 *Woolacombe*
21C145 *Ottery St Mary*
21C146 *Braunton*
21C147 *Callington*
21C148 *Crediton*

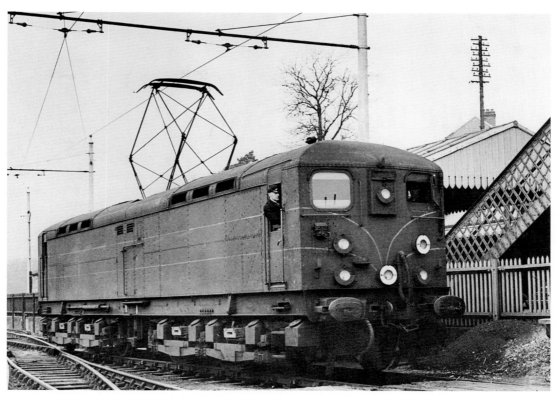

Uncertainties over how an electric locomotive would cope with gaps in the conductor rail meant that the Southern didn't really benefit fully from electrification for its goods services until the prototypes were introduced during the Second World War. This is CC1 in a siding. Note the absence of the third rail and the use of overhead wire for the safety of the shunters. *(NRM BTC-collection 814/56)*

'Battle of Britain' class

21C149 *Anti-Aircraft Command*
21C150 *Royal Observer Corps*
21C151 *Winston Churchill*
21C152 *Lord Dowding*
21C153 *Sir Keith Park*
21C154 *Lord Beaverbrook*
21C155 *Fighter Pilot*
21C156 *Croydon*
21C157 *Biggin Hill*
21C158 *Sir Frederick Pile*
21C159 *Sir Archibald Sinclair*

21C160 *75 Squadron*
21C161 *73 Squadron*
21C162 *17 Squadron*
21C163 *299 Squadron*
21C164 *Fighter Command*
21C165 *Hurricane*
21C166 *Spitfire*
21C167 *Tangmere*
21C168 *Kenley*
21C169 *Hawkinge*
21C170 *Manston*

Again, both of the above classes were renumbered by BR, and no fewer than forty additional locomotives were built.

Electric engines

CC1
CC2

A third was also built, entering service in 1948 after nationalisation.

Electric Rolling Stock

On its formation, the Southern Railway inherited from its constituent companies 460 carriages suitable for use in suburban electric trains, by far the greatest proportion coming from the LSWR. The total number of carriages comprised:

LSWR Waterloo & City	30
LSWR three-coach motor sets	252
LSWR two-coach trailer sets	48
LBSC south London line	32
LBSC Crystal Palace	98
Total	460

In addition to these, in anticipation of extending electrification, the LBSC had a number of driving trailers, each with four first- and four third-class compartments as well as the driving cab. These were surplus to use at the time and pending a decision on further electrification, the carriages were all converted for use in steam trains, with the motorman's compartment locked and the windows painted over.

The AC rolling stock was designated by the Southern as SL for that used on the south London line; CP for the Crystal Palace services; and CW for those with motor vans, as would be used on the Coulsdon North and Sutton extensions.

The Coulsdon North and Sutton extensions of the LBSCR overhead, or 'elevated electric', schemes were sufficiently far advanced on grouping for work to be continued. For these, the Metropolitan Carriage, Wagon & Finance Co. at Birmingham built 21 motor vans, 60 driving trailers and 20 trailers. The motor vans were nicknamed 'milk vans', were 42 ft long and weighed 62 tons. Although they included driving cabs, the trains were usually driven from the trailer's guard's compartment, and had two overhead bow collectors powered by four 250 hp motors which, with the rest of the electrical equipment, was supplied by the General Electric Company, later to become GEC. There were thirty each of two different types of driving trailer, of 51 ft 7 in and 57 ft 7 in. The shorter version had eight third-class compartments in addition to the motorman's compartment, and the longer had four first- and four third-class compartments. In service, these carriages formed loosely coupled five-car trains, each with a third-class and a composite driving trailer coupled to a composite trailer. Off-peak, a single set comprised a train, but two sets would provide a ten-car, or eight passenger carriage, train in the peak. Despite using new rolling stock, the trains must have had an unsatisfactory appearance, with some carriages painted in Southern green, others in LBSCR umber brown.

Southern Railway Suburban Electric Stock

1201–84: Designated 3 SUB, LSWR three-car motor sets could be operated either on their own or in tandem, or with a trailer set sandwiched between the two, and this LSWR practice was adopted by the Southern for its early suburban electrification projects. Only the motor sets included first-class compartments, with the trailer sets being all-third class and intended for peak period strengthening. In the motor sets, only the end bogies of the two end cars were powered, each with two nose-suspended 275 hp motors. With two motor sets and a trailer set, 54 mph could be attained on level track. Starting in 1934, these were rebuilt, with the bodies lengthened and mounted on standard 62 ft steel frames with new motor and trailing bodies. They had approximately 56 first-class and 180 third-class seats, although considerable variations in accommodation occurred between sets. Generally, third-class accommodation was improved, while first-class was reduced in size. Overall weight also varied between 109 and 114 tons, while length was usually around 193 ft to 193 ft 8 in.

1001–1024: Two-car trailer sets to work with the above.

1285–1310: Designated 3 SUB, these were three-car motor sets introduced in 1925 for the Western Section. The driving motor coaches were built by Metropolitan Carriage, Wagon & Finance (MCWF), with Metropolitan-Vickers (Metrovick) electrical equipment, and each had a motorman's, guard's and seven third-class compartments, weighing 39 tons. The trailer was sandwiched between them with one third-, six first- and then two third-class compartments, weighed 27 tons, and had an overall length of 180 ft 8 in. Built of teak frames with steel panels and rounded driving ends, they were sometimes referred to as the 'torpedo' type, and were similar in appearance to 1201 mentioned above, an impression further enhanced by many axle boxes having the impression 'LSWR'. Third-class compartments had five seats on either side; and first class had four on either side. There were MCB automatic couplers between carriages. On these and subsequent motor sets, the small side outlooks for guards were replaced by periscopes from 1929 onwards, increasing the number of routes on which these sets could be operated.

1025–37: Two-car trailer sets to be operated between pairs of the above, these were converted from nine-compartment stock built by the LBSC at Lancing in 1921. Each carriage had nine third-class compartments and weighed 25 tons, with an overall length of 115 ft 2 in.

1496–1524: Designated 3 SUB, these were three-car motor sets introduced in 1925 for the Eastern Section. The driving motor coaches were built by MCWF, with 300 hp motors by English Electric and other electrical equipment by Metrovick, and each had a motorman's, guard's and eight third-class compartments. Trailers built by Birmingham Railway Carriage & Wagon (BRCW) were sandwiched between with one third-, seven first- and one further third-class compartment. Overall length was 193 ft 8 in, and the weight was 109 tons. They also introduced bowed driving ends which were used on succeeding stock.

1401–95/1525–34: Designated 3 SUB, these were additional sets introduced in 1925–6 for the Eastern Section. Bodies were taken from ex-SECR six- and four-wheeled stock and rebuilt on new frames at Ashford with completion at Brighton, resulting in arrangements similar to the 1496 series above. Interior finish reflected SECR style, including 'SERCo' displayed on many fittings and fixtures.

1051–1120: Two-car trailer sets for the Eastern Section 1925–6 electrification, converted from ex-LBSC nine-compartment third-class stock, like the 1025 series, but originally a mix of LBSC and MCWF manufacture. Initially a few were split up and provided a fourth trailer on the motor sets until sufficient trailers were available to make complete trailer sets – an arrangement that provided a surfeit of first-class accommodation. Overall weight was 50 tons and length 115 ft 2 in.

1601–30: Designated 3 SUB, these three-car motor sets for the Central Section 1928 electrification were converted from ex-SECR stock and were similar to the 1401 series, but with 275 hp Metrovick motors. Automatic couplers between carriages followed the

This is a later version of the 4 SUB with the rounded effect carried through the driver's cab to produce a far more attractive look. This design also remained in production for the early 4 EPB stock. (*NRM BTC-collection 145/64*)

Southern design of a central buffer and coupling bar, and eventually this design was introduced to all of the above.

1631–57: Designated 3 SUB, these additional sets for the Central Section 1928 electrification were converted from ex-LBSC seven-carriage suburban units, with motor coaches converted from brakes with eight third-class compartments and trailers with seven first-class and two third-class compartments. Metrovick electrical equipment included 275 hp motors. The motor coaches weighed 39 tons and the trailers 26 tons, with an overall length of 193 ft 5 in.

1658–1701: Designated 3 SUB, these additional three-car motor sets were similar to the 1201 series, but weighed 108 tons overall, and were converted in 1928 from ex-LSWR four-coach suburban sets, giving one motor coach with eight third-class compartments, a trailer with five third- and five first-class compartments, and, for the first time, a motor coach with two first- and five third-class compartments. An exception was 1695, with a trailer with six first- and four third-class compartments, and three first- and four third-class in the composite motor. Metrovick 275 hp motors were fitted. Overall weight was 110 tons and length was 193 ft 8 in.

1773–85: Designated 3 SUB, these three-car motor sets were introduced in late 1930 and were identical to the 1695 series, although an exception was 1783, which matched the 1658 series.

1786–96: Designated 3 SUB, these three-car motor sets were introduced in early 1931. While their appearance was similar to those above, they were in fact converted from ex-LSWR six-wheeled suburban carriages, some dating back to 1901, with the motor cars having eight third-class compartments and the trailers seven first- and two third-class compartments.

1702–72: Designated 3 SUB, these were three-car motor sets for the 1928–30 electrification schemes, with 1760–69 used for the Windsor electrification, and converted from ex-LBSC

Bulleid's wide-bodied design originally intended for the 4 SUB series was continued on to the mechanically different 4 EPB series, easily distinguished from later 4 SUB units by the driver's cab being accessed through the guard's compartment. The designation 4 EPB was retained when deliveries of suburban electric multiple units based on BR's Mk I body design followed. This unit is at Eastleigh carriage works. *(HRMS AEN230)*

stock. They consisted of a motor coach with eight third-class compartments, a trailer with six third- and four first-class compartments, and a motor with four third-class and three first-class compartments. Nos 1702–16 and the motor coaches of 1770–1 were converted from the seven-coach suburban stock, as earlier, but the remainder were converted from LBSC electric stock. They had Metrovick electrical equipment, an overall weight of 104 tons and a length of 193 ft 5 in.

1121–67: Trailer sets for the 1928–9 electrification schemes, with a hybrid arrangement of an ex-SECR eight-compartment close-coupled to a nine-compartment ex-LSWR, with two compartments added, giving an overall weight of 49 tons and a length of 113 ft 8 in.

1168–87: Two-car trailer sets converted from ex-LBSC stock in 1929–30. 1168–80 and 1187 were former electric stock with nine third-class compartments, while the remainder had one carriage of this type coupled to a former steam composite driving trailer converted to give eight third-class compartments and a five-seat 'coupe'. Overall length was 115 ft 2 in, with the 1168 series weighing 50 tons and the 1181 series 49 tons.

1188–94: Similar to the 1121 series, but completed in 1930–1.

1797–1801: Five additional sets identical to the 1631 series and introduced in 1931–2, with No. 1801 renumbered 1600 in 1934.

1801–8: Two-car motor sets converted from overhead electrification stock intended for the south London line, to which they returned in 1929. The motor coaches included a motorman's, guard's and seven third-class compartments, with the driving trailers having two first-class, six third-class and a guard's compartment with a partitioned-off space for the motorman. In both carriages the third-class compartments were connected by a side corridor. Electrical equipment, including two 275 hp motors, was by Metrovick. These sets were originally numbered 1901–8, but the numbers changed in 1934. Overall weight was 78 tons and length 127 ft 2 in. The sets operated as single units off-peak, but as pairs in peak periods.

1195–8: Two-car trailer units converted in 1934 from ex-LSWR eight-compartment third-class carriages, with two extra compartments added, giving an overall weight of 54 tons and a length of 129 ft 4 in. These had a brief service life before the major conversion programme of trailer sets started in 1934.

1038–1120: Two-car trailer sets rearranged starting in 1934. A total of fifty-one sets were rearranged with close-coupling of ex-LBSC nine-compartment and ex-LSWR ten-compartment coaches, similar to those in the 1195 series, although overall lengths varied between 117 ft 6 in and 121 ft 6 in, and weights from 49 to 51 tons. Some ex-LBSC vehicles were withdrawn, others replaced one of the carriages in the 1195 series, and a few survived to form additional trailer sets 1199–1200 and 989–1000 formed in 1937–8, again coupled to ten-compartment ex-LSWR carriages.

1585–99: Designated 3 SUB, these additional three-car motor sets were converted in 1934–5 from ex-LSWR stock at Eastleigh with seven third-class compartments and a five-seat coupe in the motor coaches, and the trailers having a third, seven first and a further third. Overall weight was 109 tons and length 193 ft 8 in.

1579–84: Designated 3 SUB, these additional three-car motor sets were converted in 1934–5 from ex-LSWR stock at Eastleigh, with eight third-class compartments in the motor coaches. Otherwise they were like the 1585 series, except that the electro-pneumatic control gear was mounted under the motor coaches, and the overall weight was 112 tons.

Southern Railway Main-Line Electric Stock

Although initially some sets for local services were converted from earlier stock, without exception the fast and semi-fast main-line rolling stock was built from new, and in each case powered multiple units were used without any trailer sets. It also marked the introduced of

A twelve-car train for Hastings at Three Bridges in 1934, almost certainly comprised of a combination of 6 PAN and 6 PUL units. *(HRMS AAF122)*

The Eastbourne electrification scheme saw the introduction of the 6 PAN express electric multiple units, although these usually worked in conjunction with a 6 PUL on both the Brighton and Eastbourne electric services. This is 2030 on an Up working in 1935. *(HRMS AAE520)*

the Southern Railway's designations for different types of multiple unit rolling stock, using a combination of figures to indicate the number of carriages and an abbreviated designation usually based on a feature of the rolling stock.

1921–53: Designated 4 LAV and built at Eastleigh in 1931–2 for the Brighton electrification scheme to work semi-fast and slow trains to Brighton and Worthing. The end motor coaches were identical, each with a compartment for a motorman and a guard, with seven third-class compartments, with one trailer having four third- and five first-class compartments, and the other having five first- and three third-class compartments linked with a side corridor to a lavatory at each end, giving a total of 70 first- and 204 third-class passengers. The overall weight was 139 tons and length was 257 ft 2 in. Underframes were built of steel sections, with steel panels on hardwood frames for the bodies. The electrical equipment was the same as that for most suburban stock, by Metrovick, with two 275 hp motors on each motor coach. From the start, the guard had a periscope in each of the guard's compartments, and an armchair. In 1940 another two units, 2954 and 2955, were built, but in appearance and electrical equipment these resembled the 2 HALs.

2001–20 (3001–20 from January 1937): Designated 6 PUL, these were built in 1932 to operate the fast services to Brighton and Worthing, and while all the conventional trailers were built at Eastleigh, the motor coach order was divided equally between the Metropolitan-Cammell Carriage, Wagon & Finance Co. and the Birmingham Railway Carriage & Wagon Co. For the first time, centre gangway motor coaches were provided, each carrying fifty-two passengers in six sets of facing seats on each side, with an end set of four seats on each side facing the seat back of the next set. A speedometer was provided for the driver, with a bar at 75 mph, the maximum speed permitted for these units. Another departure was the use of

Another train of 6 PAN and 6 PUL units passes at speed through East Croydon in 1934. *(HRMS AAF123)*

four 225 hp English Electric motors in each motor coach, with electro-pneumatic equipment by British Thomson-Houston. The motor coaches were of all-steel construction.

The standard trailers used the same type of steel underframes with steel cladding on hardwood framing for the bodies. The trailers consisted of one with eight compartments and a coupe for four third-class passengers, and two for five first-class and three third-class passengers, with all three having lavatories at each end. The sixth carriage was a Pullman, built by the Metropolitan-Cammell Carriage, Wagon & Finance Co., with twelve first-class and sixteen third-class seats out of the unit's total of 72 first- and 236 third-class seats, as well as a pantry at each end and a kitchen at the first-class end, with a lavatory between the two classes. The Pullman cars were 8 ft 11½ in wide and 68 ft 8¾ in long.

2041–3: Designated 6 CITY sets, these were built at the same time as the 6 PUL, but differed in having all three trailers as seven-compartment firsts with end lavatories, giving a total of 138 first-class and 120 third-class seats in 2040 and 124 third-class in 2041–2, each of which used 56-seat motor coaches from an experimental train, and of which once again twelve and sixteen respectively were in the Pullman car. The high proportion of first-class seats was due to these trains being allocated to services from Brighton to London Bridge, with a very high number of first-class season ticket holders, and the usual arrangement was for a 6 PUL and a 6 CITY to be coupled together.

2051–3 (3051–3 from January 1937): Designated 5 BEL, these were originally intended for the 'Southern Belle' all-Pullman trains between Victoria and Brighton, the first all-electric Pullmans anywhere, and soon renamed the 'Brighton Belle'. The trains consisted of two motor third brakes with motorman's and guard's compartments as well as forty-eight seats, two first-class cars with twenty seats, kitchen and pantry, and a motor third with fifty-six seats. Overall weight was 249 tons, with each motor coach weighing 62 tons, and length was 335 ft. Two sets operated together with a third in reserve.

Pullman Cars: Composite and first-class Pullman cars carried girls' names in accordance with Pullman Car Co. tradition. These were:
6 PUL: 2001, *Anne*; 2002, *Rita*; 2003, *Grace*; 2004, *Elinor*; 2005, *Ida*; 2006, *Rose*; 2007, *Violet*; 2008, *Lorna*; 2009, *Alice*; 2010, *Daisy*; 2011, *Naomi*; 2012, *Bertha*; 2014, *Enid*; 2015, *Joyce*; 2016, *Iris*; 2017, *Ruth*; 2018, *May*; 2019, *Peggy*; 2020, *Clara*.
6 CITY: 2041, *Gwladys*; 2042, *Olive*; 2043, *Ethel*.
5 BEL: 2051, *Hazel and Doris*; 2052, *Vera and Audrey*; 2053, *Mona and Gwen*.

1813–90: Designated 2 NOL and converted from ex-LSWR steam stock at Eastleigh between 1934 and 1936, these had two close-coupled carriages, with the motor coaches having compartments for the motorman and the guard as well as a coupe third and another seven third-class compartments, and the driving trailers having a motorman's, three first- and six third-class compartments. The motor coaches each had two 275 hp English Electric motors, with the remaining electrical equipment supplied by Metrovick. Overall weight was 70 tons, and length 129 ft 6 in. These were used initially to replace the 1201 series on services between Brighton and West Worthing from 1934, taking fifteen sets, with a further thirty-three in 1935 taking over local services in the area bounded by Brighton, Seaford, Horsted Keynes, Eastbourne and Ore. The remainder were allocated to the Waterloo to Windsor and Weybridge services, displacing Nos 1760–69.

2021–37 (*3021–37* from January 1937): Designated 6 PAN and built for the Eastbourne and Hastings electrification of 1935, once again the trailers were built at Eastleigh, while the motor coach order was divided equally between the Metropolitan-Cammell Carriage, Wagon & Finance Co. and the Birmingham Railway Carriage & Wagon Co. The most obvious difference with the 6 PUL sets was the replacement of the Pullman composite by a first-class trailer with a pantry, staffed by the Pullman Car Co., for light refreshments. While the motor coaches were identical to the 6 PUL, the other trailers consisted of two third corridors with eight compartments and a coupe, a first corridor with seven compartments and the pantry car, which had end doors only and the equivalent of five first-class compartments. An obvious difference with the 6 PULs was that the motor coaches had fixed windows with 'Airstream' ventilators, sliding glass panels intended to provide draught-free ventilation. Overall weight was 244 tons, with a length of 392 ft 2 in.

The introduction of these units meant that the Brighton and Worthing carriage rosters were rearranged to allow 6 PUL services to Eastbourne, so that the standard train formation became 6 PUL and 6 PAN for services to the Sussex Coast.

1891–1900 (*2001–10* from January 1937)/*2011–48*/*2049–2116*/*2117–52*: These were designated 2 BIL and built in four distinct batches for the Eastbourne electrification of 1935, in 1936 for the following year's Portsmouth and Alton electrification, in 1937 for the Portsmouth via Arundel electrification, and in 1938 for the Reading and Ascot electrification. The initial order was for ten two-car sets, and once again the motor coaches were divided between the Metropolitan-Cammell Carriage, Wagon & Finance Co., Metro-Cammell and the Birmingham Railway Carriage & Wagon Co, while the driving trailers were built at Eastleigh. Intended for semi-fast services, the motor coaches had a motorman's, guard's and seven third-class compartments with a side corridor to an end lavatory, while the driving trailers had a motorman's compartment, with four first- and four third-class compartments connected by a side corridor to an end lavatory. Once again, the proven combination of two 275 hp English Electric motors and Metrovick electrical equipment was used. Later batches saw the motor coaches having a coupe compartment and six third-class compartments, increasing the space for mail and luggage. With the two Portsmouth electrification schemes, these trains usually operated the stopping services, albeit usually fast between Waterloo and Surbiton.

3101–29/*3130–55*: Designated 4 COR, these were built at Eastleigh with the first batch for the 1937 electrification of the Portsmouth Direct, the main route to Portsmouth from Waterloo via Guildford, while the second batch was built for the 1938 electrification of the Victoria to Portsmouth route via Arundel and Chichester. For the first time a corridor connection was provided through the driving cab ends, allowing access throughout the train, even when two or three sets were operated together. Each unit had two 52-seat third open motor coaches with compartments for the driver and guard, a composite trailer with five first- and three third-class compartments, and a third-class trailer with eight compartments and a four-seat coupe; both trailers had lavatories at each end. The through corridor connection meant that the headcode was offset to the left, leaving just one window facing forward, and earning these sets and both the 4 RES and the later 4 BUF the nickname of 'Nelsons'. Electrical equipment was provided by English Electric, including the two 225 hp motors fitted to the leading bogie. Overall, these sets weighed 170 tons and were 265 ft long, with accommodation for 30 first-class and 196 third-class passengers. The low proportion of first-class passengers reflected the fact that Portsmouth itself was just a little too far to be a commuter traffic generator and that it also had a very substantial service traffic, although there was substantial commuter traffic along the line, especially from Haslemere, Guildford and Woking.

3054–72: Designated 4 RES, these were also built for the Portsmouth electrification and the motor coaches, identical in every respect to those of the 4 COR, were also built at Eastleigh, but the restaurant cars were built by Metro-Cammell and the third-class trailers by the Birmingham Railway Carriage & Wagon Co. The restaurant cars included five first-class compartments, a pantry and a kitchen, with a dining section with twelve first-class seats, and a lavatory at the opposite end. No doubt the first-class dining facility reflected not only the upper end of the business and commuter markets, but also the Admiralty's willingness to pay for first-class travel for naval officers, but not the Pullman surcharge! It may also have been that the longer journey time meant that more than one serving of a meal, especially a light meal such as morning coffee or afternoon tea, could be made. The third-class trailers were the same as those on the 4 COR. Overall weight was lower than the 4 COR at 162 tons, but the length was the same, while there were 42 first-class seats and 140 third-class. Normally, one 4 RES would work with one or two 4 CORs, and in the latter case would usually operate as the middle unit.

3073–85: Designated 4 BUF, these were built at Eastleigh for the Victoria–Portsmouth electrification, and were identical to the 4 COR sets other than for the fact that the third-class trailer was replaced by an open buffet car, painted light green rather than olive. The buffet cars consisted of a pantry, a bar with ten revolving stools and a saloon with four specially shaped tables each with four revolving chairs set against scalloped edges. Overall, these sets were lighter at 164 tons and slightly shorter, at 264 ft 6 in. Seating totalled 30 first-class and 128 third-class, with another twenty-six seats in the buffet. The Victoria services were less heavily used than the Waterloo services, and it was usual for a 4 BUF and a 4 COR to operate together, with one unit dividing at Arundel or Barham (it varied over the years) for Bognor.

2601–76/2677–92: Designated 2 HAL, the initial batch was built at Eastleigh for the 1939 electrification to Maidstone and Gillingham (Kent), the final electrification before the outbreak of war and the last main-line electrification in the south of England for some twenty years. While the bodies were once again of steel panelling on timber frames on an underframe of steel sections, for the first time the driving ends were domed and of rolled steel sections, while a more modern appearance was conveyed by windows flush with the sides and large radii curves. The motor coaches contained a motorman's and a guard's compartment, as well as seven third-class compartments, while the driving trailers had a compartment for the motorman and four first- and four third-class compartments, with a side corridor and a lavatory at the inner end. Once again electrical equipment was by English Electric, with two 275 hp motors. Overall weight was 76 tons, and length was 129 ft 6 in, with accommodation for 32 first-class and 102 third-class passengers. An additional sixteen sets, Nos 2677–92, were brought into service shortly after the outbreak of war, during the winter of 1939–40.

Appendix VI

Utility Stock and Beyond

Wartime conditions brought changes to the Southern's operations, with severe cuts in many services, especially off-peak. Eventually Pullman trains were withdrawn and the Pullman carriages in other multiple units placed in storage. There were, of course, many special additional trains for the military, and also some special trains for use by senior members of the War Cabinet, and it could be that some of the Pullman stock found its way into these.

There were severe wartime production controls to minimise waste and also to allow full use of materials and manufacturing resources for the war effort. Initially, the only new transport equipment authorised for civilian use was for equipment already under construction, which could be completed. In this way, the Southern railway completed the additional sixteen 2 HAL units mentioned at the end of Appendix V. It also received another two 4 LAV units, Nos 2954 and 2955, in the winter and spring of 1940, which, despite sharing their designation and number of seats with the earlier trains of this class, were in appearance and electrical equipment similar to the 2 HAL class, reflecting some eight years of development in main-line multiple unit stock.

Even before the outbreak of war, continued strong growth in rush-hour traffic was causing the Southern to evaluate new trains, and also to see if better use could be made of space. At Eastleigh works, investigation into the use of welding to reduce the thickness of the sidewalls and the use of curved sides, led to the conclusion that up to six passengers could be seated abreast in reasonable comfort on short suburban journeys. As the war progressed, demands on the available rolling stock and the inevitable losses due to enemy action meant that new transport equipment could be authorised providing it was completed to an austere 'utility' specification – the wartime utility buses by Guy, Bristol and Daimler became well known. The Southern Railway was prominent in producing the railway equivalent.

4101–10: Initially undesignated, but later becoming 4 SUB, these were of all-metal construction using welding and curved body sides to increase capacity. The first appeared early in 1941, with two motor coaches having a motorman's compartment, a guard's compartment and nine third-class compartments each with seats for twelve passengers, a trailer with two third-, six first- and two third-class compartments, with the first-class compartments each having ten seats, and another trailer with eleven third-class compartments. Overall width was 9 ft 3 in, although the front ends were narrower and resembled those of the 2 HAL sets, while the overall weight was 144 tons and length was 257 ft 4½ in. There was accommodation for 60 first- and 396 third-class passengers. The usual 275 hp English Electric motors were fitted. Later that year, by which time all London suburban services had become third-class only by official decree, a second set, No. 4102, appeared with third-class seating throughout, giving a total of 468 seats, indicating that the numbers of compartments and their dimensions were the same as on the original, so that conversion back to first- and third-class accommodation could be made after the war: a further seven sets were built to this specification between January and April 1945.

Other wartime expedients included adding a fourth carriage to three-coach sets, starting in

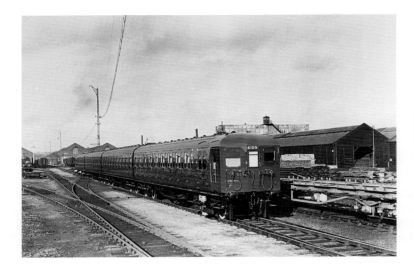

Another way of cramming more passengers into the available space was to widen the carriages at waist level, as in this 4 SUB, of a type that first appeared during the Second World War, so that in compartment stock passengers could sit six rather than five-abreast. One carriage would have eleven instead of ten compartments. (*NRM 42/00*)

1942, utilising carriages from the trailer sets, many of which had been left idle due to wartime cuts in services. These included:

4131–71: Rebuilt 1201 series compartment stock with an ex-LSWR ten-compartment trailer added, giving 353 seats in a total weight of 139 tons, length of 256 ft 8 in and width of 9 ft.

4195–4234: Rebuilt 1201 series saloon stock with an ex-LSWR eleven-compartment trailer added, giving 350 seats and dimensions of 257 ft 5 in by 9 ft.

Many of the 2 NOL sets had their coupe compartment converted to increase luggage accommodation.

3156–8: Additional 4 COR stock. The war cost the Southern fifty-one suburban and thirty-two main-line electric carriages, including three restaurant cars and one buffet, with no fewer than twenty of this total being destroyed in Portsmouth alone at the height of the blitz. A combination of stock transfers and some new stock meant that the three additional 4 CORs could be provided at the cost of three 4 RES units, since the restaurant cars were never replaced, even though this facility was reinstated on 7 January 1946, with Pullman cars following on 1 May.

4172–94/4235–49/4250–57: These were 1658 series units with the addition of an ex-LSWR ten-compartment trailer and then renumbered during 1947–8, with 4250 onwards consisting of vehicles from war-damaged units. In their new form these units had an overall weight of 139 tons and a length of 257 ft 5 in, with 370 seats, except for the 'war-damaged' series, which had 340 seats.

4300–25/4326–54: Conversions initially based on the 1285 series starting in 1945, with each having a ten-compartment 'wide-bodied' trailer built at Eastleigh, with the second batch based on the 1496 series completed in late 1945 and 1946. The first batch weighed 133 tons and were 245 ft long overall with seats for 350 passengers, while the second batch was 4 tons heavier and 257 ft 5 in long with 370 seats.

4401–4594/4601–08/4613, 4614: These were mainly converted from steam or ex-LBSC electric stock, with the addition of nine- or ten-compartment trailers, and showing some variety between units even within the same series. Some of these were to have a relatively short life, as postwar construction of new electric multiple units got under way.

4111–20/4364–76: Built at Eastleigh in two batches in 1946 and 1947 to provide additional standing room at the front of morning Up trains and the rear of evening Down trains. The two motor coaches had eight compartments each with one nine-, in case first class returned to inner suburban duties, and one ten-compartment trailer. The sets didn't have the domed and squared-off fronts of the 4101 series, while the body painting continued over the sides to the roof, and the by now standard English Electric equipment was retained. Overall dimensions were the same as for the 4101 series, or 4 SUB, while weight was 142 tons with 420 seats.

4121–30: 4 SUB: a variation on the above built at Eastleigh in 1946, but with the motor coaches divided into two groups of four compartments each, with a central gangway and two- and three-abreast seating. The ten-compartment trailer was divided into groups of three, four and three compartments, reducing seating to 382 passengers. No. 4130 used a new ventilated lightweight motor designed to provide for higher speeds and heavier loads, and intended to be suitable for both suburban and main-line operations.

4277–99: A variation of the above, but built on reclaimed bogies and underframes from withdrawn stock and with a through gangway linking all eight compartments in the motor coaches and all ten compartments in one of the trailers, leaving the other trailer with ten 'traditional' compartments. The weight was reduced to 134 tons and seating to 386 passengers, and the set used the new lightweight English Electric motors pioneered on 4130. These were built at Eastleigh during 1948 and 1949, so entering service after nationalisation, part of the Southern Railway's legacy to British Railways.

CC1/2: The first two out of three electric engines, with the third arriving after nationalisation. These were based on two three-wheel bogies, each powered by a 245 hp pressure-ventilated motor. In contrast to some experimental diesel locomotives, these had cabs at both ends. Interesting features included a pantograph, so that sidings could be equipped with overhead wires allowing for safer working for the shunters, and a booster set for each bogie that included a heavy flywheel capable of providing enough energy to cope with the longest gap in the conductor rail. These were primarily used for freight work, proving far more capable than steam locomotives, but with a 75 mph top speed they also made appearances on the Victoria–Newhaven boat train, and of course they were also in demand for special workings.

Appendix VII

Maps of the
Southern Electric

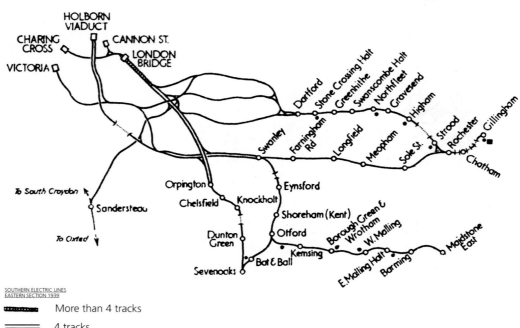

SOUTHERN ELECTRIC LINES
EASTERN SECTION 1939

More than 4 tracks

4 tracks

Double track

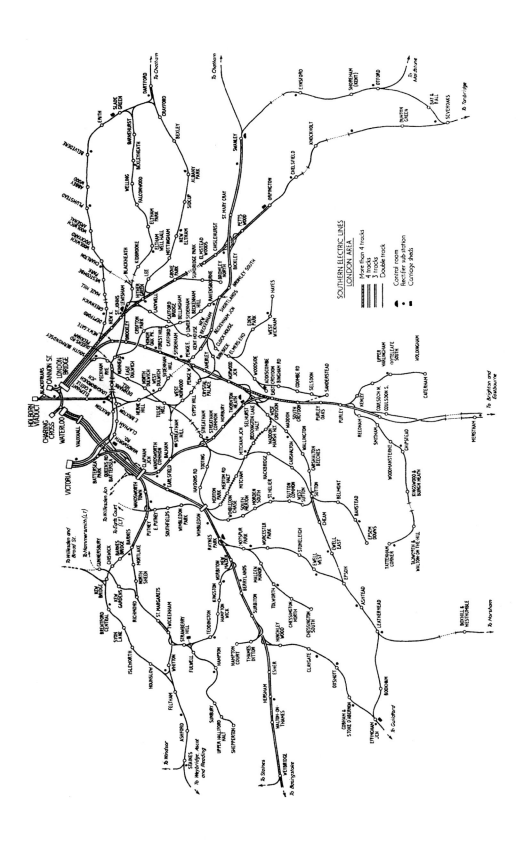

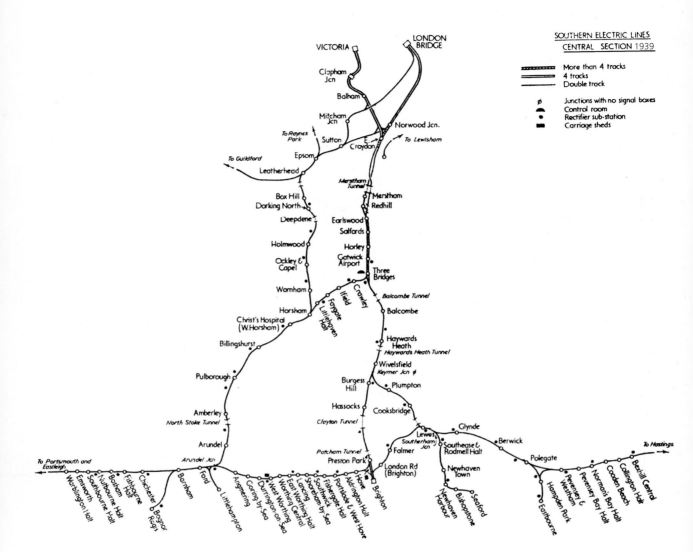

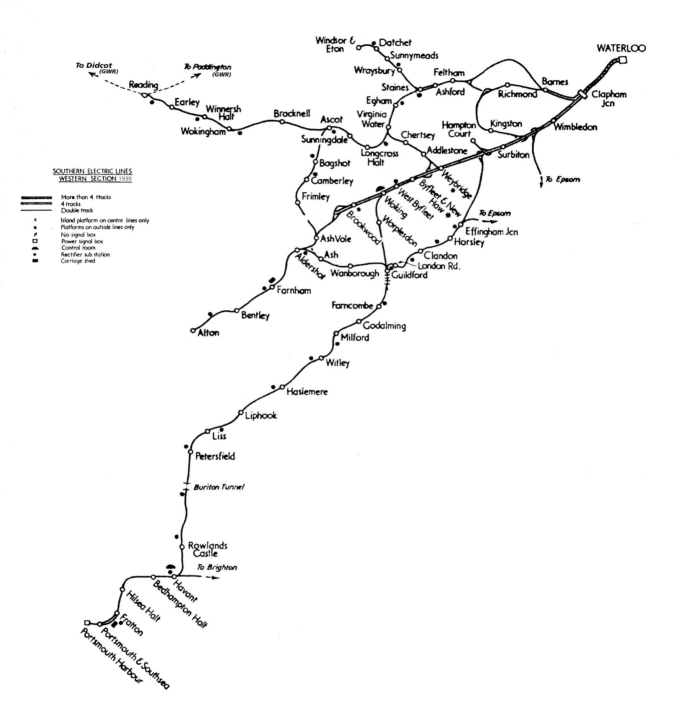

SOUTHERN ELECTRIC LINES
WESTERN SECTION 1939

More than 4 tracks
4 tracks
Double track

x   Island platform on centre lines only
     Platforms on outside lines only
     No signal box
□   Power signal box
     Control room
•   Rectifier sub station
■   Carriage shed

Bibliography

Allen, Cecil J., *Salute to the Southern*, Ian Allan, Shepperton, 1974

Allen, Cecil J. and Townroe, S.C., *The Bulleid Pacifics of the Southern Railway*, Ian Allan, Shepperton, 1951 and 1974

Allen, P.C. and Macleod, A.B., *Rails in the Isle of Wight*, Allen & Unwin, London, 1967

Bradley, D.L., *Locomotives of the Southern Railway*, 2 vols, The Railway Correspondence & Travel Society, 1977

Bradshaw's Railway Guide, published monthly with reprints available for key dates

Course, Edwin, *The Railways of Southern England: The Main Lines*, Batsford, London, 1973

Course, Edwin, *The Railways of Southern England: Secondary and Branch Lines*, Batsford, London, 1974

Darwin, Bernard, *War on the Line, The Story of the Southern Railway in War-Time, including D-Day on the Southern*, Southern Railway, London, 1946

Dendy Marshall, C.F., *A History of the Southern Railway*, Southern Railway Company, London, 1936

Elliot, Sir John, *On and Off the Rails*, George Allen & Unwin, London, 1982

Gould, D., *Bulleid's Steam Passenger Stock*, Oakwood Press, Salisbury, 1980

Gould, D., *Maunsell's Steam Passenger Stock, 1923–1939*, Oakwood Press, Salisbury, 1978

Haresnape, Brian, *Maunsell Locomotives*, Ian Allan, Shepperton, 1977

Haresnape, Brian, *Bulleid Locomotives*, Ian Allan, Shepperton, 1977

Jackson, Alan A., *London's Termini*, David & Charles, Newton Abbot, 1969

Kidner, R.W., *The Southern Railway*, Oakwood Press, Salisbury, 1958 and 1974

Klapper, Charles F., *Sir Herbert Walker's Southern Railway*, Ian Allan, Shepperton, 1973

Moody, G.T., *Southern Electric 1909–1979*, Ian Allan, Shepperton, 1979

Newberry, Peter, *The Vectis Connection: Pioneering Isle of Wight Air Services*, Waterfront, Settle, 2000

Nock, O.S., *Britain's Railways at War, 1939–1945*, Ian Allan, Shepperton, 1971

St John Thomas, David, *Regional History of the Railways of Great Britain, Vol. 1, The West Country*, David & Charles, Newton Abbot, 1960

Simmons, Jack and Biddle, Gordon, *The Oxford Companion to British Railway History*, Oxford University Press, Oxford, 2000

Southern Railway Passenger Services, October 6th, 1947; reprinted Ian Allan, Shepperton

Tavender, L., *HRMS Livery Register No. 3, LSWR and Southern*, Historical Model Railway Society

Townroe, S.C., *The Arthurs, Nelsons and Schools of the Southern*, Ian Allan, Shepperton, 1973

White, H.P., *Regional History of the Railways of Great Britain, Vol. 2, Southern England*, David & Charles, Newton Abbot, 1961

Winkworth, D.W., *Southern Titled Trains*, David & Charles, Newton Abbot, 1988

Wragg, David, *Railways at War*, Sutton, Stroud, 2006

Commuter City – How the Railways Shaped London, Wharncliffe, 2010

Index

Full details of locomotives and electric multiple units are given in the appendices, as are locomotive headcodes and station name changes. The references below relate to the narrative text.